J. Albert Robbins, editor of the volume, is Professor of English at Indiana University. A former contributor to the annual, he is co-author of *American Literary Manuscripts* and chairman of a committee commissioned to revise that volume. For many years he was bibliographer for the American literature section of the MLA Bibliography. He has contributed to *Studies in Bibliography*, *University of North Carolina Studies in Comparative Literature*, *Modern Fiction Studies*, and other scholarly journals.

# American Literary Scholarship

## 1969

# American Literary Scholarship

## *An Annual* / 1969

*Edited by* J. Albert Robbins

*Essays by* John C. Broderick, Roy R. Male, Merton M. Sealts, Jr., Bernice Slote, Hamlin Hill, William T. Stafford, Michael Millgate, William White, Richard Beale Davis, J. V. Ridgely, Patrick F. Quinn, Warren French, James H. Justus, Richard Crowder, A. Kingsley Weatherhead, Walter J. Meserve, John T. Flanagan, G. R. Thompson.

*Indexed by* Richard D. Rust

*Duke University Press,* Durham, North Carolina, 1971

# Foreword

This is the seventh volume of *American Literary Scholarship* and only one contributor has been with us from the start—Richard Beale Davis, of the University of Tennessee. At the moment that he achieves this long and useful service, he asks to be relieved of the duty, to invest the time in other commitments. I shall hate to see his name disappear from our table of contents but he has truly earned his sabbatical. Professor J. A. Leo Lemay, of the University of California, Los Angeles, will succeed Professor Davis as author of Chapter 9, Literature to 1800, in next year's volume.

Two others have been associated with the series for six years. One of these, William T. Stafford, is currently teaching in Yugoslavia and has asked for a year's leave. Professor Robert L. Gale, of the University of Pittsburgh, will contribute the James chapter in next year's volume. The other, Joseph M. Flora, faithfully provided the index for the first six volumes and has asked to be relieved of this responsibility. His successor, whose work appears in this volume, is his colleague at Chapel Hill, Professor Richard D. Rust.

While the subject is length of service, I should note that Professor John T. Flanagan, of the University of Illinois, has contributed the survey of folklore scholarship for the five years since this chapter was added in *ALS 1965*.

Readers will discover five new contributors in this year's volume and, I am sure, with me welcome them to the series. They are Bernice Slote (Whitman and Dickinson), Hamlin Hill (Mark Twain), Michael Millgate (Faulkner), Richard Crowder (Poetry: 1900 to the 1930's) and G. R. Thompson (Themes, Topics, and Criticism).

Because the production schedule of volumes in this series has been a mystery to some, it might be useful to indicate why a volume covering scholarship published in 1969 does not appear until 1971. As I indicated in the Foreword of last year's volume, the MLA Bibliography is vital to us. A contributor can begin reading and writing during the year but he really does not know what he has to deal with until he receives appropriate citations in the Bibliography. Professor Harrison T. Meserole, general editor of the MLA Bibliography, assists us greatly by providing a set of advance galleys of the American section, thereby giving us important lead time in our work. These galleys arrive in March and contributors have until mid-August to do their reading and writing. Editing by the series editor and by the press editor takes a month or month and a half, which means that the manuscript goes to the printer around mid-October (or, if delays are involved, in November). Galley proof is ready in January or February. (Observe that this brackets the Christmas season, when compositors close shop for the holiday.) Correcting galleys, correcting page proof, indexing, correcting index copy, and production of the actual volume require two and a half or three months—which means that publication is reached in April or May. This brief outline of the sequence assumes ideal conditions, with no snags or delays. In actuality, delays, alas, seem inevitable. Just one late contributor, of course, can delay the entire project and not all delays are foreseeable —for people do fall ill, have accidents, and get involved in unexpected academic duties. It would be ideal if, for example, *ALS 1969* could appear in 1970, rather than 1971, but the realities make it impossible. Our contributors have to fit this demanding responsibility into their already heavy schedules and there are no steps in the editing and production schedule which could be eliminated without imperiling accuracy and quality.

*J. Albert Robbins*

Indiana University

# Table of Contents

# Key to Abbreviations

ABC / American Book Collector
ABR / American Benedictine Review
Afterwords / Thomas McCormack, ed., Afterwords: Novelists on Their Novels (New York, Harper & Row)
Agenda
AH / American Heritage
AL / American Literature
ALR / American Literary Realism, 1870–1910
ALS / American Literary Scholarship: An Annual
ALT / African Literature Today
American Poets / Hyatt H. Waggoner, American Poets from the Puritans to the Present (Boston, Houghton Mifflin, 1968)
Amerikanische Erzählungen / Paul G. Buchloh, ed., Amerikanische Erzählungen von Hawthorne bis Salinger: Interpretationen. KBAA 6. (Neumünster, 1968)
AN&Q / American Notes and Queries
AQ / American Quarterly
AR / Antioch Review
Archiv / Archiv für das Studium der neueren Sprachen und Literaturen
ArkHQ / Arkansas Historical Quarterly
ArlQ / Arlington Quarterly
ArQ / Arizona Quarterly
ArW / Arizona and the West
ASoc / Arts in Society (Univ. of Wis.)
Aspects of the Renaissance / Archibald R. Lewis, ed., Aspects of the Renaissance: A Symposium (Austin, Univ. of Texas Press, 1967)
AtM / Atlantic Monthly
ATQ / American Transcendental Quarterly

AW / American West
AWR / The Anglo-Welsh Review (Pembroke Dock, Wales)
BaratR / Barat Review (Barat College)
BB / Bulletin of Bibliography
BBr / Books at Brown
BFLS / Bulletin de la Faculté des Lettres de Strasbourg
Bibliographical Guide / Louis D. Rubin, Jr., ed., A Bibliographical Guide to the Study of Southern Literature (Baton Rouge, La. State Univ. Press)
BJA / British Journal of Aesthetics
Black American Writers / C. W. E. Bigsby, ed., The Black American Writers: Volume II, Poetry and Drama (Deland, Fla., Everett/Edwards)
BNYPL / Bulletin of the New York Public Library
BP / Banasthali patrika
BRMMLA / Bulletin of the Rocky Mountain Modern Language Assn.
BST / Brontë Society Transactions
BSUF / Ball State University Forum
BuR / Bucknell Review
BYUS / Brigham Young University Studies
BzJA / Beihefte zum Jahrbuch für Amerikastudien, (Heidelberg, Winter)
Cabellian / The Cabellian: A Journal of the Second American Renaissance
Caliban (Toulouse)
CE / College English
CEA / CEA Critic (College English Association)
CEAAN / Center for Editions of

American Authors Newsletter
(MLA)

CentR / The Centennial Review
(Mich. State Univ.)

CHA / Cuadernos Hispanoamericanos
(Madrid)

CimR / Cimarron Review (Okla.
State Univ.)

Cithara (St. Bonaventure Univ.)

CL / Comparative Literature

CLAJ / CLA Journal (College
Language Assn.)

Classical Studies / Classical Studies
Presented to Ben Edwin Perry by
His Students and Colleagues at
the University of Illinois, 1924–60.
ISLL 58. (Urbana, Univ. of Ill.
Press)

CLJ / Cornell Library Journal

CLQ / Colby Library Quarterly

CLS / Comparative Literature Studies

ColQ / Colorado Quarterly

Commonweal

ConL / Contemporary Literature
(supersedes WSCL)

ConnR / Connecticut Review

Contemporanul (Bucharest)

CP / Concerning Poetry (Western
Wash. State College)

CQ / The Cambridge Quarterly

Cresset (Valparaiso Univ.)

Crit / Critique: Studies in Modern
Fiction

Criticism (Wayne State Univ.)

CritQ / Critical Quarterly

CWCP / Contemporary Writers in
Christian Perspective (Grand
Rapids, Mich., William B.
Eerdmans)

DA / Dissertation Abstracts

Delos: A Journal on & of Translation

Discourse (Concordia College)

DR / Dalhousie Review

DramS / Drama Survey

DuR / Duquesne Review

DVLG / Deutsche Vierteljahrsschrift
für Literaturwissenschaft und
Geistesgeschichte

EA / Etudes anglaises

EAL / Early American Literature

ECS / Eighteenth-Century Studies

EIHC / Essex Institute Historical
Collections

EJ / English Journal

ELH / ELH, Journal of English
Literary History

ELN / English Language Notes
(Univ. of Colo.)

EN / English Notes

Encounter (London)

ER / English Record

ES / English Studies

ESA / English Studies in Africa
(Johannesburg)

ESQ / Emerson Society Quarterly

Essays / Thomas G. Burton, ed.,
Essays in Memory of Christine
Burleson in Language and Litera-
ture by Former Colleagues and
Students (Johnson City, Research
Advisory Council, East Tenn. State
Univ.)

ETJ / Educational Theatre Journal

Europe

Expl / Explicator

FH / Forest History

FHA / Fitzgerald-Hemingway Annual

Fifteen Modern American Authors /
Jackson R. Bryer, ed., Fifteen
Modern American Authors: A
Survey of Research and Criticism
(Durham, N. C., Duke Univ.
Press)

FMLS / Forum for Modern Language
Studies (Univ. of St. Andrews,
Scotland)

FN / Filologicheskie Nauki (Moscow)

Forms Upon the Frontier / Austin E.
and Alta S. Fife and Henry Glassie,
eds., Forms Upon the Frontier
(Logan, Utah State Univ. Press)

ForumH / Forum (Houston)

FPt / The Far Point (Univ. of
Manitoba)

Frontiers / Ray B. Browne et al., eds.,
Frontiers of American Culture
(Lafayette, Ind., Purdue Univ.
Studies, 1968)

FurmS / Furman Studies

GaR / Georgia Review

Genre (Univ. of Ill. at Chicago Circle)

GorR / The Gordon Review (Wen-
ham, Mass.)

GQ / German Quarterly
HC / The Hollins Critic (Hollins
   College, Va.)
Historian / The Historian: A Journal
   of History
HLB / Harvard Library Bulletin
HLQ / Huntington Library Quarterly
HSE / Hungarian Studies in English
   (L. Kossuth Univ., Debrecen)
HSL / Hartford Studies in Literature
HTR / Harvard Theological Review
HudR / Hudson Review
HussonRev / Husson Review (Husson
   College)
Ibadan (University of Ibadan, Nigeria)
IEY / Iowa English Yearbook
IF / Indiana Folklore
Indian Essays / Sujit Mukherjee and
   D. V. K. Raghavacharyulu, eds.,
   Indian Essays in American Litera-
   ture: Papers in Honour of Robert
   E. Spiller (Bombay, Popular
   Prakashan)
Indian Response / C. D. Narasim-
   haiah, ed., Indian Response to
   American Literature (New Delhi,
   United States Educational Foun-
   dation in India, 1967)
ISLL / Illinois Studies in Language
   and Literature
JA / Jahrbuch für Amerikastudien
JAAC / Journal of Aesthetics and
   Art Criticism
JAF / Journal of American Folklore
JAmS / Journal of American Studies
JEGP / Journal of English and
   Germanic Philology
JFI / Journal of the Folklore Institute
   (Ind. Univ.)
JGE / Journal of General Education
JHI / Journal of the History of Ideas
JHS / Journal of Historical Studies
JLN / Jack London Newsletter
JNH / Journal of Negro History
JPC / Journal of Popular Culture
KAL / Kyushu American Literature
   (Fukuoka, Japan)
KanQ / Kansas Quarterly
KBAA / Kieler Beiträge zur Anglistik
   und Amerikanistik
KFQ / Keystone Folklore Quarterly
KFR / Kentucky Folklore Record

KM / Kansas Magazine
KN / Kwartalnik Neofilologiczny
   (Warsaw)
KR / Kenyon Review
L&P / Literature and Psychology
   (U. of Hartford)
LaHist / Louisiana History
Landmarks / Hennig Cohen, ed.,
   Landmarks of American Writing
   (New York, Basic Books)
Lang&S / Language and Style
LangQ / Language Quarterly (Univ.
   of South Fla.)
LauR / Laurel Review
LC / Library Chronicle (Univ. of Pa.)
LE&W / Literature East and West
LHR / Lock Haven Review (Lock
   Haven State College, Pa.)
Literatur und Sprache / Hans
   Helmcke, Klaus Lubbers, and
   Renate Schmidt-von Bardeleben,
   eds., Literatur und Sprache der
   Vereinigten Staaten: Aufsätze zu
   Ehren von Hans Galinsky
   (Heidelberg, Winter)
Maekawa / Maekawa Shunichi kyōju
   kanreki kinen-ronbunshū [Essays
   and studies in commemoration of
   Professor Shunichi Maekawa's
   sixty-first birthday] (Tokyo,
   Eihōsha, 1968)
Markham Rev / Markham Review
   (Wagner College)
MASJ / Midcontinent American
   Studies Journal
MD / Modern Drama
Meanjin / Meanjin Quarterly (Univ.
   of Melbourne)
MFS / Modern Fiction Studies
MinnR / Minnesota Review
MissQ / Mississippi Quarterly
MLQ / Modern Language Quarterly
MLR / Modern Language Review
Mosaic: A Journal for the Comparative
   Study of Literature and Ideas
MP / Modern Philology
MQ / Midwest Quarterly
MQR / Michigan Quarterly Review
MR / Massachusetts Review
MSE / Massachusetts Studies in
   English
MSS / Manuscripts

MTJ / Mark Twain Journal
NALF / Negro American Literature Forum
Names
NASRC / Newsletter, American Studies Research Centre (Hyderabad)
Nassau Rev / Nassau Review (Nassau Community College)
N&Q / Notes and Queries
NCF / Nineteenth-Century Fiction
NCHR / North Carolina Historical Review
NebrHist / Nebraska History
NegroD / Negro Digest
Neophil / Neophilologus (Groningen)
NEQ / New England Quarterly
NF / Northwest Folklore
NL / Nouvelles littéraires
NLH / New Literary History
NMHR / New Mexico Historical Review
NMW / Notes on Mississippi Writers
NoCF / North Carolina Folklore
Novel: A Forum on Fiction
NovM / Novyi mir (Moscow)
NRF / Nouvelle revue française
NS / Die neueren Sprachen
NYFQ / New York Folklore Quarterly
NYHSQ / New York Historical Society Quarterly
NYTM / New York Times Magazine
OL / Orbis litterarum
OSUTCB / Ohio State Univ. Theatre Collection Bulletin
OUR / Ohio University Review (Athens)
PAAS / Proceedings of the American Antiquarian Society
PAH / Perspectives in American History
P&R / Philosophy and Rhetoric (Pa. State Univ.)
PBSA / Papers of the Bibliographical Society of America
Person / The Personalist
Perspectives / Jagdish Chander, ed., Perspectives in American Literature (Ludhiana, India, Lyall Book Depot)
PF / Pennsylvania Folklife
Phylon

PLL / Papers on Language and Literature
PMHB / Pennsylvania Magazine of History and Biography
PMHS / Proceedings of the Massachusetts Historical Society
PMLA / PMLA, Publications of the Modern Language Association
PN / Poe Newsletter (Wash. State Univ.)
Poetic Theory / Poetic Practice / Robert Scholes, ed., Poetic Theory / Poetic Practice: Papers of the Midwest Modern Language Association
PoetryR / Poetry Review (London)
PQ / Philological Quarterly
PR / Partisan Review
PrS / Prairie Schooner
PSA / Papeles de Son Armadans (Mallorca)
PsyR / Psychoanalytic Review
PULC / Princeton University Library Chronicle
Quest (Bombay)
RACHSP / Records of the American Catholic Historical Society of Philadelphia
Radical Sophistication / Max F. Schulz, ed., Radical Sophistication: Studies in Contemporary Jewish-American Novelists (Athens, Ohio Univ. Press)
Renascence
Rendezvous: Journal of Arts and Letters
RES / Review of English Studies
RLC / Revue de littérature comparée
RLM / La revue des lettres modernes
RLV / Revue des langues vivantes
RS / Research Studies (Washington State Univ.)
SA / Studi americani
SAB / South Atlantic Bulletin
SAQ / South Atlantic Quarterly
SB / Studies in Bibliography: Papers of the Bibliographical Society of the University of Virginia
SDR / South Dakota Review
SELit / Studies in English Literature (English Literary Society of Japan, Univ. of Tokyo)

*Serif* / *The Serif* (Kent State Univ., Ohio)
*SF&R* / Scholars' Facsimiles and Reprints
*SFQ* / *Southern Folklore Quarterly*
*SG* / *Studium Generale*
*Shenandoah*
*SHR* / *Southern Humanities Review*
*Sigma: Revista trimestrale di lettera- tura* (Turin)
*SIR* / *Studies in Romanticism*
*Sixties* (Madison, Minn.)
*SLitI* / *Studies in the Literary Imagination* (Ga. State College)
*SLJ* / *Southern Literary Journal*
*SLN* / *Sinclair Lewis Newsletter*
*SN* / *Studia Neophilologica*
*SNL* / *Satire Newsletter*
*SNNTS* / *Studies in the Novel* (North Texas State Univ.)
*SoQ* / *The Southern Quarterly* (Univ. of Southern Miss.)
*SoR* / *Southern Review*
*SoRA* / *Southern Review: An Aus- tralian Journal of Literary Studies* (Univ. of Adelaide)
*Soundings: A Journal of Interdis- ciplinary Studies*
*SovL* / *Soviet Literature*
*SP* / *Studies in Philology*
*Spirit: A Magazine of Poetry*
*SR* / *Sewanee Review*
*SRAZ* / *Studia romanica et anglica zagrabiensia*
*SSF* / *Studies in Short Fiction*
*SSJ* / *Southern Speech Journal*
*StN* / *Steinbeck Newsletter*
*StQ* / *Steinbeck Quarterly* (Formerly *Steinbeck Newsletter*)
*Studiekamraten* (Lund)
*Studies in American Literature* / Robert Partlow, ed., *Studies in American Literature in Honor of Robert Dunn Faner, 1906–1967* *PLL* 5sup:1–172)
*Style*
*SUS* / *Susquehanna University Studies*
*SWR* / *Southwest Review*
*SWS* / *Southwest Writers Series* (Austin, Texas, Steck-Vaughn Co.)
*TA* / *Theater Annual*
*TCL* / *Twentieth Century Literature*

*TFSB* / *Tennessee Folklore Society Bulletin*
*The Forties* / Warren French, ed., *The Forties: Fiction, Poetry, Drama* (Deland, Fla., Everett/Edwards)
*Themes and Directions* / Ray B. Browne and Donald Pizer, eds., *Themes and Directions in Ameri- can Literature: Essays in Honor of Leon Howard* (Lafayette, Ind., Purdue Univ. Studies)
*Thought*
*TJQ* / *Thoreau Journal Quarterly*
*TLS* / *Times Literary Supplement* (London)
*To Find Something New* / Henry Grosshans, ed., *To Find Something New: Studies in Contemporary Literature* (Pullman, Wash. State Univ. Press)
*Topic* (Washington and Jefferson College)
*TPJ* / *Tennessee Poetry Journal*
*TQ* / *Texas Quarterly*
*Tradition: A Journal of Orthodox Jewish Thought*
*TriQ* / *Tri-Quarterly*
*TSB* / *Thoreau Society Bulletin*
*TSE* / *Tulane Studies in English*
*TSL* / *Tennessee Studies in Literature*
*TSLL* / *Texas Studies in Literature and Language*
*TUSAS* / Twayne United States Authors series (New York, Twayne Publishers)
*TWA* / *Transactions of the Wisconsin Academy of Sciences, Arts, and Letters*
*UDR* / *University of Dayton Review*
*UMPAW* / University of Minnesota Pamphlets on American Writers
*Univ* / *Universitas* (Stuttgart)
*UR* / *University Review* (Kansas City, Mo.)
*UWR* / *University of Windsor Review* (Windsor, Ontario)
*Variations* / Darshan Singh Maini, ed., *Variations on American Literature* (New Delhi, U.S. Educational Foundation in India, 1968)

*Part  I*

# 1. Emerson, Thoreau, and Transcendentalism

## John C. Broderick

In last year's chapter I expressed concern at the proportion of brief notes to substantial articles and books. My gloomy forecast then was that, both in numbers and in proportion, they were likely to increase. And so they have. The satisfaction which ordinarily accompanies accurate prophecy has been tempered in this case by the necessity of somehow arching this flood of publication. At least fifty separate bibliographical entries could be listed merely from the *American Transcendental Quarterly*, which published its first issues in 1969. (Not one of these, by the way, appears in the MLA International Bibliography.) There were well over a hundred and fifty in all. Selectivity of citation and commentary, even more rigorous than in the past, has been the *sine qua non* for 1969.

In these circumstances, it is a pleasure to call attention first to Lewis Mumford's general essay in praise of Emerson, "Have Courage!" (AH 20,ii:104–11). Broadly informed in the facts of Emerson's life, his works, and his place in the Western literary tradition, Mumford exhibits a range and perspective noticeably absent in much literary scholarship. A poet "who used the materials of other arts and disciplines to provide colors for his own palette," Emerson is called "the most liberated mind that the West had produced in several centuries, as liberated as Shakespeare's." He radically challenges "our conformity, our timidity, our docility—or those fashionable negative images of these same traits, our mindless anarchies, our drug-excited audacities, our aimless violence." Mumford's essay adds almost nothing to knowledge of Emerson but makes possible a more nearly complete understanding of the man, his work, and his relevance for our own times.

### *i.* Texts, Editions, Bibliographies

The publication of Volume VII of *The Journals and Miscellaneous Notebooks of Ralph Waldo Emerson*, edited by A. W. Plumstead and Harrison Hayford (Cambridge, Mass., Harvard Univ. Press, Belknap Press), brings to a welcome end the three-year hiatus in this great edition. There have been changes in the organization of the editorial board in the interim, but apparently none in the consistently high editorial standards. Volume VII, a continuation from Volume V (the intervening volume consisting entirely of "miscellaneous notebooks"), prints journals D, E, and F2, and covers the period 1838–42 (largely 1838–40). Since Emerson in that period delivered the "Divinity School Address" and underwent its controversial sequel, harbored Jones Very during his difficult interval, passed his own crisis with Margaret Fuller and her circle, published *Essays: First Series*, and lost his son Waldo, Volume VII vies with Volume V for intrinsic interest. (Passages on the death of Waldo do not appear in this volume.) The editors' introduction forthrightly indicates the various personal and intellectual concerns of Emerson during these years without preempting their interpretation. Their characterization of this period as one of "consolidation" seems apt. Nevertheless, they write, "these were not years of stasis. His ideas were put to the test in experience." Because of Emerson's habit of using overlapping journals for different purposes, the record of these crucial years will remain incomplete until the appearance of Volume VIII.

*The Letters of A. Bronson Alcott*, edited by Richard L. Herrnstadt (Ames, Iowa State Univ. Press), provides the text of 1,074 letters, an Alcott genealogy, and other information useful to advanced study of Alcott. The weighty and expensive book, with nearly as many pages as letters, represents scholarship of a different era from that of Odell Shepard, who in 1938 almost apologetically offered his rigorous selection from Alcott's voluminous journals. Despite the apparent comprehensiveness, however, more than three-quarters of the total number of letters are dated 1860 or later. Moreover, there are no letters to Thoreau, Hawthorne, Brownson, or Margaret Fuller, only one each to Theodore Parker and Ellery Channing, and two to Whitman. There are eight letters to Emerson, all but one in 1837. Alcott wrote a sizable number of letters to only three correspondents: William Torrey Harris (108 letters plus 3 known lost); Mrs. Alcott

(113 plus 12 lost; also 2 to Mrs. Alcott and the daughters); and Ellen A. Chandler (79). Despite the care with which the editor has gathered and transmitted his material, therefore, the net result is somewhat disappointing. Alcott appears to better effect in the selected *Journals* and even in Emerson's *Journals* than in his letters.

*The Variorum Civil Disobedience*, edited by Walter Harding (New York, 1967; see *ALS, 1967*, p. 7) is the subject of George Hendrick, "Thoughts on the Variorum Civil Disobedience" (*ESQ* 56:60–62; also printed in *New Approaches to Thoreau*, edited by William Bysshe Stein, as explained in section *iii* below). Hendrick finds the edition faulty in text, annotations, and interpretive selections. He is especially critical of the treatment of Gandhi's indebtedness to the essay, a subject about which there is as yet no consensus (see section *iii* below). Discussion of Thoreau's use of "delugeous" ("deutergeous"?) in the essay on Carlyle, begun in 1968, continued with two notes in the *CEAAN*.

Two unknown caricatures of Thoreau are among the annotations in the copy of *Walden* owned by Daniel Ricketson and recently acquired by the Houghton Library. These facts are recounted, the annotations are printed, and one of the caricatures is reproduced in the hitherto overlooked article by Walter Harding, "Daniel Ricketson's Copy of *Walden*" (*HLB* 15[1967]:401–11). An overlooked partial printing of Thoreau's letter of 16 July 1860 to Charles Sumner is pointed out by Douglass Noverr in *TSB* 107:2. The usual specialized checklists appear in *ATQ*, no. 2, and *TSB*, all issues.

Histories and records of the Salem and Concord Lyceums, the Lowell Institute, and other organizations are reprinted and/or edited by Kenneth Walter Cameron in *The Massachusetts Lyceum During the American Renaissance: Materials for the Study of the Oral Tradition in American Letters: Emerson, Thoreau, Hawthorne and Other New-England Lecturers* (Hartford, Conn., Transcendental Books).

### *ii.* Criticism: Emerson

Does Emerson speak to our own times? The answers vary. Even those who would answer "Yes" do so in many different ways. Lewis Mumford, cited above, assumes that the Emersonian essay remains accessible to a perceptive reader in all its literary and intellectual fullness. Others, however, would educate the response to Emerson by demonstrating the interchangeability of his message with messages of more recent or more fashionable mentors. One procedure has been to convert Emerson's traditionalist theological language to one that proves less an obstacle to twentieth-century readers. Paul Lauter's "Emerson Through Tillich" (see *ALS 1963*, p. 6) is one example. Last year's report discussed Harold Fromm's study of Emerson and Kierkegaard (see *ALS 1968*, pp. 10–11), which made large and persuasive claims for the coherence and contemporary relevance of Emerson's intellectual formulations.

Very much in this scholarly tradition is William E. Bridges's "Transcendentalism and Psychotherapy: Another Look at Emerson" (*AL* 41:157–77). The essay considers Emerson "as a forerunner of those who concern themselves with the potentialities of, and the dangers to, selfhood: psychotherapists like Carl Rogers, Erich Fromm, and Frederick Perls, and theologians like Martin Buber and Paul Tillich." Part of Bridges's work is finding modern equivalents for some terms in Emerson's terminology (e.g., "decorum" equals Riesman's "other-direction"; "seeming" equals personal inauthenticity, etc.). Bridges insists that in Emerson's work "intuition" is not opposed to "rationality," if these are understood as different elements of the person, self-recovery not being recovery of a thing but a reopening of lines of communication and personal responsiveness. He concludes that "Transcendentalism is an appeal to alienated man to recover and trust his own responses to experience—to take a stance . . . of total confrontation and total awareness." In these terms, "Transcendentalism provides a still impressive analysis of the psychic strains of life in a mass society and . . . a system of self-therapy." (Most frequently cited as a modern analogue to Emerson is Carl Rogers's *On Becoming a Person*.)

How Emerson arrived at his own rhetoric is the subject of Sheldon W. Liebman's "The Development of Emerson's Theory of Rhetoric, 1821–1836" (*AL* 41:178–206), a companion piece to his study of Emerson's philosophical transformation in the 1820's (see *ALS 1968*, pp. 9–10). Liebman shows how the young Emerson accepted the precepts of Edward T. Channing and the rhetorical principles of Hugh Blair throughout most of the 1820's. By the early 1830's, however, he cited the work of Archibald Alison as an alternative to Blair. He began to admire the eloquence of colloquialism and its practitioners (Montaigne, Carlyle), and sought a primitive vocabulary in the manner of Father Taylor and through the image-making power of the imagination. By 1836 he had evolved a new manner of writing suited to his changed philosophical views. Another favorite subject of study is Emerson's second transformation (from the 1830's to the 1850's). Ever since Stephen Whicher's *Freedom and Fate*, the subject has been prominent in doctoral dissertations, critical essays, and a few books. Theodore L. Gross ("Under the Shadow of Our Swords: Emerson and the Heroic Ideal," (*BuR* 17,i:22–34) detects a significant change in the heroic ideal depicted in the early Transcendental manifestoes as opposed to the "extraordinary, powerful man of the later work." Gross interprets the change to indicate Emerson's "decreasing faith in the potential heroism of the common American," a factor in "the failure of idealism in nineteenth-century American thought." (Gross's analysis would have been more convincing if he had included some comment on the early lecture series on biography, which tests his conclusions considerably.)

A pair of complementary essays on organicism and the organic method, although not incompatible, approach the subject with different predispositions and emerge with different results. Richard P. Adams's "The Basic Contradiction in Emerson" (*ESQ* 55:106–10) begins with the contradiction inherent in organicism as defined by Stephen Pepper, i.e., that between a static perfection and a dynamic diversity, both of which are characteristic of organicism and both of which Emerson employs. Adams finds the contradiction not only in *Nature* (its famous locus) but in several other essays as well. Despite its logical inadequacy, the contradiction "dramatizes the human condition of being in a flux of chaotic and perhaps meaningless motion and having to comprehend and govern the situation by whatever means we can invent. The organic metaphor is as good as any and better than most of the patterns we arbitrarily devise or select and use." In "Emerson's Use of the Organic Method" (*ESQ* 55:18–24), Carl F. Strauch celebrates Emerson's "fundamental accommodation" of Neoplatonic emanation and biological evolution as an "impressive cosmic view: emanation flowing down through lessening degrees of the divine . . . and biological evolution thrusting upward from the lowest forms to man, and, idealistically interpreted, yielding evidence of a purposive universe." Discussion of Emerson's reconciliation of ancient and modern thought, and especially of the role of the poet-seer and the organic plant analogy in the accommodation, is pre-

liminary to a consideration of the octosyllabic couplet, Emerson's
favorite measure. An extended analysis of "The Problem" demonstrates its suitability within the cosmic view Emerson achieved and
the organic method which he employed for its utterance. (Strauch
also provides the intellectual background for two other poems,
"Written in Naples" and "Written in Rome," in "Emerson and the
Longevity of the Mind," *ESQ* 54:60–68.)

### *iii.* Criticism: Thoreau

Hubert H. Hoeltje, a careful student of the Concord group for more
than twenty-five years, enters a minority report in "Misconceptions in
Current Thoreau Criticism" (*PQ* 47[1968]:563–70). The misconceptions specified are (i) that Thoreau is a great social seer, (ii) that
Emerson impeded Thoreau's reputation, (iii) that nature takes up
little space in the journals, (iv) that nature writing can be separated
advantageously from Transcendentalism, and (v) that Walter Pater
is Thoreau's spiritual kin. Chapter and verse follow, persuasively
argued. Hoeltje concludes, with Arthur Christy, that Thoreau's place
is "with the mystics." His discussion of "Thoreau's erratic political
commentary" may be more nearly in the mainstream than he would
have suspected at the time he prepared his article (see below). In
other respects as well, Hoeltje articulates some common-sense reactions to much recent criticism.

Several essays prepared for the *Emerson Society Quarterly*, no.
56, have been published simultaneously in a gathering, *New Approaches to Thoreau: A Symposium*, edited by William Bysshe Stein
(Hartford, Conn., Transcendental Books). The approaches are not
particularly new, being chiefly close readings of literary works, with
an emphasis on symbol, structure, and language, but there is a refreshing preoccupation with minor items in the Thoreau canon. There
are thus two essays (by Bernard Rosenthal and B. Bernard Cohen)
on "Autumnal Tints"; two (by Gordon Bigelow and James Morse
Marshall) on "A Winter Walk"; and one each on "The Landlord,"
"Walking," and "A Walk to Wachusett" (by Joseph M. DeFalco,
Frederick Garber, and Donald R. Swanson, respectively). The
major items are not entirely slighted: Donna Gerstenberger has some
interesting things to say about paradox in *Walden*, and Joseph Schiffman reviews the sociology of literary taste as revealed in critical

understanding of *Walden* and "Civil Disobedience" (see below). There is also an introductory essay by Stein on Thoreau's use of language.

Of one essay in the volume, however, it can be said that it is a "new approach." Robert O. Evans's "Thoreau's Poetry and the Prose Works" is a detailed and closely argued discussion of Thoreau's poetry, in which Evans convincingly finds fault with almost all previous commentators. He asks a number of fundamental questions about the poetry and provides some remarkable answers, which need not necessarily be accepted to be liberating and instructive. Briefly, he finds that Thoreau's poems, far from being a "pendant" to the prose or "fillers" (as Carl Bode is said to regard them), are "the core which bears the meaning," though they are "not the only way meaning is expressed." (In an exemplary reading of "Smoke," for example, he persuades me that the poem is not really about smoke at all, but about *Walden*.) Thoreau is said to have worked toward his innovative technique of intermixture of poetry and prose in *A Week* but to have realized the book's inadequacy in this fundamental respect even as he was completing it. *Walden*, however, was a success. The wide-ranging essay seems certain to be a seminal one, leading to further publication by Evans himself as well as others. For example: Evans refers several times to Thoreau's "modesty." Although it is possible to see what he means by it, the term is so foreign to the customary impression that it deserves elaboration in a separate essay.

As if to validate his disagreement with Evans, in the Leon Howard festschrift Carl Bode has discussed the poetry from a quite different point of view. In "Thoreau and the Borrowed Reeds" (*Themes and Directions*, pp. 58–68), Bode emphasizes the self-revealing character of the poetry, demonstrating as it does Thoreau's literary enthusiasms (the Metaphysicals, Milton, Wordsworth, Emerson), his eclecticism of method coexisting with organic theory, and his central belief in the superiority of the poet's life to his work. ("Smoke," by the way, in Bode's essay, is treated as a poem in which nature is both subject and comparison.)[1] Both Bode and Evans enlarge perspectives on the poems, each in his own way.

There were other discussions of minor items in the Thoreau canon, in addition to those gathered in *New Approaches*. Lauriat

---

1. Lyle Glazier ("Thoreau's Rebellious Lyric" *ESQ* 54:27–30) emphasizes the poem's "rebelliousness" metrically, metaphorically, etc.

Lane, Jr. ("Thoreau's Two Walks: Structure and Meaning," *TSB* 109:1–3) contrasts "A Walk to Wachusett," a "transcendental allegory" involving "a quest, linear, exploratory, through the unfamiliar toward revelation," and "A Winter Walk," "a ramble, orbital, responsive, through the familiar toward completion." The latter points more clearly toward *A Week* and *Walden*. In " 'Ktaadn'—A Record of Thoreau's Youthful Crisis" (*TJQ*, 1,iv:1–6) John F. Jaques insists that Thoreau's mountain-top experience was no "thrilling epiphany" but "the grim awareness of bare matter." Thoreau suppressed its effect on him in his essay, a response which turned him inward.

Because of the special focus of the Stein symposium and the apparent diversion of some scholarly energies to secondary works by Thoreau, there was less abundant commentary on *Walden* than in recent years. One essay taking a new approach, however, was Lauriat Lane, Jr.'s "*Walden*, the Second Year" (*SIR* 8:183–92). Lane points out that the second year at Walden was not like the first. Some of the differences are implied in *Walden*; others are suppressed. One (the account of his jailing) was shifted from 1846 to 1845. Lane understands Thoreau's refusal to include the struggles and disappointments of the second year to indicate that *Walden* is essentially a mythic narrative of purification, to be analyzed and criticized as such. He implies that *Walden* might have been a richer book had its author been able to synthesize the experience of the first and second years, but he does not insist upon that point of view. C. E. Pulos ("The Foreign Observer in *Walden*," *ELN* 7:51–53) relates the occasional indication of detached points of view to eighteenth-century travel narratives, the difference being that Thoreau uses the distancing not merely for social satire but to authenticate his own emancipation. In an article inadvertently omitted from last year's report, "Emerson, Thoreau, and the Double Consciousness" (*NEQ* 41[1968]:40–50) Joel Porte relates several features of *Walden* to the inner conflict between the spiritual and sensual selves dramatized in Goethe's *Faust*. The chapter "Solitude," the encounter with the Canadian woodchopper, the colloquy with himself in "Higher Laws," and the elemental imagery of "Spring" all reveal Thoreau's preoccupation with the manifestation of vital energy at all levels of nature (including "the low") and its unison with the highest spiritual insight.

There was considerable commentary on Thoreau's work and thought by Indian scholars in 1969, which, despite its variety, it seems proper to consider as a unit, demonstrating in part the worldwide interest in the Transcendentalists. Two of the most substantial appear in the festschrift for Robert E. Spiller (*Indian Essays*). K. R. Chandrasekharan discusses "Thoreau's Literary Art and His Philosophy" (pp. 41–54), stressing Thoreau's claim to be regarded as "a Modern Hindoo," as he called himself. In "The Question of Form in Thoreau's *A Week on the Concord and Merrimack Rivers*" (pp. 99–112), V. K. Chari questions the interpretations of the book by Sherman Paul and Carl Hovde, especially their stress upon its contemplative character, a tactic to defend *A Week* against its detractors, according to Chari. He finds Thoreau occasionally successful in shifting naturally from the facts of the voyage to meditations suggested by them, but often not successful at all. He questions also the claims made for a structure based on days of the week, the analogies of which are unconvincing. The structure of the book, Chari insists, is based on the irreversible order of the voyage, around which Thoreau, with mixed success, built the substance of the book.

*Perspectives in American Literature*, edited by Jagdish Chander (Ludhiana, Lyall Book Depot), is a gathering of about forty essays on American literature, papers presented at a seminar on the subject at Simla in 1967 and sponsored by the U.S. Educational Foundation in India. Since the essays are by Indian students and scholars at all levels, they vary considerably in value. There are nine essays on Emerson, Thoreau, and Transcendentalism, all but two of which concern Thoreau exclusively. Throughout, Thoreau is treated more as modern gospel than literature. The words of Satwant Grewal typify the approach: "For Indians *Walden* takes on a special meaning. It advocates ideas and values of life similar to their own." Nevertheless, the most famous instance of Thoreau's affinities with Indian thought is challenged in Nissim Ezekiel's "The Thoreau-Gandhi Syndrome: An Ambiguous Influence" (*Quest* 58[1968]:21–26), in which accounts of Thoreau's influence on Gandhi are called exaggerated and sentimental, based in part on American chauvinism and in part on Indian attempts to win American support for Gandhi's movement for national independence. The argument is based chiefly on marked temperamental and philosophical differences between the two men themselves.

Despite the number of Indian essays on Thoreau's writings, the principal contribution in criticism by a foreign scholar among those to be considered here is Enrico Forni (*Mito contro ideologia: Nota su Thoreau*, Rome, Silva, 1968). Forni is charmed by Thoreau's "attualità," as opposed to the faintly breathing academic organism represented by Emerson. The one manifests vital myth; the other, pale ideology. Thoreau's naturalistic existentialism is praised in terms lately employed by Harold Fromm and William Bridges to depict the achievement of Emerson. It is unfortunate that Emerson's role in the book is that of mere foil to Thoreau, because the dialectic necessitates some distortion of Emerson not at all essential to the praise of Thoreau's "wildness," primitivism, and aesthetic vitalism. Concerning the structure of *Walden* Forni introduces the helpful analogy of the medieval travel narrative in three stages: the dark forest, the rediscovery of nature, and the discovery of supreme laws. There are other *obiter dicta* of interest, especially in discussion of the cyclic myth of death and rebirth and the archetypal gnosis of return.[2]

There is little constancy at present in the interpretation of Thoreau's political essays. In "Thoreau and American Power" (*AtM* 223,v:60–68) Alfred Kazin attributes the stirring character of "Civil Disobedience" to its personal urgency, but finds it no guide to political action, because it rests on an unacceptable literary anarchism. Thoreau, he writes, did not anticipate the modern state; he distrusted government and did not understand it. Kazin finds it ironical that Thoreau is widely read in modern America. Identifying power with individual spiritual power, Thoreau did not understand massive state power. A much more sympathetic view of Thoreau is found in Staughton Lynd, *Intellectual Origins of American Radicalism* (New York, Pantheon, 1968). Lynd's general argument is that there was a radical content to the Declaration of Independence deriving from British dissenters. Nineteenth-century reformers, especially Abolitionists, renewed the radicalism of the Declaration and, in doing so, anticipated many positions of existential radicalism of the 1960's. Thoreau is frequently and admiringly quoted, especially on active civil disobedience and the Jeffersonian concept that "the earth belongs to the living."

So wide a variance suggests that analytical scholarship has not completed its tasks. A return to *explication de texte* is attempted by John A. Christie ("Thoreau and Civil Resistance," *ESQ* 54:5–12).

2. I acknowledge gratefully the assistance of my colleague John Finzi in dealing with the subject matter of Forni's book.

Christie points out numerous ways in which Thoreau's political essays have been distorted or misconstrued and particularly distinguishes the reservations and misgivings with which Thoreau offered civil resistance. Joseph Schiffman in "*Walden* and *Civil Disobedience*: Critical Analyses" (*ESQ* 56:57–60) synthesizes the points of view of Kazin and Christie. Thoreau's doctrine of conscience is said to suffer from "a dangerous glibness" and a lack of social safeguard, "especially when conscience is less than pure." But his strictures apply to civil disobedience as theory, not Thoreau's practice, which was "noble." Civil disobedience used with militant reprisal and contempt for law is anti-Thoreauvian, ignoring as it does the moral and renovative character of the practice in Thoreau's use.

### iv. Criticism: Other Transcendentalists

Two book-length studies of Margaret Fuller, one essentially biographical, the other a survey of her criticism, could hardly offer sharper contrasts between the academic mode of scholarship and its opposite. *The Roman Years of Margaret Fuller: A Biography* (New York, Crowell) is the work of Joseph Jay Deiss, formerly vice-director of the American Academy in Rome, who brings to his biographical task important assets: familiarity with Italy, its language, its scenes, and its history; access to the Ossoli–della Torre family archives as well as Fuller papers in Boston and Cambridge and the ability to use them to good advantage; and a loyal interest in the subject. Unfortunately, his apparent unfamiliarity with the American background leads to some avoidable blunders, such as the reference to "kindly old" William H. Channing in the context of March 1848. Deiss stresses and documents the respectability of the Ossoli family and the significance of its name; Margaret's extremely close friendship with Mazzini, Mickiewicz, and other republican leaders; her espousal of radicalism (Mrs. Browning called Margaret "one of the out and out Reds"); and the pathos and incredible bad luck leading to her death at sea. He is also able to fix the approximate date of her marriage (fall 1849), about a year after the birth of Angelino. The book is overdramatic, however, especially the first half, as Deiss presents Margaret as an archetypal Puritan spinster who achieves sexual emancipation and radicalization in sunny Italy. (There is, of course, something to this view, but it need not be comprehended or presented simplistically.) As usual, Emerson comes off badly in a biography of one of his circle; he is the cold fish, arch-representative of Margaret's Puritan background, unable to anticipate her potential and unable to understand her after her liberation. *The Roman Years of Margaret Fuller* must be regarded as an important, though not completely satisfactory, book.

In *Margaret Fuller, Citizen of the World: An Intermediary Between European and American Literature* (Heidelberg, Carl Winter), on the other hand, Russell Durning surveys Margaret's interest in and comments about European literature, arriving at conclusions entirely predictable and indeed forecast by his subtitles. The work, which was a 1964 dissertation at North Carolina, will be consulted less for new information or insight than for its solid reliability as a reference or, more specifically, bibliographical tool.

Vivian C. Hopkins also pays tribute to "Margaret Fuller: American Nationalist Critic" (*ESQ* 55:24–41), a rapid-fire summary of her critical opinions about literature and culture, with a highly useful set of bibliographical notes, 100 in number. There is relatively little commentary, but Miss Hopkins identifies a number of criteria Margaret shared with other Transcendentalists: the distinction between genius and talent, the value placed on newness of inspiration, the demand for organic form, etc. Unlike other Transcendentalists, however, she valued passion as a literary component, criticized overt moralism, and even tolerated light literature of escape. Her critical theories also figure in Sidney Poger's "The Critical Stance of *The Dial*" (ESQ 57:22–27). Poger finds that *The Dial* under Margaret Fuller's editorship included more statements of critical principles than under Emerson's, but the "critical stance" was remarkably uniform throughout its brief publishing history. Complementing the studies cited above is John B. Wilson's "The Aesthetics of Transcendentalism" (*ESQ* 57:27–34), which surveys a variety of comments on aesthetics by a number of Transcendentalists but emphasizes Margaret Fuller and Elizabeth Peabody, upon both of whom Wilson finds the influence of Washington Allston to have been strong, almost decisive, in aesthetics. In a general essay of slight interest, "A Study in Contrast: Effie in Venice and the Roman Spring of Margaret Fuller" (*AR* 28:461–76), Helen Barolini contrasts the reaction to Italy and things Italian by Margaret Fuller and Mrs. John Ruskin.

The once-neglected lesser Transcendentalists were the subject of a number of interesting essays. Two dealing with William Ellery Channing the Elder propose almost identical statements of purpose and remarkably similar conclusions. Nathan Lyons ("The Figure of William Ellery Channing," *MQR* 7[1968]:120–26) seeks to account for the pale impression which Channing makes despite his reputation among his contemporaries and concludes that because Channing "trafficks endlessly in abstractions which want pith" his prose obscures his impact upon his own times. Similarly, Mary W. Edrich, ("The Channing Rhetoric and 'Splendid Confusion,'" *ESQ* 57:5–12) attributes to Channing's "lack of artistic adventurousness" the impression that he was indifferent to social action. Miss Edrich traces the weakness of Channing's prose style to the theories of Blair and Kames, which Channing followed slavishly. Nevertheless, his rhetoric was exciting to the younger generation.

According to Robert D. Arner ("Hawthorne and Jones Very: Two Dimensions of Satire in 'Egotism; or, The Bosom Serpent,'" *NEQ* 42:267–75), Very, not Edgar Allan Poe, is the object of satire in Hawthorne's story. The evidence (generally from secondary sources) is found in correspondence of Very and Elizabeth Peabody and some verbal parallels. The post-1840 Very is studied in Paschal Reeves's "Jones Very as Preacher: The Extant Sermons" (*ESQ* 57:16–22). There are 134 manuscript sermons of Very in existence (105 at the Houghton Library, 28 at Brown, and 1 in the Essex Institute). Analysis of them reveals Very's wide acquaintance with the Bible and secular Western literature, his theological conservatism and opposition to Catholicism, and the absence of the intense mysticism which informed his early poems.

Orestes Brownson was also conservative in many ways. One of these was his lack of sympathy with advocacy for women's rights. Late in life he wrote two articles on "The Woman Question" (1869, 1873). These are analyzed by Arlene Swidler ("Brownson and the 'Woman Question,'" *ABR* 19[1968]:211–19). According to Brownson, there was not "a single Christian believer" among the advocates of women's rights. Distinguishing between natural rights and civil rights (which included suffrage), Brownson took a position toward women's rights similar to that toward Negro suffrage. In the end Brownson was not so much refuted as ignored.

Bronson Alcott is also ignored, but with less justification, according to Charles Strickland, "A Transcendentalist Father: The Child-

Rearing Practices of Bronson Alcott," *PAH* 3:5–73. His record of observations of his daughter Anna "clearly mark the beginnings of child psychology in America, a full half-century before G. Stanley Hall." Not only did both Anna and Louisa turn out well, the concept of the family which directed their rearing was a refuge to Alcott himself.

Finally, John B. Wilson ("Elizabeth Peabody and Other Transcendentalists on History and Historians," *Historian* 30 [1967]:72–86) indicates how thoroughly informed Elizabeth Peabody was in history and historical theory and how influential she was in advocating its teaching. For nearly fifty years she wrote and talked about history. (A series of articles in the 1830's in the *Christian Examiner* betoken her early interest; her final publication on history was in the *Journal of Speculative Philosophy*, 1881.) Wilson includes some commentary on Parker, Ripley, and James Freeman Clarke, only to conclude that all were dilettantes compared to Miss Peabody. (This, despite Parker's having spent months verifying references and reading the sources before reviewing W. H. Prescott's eight-volume Spanish history, the scholarship of which Parker found faulty.)

### v. Sources and Influence

There were a great many brief comments during the year in which this or that author or work (from Socrates and Marcus Aurelius on down) was found to be the source of a sentiment or technique in Emerson or Thoreau or in which this or that author or work was thought to be influenced by them. Most of these are of slight interest. A few of the more substantial contributions are noticed below.

Andrew M. McLean ("Emerson's 'Brahma' as an Expression of Brahman," *NEQ* 42:115–22) is less concerned with Emerson's sources than with exegesis of the Hindu mythological content of the poem, which captures "the essence of the Hindu religious spirit." According to John Homan, Jr. ("Thoreau, the Emblem, and the *Week*," *ATQ* 1,i: 104–08), Thoreau "consistently employs an approximation of the emblem to illustrate his impressions of nature, comment aphoristically on the corresponding idea, and elaborate the practical and moral applications." Since Thoreau's interest in Quarles has been a scholarly commonplace, interest in Homan's article will reside in the many examples which he provides to validate his thesis of a consciously emblematic prose in *A Week on the Concord and Merri-mack Rivers*.

Perry Westbrook ("John Burroughs and the Transcendentalists," *ESQ* 55:47–55) surveys interest in Emerson, Thoreau, and Whitman by Burroughs, who wrote over fifty essays on the three writers and thus "forms an extremely important link in the continuity of our literary and intellectual life." R. Majumdar ("Virginia Woolf and Thoreau," *TSB* 109:4–5) reminds us of the somewhat surprising interest on the part of the British novelist, typified by her centennial essay on Thoreau in *TLS*. The interest of Marcel Proust in Thoreau's work has been known since F. O. Matthiessen's *American Renaissance* (1941) at least. However, there are new revelations of the extent of Proust's enthusiasm in Laurence Vernet's "Proust admirateur imprévu de Thoreau" (*Europe* 477:217–24). Apparently Proust would have translated Thoreau if he had not been anticipated by the Princesse de Polignac, the daughter of Isaac Singer, whose translations appeared in Paris periodicals in the early years of the twentieth century.

## vi. Dissertations

Only seven dissertations specifically on Emerson, Thoreau, and Transcendentalism were abstracted in *Dissertation Abstracts*. This represents a very steep decline from the level of the past two years. Almost as surprising, only one of these has Emerson as its subject: "Emerson's Proverbial Rhetoric: 1818–1838" by Ralph Charles La-Rosa (*DA* 30:1140A).

Thoreau, on the other hand, continues to attract considerable attention at the doctoral level. There were five dissertations in which Thoreau's work or thought was the principal or a coordinate subject. In addition, Thoreau serves as principal foil in Eugene William Chesnick's "The Amplitude of Time: A Study of the Time-Sense of Walt Whitman" (*DA* 29:3969A–70A). He is a principal in Ronald Milburn Fields's "Four Concepts of an Organic Principle: Horatio Greenough, Henry David Thoreau, Walt Whitman, and Louis Sullivan" (*DA* 29:3929A), a Fine Arts dissertation at Ohio University. And, along with Emerson, he figures prominently in Bernard Rosenthal's "Nature's Slighting Hand: The Idea of Nature in American Writing, 1820–1860" (*DA* 30:2226A).

Of the five dissertations more exclusively concerned with Thoreau, two studies, apparently complementary in outlook and method, pertain to nature and the naturalist tradition. They are L. Gary Lambert's "Rousseau and Thoreau: Their Concept of Nature" (*DA* 30:1988A), and Kichung Kim's "Thoreau's Involvement with Nature; Thoreau and the Naturalist Tradition" (*DA* 30:1985A). Two others concern the continuity, fore and aft, of literary traditions in which Thoreau has a place. They are Gordon Emmett Slethaug's "Thoreau's Use of the Pastoral and Fable Traditions" (*DA* 29:4504A–05A) and Lyle D. Domina's "Frost and Thoreau: A Study in Affinities "'(*DA* 29:2705A–06A). The fifth is a survey of critical opinion of Thoreau: Theodore Haddin's "The Changing Image of Henry Thoreau: The Emergence of the Literary Artist" (*DA* 30:724A–25A).

A general study is Roger Chester Mueller's "The Orient in American Transcendental Periodicals, 1835–1886" (*DA* 29:2681A). Dr. Channing and Emerson are among those studied in John Joseph Seydow's "The Objective Aesthetic in American Literature, 1828–1838" (*DA* 29:3109A–10A).

### *vii.* Miscellaneous

Students of Transcendentalism will not wish to neglect Marjorie J. Elder's *Nathaniel Hawthorne, Transcendental Symbolist* (Athens, Ohio Univ. Press), which is noticed in chapter 2 below. Like some other recent publications, it rejects the traditional simplistic polarity of Hawthorne-Meville versus Emerson-Thoreau. Also not to be overlooked is *Emerson's Nature—Origin, Growth, Meaning*, edited by Merton M. Sealts, Jr., and Alfred R. Ferguson (New York, Dodd, Mead). The volume, which is to "casebooks" as "The American Scholar" is to the ordinary commencement address, may be regarded as pedagogical first fruits of the Belknap Press edition of Emerson's journals, of which Sealts and Ferguson have been two of the principal editors.

Amid and perhaps because of the welter of publication on Emerson, Thoreau, and Transcendentalism, it is reassuring that a number of scholars and critics concern themselves with central rather than peripheral questions. In 1969, it seemed, they were more vocal than in the recent past—and with justification.

*Library of Congress*

# 2. Hawthorne

## Roy R. Male

Each year roughly one-eighth of the work done on Hawthorne is of considerable significance. The remainder consists of dissertations (which in distilled form may later prove to be significant), forced publications by young scholars, commercial casebooks and reprints, articles done on assignment or with their left hands by established critics, and miscellaneous bits and pieces of information or interpretation, often useful, but limited in scope. In reviewing Hawthorne studies for 1969, I discriminate more sharply between these two categories by placing the major work in a broad and unified context; the minor work—much of it eminently respectable, but limited in its implications—I have arranged in alphabetical order under subject headings.

### i. New Trends

Put briefly, the major issue that plagued and fascinated Hawthorne in his life and work is this: What is the relation between inner experience, particularly daydreaming, and the reality of ordinary life? How does the magical power of the imagination impinge upon the apparent objectivity of the institutionalized world? That such a theme should strike us once again as being centrally important reminds us not only of our debt to the Romantics but, more specifically, of the ways in which Hawthorne's work has responded to rapidly shifting expectations during the last two decades.[1] In the fifties it rewarded the explicatory and mythic analyses of the New Critics; in the mid-sixties it survived, at the cost of some diminution, the rigorous inquest of the new historicists and the neo-Freudians; and now his

---

1. Hyatt H. Waggoner's revised edition of Hawthorne's *Selected Tales and Sketches* (New York, Holt, Rinehart and Winston, 1970), provides both in its new introduction and in its contents a valuable summary of changes in critical perspective.

fiction seems more vital than ever for readers aware of new developments in psychology and related fields.

The developments I have in mind are better indicated by a representative book list than by any label: Jerome L. Singer, *Daydreaming* (1966) and his article "Fantasy" in the *International Encyclopedia of the Social Sciences*; M. D. Vernon, *The Psychology of Perception* (1962); E. H. Gombrich, *Art and Illusion* (1960); Mario Praz, *Mnemosyne* (1970); Peter Berger and Thomas Luckmann, *The Social Construction of Reality* (1966); J. H. Van Den Berg, *The Phenomenological Approach to Psychiatry* (1955); Paul Brodtkorb, *Ishmael's White World* (1965); Robert Scholes and Robert Kellogg, *The Nature of Narrative* (1966); and Scholes, *The Fabulators* (1967).

If we add to this highly respectable list such popularizations as textbooks like *Montage* (New York, Macmillan, 1970) and Marshall McLuhan's burgeoning bibliography of antibooks, we have a fairly accurate model of the insights and expectations that many readers are now bringing to Hawthorne's works. Among them are the following: that the processes of perception and cognition are complicated, fascinating, and still not completely understood; that one rewarding way of approaching these processes is by studying the relation between pictorial and verbal art forms; that believing is seeing, or as Gombrich says, "all culture and all communication depend on the interplay between expectation and observation";[2] that fantasizing or daydreaming, instead of being either a trivial activity or a disguised form of drive gratification, may well be a major human function, a cognitive skill integrated with other aspects of mental life; that subjective identity is precarious, dependent upon the individual's relations with equally precarious others and "continually threatened by the 'surrealistic' metamorphoses of dreams and fantasies";[3] and that the reality of ordinary life which we must take for granted is, nevertheless, essentially a human and social construction.

To speak of "new" developments in psychology in the same breath as we return to the classical problems of consciousness that Hawthorne brooded over may seem anachronistic. But one characteristic of our time is that with the aid of electronic machinery we have arrived at or returned to a less hydraulic, less simplistic view of man.

2. *Art and Illusion* (New York, Pantheon, 1960), p. 60.
3. Peter L. Berger and Thomas Luckmann, *The Social Construction of Reality* (New York, Doubleday, 1966), p. 100.

After years of domination by the behaviorists, who saw man essentially as an empty organism controlled by conditions of stimulus and response, and by the Freudians, who saw man as an organism controlled chiefly by states of drive deficit, psychology has been enriched and complicated by the neurophysiologists and by the designers of computers. Seeking a systematic means of studying mental life, the neurophysiologists explored the site of consciousness with electrodes and amplifiers, discovering there a complex network of filters and circuits. At the same time, interest in consciousness and cognition in general was greatly augmented "'when it was demonstrated that computers could be programmed to simulate complex thought processes. . . . Neither the brain as revealed by contemporary neurophysiology nor the brain as simulated by the modern high speed computer gave any support or comfort to the simplistic conceptions of the nature of the human being which had dominated American psychology for thirty years."[4]

For literary critics probably the most significant aspect of this activity in psychology is the work that Jerome L. Singer and others have done on fantasy during the past fifteen years. The starting point was Freud's early papers (1908 and 1911) on the poet and daydreaming which set forth two influential hypotheses: (i) daydreaming grows out of an unsatisfied wish, and (ii) all processes of thought, including fantasy, by allowing partial satisfactions, partially reduce the drive, and this permits delay in its discharge. Recent research having produced telling evidence against this catharsis theory, Singer decided to take a fresh look at the origin of fantasy "without the burden of concepts of cathectic dynamics or neutralized versus libidinized energy." He proposed instead to begin by regarding the development of fantasy behavior as a cognitive skill, a capacity for gradual internalization of response, for "practicing a complex series of skills related to what Kurt Goldstein has called 'the attitude toward the possible.'"[5]

By shucking the therapeutic bias of psychoanalysis, by subjecting its speculative hypotheses to controlled experiment and large-scale data gathering, Singer and his colleagues have effectively countered

4. Foreword by Sylvan Tomkins in Jerome L. Singer, *Daydreaming* (New York, Random House, 1966), p. viii.

5. Singer, "Fantasy," in *The International Encyclopedia of the Social Sciences*, edited by David L. Sills (New York, MacMillan, 1968), 5:331–32.

the typical American conception of the daydream as being either
trivial, pathological, or sublimated gratification. Yet, given our ex-
troversive ideology, doubts concerning the value of fantasy, some
of them well-founded, will remain. And with this ambivalence, we
are back in the world of Hawthorne's notebooks, prefaces, and
fictions.

### ii. Major Work

That world is in the process of being rediscovered and redefined. In
" 'Young Goodman Brown' and Hawthorne's Theory of Mimesis"
(*NCF* 23:393–412), surely one of the best articles ever written on
Hawthorne's art, Taylor Stoehr has shown that its central struggle
"is to maintain a tension between the terms of his symbols, to enliven
dead metaphors, to force his daydreams into a certain relation with
everyday life without giving up their essential strangeness." Stoehr
begins by distinguishing the American tellers of tales from the writers
of short stories. The former, writers like Poe, Hawthorne, Melville,
and the later Mark Twain, "construct their fictions around some single
and striking figure of speech, at once abstract and concrete, an idea
embodied in an action, object, circumstance, or the like, so that it
becomes, as it were, a trope of life." Hawthorne's special use of
language is a heavily metaphorical style in which the literal is forever on the verge of turning into figurative description, and in his
best tales he puts the confrontation between the imaginary and the
real directly into his plots.

Following up an observation originally made by Harry Levin,
Stoehr maintains that the best of Hawthorne's tales are "hypothetical"
rather than purely allegorical in method. They are simulations: "we
are required to put an 'as if' construction on everything, to begin the
experience with a silent 'supposing that . . .' which determines our
attitude toward what we read." For characters like Young Goodman
Brown and Giovanni Guasconti, mind and attitude actively partici-
pate in the constitution of "fact," and Hawthorne's technique "puts
us in nearly the same position as his characters, except that we are
given some additional hints as to how we should come to terms with
*our* dream, the tale we are reading." Stoehr is not the first to read
"Young Goodman Brown" as essentially a tale about the relation of
fiction and reality. But his sketch of Hawthorne's theory of mimesis

is so deftly drawn and so solidly based on a lucid reading of all of Hawthorne that his article wins first prize (an imaginary trip to Salem) in this year's competition.

Equally impressive is the same author's "Hawthorne and Mesmerism" (*HLQ* 33:33–60), a model of what a first-rate article should be. It turns up some new and extremely interesting material about the impact of mesmerism upon Emerson and his contemporaries, offers a fascinating case history of Sophia Hawthorne, and sensitively interprets Hawthorne's reaction to the magnetic peril by placing *The House of the Seven Gables* and *The Blithedale Romance* in the context of other novels dealing with mesmerism. Stoehr concludes that "the magical power of imagination was Hawthorne's chief theme in all of his writings, and the usefulness of the new pseudoscience lay in its adaptability to this theme. His art could be taken as a variety of mesmerism, a spell he wove over his readers, which might change their lives, and for which he might be responsible." Hawthorne saw the ways that "mesmerism expressed his own ambivalent position on questions of will, imagination, and reality, and he made what use he could of it to bring his own problems as a writer into the center of *The House of the Seven Gables* and *The Blithedale Romance*, where, if he could not solve them (no more could his characters) he could at least continue, tentatively and equivocally, to practice the art he mistrusted."

Proceeding from somewhat similar premises, an important article by Darrel Abel, "Black Glove and Pink Ribbon: Hawthorne's Metonymic Symbols" (*NEQ* 42:163–80), complements Stoehr's work and gives it historical dimensions. Working adeptly with the metonymic symbols of the black glove in *The Scarlet Letter* and the pink ribbon in "Young Goodman Brown," Abel shows how Hawthorne's "brilliant historical imagination is displayed in these stories. His insight is that history's inner meaning is in that complex of ideas which in any given historic scene patterns events to the perception of the actors in the scene." Events, in short, do not possess their own absolute pattern; as anyone who has participated in recent history knows, they have patterns projected by the consciousness of persons who move them and are moved by them in a community of thought and action.

Thus Abel maintains that it is "beside the point to ask what the 'real' meaning of Young Goodman Brown's adventures is, or to consider whether he 'had only dreamed a wild dream,' as the author deprecatingly invites us to do." Since every real meaning exists only insofar as it seems real to persons involved in the world of their imagination, "all interpretations of experience are dreams of meaning. Hawthorne's genius was in his ability to dream his way back into the Puritan reality and to furnish us the means of dreaming their dreams as well." Thus the inner meaning of historical events in *The Scarlet Letter*, occurring in the capital of Puritan faith at a time when venerated personages of the first generation of Puritans were at the height of their authority, differs from that of "Young Goodman Brown," laid in Salem in the witching times of 1692.

Compiling a list of examples which, as he says, could be multiplied, Abel persuasively argues that Hawthorne's most insistent theme is "that every reading of facts, every version of 'truth,' is an arbitrary determination." The point here is not simply that Hawthorne admits this epistemological uncertainty; he "deliberately exposes and artfully exploits it in his tales." Abel's other major article, "Giving Lustre to Gray Shadows: Hawthorne's Potent Art" (*AL* 41:373–88), is a densely illustrated piece, important for those who would understand the specific workings of Hawthorne's imagination. After examining some of his less successful methods of constructing vehicles to move his readers' imaginations, Abel concludes that for Hawthorne "the most potent datum was some relic of human action and character, now an anachronism, but found in a place where it was once the most significant feature of a full and living scene, so that it retains a metonymic capability of recalling the entire fabric of reality to which it belonged." In its emphasis upon the metonymic symbol, Abel's work corroborates Edward M. Clay's article reviewed in *ALS 1968*, p. 29.

Since imaginative literature exists midway between painting and music, a writer's style may be defined to some extent by the way he presses toward one or the other of these kindred art forms. Hawthorne's medium has long been recognized as essentially pictorial, but in the past year the work of Richard H. Fogle and Leo B. Levy has enriched this recognition.

Fogle's book, *Hawthorne's Imagery: The "Proper Light and Shadow" in the Major Romances* (Norman, Univ. of Okla. Press), is, as the author indicates in a pleasantly candid and polemical preface, narrower than his *Hawthorne's Fiction*, which it supplements.

After an excellent introductory chapter which offers a close analysis of the prefaces and "Main Street," Fogle patiently unfolds the patterns of light and darkness that inform the four major romances. Except for this guiding orientation little critical pressure is applied to the text. Fogle seems more determined than ever to let Hawthorne's fiction speak for itself. The result is a great deal of quotation, which, even though it is aptly chosen, risks becoming tiresome. Put differently, the text does not offer enough resistance to Fogle's analysis. Hawthorne's fundamental figure was, as Fogle argues, pictorial. Light and darkness in the fiction are interdependent, but framed by absolutes outside the picture, i.e., the human dimension. What I miss here is a full account of the image-making process itself and Hawthorne's ambivalent attitude toward it, placed in the context of the Romantic movement. Since no one is better qualified to write on Hawthorne and Coleridge than Professor Fogle, it is hoped that his next book will satisfy this need.

In a corollary essay, "Weird Mockery: An Element of Hawthorne's Style" (*Style* 2[1968]:191–202), Fogle offers an urbane, acute analysis of the ways in which Hawthorne "inveterately 'keeps his cool'. . . . He says what abstractedly may be regarded as some quite wonderful and terrible things, but he says them very calmly." Building upon the observations of James, Trollope, and Melville, Fogle points to the element of weird and delicate playfulness present in the style of "Young Goodman Brown" and "My Kinsman, Major Molineux."

In "The Landscape Modes of *The Scarlet Letter*" (*NCF* 23:377–92) Leo Levy continues his low-keyed but important series of articles on the sublime and the picturesque in Hawthorne's fiction. Examining the settings of *The Scarlet Letter*, Levy describes the ways in which Hawthorne "transcends landscape through an extension of the principles by which he visualizes it." A companion essay, "*The Blithedale Romance*: Hawthorne's 'Voyage Through Chaos'" (*SIR* 8[1968]:1–15), suggests that the characters and themes of the book may be understood as the sum of the conflict between the picturesque, "associated with a dying agrarian order and utilitarian science, foreshadowing the appearance of an urban and technological age." Thus the romance generates its force from the paradox of a future based upon the restoration of a simpler mode of life, derived from the values of an earlier time. Rarely is it necessary these days to urge that a scholar collect his essays in a book, but I think we would all profit if Professor Levy were to do so.

The subtitle of Hugo McPherson's *Hawthorne as Myth-Maker: A Study in Imagination* (Toronto, Univ. of Toronto Press) promises more than the book delivers, but it is nevertheless a significant addition to the shelf of critical works on Hawthorne. The book attempts to define the nature of Hawthorne's "inward vision" by studying the myth-making nature of his imagination. McPherson claims that his prime concern is not to study Hawthorne's art "in terms of an external frame of ideas but to allow the character types, image patterns, and narrative configurations of his art to speak for themselves." Like all such disclaimers, this one is a cover for the critical framework McPherson does use. He even includes a chart of character types and refers to his own broad "outline map." No—truly to let character types, image patterns, and narrative configurations speak for themselves, the critic would have to remain silent and let his reader read Hawthorne. But McPherson does spare us the usual grandiose references to Campbell and Eliade that afflict writers on myth, and he stays with the Greek myths that most appealed to Hawthorne.

In synopsis, Hawthorne's personal myth was this: the young, fatherless artist-hero, Oberon,' menaced by his aged 'fathers,' goes on a twelve-year quest in an illusive world of spectres, and finally returns to claim his place and marry a 'princess.'" Deliberately cast in the language of fairy tale, this account nevertheless does permit McPherson to place in new perspective several prime features of Hawthorne's work: his obsession with the past, his view of the rising democracy of the present, his suspicion of transcendentalism, and his conviction that artists indeed are the "unacknowledged legislators of the world."

### iii. Minor Work: General

B. Bernard Cohen's *The Recognition of Nathaniel Hawthorne: Selected Criticism Since 1828* (Ann Arbor, Univ. of Mich. Press) offers a well-balanced collection of reprinted criticism, including some relatively unfamiliar early reviews. The selections from modern critics emphasize the controversy of the mid-sixties. In *Nathaniel Hawthorne: Transcendental Symbolist* (Athens, Ohio Univ. Press)

Marjorie J. Elder summarizes transcendental aesthetic theory and Hawthorne's supposed application of it in his tales. The thesis throws Hawthorne's work out of balance by leaning too heavily upon the assumed Emersonian influence. But the main objection is that the book does no penetrating; Miss Elder is content to quote, summarize, and paraphrase. There is no indication that she has read Fogle, Waggoner, Crews, or any recent criticism. This book did not need to be published. Theodore L. Gross's "Nathaniel Hawthorne: The Absurdity of Heroism (*YR* 57[1968]:182–95) is a gracefully composed essay that focuses upon a recurring theme in Hawthorne's work: heroism and absurdity cannot be easily distinguished. The sense of the actual forced Hawthorne to modify the intensity of his tragic vision and conditioned his attitude toward heroes. The work which most clearly demonstrates the limitations of heroism is *The Blithedale Romance.*

In Benjamin Lease's "Hawthorne and *Blackwood's* in 1849: Two Unpublished Letters" (*JA* 14:152–54) the first is a letter from Horatio Bridge to a New York lawyer, John Jay, on June 12, 1849, suggesting that *Blackwood's* employ Hawthorne as a regular or occasional contributor. Jay's letter to *Blackwood's* indicates that Hawthorne has been advised, through Bridge, to send one or two articles written expressly for the magazine. Nothing ever came of Bridge's overture. Paul McCarthy ("The Extraordinary Man as Idealist in Novels by Hawthorne and Melville," *ESQ* 54:43–51) divides the idealists into yea-sayers and nay-sayers and pairs off characters from the major novels of Hawthorne and Melville. The arrangement resembles Merlin Bowen's in *The Long Encounter.* But it seems flat because the article treats these characters as if they were real people and ignores the complexity of the literary context in which they appear. Examining "The Textual Editions of Hawthorne and Melville" (*SLitI* 2,i:27–41), Thomas L. McHaney sees both editions as "monuments of hard work and scholarship" and offers a good clear statement of the problems confronted by the editors of the Centenary Edition. James E. Rocks's "Hawthorne and France: In Search of American Literary Nationalism" (*TSE* 17:145–57) is a useful survey of Hawthorne's critical reception in France in the nineteenth century. The reviews of French critics like Louis Etienne and Emile Montegut tended to exaggerate the importance of the New England Puritan heritage on Hawthorne's work. Hyatt H. Waggoner presents a brief,

clear, and authoritative discussion of Hawthorne's religious ideas in
relation to those of Emerson and Thoreau (" 'Grace' in the Thought
of Emerson, Thoreau, and Hawthorne," *ESQ* 54:68–72). At once
more traditional than they in his emphasis on universal guilt and
more conventional in his emphasis on the redemptive power of
domesticity, Hawthorne agreed that grace was unknowable to intellect and impossible to will.

### *iv.* Minor Work: The Tales.

Alexander W. Allison's "The Literary Contexts of 'My Kinsman,
Major Molineux' " (*NCF* 23[1968]:304–11) identifies a pattern of
balanced allusions to classical and Christian traditions in the story.
Robin is linked with Odysseus, Aeneas, and Heracles but in a mock-
heroic way as in Fielding. Walter E. Bezanson's "The Hawthorne
Game: 'Graves and Goblins' " (*ESQ* 54:73–77) is a light, breezy
analysis of one of Hawthorne's failures, first published in the *New
England Magazine*. Bezanson mocks Hawthorne's mockery of the
gothic and gift-book styles but rightly suggests that the latter sometimes became "more than protective coloring. With so limited an
audience there was not much pressure to distinguish between parody
and outright concession." In " 'The Minister's Black Veil': Symbol,
Meaning, and the Context of Hawthorne's Art" (*NCF* 24:182–92)
W. B. Carnochan argues persuasively that Hawthorne's familiar
formula of multiple choice is really designed to prevent, not to encourage, speculation. The story is "concerned above all with the veil
as a symbolic object pointing toward questions that cluster about the
notion of a symbol itself." Thus to insist upon a single meaning or
explanation of the veil is to be like the townspeople of the story.
    Comparing "Young Goodman Brown" and "My Kinsman, Major
Molineux" as companion pieces, Richard C. Carpenter ("Hawthorne's Polar Explorations,' *NCF* 24:45–56) sees them as organized
by a typical quest pattern. The former pursues the idea of isolation
as far as was artistically feasible; the latter follows the idea of corruption by society. Joe Davis in "The Myth of the Garden: Nathaniel
Hawthorne's 'Rappaccini's Daughter' " (*SLitI* 2,i:3–12) offers a
reading of the tale as myth, supported by the usual references to
Joseph Campbell and Mircea Eliade. Davis concentrates on the two
motifs of the lost Eden and the task of redeeming it through selfless

acts. Though essentially sound, the article seems well-worn after fifteen years of mythy explications.

J. M. Ferguson, Jr. ("Hawthorne's 'Young Goodman Brown,'" (*Expl* 28: item 32) reminds us that the pink ribbons, being neither scarlet nor white but of a hue somewhere between, suggest neither total depravity nor innocence, but the universal human condition somewhere between.

Robert H. Fossum skillfully extends earlier readings of "Alice Doane's Appeal" by Waggoner, Crews, and others to show how it illustrates Hawthorne's dilemmas as a writer of historical romance ("The Summons of the Past: Hawthorne's 'Alice Doane's Appeal,'" *NCF* 23[1968]:294–303). Fossum is particularly sensitive to the relation between "mind" and setting, structure and meaning, as he traces Hawthorne's efforts to make his recreation of the past plausible, yet sufficiently colored by the imagination to seem legendary. In "A Writer's Workshop: Hawthorne's 'The Great Carbuncle'" (*SSF* 6:157–64) Patrick Morrow effectively shows that we can profit from analyzing one of Hawthorne's failures. Though the story lacks moral ambiguity, psychological revelation, and complexity, it assembles a group of characters and situations that Hawthorne "will find portable." Julian Smith ("Hawthorne's *Legends of the Province House*," *NCF* 24:31–44) analyzes Hawthorne's only successful use of the framing device and shows that he was highly ambivalent toward and sometimes critical of the American Revolution. Dwayne Thorpe ("'My Kinsman, Major Molineux': The Identity of the Kinsman," *Topic* 18:53–63) emphasizes the nobility of the Major and the injustice of the mob that humiliates him. Writing with a curious combination of shrewdness and naiveté, Thorpe makes the dubious suggestion that the apparently benevolent guide who joins Robin near the end of the story is not to be trusted. In "'Roger Malvin's Burial': The Burial of Reuben Bourne's Cowardice" (*RS* 37:112–21) Robert E. Whelan, Jr., attempts to correct Crews' reading by stressing the allegorical significance of Cyrus, who reflects his father's inner life. His role, therefore, is "to mirror the struggle between cowardice and truth within his father's heart." Identifying with this handsome youth, many a reader has overlooked the figurative meaning of his death. William M. White ("Hawthorne's Eighteen-Year Cycle: Ethan Brand and Reuben Bourne," *SSF* 6:215–18) rather tenuously yokes the two stories as companion pieces, ignoring their dates of composition.

In "Hawthorne and His Artist" (*SIR* 7[1968]:193–206) R. A. Yoder argues that Hawthorne's view of the artist in "The Artist of the Beautiful" is closer to Emerson's that it is to the ironist critics. Yoder offers little that was not present in Fogle's article of 1949 except that more emphasis is placed upon Warland's triumph as a man. Sherry Zivley ("Hawthorne's 'The Artist of the Beautiful' and Spenser's 'Muiopotmos,'" *PQ* 48:134–37) establishes parallels between Spenser's and Hawthorne's butterflies and clarifies mythological allusions in Hawthorne's story.

### v. Minor Work: The Romances

John M. Bell ("Hawthorne's *The Scarlet Letter*: An Artist's Intuitive Understanding of Plague, Armor, and Health," *Journal of Orgonomy* 3,i:102–15) reads it as a radical book, one which "embodies a remarkable understanding of both human armoring and the social origins of that armoring." The most valuable part of the article is Bell's treatment of "The Custom House" and its relation to the rest of the book. The remainder of the article is thesis-ridden, thrown out of shape by the author's insistence that Hawthorne anticipated the insights of Wilhelm Reich. William B. Dillingham sees "Arthur Dimmesdale's Confession" (*SLitI* 2,i:21–26) as the final irony of his alienated life. "He was too weak to be true in life and therefore *could* not be true when it was time for him to die." Seymour Katz ("'Character,' 'Nature,' and Allegory in *The Scarlet Letter*," *NCF* 23 [1968]: 3–17) argues that neither the manner of construction nor the characters can be accurately described as being allegorical. Instead Hawthorne posited for each person a nature—the amount and kind of physical, emotional, and intellectual potentialities with which the individual is born—and a character—those internalized principles which control and direct the potentialities of nature. Considering "Character and Motive in *The Scarlet Letter*" (*CritQ* 10[1968]:373–84), A. N. Kaul covers familiar territory, but this is a closely reasoned analysis of the "story" in the book. It focuses on three questions: (i) Why doesn't Hester leave Boston? (ii) Why and under what altered circumstances does she at a later date settle on a plan of flight? (iii) And finally, why does the flight not materialize, or rather, why does it strike us as a futile and doomed venture? More valuable, perhaps, than Kaul's answers are his thoughts about where and how we find them. He shows that the expository chapters are "dramatized to the extent to which the author's communication in them is complicated by the character's represented point of view." Katsumi Okamoto (*"The Scarlet Letter*: Struggle Toward Integrity," *SELit* 46:45–61) relates the ending to the rest of the book, covering all the old ground once again. The author proves that he has read the book with care and sensitivity, but his account of the tensions found there is old stuff, smoothly rehearsed. Kathryn Whitford ("On a Field Sable, the Letter "A," Gules,'" *LHR* 10[1968]:33–38) claims that Hester's return to Boston becomes more comprehensible if it is viewed within the framework of Puritan theology, specifically the belief in the resurrection of the flesh.

Of the two essays on *The House of the Seven Gables*, one by Donald R. Swanson ("On Building *The House of the Seven Gables*," *BSUF* 10,i:43–50) traces the sources of the book in the *American Notebooks*. Swanson accepts Thomas Morgan Griffiths's idea (*NEQ*, 1943) that the house was patterned after the Knox mansion, Montpelier. Arthur E. Waterman ("Dramatic Structure in *The House of the Seven Gables*," *SLitI* 2,i:13–19) discovers a five-act structure, points to various theatrical devices, and concludes that the book is patterned after a well-made play, a domestic melodrama. This, according to Waterman, is what is wrong with the ending, because in completing his "well-made structure according to accepted dramatic practice, Hawthorne has not resolved the ideological questions the novel raises."

Robert K. Martin ("Hawthorne's *The Blithedale Romance*," *Exp* 28:item 11) notes Moodie's movable eyepatch, mentioned in chapter 2 of *ALS 1968*, p. 28. Julian Smith asks "Why Does Zenobia Kill Herself?" (*ELN* 6[1968]:37–39) and also, was Zenobia pregnant? Smith finds "solid clues" in the book, but they involve reading some of her comments with a double meaning. External evidence is interesting but inconclusive. Claire Sprague's note, "Dream and Disguise in *The Blithedale Romance*" (*PMLA* 84:596–97) highlights Coverdale's dream of Zenobia and Hollingsworth standing on either side of his bed and bending across it to exchange a passionate kiss. The author argues that this dream within a dream uncovers Miles's own disguises.

Sacvan Bercovitch's "Miriam as Shylock: An Echo from Shakespeare in Hawthorne's *Marble Faun*" (FMLS 5:385–87) is another

brief indication of the way Hawthorne used bits from his reading
to build his characters. Walter Blackstock ("Hawthorne's Cool,
Switched-On Media of Communication in *The Marble Faun*," *LangQ*
7, iii–iv:41–42), who joins in the current effort toward making
"media" a singular noun, also argues that *The Marble Faun* constitutes "authentic existentialist evidence." The rest should have been
silence but instead is plot summary. In "When the Deity Returns:
*The Marble Faun* and *Romola*" (*Studies in American Literature*,
pp. 82–100), Curtis Dahl sees in both novels the idea of a classical
deity who returns to later times. Further comparison reveals the
concept of recurrent human experience, mythic parallels, autobiographical elements, and gothic trappings. Sidney P. Moss ("The
Symbolism of the Italian Background in *The Marble Faun*," *NCF*
23[1968]:332–36) connects Hawthorne's tripartite representation of
the Italian background—Etruscan, Roman, Christian—with the three
stages of Donatello's spiritual progress. Moss says, however, that
Hawthorne's intention here was not realized. He should have been
more selective, offering only those details of Italian background that
would delineate the setting as a mirror image of Donatello's development. Cushing Strout's "Hawthorne's International Novel" (*NCF*
24:169–81) is a gracefully composed essay which reads the book as
an intricately designed encounter between American innocence and
European experience. "It is not so much the Adamic significance of
the Faun's fall that organizes the novel as it is the varied meanings
which this event has for two couples from different cultures."

*University of Oklahoma*

# 3. Melville

## Merton M. Sealts, Jr.

The anniversary year 1969 brought a spate of books and articles on Melville. Two American journals, *Studies in the Literary Imagination* and *Studies in the Novel*, published issues featuring Melville, as did *Eigo Seinen* (*The Rising Generation*) in Japan. *Soviet Literature* marked the occasion with a survey of recent Russian translations and criticism of Melville by Boris Gilenson ("Melville in Russia: For the 150th Anniversary of His Birth," 9:171–73). Emphasis fell once again on Melville's work after 1850, especially *Moby-Dick* and *The Confidence-Man*, with the latter receiving unusually rewarding but divergent analysis; and there were two monographs devoted entirely to the once-neglected *Israel Potter*. Exclusive of dissertations, I have counted ninety-six individual items either published during 1969 or not previously listed in the annual MLA bibliographies; my figures for 1967 and 1968 were eighty-six and eighty-one, respectively. Ten new dissertations concerned wholly or partly with Melville were listed in *Dissertation Abstracts* through 1969 beyond the eleven surveyed in *ALS 1968*; in addition, *DA* 29 and 30 reported seven older dissertations, all written at Yale in the 1940's, that have now been microfilmed. In view of the great number of items this year and the need to conserve space in *ALS*, I have felt obliged to concentrate on only the more important published work, touching on seventy-five items, and to omit the survey of dissertations with which Professor Thorp and I have previously concluded our chapters on Melville. (A new directory of Melville dissertations that will bring up to date the earlier compilations of Tyrus Hillway and Hershel Parker is in preparation by Joel Myerson.

### i. Books

A third volume of the Northwestern-Newberry edition of Melville appeared in 1969: *Redburn*, edited by Harrison Hayford, Hershel

Parker, and G. Thomas Tanselle (Evanston, Ill., Northwestern Univ.
Press). Its methodology and format follow the pattern and standards
established by its predecessors, *Typee* and *Omoo* (see *ALS 1968*, pp.
30–31). The two monographs dealing solely with *Israel Potter* are
covered in section *vi* below. A third monograph, extending the
previous work of George Creeger and others on the nature and significance of Melville's use of light and color, is Max Frank's *Die Farb-
und Lichtsymbolik im Prosawerk Herman Melvilles* (Heidelberg,
Carl Winter, 1967). Frank's well-considered discussion, narrowly
focused but illustrated with generous quotations from Melville and
accompanied by four frequency tables, examines prose from the early
"Fragments" to *Billy Budd, Sailor*, passing over *Israel Potter*, *The
Confidence-Man*, and most of the shorter fiction—the center of much
recent discussion—as well as the poetry and miscellaneous writing.
Further analysis along similar lines should be undertaken once the
Northwestern-Newberry edition has been completed and a much-
needed concordance to the entire Melville canon compiled.

Jay Leyda's invaluable work of 1951, *The Melville Log*, is now
back in print (2 vols.; New York, Gordian Press) with a new supplement (2:901–66) adding reviews and other documents turned up
since the first edition appeared and incorporating corrections and
amplifications chiefly occasioned by publication of the *Letters* and
by research on Melville's library and lectures.

Alice P. Kenney (*The Gansevoorts of Albany: Dutch Patricians
in the Upper Hudson Valley*, Syracuse, N.Y., Syracuse Univ. Press)
offers students of Melville a wealth of material about his mother's
family, its Dutch traditions, and the individual relatives whom he
knew best. The chapter treating Melville himself (pp. 214–43) turns
on the "psychological and social conflict" that Miss Kenney detects
"between the Dutch and American traditions" of his ancestry. She
believes that his recurrent rheumatic complaints "probably represented a hereditary weakness," noting that a number of the Gansevoorts suffered similar physical disabilities. She associates Melville's
powers of direct observation and his "highly visual" imagery with
the traditional Dutch emphasis on physical details rather than intellectual abstractions, citing Peter Gansevoort's fondness for *Typee*
and drawing an analogy between the book and Dutch genre painting.
More speculatively, she links both Melville's concern with religion

primarily "as a motivation of right human conduct" and his insistence on the supremacy of heart over head with a characteristic Dutch exaltation of the conscience rather than the reason. Miss Kenney comments succinctly on *Moby-Dick, Pierre,* and *Clarel* as dealing respectively with those aspects of life that the Albany Dutch regarded as fundamental: "fortune, family, and religion"; the conclusion of *Clarel* suggests to her that Melville had "escaped from the Albany Dutch tradition physically and intellectually only to return to it emotionally and spiritually."

Two books treating Melville among other American writers also emphasize his concern with religious and philosophical issues. A phrase from *Moby-Dick* suggested the title of Edward Stone's *A Certain Morbidity: A View of American Literature* (Carbondale, Southern Ill. Univ. Press); one of Stone's essays (pp. 16–42) concentrates on the dark world-view expressed in Ahab, Ishmael, and Bartleby, whom Stone groups "with the Preacher and Albert Camus" in their common recognition of "an absurdity, an indifference in our universe." As the catastrophe in *Moby-Dick* approaches, Ahab and Ishmael gradually diverge, Stone thinks: Ishmael is retrieved by faith and brotherhood into a resignation and acceptance that Ahab cannot match. Ahab, unable to love, must perish; as for Bartleby, "learning the truth that the universe in which he is sentenced to live has no temple destroys his mind." John T. Frederick's chapter on Melville in *The Darkened Sky: Nineteenth Century American Novelists and Religion* (Notre Dame, Ind., Univ. of Notre Dame Press, pp. 79–122) examines a larger canvas than Stone's, tracing Melville's own "lifetime preoccupation with religious problems" and noting incidentally that the Albany years were crucial ones in his development. The discussion covers familiar ground, synthesizing applicable scholarship. "Broadly speaking," Frederick observes, Melville "was to express in *Moby Dick* his assertion of the individual freedom of the human mind; in *Pierre* and *The Confidence-Man* his conception of the failure of Christianity to meet the needs of the thoughtful man in the life of the actual world; and in *Clarel* and thereafter to seek a reconciliation and resolution of those needs." Frederick sees a significant change in the later Melville that is reflected in *Billy Budd,* though overlooked by those who read it only ironically. Melville, he concludes, finally "found peace—neither through victorious resolution of his dilemma nor in mere resignation, but in the clear-sighted recognition of gains as well as losses and the acceptance of the total given fact of life itself."

Another approach to Melville, as a writer of romances using "all of the familiar romance themes," is taken by Joel Porte in *The Romance in America: Studies in Cooper, Poe, Hawthorne, Melville, and James* (Middletown, Conn., Wesleyan Univ. Press, pp. 152–92). Somewhat surprisingly, having stressed Melville's need as a romancer "to define, within his own fictions, both his role as a creator and the relation of experience to his productions," Porte does not consider the relevant material of *Moby-Dick* and the earlier books that draw directly on Melville's years at sea; instead, he concentrates on four of the later works: first "The Piazza" and then *The Confidence-Man, Pierre,* and *Billy Budd,* in that order. The pivotal book in his discussion is *The Confidence-Man,* which he reads as "a complex exercise in self-satire such as only the bitterest, most disappointed, and most brilliant romancer could ever have conceived"; it is at once "a lecture with illustrations . . . on the theory and practice of romance" and "a bizarre portrait of the artist as a gay Devil, the confidence-man supreme." Like other recent critics such as Edgar Dryden and Helmbrecht Breinig (see *ALS 1968,* pp. 32–33, 41–42), Porte sees Melville coming to a dead end as a romancer in the mid-1850's; but he takes a different view of *Billy Budd* as reasserting the essential realism of romance by once again pointing to that "something ineluctably and terrifyingly mysterious at the bottom of human experience" that had long fascinated Melville. The problems of his protagonist, Vere, confronting in Billy and Claggart apparent embodiments of good and evil, light and dark, reason and the irrational, are "the stock in trade of the committed romancer." As in *Pierre* and *The Confidence-Man,* according to Porte, Melville uses another device of the romancer, that of a dream-vision, in the concluding ballad, "Billy in the Darbies," which for Porte recalls Prospero's words in *The Tempest* suggesting the visionary quality of life itself. If the allusion was intentional, he concludes, then "the poetic finale of *Billy Budd* is indeed the fitting testament of a writer who devoted his career to seeking the 'ungraspable phantom of life' in the 'baseless fabric' of a romancer's shifting vision." Porte's depiction of Melville as a persistent romancer rather than the literal observer who pleased Peter Gansevoort is in more than one sense a partial portrait. His discussion suffers from limitations of space and consequent foreshortening in its selective glimpses of the Melville canon; moreover, as Newton Arvin once observed, Melville's mind was both sympathetic to poetry and romance and at the same time biased toward "facts" and materiality. Nevertheless, it is illuminating to study Melville among the romancers as among the Gansevoorts, and both Porte and Miss Kenney thus contribute to our sense of the man and the range of his mind and art.

The need to condense also hampered Howard P. Vincent in *The Merrill Guide to Herman Melville* (Columbus, Ohio, Merrill), a brief pamphlet for student use (42 pages). The discussion, though frequently eloquent, is uneven in comparison with Leon Howard's similar treatment (1961, 1968) and is marred by inaccuracies and typographical errors. Two companion pieces are *The Merrill Studies in "Moby-Dick,"* in which Vincent brings together a fine brief sampling of representative criticism from 1851 to the present; and *The Merrill Checklist of Herman Melville*, Vincent's selective compilation of works by and about Melville, conveniently organized but also marred by misprints and by his omission of key editions of several individual works. In treating secondary materials the *Checklist* is less inclusive than other recent compilations, such as that by Maurice Beebe, Harrison Hayford, and Gordon Roper (*MFS* 8[1962]:312–46) or "A Selected Checklist of Melville Criticism, 1958–1968," by J. Don Vann (*SNNTS* 1:507–35).

### *ii.* Before *Moby-Dick*

Among the few articles of 1969 dealing with Melville's first five books the most significant is a reassessment of *Typee* by Charles R. Anderson: "Melville's South Sea Romance," the single English-language contribution to the Melville issue of *The Rising Generation* (115:478–82, 564–68). While praising the book's "freshness and spontaneity of style" as the source of its special charm, Anderson is clearly not in sympathy with much of the criticism of *Typee* that has appeared since the publication of his *Melville and the South Seas* thirty years earlier. He takes issue particularly with those who find virtue in either its craftsmanship, which he thinks careless, or its supposed symbolism: "The technique of interpreting symbols in a literary creation," he declares flatly, "becomes meaningless when applied to the accidents of a real adventure." Anderson's analysis of *Typee* stresses the fundamental dichotomy that he senses between its theme, identified as a "whole-hearted defense of the Noble Savage and a eulogy of his happy life," and a purely structural device, as he calls it, that Melville introduced to create suspense in the absence of a genuine plot: his alternative suggestion that the admired islanders "may be after all ferocious cannibals." The young author, Anderson feels, did not fully understand either what he had experienced in the Marquesas or the basic demands of his "lifelong problem," literary form. In his first book Melville wrote not a novel but "at best a loose fictional chronicle" that exhibits an "almost complete failure in form —not so much from awkwardness as from indifference."

Taji as "The Artist in Melville's *Mardi*" (*SNNTS* 1:459–67) is studied by Barbara Meldrum with particular reference to "the impersonality of the artist," as in her dissertation (see *ALS 1967*, p. 47). In Taji and Babbalanja she sees Melville working toward his later characterizations of Ahab, Ishmael, and Pierre.

### iii. Moby-Dick

Several brief studies single out various passages of *Moby-Dick* as touchstones. For Howard P. Vincent ("Ishmael, Writer and Art Critic," *Themes and Directions*, pp. 69–79) the painting in the Spouter Inn that Ishmael the Writer analyzes "serves as a ritual icon of the *Pequod*'s quest"—"a graphic frontispiece to the book, a parallel in visual art to the verbal functions and effect of 'Extracts'"—that summarizes and comments on *Moby-Dick* itself. ("Perhaps Ishmael insists so strongly that the whale is the subject," Vincent remarks, "because he knew that the fundamental subject was Ishmael himself.") Sanford Sternlicht ("Sermons in *Moby Dick*," *BSUF* 10,i:51–52) holds that not Father Mapple addressing his congregation but Fleece preaching to the sharks delivers "the true sermon of life as Melville saw it" in his "darkly pessimistic view of man's role and fate." William K. Spofford in "Melville's Ambiguities: A Re-evaluation of 'The *Town-Ho*'s Story,'" (*AL* 41:264–70) thinks critics have been misled by possible correlations between that chapter and *Billy Budd*. He sees it as "a microcosmic presentation" of issues that both chapter and book leave indeterminate: Is God just or unjust? Is the whale agent or principal?

Melville's knowledge of theology and complex responses to it make a starting point for three longer essays on *Moby-Dick*. T. Walter Herbert, Jr. ("Calvinism and Cosmic Evil in *Moby-Dick*," *PMLA* 84:1613–19) finds him drawing on both Calvinist and anti-Calvinist materials in his handling of cosmic evil in terms of Ahab's conflict with the godlike whale: the portrait of Ahab himself reflects Calvin's treatment of the biblical King Ahab, according to Herbert, and his "cosmic fury" is related to "the angry reactions which Calvin's doctrine of God typically provoked"—for example, in such a book as John Taylor's anti-Calvinist *Scripture Doctrine of Original Sin*, which Melville owned. Thomas Werge ("*Moby-Dick* and the Calvinist Tradition," *SNNTS* 1:484–506), although disagreeing with Herbert's "definition of an 'actual cosmic evil'" in the book, endorses his general approach as a way of illuminating Melville's writings. Though not himself a Calvinist, "Melville—often reluctantly—acknowledges and sympathizes with Calvinist ideas and emphases," Werge argues here as in his recent dissertation (see *ALS 1968*, p. 48): in *Moby-Dick* the epistemological emphasis and even the book's total coherence "are inseparable from the preoccupations, language and dialectic of the Calvinist tradition" to which it "consistently refers and on which it consciously depends." Gregory H. Singleton ("Ishmael and the Covenant," *Discourse* 16:54–67) treats Ishmael and his story in relation to Melville's familiarity with "covenant" theology. Like the biblical prototype whose name he deliberately assumes, Ishmael is an individual "in a peculiar relationship to a covenanted people," specifically the crew of the *Pequod* led by Ahab. Ever the lone man, the outsider, he is neither entirely *of* the covenant nor completely separated *from* it, until the final catastrophe, being "in community with the crew, mankind, and nature" but excluded from "the covenant of death aboard the *Pequod*." Ishmael's survival, Singleton thinks, is "Melville's final irony, . . . his greatest inversion of the Christian-Calvinist cosmology—the salvation by exclusion."

William Glasser ("Moby Dick," *SR* 77:463–86) attempts to "clarify" the book in terms of the world-views held by its characters, Ahab and Ishmael in particular. Ahab's obsessive conflict with the whale is really a conflict with God; at various times he expresses contradictory views on the questions of free will and fate. Ishmael is more objective in facing the world, which he sees as both dark and bright; his allowance for necessity, free will, and chance in "The Mat-

Maker" helps to offset Ahab's errors. Even so, his "clarifying view" of the world "is a limited one," and "God remains, as Ishmael says, 'inscrutable.'" As for Ahab, despite his mistakes he deserves admiration, Glasser concludes, as "a rare individual, a 'mighty pageant creature.'" A quite different reading, one which sees archetypal parallels between *Moby-Dick* and the Grail legend, is that of Janet Dow in "Ahab: The Fisher King" (*ConnR* 2,ii:42–49). H. B. Kulkarni examines the book in the perspective of other world religions than Christianity. In "Significance of Sacrifice in *Moby Dick*" (*Indian Response*, pp. 29–37), Kulkarni holds that if the repeated pattern of sacrifice that he sees in the book "is duly emphasized, the meaning of *Moby Dick* undergoes a radical change" and the book becomes "a 'mystical treatise' on the quest for God and the meaning of creation and its realization through complete surrender and sacrifice." His exposition of this thesis deals with Ishmael, Queequeg, and Pip, but is especially impressive in treating Ahab and that "most misunderstood" of the characters, Fedallah. The Parsee, whose name in Arabic means "'Bounty of God' or 'the sacrifice of God,'" seemingly has but one aim in life: "to offer himself as sacrifice to his God of Fire," which Ahab also worships—not in love but in hate and defiance. "Death is inevitable, but death at the hands of divinity is the most desirable consummation of devotion to God," as in Hindu mythology, where stories of Vishnu's incarnations (once as a whale) are marked by "hate as a method of worship." Thus Ahab "prepares himself for death . . . with all his heart and soul" in a mood "akin to that of intense prayer where hate has been purged of its impurities and keeps burning like a pure flame of grand devotion. His death, therefore, has all the spiritual associations which transform a brutal assassination into an act of religious sacrifice." Recalling Melville's reported interest in "East India religions and mythologies," I am struck by Kulkarni's challenging reinterpretation; even if not entirely persuasive to Western readers it seems well worth pondering.

Not theology or mythology but popular superstition as an ingredient of the book Melville called "wicked" is studied by Helen P. Trimpi in an article based on her 1965 dissertation (see *ALS 1967*, p. 46): "Melville's Use of Demonology and Witchcraft in *Moby-Dick*" (*JHI* 30:543–62). Beginning with a glance at Melville's jottings about devil lore in his set of Shakespeare, Mrs. Trimpi specifies no fewer than nineteen ideas found in the European history of witchcraft and demonology that "enter significantly into the structure and the characterization of *Moby-Dick.*" Turning to non-European superstitions, she suggests that Melville's knowledge of one of them—Obeism, which some writers of his day equated with devil worship—may account for his "otherwise inexplicable change of 'Mocha Dick' to 'Moby Dick,'" which for "the alert contemporary reader . . . would emphasize the Whale's role as Devil." Mrs. Trimpi associates *Moby-Dick* and its hero with popular romances of Melville's day, citing Walter Scott's essay on "Romance." Robert D. Hume ("Gothic versus Romantic: A Revaluation of the Gothic Novel," *PMLA* 84:282–90) places the book somewhat differently, calling it "perhaps the greatest of Gothic novels, and an almost perfect example of the form." In Hume's reading, Ahab is "the completely dominant villain-hero" whose monomania will destroy him and his companions; Moby Dick is for Ahab "what the monster is for Frankenstein"; Ishmael's narration draws the reader into the world of the *Pequod* much as Lockwood's leads him into that of *Wuthering Heights*; both tales end, like gothic novels generally, leaving us "with great ambiguities" rather than some final statement. Hume sees a basic difference between romantic writing, "the product of faith in an ultimate order," and gothic writing, "a gloomy exploration of the limitations of man."

The question of Melville's reaction to the romantic sensibility and particularly to Transcendentalism continues to preoccupy interpreters of *Moby-Dick*, though what is seen in that doubloon obviously varies with the predispositions of the critic. For Michael J. Hoffman ("The Anti-Transcendentalism of *Moby-Dick*," *GaR* 23:3–16) the issue is scarcely in doubt: the book, "almost totally ironic," mocks "the Transcendental style"; "its major 'symbol' symbolizes absolutely nothing"; its "central figure" is a man "blinded by his own vision" who "mouths the ideas of an author whom Melville thought 'a humbug,' and is ultimately a parody of the Transcendentalist 'great man.'" In sum, "the *Pequod*'s quest means nothing and the fate of its crew little. Whatever meaning the novel has lies in the paradigm presented to us by Ahab's quest and failure—that all attempts to force meaning upon the world are futile, are indeed more than futile: they are destructive." The specifically political implications of American Romanticism then and now come under Milton R. Stern's examination in "*Moby Dick*, Millennial Attitudes, and Politics" (*ESQ* 54:51–60), which sees Ahab as "both very Romantic and

very American." Having dealt elsewhere with metaphysical, onto-
logical, and epistemological implications of Melville's writings, Stern
chooses here to read *Moby-Dick* "narrowly," for among other things
it appears to him "a deeply political novel" in which "the political
Ahab" provides "one more glimpse into the heart of the American
Renaissance," with Melville himself challenging its "millennial assumptions" as Ahab's "ideological crusade" reflects them. In Stern's
treatment, which broadly implies that Ahab has at least one twentieth-
century political counterpart, the book becomes a kind of cautionary
tale. If its metaphysics "prescribes anything," he remarks at one
point, "it prescribes relativism"; in concluding his essay he holds that
"the core of the politics is the same," its message being this: "Beware
of the absolute vision; beware of the great causes and men who make
the abstract principle more important than people, more real than
the common world of human necessity."

Where Glasser finds something to praise in both Ahab and Ishmael, Stern sees Ahab as dangerous to humanity. Ishmael is an exemplary figure for Stern, as he has previously affirmed (see *ALS 1967*, p.
35); in this study Ishmael is the praiseworthy realist and relativist
who "takes a warmer view of man and a humbler view of will" than
Ahab, his "usurping leader." Hoffman also exalts Ishmael, hailing
him as "the new post-Transcendental man, whose ultimate ironic detachment will become a commonplace pose for the new 'hero' of the
'realist' novel"; but another "political" reading of *Moby-Dick* brings
in a strongly dissenting report on what Ishmael is and does: Cecil M.
Brown ("The White Whale," *PR* 36:453–59) sees him as forerunner
of "the white, disembodied, overliterate, boring, snobbish, insipid,
jew-bastard, nigger-lover, effete, mediocre, assistant-professor-type,
liberal." The book appears less political or metaphysical than psychological or existential in an essay by Carl F. Strauch, "Ishmael: Time
and Personality in *Moby-Dick*" (*SNNTS* 1:468–83); through Ishmael's changing vision, in Strauch's words, it moves "away from
metaphysical speculation toward existentialist affirmation of a living
universe, an acceptance of the simple and primitive physical world
of whale and savage." Ishmael and Ahab he regards as "archetypal
twins exemplifying the dual theme of destruction and survival"; in
"The Try-Works" Ishmael liberates himself just in time from Ahab's
"suicidal quest for meaning in a possibly meaningless universe."

Strauch finds "the crown of Ishmael's wisdom" in "The Gilder" and its pivotal passage on "mankind's pondering repose of If"—a word best left undefined, he thinks, "though it is the most important word in *Moby-Dick*." What Ishmael has achieved "through love of the whale universe and the primitivism of Queequeg" involves a "Romantic awareness of organic relations and of freely flowing association"; in his "self-healing" Ishmael "rejects metaphysical Romanticism" but "vigorously champions psychological Romanticism." Future commentators will do well to consider Strauch's recognition of differing aspects of Romanticism—and to clarify their own terminology—before making sweeping statements about Ishmael, Ahab, and Melville himself as romantic, antiromantic, Transcendental, anti-Transcendental, or post-Transcendental.

### iv. Pierre

Nicholas Canaday, Jr., extends his study of Melville and authority (see *ALS 1968*, pp. 31–32) beyond *Moby-Dick* in "Melville's Pierre: At War with Social Convention" (*PLL* 5:51–62). "Out of Pierre's obedience to a moral imperative in defiance of society," he observes, come both "heroism and foolishness, knowledge and grief, independence and death"; toward Pierre and his "war" Melville's attitude is "ambivalent." In the course of his discussion Canaday takes the position that because there is no physical consummation in Pierre's relations with Isabel he "has not violated any standard of morality or the law"; Melville, he thinks, "does not approve Plinlimmon's pamphlet" as a guide for conduct. R. K. Gupta continues to publish the findings of his dissertation (see *ALS 1965*, p. 43), concentrating on the Memnon Stone and the vision of Enceladus in "Pasteboard Masks: A Study of Symbolism in *Pierre*" (*Indian Essays in American Literature*, pp. 121–28). R. L. Carothers ("Melville's 'Cenci': A Portrait of *Pierre*," *BSUF* 10, i:53–59) argues that "the incestuous motive" lies at the heart of "the conflict that eventually destroys Pierre"; his analysis examines Pierre's wish for a sister and his "basically sexual" image of his father as preparing the way for his difficulties. On the thematic level, Pierre must confront God as well as his father, "the relation of father to son, Father to Son," being "the central and unifying metaphor" of this book by "the violently anti-Christian Melville," as Carothers calls him.

### v. Tales

"Bartleby," which a contemporary reviewer considered "a Poeish tale," is illuminated through comparison with "The Raven" by James L. Colwell and Gary Spitzer in " 'Bartleby' and 'The Raven': Parallels of the Irrational" (*GaR* 23:37–43). Both works relate a narrator's encounter with "unreason." Melville's "double allusion" in the story to Edwards and Priestley and his juxtaposition of *will* and *necessity* are the starting points for Walton R. Patrick's study, "Melville's 'Bartleby' and the Doctrine of Necessity" (*AL* 41:39–54), which finds the title character " 'programmed' . . . to will as he wills" despite his "dogged assertion of preferences." But the focus, Patrick contends, is not on Bartleby alone; the story concerns his relationship with the attorney and the latter's possibly predestined awakening "from a smug self-complacency to a painful and profound sense of compassion and sympathy for all mankind." Kingsley Widmer ("Melville's Radical Resistance: The Method and Meaning of *Bartleby*," *SNNTS* 1:444–58) denies that the lawyer achieves "authentic awareness" either of Bartleby or of humanity in general. This "high point" of Melville's art Widmer takes as "a reasoned exploration of the irrational situation of man," but his frame of reference is the nihilism of "our contemporary existential thinkers" rather than the prose or poetry of Poe. Bartleby and the narrator are doubles ("like Delano-Cereno, Vere-Budd, Ahab-Ishmael, etc."), paired by Melville in "a grotesque version of the Faust theme" to form a "duality of consciousness in which only the spirit of negation continues the human striving." In this reading Bartleby is "an archetypal figure" of "the ultimate passive resistor" who renounces "life based on false consciousness" in "a vicious civilized order." The "blandly benevolent" lawyer is subjected to Melville's "sympathetic but ironical critical analysis" as "a decent, well-meaning, prudent, rationalizing enforcer of established values"—in short (like Cecil Brown's Ishmael?), "a representative liberal American." "Melville thus indicts," Widmer believes, "one of the major traditions of what has passed for normal reasonableness, in our time as well as in his time."

Reidar Eknar ("*The Encantadas* and *Benito Cereno*—On Sources and Imagination in Melville," *Moderna Språk* 60[1966]:258–73) examines the nature and effect of Melville's adaptations of his principal literary sources in the two works; concerning the story of Hunilla in the eighth sketch of "The Encantadas" he also sees a resemblance both to an actual event of 1852 on Chatham Island and to the unpublished story of Agatha as Melville had presented it to Hawthorne. Charles N. Watson, Jr., pursues the latter parallel in "Melville's Agatha and Hunilla: A Literary Reincarnation" (*ELN* 6[1968]:114–18), arguing that Melville consciously took over for the sketch "not only a central character and a general theme, but also a number of details of plot, setting, and minor characterization." Robert J. Brophy ("Benito Cereno, Oakum, and Hatchets," *ATQ* 1:89–90), noting that the oakum-pickers and hatchet-scourers are among Melville's additions to "Benito Cereno," detects in them allusions to two of "the Parcae of classical lore."

Paul Deane ("Herman Melville: Four Views of American Commercial Society," *RLV* 34[1968]:504–07) sees specific social criticism in four tales: "The Paradise of Bachelors," "Bartleby," "Jimmy Rose," and "The Fiddler." Beryl Rowland ("Melville's Bachelors and Maids: Interpretation Through Symbol and Metaphor," *AL* 41:389–405) finds the organizing symbol of "The Paradise of Bachelors" and "The Tartarus of Maids" to be that of the mill taken as a sexual symbol. In this reading, like that of Alvin Sandberg (see *ALS 1968*, p. 41), the diptych conveys the narrator's "pleasure in the bachelors' world and his recoil from the world of women"; although that "solitary deviate" leaves "no doubt as to the world he wants," he "never understands his motivation." Merton M. Sealts, Jr., in "Melville's Chimney, Reexamined" (*Themes and Directions*, pp. 80–102) traces "the main lines of analysis" of "I and My Chimney" up to 1967; Richard D. Lynde has a good word to say for a neglected tale in "Melville's Success in 'The Happy Failure: A Story of the River Hudson'" (*CLAJ* 13:119–30). An overview by Bert C. Bach ("Melville's Theatrical Mask: The Role of Narrative Perspective in His Short Fiction," *SLitI* 2, i:43–55), although attempting too much in brief compass, has some interesting generalizations. Each of the fifteen narrators of the tales, by choice or by nature, is a bachelor or at least bachelor-like, in Melville's special sense of the word; he is recalcitrant toward change and fearful of "either the enthusiast's or the institution's definitions of moral or ethical concepts." But "either by personal volition or by circumstance," Bach affirms, each "is led to confront reality as it exists in some perspective alien to his earlier beliefs."

### vi. Israel Potter

The interrelations of Melville's work between *Pierre* and *The Con-fidence-Man* are stressed in two articles by Frederick W. Turner, III. His "Melville's Post-Meridian Fiction" (*MASJ* 10:60–67) treats "Bartleby," "The Encantadas," "Benito Cereno," *Israel Potter*, and *The Confidence-Man* as exploratory studies of the American scene in which Melville, seeking an explanation for the poor reception of *Moby-Dick* and *Pierre*, found the source of failure in his country's culture and national character. In "Melville and Thomas Berger: The Novelist as Cultural Anthropologist" (*CentR* 13:101–21) Turner con-centrates on *Israel Potter*, which he reads in conjunction with Berger's *Little Big Man* (1964) as "an extended cultural parable" treating a century of American experience beginning with the Revolution. Is-rael's cultural displacement—he is both British and American and he is neither—is taken as Melville's "vehicle for the expression of cultural relativism." The American revolutionaries as he depicts them exhibit "almost barbaric qualities" in their encounters with Europeans; Israel in company with the British king is "the American barbarian in civili-zation," and when he meets Franklin and John Paul Jones he is seeing epitomized in turn the past (the Enlightenment) and the future (the American West). The battle chapters illustrate Melville's view that "civilization *is* but an 'advanced stage of barbarism'" and that "in the community of nations America is least removed from barbarism." On the basis of sheer vitality the near-savage Americans may be prefera-ble to the denizens of London as Israel comes to know them, Turner observes, but in his role as writer Melville nevertheless had misgiv-ings: "Where was the place for the arts in such a half-civilized state?"

A longer, more detailed study by Arnold Rampersad, *Melville's "Israel Potter": A Pilgrimage and Progress* (Bowling Green, Ohio, Bowling Green Univ. Popular Press), sees the book as Melville's "most complete statement of the responsibilities and rewards of the common man." Rampersad's monograph (which is both unevenly written and carelessly printed) proceeds methodically to relate *Israel Potter* to Melville's previous writing and to survey his adaptation of and additions to its principal source, Potter's *Life and Remarkable Adventures*. One chapter considers Melville's use of Dante's City of Dis and such possible literary analogues as medieval dream narra-tives and *The Pilgrim's Progress*. Melville's depiction of Israel himself and his contrasting portraits of Franklin, Jones, and Ethan Allen constitute for Rampersad his "evaluation of a variety of ways of life," with Allen's representing his own loftiest ideals: "frankness, conviviality, honor and brotherhood." All in all, Rampersad concludes, the book "simultaneously spurns despair and rejects social, religious or economic liberalism." Like Turner he recognizes its aesthetic shortcomings, but he praises its "artistic and ideological honesty."

Alexander Keyssar's *Melville's "Israel Potter": Reflections on the American Dream* (Cambridge, Harvard Univ. Press) is a briefer study of both themes and techniques that approaches the book as Melville's reappraisal of "the value of civilization," particularly in America: "Israel Potter fights for the creation of America and spends the rest of his life unsuccessfully trying to cash in on America's promise. Why he is unsuccessful is the subject of Melville's book." Keyssar sees the narrative as "an exemplum punctuated by symbolic episodes that function as commentary" and singles out for analysis Melville's images of the garden and of "captivity, immurement, and enclosure," along with the "motif of changing clothes." Most of the "interpolated historical or social passages" as Keyssar sees them deal with "the reality and myth of America": Franklin and Jones are likened respectively to America's "super-ego" and "id" while the "optimistic" sketch of Ethan Allen and his "Western spirit" is regarded as undeveloped; more dubiously, Israel as the common man laboring in the brickyard reveals "the inhumane working conditions that accompanied the rise of industrial assembly-line production" as well as "the existent inequities between economic classes." *Israel Potter* as a whole has structural weaknesses, Keyssar notes. Ironic and even satirical in tone, it combines a "strange and pessimistic pathos" with its "comic adventures and symbols." Melville "could not write tragedy about the common man," Keyssar holds, "because he could not honestly believe that the deaths of such men were meaningful or redemptive." His "perceptions of the American reality and its relationship to the common man have an ominous relevance," according to this study, "to the turmoil and crisis of the modern world."

### vii. The Confidence-Man

Except for a glance at the narrative modes of *The Confidence-Man* by Bert C. Bach ("Melville's Confidence-Man: Allegory, Satire, and the Irony of Intent," *Cithara* 8:28–36), recent discussion of the book exhibits some unity in its diversity by a common focus on the title character. As noted in section *i* above, Joel Porte identifies him with the artist himself; Joseph Baim ("The Confidence-Man as 'Trickster,'" *ATQ* 1:81–83) sees him as an archetypal figure "in whom all opposition is resolved"; Johannes D. Bergmann ("The Original Confidence Man," *AQ* 21:560–77) traces his origins to "a particular real life criminal so well known in the 1850s that many readers . . . could not have helped but connect him with the novel." Bergmann's fascinating report on this man, known as William Thompson, is drawn from the findings of his 1969 dissertation (*DA* 30:678A–79A). Citing contemporary reviews of Melville's book, he makes the point that readers thought of it "in a singular sense, that the impression grew that the 'Original Confidence Man' of 1849 appeared and reappeared, ubiquitously and almost supernaturally." In this way he is indeed archetypal: as Bergmann puts it, he "illuminated for the age . . . the confidence man principle."

Pursuing Elizabeth Foster's suggestion that Melville's various dealers in "confidence" satirize different forms of philosophical optimism, Fred E. Brouwer ("Melville's *The Confidence-Man* as Ship of Philosophers," *SHR* 3:158–65) argues that he has in mind "specific philosophers": eighteenth-century ethical thinkers who wrote in reaction to Thomas Hobbes. Brouwer's statement of the issues—"egoism versus altruism, self-love versus love of others"—is more persuasive than his identifications of the barber with Hobbes and particular appearances of the title character with Shaftesbury, Berkeley, Bishop Butler, Schelling, and Paley. In contrast to Brouwer, Merlin Bowen ("Tactics of Indirection in Melville's *The Confidence-Man*," *SNNTS* 1:401–20) accounts for the narrator's ingenious evasions on the ground that the Protean title character is really "God—an amoral God not merely permissive of evil but including it as part of His own mysterious Nature." Bowen does not regard the book, in the manner of some recent commentators, as either blackly pessimistic or a sermon on moderation. Like D. Nathan Sumner (see *ALS 1968*, p. 43) he sees a "center of affirmation" in Pitch, set over against the confidence man as "the book's antagonist and . . . only sympathetic character"; for Bowen, Pitch is "the comic hero," the Indian-hater being his tragic counterpart."

Warner Berthoff ("Herman Melville: *The Confidence-Man*,"

*Landmarks*, pp. 121–33) concentrates on the confidence man himself, not as deity or devil or even trickster but as a kind of teacher in an obscure moral world "from which the blessings of grace and of moral certitude appear to have been withdrawn." What he teaches, according to Berthoff's unorthodox formulation, is not doctrine but "the image of a way of life" that, "far from beguiling men into evil ways," constitutes an "austere and forbidding" process of dealing with the kind of world that is represented in the book. The name for his teachings "may be 'confidence,' but it is a confidence in circumstances and prospects that is only to be maintained by an unending process of testing, a constantly open-eyed examining of all signs and indications, a process of engaged watchfulness that has no resolution and from which there is, in life, no release." If one can grant this premise, then he may also accept Berthoff's speculative reading of the final chapter, in which the cosmopolitan's restraint and kindliness may express "real kindness and real sympathy, plainly given and plainly received." Perhaps, as Berthoff concludes, there is "a hopeful, benignant ending after all. It, too, is a 'masquerade,' but there may be more comfort and cheer in it, or at least less terror, than we quite dare to think."

Paul Brodtkorb, Jr. ("*The Confidence-Man*: The Con-Man as Hero," *SNNTS* 1:421–35) calls the cosmopolitan the "most likeable character" of the book and terms his tricks "as playful as they are sinister." The "ethically deceptive" world he inhabits is "satirically presented" but "not satirically condemned," Brodtkorb holds. "Rather, it is seen as inevitable, and the most appropriate response to it is not moral outrage but . . . humorous despairing serenity." Epistemologically, the "basic vision" of *The Confidence-Man* "is of masks; and underneath, masks, further masks; and under all masks there is more than a chance that there is nothing at all." Theologically, it expresses "its author's despair." Even so, "the playful con-man," as Brodtkorb calls him, makes "the spirit of the book" comic as well as misanthropic, transmuting "the underlying Melvillean despair" into the "humorous serenity" that this reading identifies as dominant. As a result, the book in Brodtkorb's eyes is "as close to being a 'testament of acceptance,' an ironic one, of course, as 'Billy Budd' is." To him it "looks anachronistically modern" because "modern ironic modes are the cultural lag of 19th Century romantic philosophies; Kierkegaard would have had no trouble understanding it."

### viii. Poems

After a year of neglect Melville's poetry is once again attracting
critical attention. Three studies deal with *Battle-Pieces*: Ralph E.
Hitt, "Melville's Poems of Civil War Controversy" (*SLitI* 2,i:57–68);
William J. Kimball, "The Melville of *Battle-Pieces*: A Kindred Spirit"
(*MQ* 10:307–16); and David J. Hibler, "*Drum-Taps* and *Battle-
Pieces*: Melville and Whitman on the Civil War" (*Person* 50:130–47).
Hitt stresses Melville's relative freedom from sectional prejudice; he
feels that the war may have brought some release from the melancholy of Melville's earlier years. Kimball thinks Melville's themes of
nationalism and reconciliation are worked out in the direction of
universality. Hibler notes a continuity with his earlier writing, though
the war heightened his "sense of suffering and death." All three commentators have reservations about the aesthetic worth of the volume.

Jane Donahue's "Melville's Classicism: Law and Order in His
Poetry" (*PLL* 5:63–72) is a more significant study that sees "a
classical theme" emerging in the poetry as early as *Battle-Pieces*:
in "Dupont's Round Fight"; I would suggest that it is visible even
earlier: in the lecture of 1857 on "Statues in Rome." Melville provides
"the clearest example in nineteenth-century American poetry of the
fruitful interaction of classical and romantic themes," she concludes,
after examining pieces of varying effectiveness from both *Battle-
Pieces* and *Timoleon* and pointing out their implications for Melville's view of society as well as of art. Douglas Robillard ("Theme
and Structure in Melville's *John Marr and Other Sailors*," *ELN* 6:187–
92) argues for the unity of Melville's volume of 1888; his discussion
would profit by associating the combination of prose and verse in
*John Marr* with Melville's other experiments of this kind, culminating
in "Billy in the Darbies" and *Billy Budd, Sailor*. What Robillard sees
as "deliberate reference" by Melville to "the themes and materials of
his earlier works" is explored with regard to both *John Marr* and
*Timoleon* in a good brief study by Lawrence H. Martin, Jr., "Melville
and Christianity: The Late Poems" (*MSE* 2:11–18). Melville's "distrust and dislike of organized Christianity" did not change in his
later years, Martin concludes; what changed was his tone, which
became quieter, more understated. Martin's discussion includes explication of six poems: "The Haglets," "The Maldive Shark," and

"The Berg" from *John Marr*; "Timoleon," "The Margrave's Birth-night," and "Herba Santa" from *Timoleon*.

### ix. *Billy Budd, Sailor*

In "*Billy Budd*: Melville's *Paradise Lost*" (*MQ* 10:173–85), Robert L. Perry explores the Miltonic strain in *Billy Budd* previously examined by Henry F. Pommer and Norman Holmes Pearson. Beginning with Pommer's comparison of Satan and Claggart, Perry also considers Billy's resemblance to prelapsarian Adam and Eve: reflecting on Milton's phrase in *Areopagitica*, "knowledge of good *and* evil," he concludes that Billy's "*real* tragic flaw" is that naive "innocence due to ignorance . . . that Milton condemned." Both writers, he holds, believed that such ignorance can be overcome "by education and experience," including the "imaginative experience" of reading—but this last prescription, contra Perry, seems more applicable to the literate Vere than to the Handsome Sailor. Parallels not with Milton but with Melville's own writing of the 1850's have been noted by several recent critics, including Edgar Dryden, Kingsley Widmer, and Charles Mitchell (see *ALS 1968*, pp. 44–46); to Karl F. Knight in "Melville's Variations of the Theme of Failure: 'Bartleby' and *Billy Budd*" (*ArlQ* 2:44–58), these two works appear "so remarkably similar that it is as if Melville had determined . . . to go back over the previous ground and make his point more tellingly." Both deal with a subordinate "sacrificed in the interest of order" by a basically good man who "has found no way to use his best knowledge in satisfying the demands of worldly society," but in *Billy Budd* Melville makes the scapegoat more sympathetic and the man of authority more credible. There is "no basis for seeing hope" in either story, according to Knight; critics who take them as optimistic overlook their common focus on failure. Nor do the parallels, he concludes, reveal any shift over the years in Melville's characteristic view of man as possessing a "dual vision of truth" and an "impossible yearning to harmonize heaven and earth" that are both his "nobility and his curse."

The current division of critical opinion about *Billy Budd* and especially about Vere is reflected in two essays which claim Melville's own warrant for exactly opposite readings. David Ketterer ("Some

Co-ordinates in *Billy Budd*," *JAmS* 3:221–37) argues "that Melville is endorsing Vere's view directly, that the 'straight' reading does more justice to Melville's intention than the ironist reading"; Vere is "the true empiricist and hero of *Billy Budd*," who, as "Melville's touchstone of pragmatism and empiricism," should guide the reader's interpretation of the action. But what Ketterer praises another critic roundly condemns. In "Melville's Judgment on Captain Vere" (*MQ* 10:189–200) Evelyn Schroth is persuaded that Melville himself "subscribed to the philosophy of humanism . . . rather than to pragmatism with its repressive, cramping, and stultifying limitations," and that he accordingly condemns Vere for being pragmatic as she understands the term. Both the ships and the characters of the story are deliberately grouped, she believes, so as to facilitate comparative judgments with reference to "the central issue of the natural or moral law versus the legal law." The man "whom Melville would have govern" is "the balanced man," "the whole man—with instinct and reason joined and head and heart reigning together," such as Nelson; Vere, by contrast, governs merely "by norms of social expediency," having "mechanized the finer instincts of his soul to the routinized enforcement of 'forms.' " There is more to her argument, and to Ketterer's as well. But the real focus of their disagreement lies less within Melville's text than in some extraliterary universe of discourse, be it semantic, philosophical, or political, where so much current discussion of *Billy Budd* is being vigorously carried on.

### x. Miscellaneous

A useful survey by G. Thomas Tanselle, "The Sales of Melville's Books" (*HLB* 18:195–215), compiles figures from Melville's contracts with publishers, their statements of account, and the business records of Murray and Bentley in London concerning the sales and profits of Melville's first seven books: between 1846 and 1887 they sold a total of 50,482 copies and yielded him in all $10,444.53; there were additional posthumous sales both at home and abroad. Accompanying tables give the data for each publisher and title. Kenneth Walter Cameron ("Scattered Melville Manuscripts," *ATQ* 1:63–64) reproduces two items from dealers' catalogues: an undated letter from Melville to Evert Duyckinck and a quoted proverb with his signature. A handsome volume, *The American Writer in England: An Ex- hibition Arranged in Honor of the Sesquicentennial of the University of Virginia* (Charlottesville, Univ. Press of Va.), lists among the Melville items displayed (pp. 50–54) a signed presentation copy from Melville to Dr. Robert Tomes of the first American edition of *Moby-Dick* and prints two of his letters: the first, written in 1852 to introduce the younger Lemuel Shaw to John Murray, is published here for the first time; the second, to Havelock Ellis in 1890, is de- scribed as "presumably unpublished" but has in fact been printed before (*Letters*, edited by Davis and Gilman, 1960, no. 258).

Concerning Melville's reading, Ruth M. Vande Kieft's " 'When Big Hearts Strike Together': The Concussion of Melville and Sir Thomas Browne" (*PLL* 5:39–50) is a well-considered study of a major influence on the early Melville. Hans-Joachim Lang ("Melvilles Dialog mit Captain Ringbolt," *JA* 14:124–39) calls attention to a little-known book Melville read in 1847: *Sailors' Life and Sailors' Yarns* by John Codman, which he reviewed in the *Literary World* along with J. Ross Browne's *Etchings of a Whaling Cruise.* Where Browne, like Dana, had sailed before the mast and speaks for the forecastle, Codman's "Captain Ringbolt" takes the quite different point of view of an officer. Beginning with this distinction, Lang con- siders parallels between Codman's work and Melville's, finding that the dialectic of Browne versus Codman in the early review repeats itself inconclusively in Melville's later writing wherever sailors con- front the authority of officers. Here Lang, like other critics such as John Bernstein and Nicholas Canaday, Jr., is dealing with the issue also raised by Theodore Gross in "Herman Melville: The Nature of Authority" (*ColQ* 16[1968]:397–412). "Much of the tension in Mel- ville's work," Gross acutely remarks, "grows out of his fear of power," ranging from the absolute authority of a captain over his crew to "the ultimate authority, the ultimate power" of nature itself. The earlier books present men who challenge all authority; in the later fictions, instead of epic heroes Gross sees "a series of victims" whose wills have broken down in the face of authority in "some adamant form." He takes *Billy Budd*, "Melville's truly considered coda to the problem," as offering a resolution in terms of "the authority that ought to be" rather than that authority which actually exists. The focus is of course Captain Vere's decision concerning Billy, which "represents

Melville's own intellectual conclusion" but is one to which he only "grudgingly assents," in Gross's phrase, as if to do so he "had to suppress the lifelong ambiguities" that mark the earlier writings.

Other aspects of Melville's social criticism are explored by Barbara Meldrum in "Melville on War" (*RS* 37:130–38). War is a subject Melville used in *White-Jacket* and after to develop his views on the theory and practice of both democracy and Christianity in a man-of-war world; though his attitudes "shifted and developed through the years," Mrs. Meldrum concludes, "his ideals did not change radically; rather, his hopes for a realization of those ideals dimmed, possibly even flickered out" by the time of *Billy Budd*. Eleanor E. Simpson ("Melville and the Negro: From *Typee* to 'Benito Cereno,' " *AL* 41:19–38), addressing a topic that has provoked much recent discussion, takes issue with Sidney Kaplan's well-known study of "Herman Melville and the American National Sin" (*JNH* 41[1956]:311–38; 42[1957]:11–37). Surveying Melville's treatment of nonwhites and of slavery in his fiction up to 1855, she finds "increasing originality in his portrayals" and "decreasing reliance on literary convention and popular stereotypes." Her article is fair to Melville and to previous scholarship—Kaplan's included—that touches on the issues at stake; though citing essays like Charles Foster's on *Moby-Dick* as an antislavery fable, she somehow overlooks Robert Forrey's "Herman Melville and the Negro Question" (*Mainstream* 15[1962]:23–32) and Priscilla Zirker's "Evidence of the Slavery Dilemma in *White-Jacket*" (see *ALS 1966*, p. 27).

Among broader examinations of Melville's development through *Moby-Dick* is an understanding study by Vito Amoruso, "Alla ricerca d'Ismaele: Melville e l'arte" (*SA* 13[1967]:169–233). John D. Seelye has written a speculative essay in which the inferences seem to me to reach beyond the evidence: " 'Ungraspable Phantom': Reflections of Hawthorne in *Pierre* and *The Confidence-Man*" (*SNNTS* 1:436–43). "The love affair between Pierre and Isabel and the gulling conversation between Frank Goodman and Charles Noble," Seelye contends, "are depicted with metaphors and allusions which link them to the undoubted portraits of Hawthorne in the *Mosses* review and *Clarel*, producing a composite pattern of psychic seduction and betrayal." Perhaps. Vicki Halper Litman ("The Cottage and the Temple: Melville's Symbolic Use of Architecture," *AQ* 21:630–38) surveys some of Melville's writing, particularly the short stories, in the light of contemporary architectural theories such as those of Andrew Jackson Downing, which established the farmhouse and the temple as architectural ideals; Melville's own "dystopian view of earthly possibilities," she observes, "meant that few, if any, perfect structures, or perfect architects, would appear in his writing." Mrs. Litman's brief discussion opens a subject well worth broader and deeper treatment.

*University of Wisconsin—Madison*

# 4. Whitman and Dickinson

## Bernice Slote

With 1969 celebrated as the hundred and fiftieth anniversary of the birth of Walt Whitman, the volume of Whitman studies was as richly expansive as that on Emily Dickinson was narrow. But there is still that fortunate dialogue in the ways of poetry: "I loafe and invite my soul," says Whitman. "The Soul selects her own Society," says Dickinson—a dialogue reflected in the ways of criticism. Whitman scholars grow cosmic and philosophical; Dickinson scholars lean to explication and a close use of lexicon and concordance. Both are needed.

### i. Whitman

*a.* **Bibliography, texts and editions, biography.** Along with the fifty Whitman items and cross references listed in the *1969 MLA International Bibliography*, nearly sixty additional items have been considered for this review. Among the works unaccountably omitted from the MLA listing are three major books, a monograph, and several special issues of periodicals. Obviously not all of these more than one hundred items can be noted here (dissertations and reviews will be generally omitted), and the Whitman student should therefore consult regularly (and especially for 1969) the "Current Bibliography" compiled for each issue of the *Walt Whitman Review* by William White.

The triumph of this anniversary year was the publication of Volumes IV and V of *Walt Whitman: The Correspondence*, Volume IV: *1886–1889*; Volume V: *1890–1892*, edited by Edwin Haviland Miller (New York, N.Y. Univ. Press), thus completing one segment of *The Collected Writings of Walt Whitman*, under the general editorship of Gay Wilson Allen and Sculley Bradley. The 2721 Whitman letters (with an addendum of sixty-five letters discovered since the publication of the first three volumes in 1961 and 1964) are arranged chronologically through the five volumes. Each volume has an introduction by the editor, a list of correspondents, an index, and appendices including a list of manuscript sources, a list of Whitman's lost letters, a calendar of letters written to Whitman, and a chronology of his life and works. Texts and notes have been meticulously handled by the editor. Uniquely combining the foresight, energy, and generosity of a private collector, Charles E. Feinberg, from whose collection the major part of the letters are taken, the skilled and knowledgeable work of its editor, and the care shown in design and production by the New York University Press, this edition of Whitman's *Correspondence* must surely be considered an example of American literary scholarship at its best.

As the editing of *The Collected Writings* continues, notes by Harold Blodgett (*CEEAN* 1[1968]3–4) and Sculley Bradley (*CEEAN* 1[1968]:9) are informative on problems of handling manuscripts and determining texts, the first indicating something of the "limitless" problems of collating the manuscript leaves and fragments and other revisions and copies, the second describing a process of "detective work" in identifying editions. See also a summary directed to scholars in India: William White, "*The Collected Writings of Walt Whitman* —A Progress Report" (*NASRC* 11:23–28).

New Whitman items continue to appear, many of them with both bibliographical and biographical interest. Three Whitman letters of 1882 concerning books ordered by Mrs. Vine Coburn are presented by Samuel A. Golden (*WWR* 15:59–60). Neda M. Westlake recounts the history of a twenty-page manuscript of Whitman's, "A Backward Glance on My Own Road," recently given to the University of Pennsylvania (*LC* 34 [1968]:100–02). An anonymous 1845 article with many characteristic Whitman touches is suggested as an attribution by Burton R. Pollin in " 'Delightful Sights,' a Possible Whitman Article in Poe's *Broadway Journal*" (WWR 15:180–87). William White reports on two interesting biographical accounts. An unsigned piece, "Walt Whitman for 1878" (*West Jersey Press*, 16 Jan. 1878), suggests Whitman's hand, though inconclusively. It is printed with an explanatory note in "Whitman or Whitmaniana?" (*ATQ* 1:120–21). And from the Feinberg Collection comes "Walt Whitman: An Unpublished Autobiographical Note," reprinted with factual corrections and dated 1891 in a note by White (*N&Q* 16:221–22).

As Harold Jaffe says in his note on the nature of Whitman's "collaboration" on Richard Maurice Bucke's 1883 *Walt Whitman*

("Bucke's *Walt Whitman*: A Collaboration," *WWR* 15:190–94), "Whitman was his own most efficient entrepreneur." A rare and out-of-print biography, James Thomson's *Walt Whitman: The Man and the Poet*, edited by Bertram Dobell (1910), is described by Glenn E. Doyle, along with John Burroughs's *Notes on Walt Whitman*, as giving the view of his life "Walt Whitman wanted projected" ("A Note on Thomson's Biography of Whitman," *WWR* 15:122–24).

Several other notes help to fill out our knowledge of Whitman's life, both as poet and as person. Edward F. Grier gives a full account of his study of Whitman's first notebook as it now appears on microfilm ("Whitman's Earliest Known Notebook," *PMLA* 83:1453–56), though the reader should also consult a note by John C. Broderick ("Whitman's Earliest Known Notebook: A Clarification," *PMLA* 84:1657) on the history of both the notebook and the microfilm in the Library of Congress. Grier finds that material for *Leaves of Grass* appeared in the notebook as early as 1847. Bert A. Thompson briefly sketches the life of Edward Wilkins, the young Canadian (and future doctor) who served as Whitman's nurse from November 1888 to October 1889 ("Edward Wilkins: Male Nurse to Walt Whitman," *WWR* 15:194–96).

Some new details on Whitman's unsuccessful adventures with New Mexico mining stock are given in William White's "Walt Whitman and the Sierra Grande Mining Company" (*NMHR* 44:223–30). Atcheson L. Hench contributes another note on Folger McKinsey's recollections of Whitman—a meeting at Camden with Richard Le Gallienne in which Whitman spoke of the West as "the real country of America" (*AN&Q* 8:53). Whitman's own trip to the West as far as Denver in September 1879 and his stop in Lawrence and Topeka for the two-day Old Settlers' celebration is described in an informative article by Walter H. Eitner, "Walt Whitman in the *Kansas Magazine*" (*Kansas Magazine*, 1968, pp. 29–31). Two of Whitman's poems had been published in the first volume of the magazine in 1872 ("The Mystic Trumpeter" and "Virginia—The West"), and there were several early notes and articles about him, but even by 1879 Whitman was not the "people's poet" in Kansas—Whittier had that distinction.

Whitman the person comes close in two articles, Peter Van Egmond's "Walt Whitman on the Platform" (*SSJ* 32[1967]:215–24) and Kenneth P. Neilson's "The 'Voice' of Walt Whitman" (*ABC* 19,iv [1968]:20–22). The first surveys accounts of Whitman as a public speaker and suggests again a difference between his own image of himself and the reality as described by others. The second article raises the problem of a Whitman ghost—his voice on a record which may—or may not—have been reproduced from an Edison cylinder recording of 1890. Neilson says only that he cannot claim the record to be authentic.

*b.* **Criticism: general.** After reading nearly a hundred articles of Whitman criticism this year, I find one statement by Roger Asselineau strangely endearing. He says, "I could in my turn draw up endless inventories of his inventories" ("Walt Whitman: From Paumanok to More Than America," *Studies in American Literature*, pp. 18–39). This admission makes kin of us all, for there is something contagious in the Whitmanian cadence, a procreant urge that leaves pages studded with cosmic glitter in vast rondures of rhetoric. Through it all, however, are repetitions of basic themes in Whitman, and more than usual evidence that readers agree, though each in his own voice, on certain elements: a pervasive duality, as well as union—not only in themes of body and soul but in distinctions of Whitman's personal and national qualities, as in Alain Bosquet's "Les deux visages de Walt Whitman" (*NL* 21[Aug]:3), or the combined appeals of his mysticism and humanism, as in P. H. Wild's "Flower Power: A Student's Guide to Pre-Hippie Transcendentalism" (*EJ* 58:62–68); the presence of some kind of structure in *Leaves*, particularly in "Song of Myself," with a movement from the actual, or physical, to the Transcendental, or spiritual; and the variable voices of "I" or the self. There have been some distinguished essays on these themes, with a number of individual insights.

The most important critical publication in current Whitman studies is *A Century of Whitman Criticism*, edited by Edwin Haviland Miller (Bloomington, Indiana Univ. Press). A compendium of significant statements by forty-six critics, beginning with Emerson's 1855 letter to Whitman and ending with the 1955 "Introduction" to *Walt Whitman's Poems* by Gay Wilson Allen and Charles T. Davis, it is both a history of Whitman criticism and an indispensable source book for students. One of my own pleasures in reading this book was to encounter again Randall Jarrell's tour de force in massing evidence of the sheer witchery of Whitman's poetry—the language itself—in *Leaves of Grass* ("Some Lines from Whitman," 1953). Least effective,

I thought, was the very nearly no-statement by Wallace Stevens (letter to Joseph Bennett, 8 Feb. 1955). Miller's introduction gives with complete clarity the changing critical views of Whitman, from the ardent hero-worship of his own time to the later preoccupation with the artist, and evaluates (sometimes disagreeing with) the selections which follow.

A half-dozen recent essays which stress Whitman's meaning for the present American deserve special notice. Roy Harvey Pearce, writing on "Whitman and Our Hope for Poetry" (*The Poetic Tradition,* edited by Don Cameron Allen and Henry T. Rowell, Baltimore, Johns Hopkins Press, 1968, pp. 123–40), chooses Whitman, the social critic, as most important for the present, but he also points to a significant continuity in the reading of Whitman: "For the history of American poetry could be written as the continuing discovery and rediscovery of Whitman, an on-going affirmation of his crucial relevance to the mission of the American poet: which is, as it is everywhere, simply to tell us the truth in such a way that it will be a new truth"; in other words, to renew us and our capacity to have faith in ourselves. His subject is particularly "that Whitman who sought the spirit 'that restores the land to productive order.'" In *Leaves of Grass,* writes James E. Miller, Jr. ("Walt Whitman: The Quest for Identity," *Quests Surd and Absurd* [Chicago, Univ. of Chicago Press, 1967], pp. 95–102), Whitman "vigorously dramatized the questions that continue to haunt the American imagination"—among them—"What does it mean, being an American?" The course of the drama is the discovery of self, or Modern Man finding his identity here and now—by rebirth into a new self (American, personal, human), by a test of maturity in the Civil War, and by insight into the meaning or fulfillment of death. The key poems in this sequence are "Song of Myself," *Drum-Taps,* and "Passage to India." The theme of Roger Asselineau's essay (cited above) is America as poem—Whitman's absorption of and identification with America. His outline of Whitman's discovery of America in *Leaves,* from the actual man to the soul which is "more than America," is very much like the stages given by Howard Mumford Jones in "The Cosmic Optimism of Walt Whitman" (*Belief and Disbelief in American Literature* [Chicago, Univ. of Chicago Press, 1967], pp. 70–93). Here the theme is also the destiny of something beyond, and the presence of a purposeful cosmic will. In Whitman there is a "universal vitalism that, by reason of its emphasis upon activism rather than passivity, is curiously American." This American quality is suggested in a perceptive contrast by Eugene Goodheart in "Walt Whitman: Democracy and the Self" (*The Cult of the Ego: The Self in Modern Literature* [Chicago, Univ. of Chicago Press, 1968], pp. 133–60). Typical of the European theme, he says, is that Baudelaire's role-playing becomes confinement, another kind of prison; Whitman's American self engages in "spiritual acrobatics" which demonstrate "the capacity of the *I* to escape reduction." *Leaves of Grass* he sees as "the spiritual-physical incarnation of the democratic possibility." Such expansive action toward something beyond is "cosmic evolution," a phrase used by George Bowering in "The Solitary Everything" (*WWR* 15:13–26). Whitman "stands in the midst of a suffused universe, not as interpreter, but as part of the action itself," himself a poem, itself an organism that changes because change and life are inseparable. That process of the making of the New World as Whitman described it, with a final emergence of true Democracy, is unfinished, concludes Mr. Bowering ("the grandest things always remain").

Other articles are variations on themes of change and movement in *Leaves of Grass* and the "I" of the poems. In "Walt Whitman's Philosophical Epic" (*WWR* 15:91–96) Charles R. Metzger again traces the central figure from hero to prophet, but also has the suggestive comment that *Leaves*, in its length, its continuous changing forms, and its multiple voices, gains some of the qualities of the anonymous folk epic. Rameshwar Gupta in "Whitman: The Poet of Cosmic Dynamism" (*BP* 4[1968],ii:95–103) emphasizes that the movement of *Leaves* is not linear but "rolling, fermenting, undulating, ebbing and flowing." In a carefully detailed article, "Walt Whitman's Ambiguities of 'I' " (*Studies in American Literature*, pp. 40–59), Philip Y. Coleman argues for the multiple and simultaneous meanings of lines and the "I" or speaker, which may be either the poet/narrator or the body of a book of poetry, or the soul or the body, or both or neither. James E. Mulqueen in "Organic Growth of *Leaves of Grass*" (*WWR* 15:85–91) attributes some of the changes observable in Whitman's successive versions of his book to "psychological changes in the poet resulting from an ebbing of the libido." The movement is "from reality to art to religion," a pattern best observable in "Proud Music of the Storm." Perhaps the best evidence of Whitman's organic *Leaves* is a long, detailed, and convincing analysis by Elizabeth Wells, "The Structure of Whitman's 1860 *Leaves of Grass*" (*WWR* 15:131–61). Between the announcement of the major themes in the opening "Proto-Leaf" and the summary in "So Long," there is a discernible order in the 1860 edition, with a progressive building of associations. This is a useful article, especially for the sense it gives of Whitman as the conscious maker and arranger of his book. The only point on which I would demur is the occasional overinsistence on the necessity of the 1860 arrangement for an accurate reading. (I, for one, do not misinterpret "Elemental Drifts," when it is out of context, as the author says a reader would.) With a link to the future, Sholom J. Kahn's "Whitman's 'New Wood'" (*WWR* 15:201–14) studies image clusters (roots, trees) which give the "organic sense of nature and growth." The "new wood" of American poetry is matter rather than style. Barriss Mills offers a definition of Whitman's hope for a "new poetry" ("Whitman's Poetic Theory," *ESQ* 55,ii:42–47) as one which is more experience than words, is more concrete than abstract, and links poet and reader. "If no other poet has used 'I' so frequently, . . . no other poet, perhaps, has written 'you' so often."

Among other general views of Whitman, from different vantage points, is Hyatt H. Waggoner's eloquent and generally convincing look at Whitman's relation to Emerson in "Signing for Soul and Body" (*American Poets*, pp. 149–80). His case is overstated only if one reads nothing else, and pertinent precisely because readers have not always been aware of the close link with Emerson. He has some excellent readings of individual poems. Howard D. Pearce sees in the line, "I lean and loafe at my ease observing a spear of summer grass," a posture symbolic of the Romantics' theory of knowledge, the poet as a passive receiver of intuited (or given) wisdom, and relates Whitman's attitude to those of Wordsworth and Emerson ("'I Lean and Loafe': Whitman's Romantic Posture," *WWR* 15:3–26). The theme of Gay Wilson Allen's "Walt Whitman's Inner Space" (*Studies in American Literature*, pp. 7–17) may not be entirely new, but it is presented in arresting terms: Whitman's imagery of the "largeness of nature" and his imagery of exploration are frequently only metaphors for *inner space*. Ideas of the "cosmic dimensions of the soul" are well supported by quotations from Whitman's notebooks. Other general notes on Whitman are Horace M. Kallen, "Of Love, Death and Walt Whitman" (*WWR* 15:171–80), Charles

Hughes, "Impact of Evil on the Poetry of Walt Whitman" (*WWR* 15:237–42), Richard D. McGhee, "Concepts of Time in Whitman's Poetry" (*WWR* 15:76–85), and Oscar Cargill, "Walt Whitman and Civil Rights" (*Essays in American and English Literature*, edited by Max F. Schulz [Athens, Ohio Univ. Press, 1967], pp. 48–58), showing with some informative examples that in his journalistic and other prose writings Whitman was likely to be ambivalent in politics, including his position on states' rights.

Turning from themes and structures to studies of style and language, we can single out two suggestive articles. In "A Prosody for Whitman?" Roger Mitchell (*PMLA* 84:1606–12) rejects a theory of stress prosody for Whitman (once suggested by Sculley Bradley some thirty years ago) and develops a scansion based on the caesura and involving rhythmic and thematic patterns of word groups within a poem. As with any system of scansion, there are difficulties when two readers do not agree on a reading (my own caesuras and patterns do not always coincide with Mitchell's), but the suggested patterning (often in a "rhythmical parabola") is worth study. Lawrence Buell in "Transcendentalist Catalogue Rhetoric: Vision Versus Form" (*AL* 40[1968]:325–39) has a helpful analysis of the catalogue in Whitman as formed primarily "to express the boundless fecundity of nature and human life" through all the senses, but with some suggestion of internal design. Primarily, they demand of the reader "a sense of abandonment." Buell relates Whitman's catalogues particularly to those in Emerson's prose (see *ALS 1968*, pp. 11–12). Other notes on style add to a reservoir of biblical influences on Whitman: James L. Livingston in "Walt Whitman's Epistle to the Americans" (*AL* 40:542–44) sees certain likenesses of rhythm and arrangement between I Corinthians 13:4–8 (beginning "Charity suffereth long") and "A Song of the Rolling Earth," and Richard J. Fein notes a reminder of Lamentations in "When Lilacs Last in the Dooryard Bloom'd" (*WWR* 15:115–17). Also on Whitman's use of language are Marian Stein's "'Comrade' or 'Camerado' in *Leaves of Grass*" (*WWR* 13[1967]:123–25) and Charles L. Cherry's "Whitman and Language: An Instance of Semantic Paradox" (*WWR* 14[1968]: 56–58).

*c.* **Criticism: individual poems.** "Song of Myself" still seems to be the key poem in considering theme, structure, and narrative voice in

*Leaves of Grass.* That "Song of Myself" has some kind of structure, and one which is closely related to Whitman's theme, is usually conceded, though it may be described variously as psychological, symphonic, narrative. An excellent general description of the poem, as well as a good introduction to Whitman, is "Walt Whitman: 'Song of Myself,'" an essay by James E. Miller, Jr., originally prepared for a series of foreign broadcasts by the Voice of America and now collected in *Landmarks* (pp. 144–56). It includes in brief form Miller's analysis of the framework of the poem as a narrative-drama of mystical experience, and stresses the importance of the "I" and the "You" involved in the poem and the value of the self which is created there ("a vision of fertile creation and a heightened sense of life's joyous vitality"), both the "I" and the "You" becoming Whitman's "robust souls." Representing the antistructural view, however, Ronald Beck ("The Structure of 'Song of Myself' and the Critics," *WWR* 15:32–38) argues that only the theme of "oneness" holds together the fifty-two separate sections of the poem (something like fifty-two ways of looking at a blackbird). But this will not do, on the basis of the poem itself. Even though Mr. Beck thinks it is unreasonable to expect some causal order (while admitting that the poem is organic), the fact is that a sequence happens: by the end of the poem the blackbird (or hawk) has circled about and flown away. In another view of the poem, John Nagle in "Toward a Theory of Structure in 'Song of Myself'" (*WWR* 15:162–71) finds a rhetorical organization, eight parts identified on the basis of transitional signals. The overall pattern is of "conflict–climax–fulfillment."

The most extensive study of a single poem is Estelle W. Taylor's "Analysis and Comparison of the 1855 and 1891 Versions of Whitman's 'To Think of Time'" (*WWR* 13[1967]:107–22), showing that Whitman developed a unified structure in which the pattern of repetitions suits the theme, "faith in the eternal cyclic scheme of things." Three articles deal with "The Sleepers." Michael S. Reynolds in "Whitman's Early Prose and 'The Sleepers'" (*AL* 41:406–14) finds that certain admired elements of the poem—"the dream journey motif, the conscious structure, and the stream-of-consciousness technique"—appear in Whitman's early prose of 1840 and 1842 and later in his newspaper pieces. Parallels to several motifs in "The Sleepers" are in Swedenborg. In "Shades of Darkness in 'The Sleepers'" (*WWR* 15:187–90), Sister Eva Mary, O.S.F., observes the predominant use of various kinds of darkness in the poem, with night as a metaphorical fulfillment, a merging of all elements. In "Whitman's 'The Sleepers' and the 'Indiana' Section of Crane's *The Bridge*" (*WWR* 15:245–48) John P. Runden notes a strong relationship in both matter and spirit between that section of Crane's poem and section 6 of Whitman's poem.

Charles Clay Doyle in "Poetry and Pastoral: A Dimension of Whitman's 'Lilacs'" (*WWR* 15:242–45) suggests that on one level the poem is about poetry, thus having the spirit if not all the conventions of the pastoral. It begins with images of confinement, followed by images of liberation and expansiveness suited to the possible emergence of the poets of democracy Whitman hoped for. "'Starting from Paumanok' as Functional Poetry" by Frances H. Bennett (*WWR* 15:117–20) is a detailed and sensitive explication of the poem, especially in its structural devices. So is "'Crossing Brooklyn Ferry': A Hundred Years Hence," by John D. Magee (*WWR* 15:38–43), though there is little that is new in the account. A brief note by Frank C. Cronin, "Modern Sensibility in Stanza 2 of 'Crossing Brooklyn Ferry'" (*WWR* 15:56–57) emphasizes the balance of flux and suspension in the poem. Larry Sutton writes on "Structural Music in Whitman's 'Out of the Cradle'" (*WWR* 15:57–59). William A. Wortman in "Spiritual Progression in 'A Sight in Camp'" (*WWR* 14[1968]:24–26) reads that poem as "a statement about the poet's recovery during war of faith in life." Harold Aspiz observes the envelope structure of "Spirit That Form'd This Scene" (*Expl* 28:item 25). Arthur Golden, reviewing Edwin H. Miller's *Walt Whitman's Poetry* (*L&P* 19,iii–iv:61–65) argues that both "As I Ebb'd" and the "Calamus" sequence relate to some emotional crisis for Whitman during the late 1850's; he has other helpful comments on "Passage to India." Sister Margaret Patrice Slattery observes in "Patterns of Imagery in Whitman's 'There Was a Child Went Forth'" (*WWR* 15:112–14) a cyclic movement of human existence through "life, death, and life in death," combined with patterns of contrast. The universality of the same poem is reinforced by Stanley Friedman's note on close resemblance of theme and imagery in Dylan Thomas's "Poem in October" ("Whitman and Laugharne," *AWR* 18:81–82). Two useful explications which focus on Whitman's use of appropriate language are "Elemental Imagery in 'Children of Adam,'" by Rosemary Stephens (*WWR* 14[1968]:26–28), and "Organic Language in 'Patroling Barnegat,'" by Raymond G. Malbone (*WWR* 13[1967]:125–27).

Whitman's attitude toward the Civil War has been studied through his poems. David J. Hibler's comparison of the war poems of Whitman and Melville (*"Drum-Taps* and *Battle-Pieces," Person* 50:130–47) is thoughtful and convincing. While Melville's view is darker throughout, his representation of war and its suffering is general, based on the known fact rather than the experienced reality; Whitman, though showing more optimism about the eventual good from the war, has the perspective of experience and communicates a shared suffering with the individual, says Mr. Hibler. Though Whitman's bardic vision of 1860 continued to hold, it was modified by "a practical sense of compassion and a new prophetic sense of America's en-masse mission." Comparing Whitman's "Reconciliation" and Wilfred Owen's "Strange Meeting," two poems with somewhat the same situation, C. N. Sastry (*NASRC* 11:54–56) shows that both poets express revolt against war and also find illumination and "the spirit of peace that reconciles discordant elements." Whitman's attitude is like Owen's condemnation rather than Rupert Brooke's glorification of war.

*d.* **Relationships, reputation, influence.** Various relationships that help to define Whitman's personal cosmos have been discussed—central links, for example, with Emerson and the Transcendentalists, with Wordsworth or Shelley and the Romantics. Other notes exploring circumferences (as Emily Dickinson might put it) suggest that Whitman may have taken the phrase "children of Adam" from Horace Greeley; that he has likenesses with Hegel; that William Michael Rossetti, Henry James, and Theodore Dreiser liked him, that Markham did not; that there are parallels in Teilhard de Chardin; that he is both like and different from Sartre. See the following articles: Harold Aspiz, "'Children of Adam' and Horace Greeley" (*WWR* 15:49–51); James L. Livingston, "With Whitman and Hegel Around the Campfire" (*WWR* 15:120–22)—Hegelian dialectic in "By the Bivouac's Fitful Flame"; Dean H. Keller, "Walt Whitman in England: A Footnote" (*WWR* 15:54–55), and R. W. Peattie, "Postscript to Charles Kent on Whitman" (*WWR* 15:107–11)—both on Rossetti and Whitman; William White, presenting two new letters from the Feinberg Collection in "Unpublished Henry James on Whitman" (*RES* 20:321–22) and "Dreiser on Hardy, Henley, and Whitman" (*ELN* 6[1968]:122–24); Harold Jaffe, "Markham on Whitman" (*Markham Rev* 2[1968]:[1]); Sister Flavia Marie, C.S.J., " 'Song of Myself': A Presage of Modern Teilhardian Paleontology" (*WWR* 15:43–49); and Stanley R. Harrison, "Sacrilege of Preference in Whitman and Sartre" (*WWR* 15:51–54).

Little has appeared on Whitman's relationship to the arts. One article of special interest, however, is Henry B. Rule's "Walt Whitman and George Caleb Bingham" (*WWR* 15:248–53), in which a source for some descriptions in Whitman is found in the works of the American painter and his "realistic pictures of common life in the Mississippi Valley." Whitman's lines on a "western turkey-shooting" in "Song of Myself" (section 15, ll. 283–84) seem to describe Bingham's *Shooting for the Beef* (1850), and, more indirectly, lines on the river boatmen's camp in "Our Old Feuillage" (ll. 38–39) suggest Bingham's popular *Jolly Flatboatmen* (1846). A good case is made for Whitman's knowing the pictures (and feeling some kinship to Bingham). The reader can judge for himself, for in the same issue of the *Walt Whitman Review* both paintings are reproduced in black and white on the back cover. In a different direction, some students might be interested in one doctoral dissertation: "A Study of Selected Choral Settings of Walt Whitman Poems" (*DA* 28:3706A) by Lou Stem Mize, which includes musical influence on Whitman as well as his influence on composers.

In Dreiser's 1902 letter on Hardy, Henley, and Whitman (see above), Whitman is called "better than oriental in his pantheism—universal I should say." The problem of defining the extent and nature of Whitman's "oriental" philosophy, or mysticism, continues to engross a number of writers, who refer generally to the two earlier studies which have been most influential: Malcolm Cowley's 1959 essay, " 'Song of Myself' and Indian Philosophy" (reprinted in *A Century of Whitman Criticism*, pp. 231–46) and V. K. Chari's 1964 *Whitman in the Light of Vedantic Mysticism*. In recent articles, Raman K. Singh writes of Whitman as "*Avatar* of Shri Krishna?" (*WWR* 15:97–102)—but a philosophical rather than a physical reincarnation. Singh stresses the Indian concept of the union of soul and body and of sex as the means to achieve spiritual freedom. V. John Mathew, "Self in 'Song of Myself': A Defence of Whitman's Egoism"

(*WWR* 15:102–07), relates Whitman particularly to Hindu mysticism and resemblances with the Bhagavad-Gita. Seeing the "*one fundamental unifying principle*" in Whitman as "the principle of selfhood," Mohan Lal Sharma describes similar themes in Rabindranath Tagore and in Pakistan's national poet, Mohammed Iqbal ("Whitman, Tagore, Iqbal," *WWR* 15:230–37). Parallels and relationships between Whitman and Kahlil Gibran are discussed in a helpful essay by Suhail ibn-Salim Hanna ("Gibran and Whitman: Their Literary Dialogue," *LE&W* 12[1968]:174–98). One might note particularly the comments, in footnotes as well as in the text, on other Arabic writers and the influence of the New England Transcendentalists. As one dissenting note in the study of Whitman and the Far Eastern philosophies, Howard Mumford Jones states that "as a mystic, Whitman lacks the humility of Oriental systems of belief. He stands imperturbable in the midst of nature" (*Belief and Disbelief in American Literature* [Chicago, Univ. of Chicago Press, 1967], p. 92).

Interest in Whitman is particularly strong in India and is rising in Japan and in certain of the Slavic countries. However, most works published in those countries must wait to be translated before they can effectively reach American scholars; even when they are in English, they are hard to find in American libraries. A welcome summary is "Whitman in Russia" by Boris Gilenson (*SovL* 5:176–81), who traces interest in Russia from Turgenev and his unpublished translations in the 1870's, through Tolstoy at the turn of the century, to critics Maurice Mendelson and Kornei Chukovsky and their latest work in the 1960's. The typical view of Whitman in the Russia of the early 1900's, when Whitman first appeared in translation, was "as a pioneer of new forms and a spiritual titan"; he was admired among the Russian futurists in the period before 1918; and since then he has been important to both poets and critics as, according to Anatoli Lunacharsky, "a huge prophetic figure at the entrance to the new world." A similar review is Stanley E. McMullin's "Walt Whitman's Influence in Canada" (*DR* 49:361–68), which describes two general kinds of response: that of the Canadian press and periodical literature, which ranged between accusations of "bestiality" and devotions to "a Homeric writer" but included balanced critics like Charles G. D. Roberts and Wilfred Campbell; and that of the "Whitman cultists," groups which derived from Canadian connections with Dr. Richard

Maurice Bucke and Horace Traubel and who, at least up to 1925, were considered radicals.

Several periodicals published special Whitman issues for the 1969 sesquicentennial anniversary of Whitman's birth. A double volume of the *Walt Whitman Review* was made possible by the support of Charles E. Feinberg, and the "Eleventh Annual Walt Whitman Pages" of *The Long-Islander* (131st year, section 3, 29 May 1969), edited by Gay Wilson Allen, had an impressive list of contributors (see the analysis of this issue in William White, "A Current Bibliography," *WWR* 15:196). A representative special issue is that of *American Dialog* 5,iii(Spring-Summer), edited by Joseph North, with Walter Lowenfels and Hugo Gellert. Among the thirty-six special articles, reprints, appreciations, poems, and illustrations are a note by Roger Asselineau; an article by Sidney Finkelstein on Whitman and his city, "Whitman's Mannahatta"; an essay by Langston Hughes, "The Ceaseless Rings of Walt Whitman," reprinted from his introduction to *I Hear the People Singing: Selected Poems of Walt Whitman* (1946); excerpts from Kornei Chukovsky's book *My Whitman*, in "What Walt Whitman Means to Me"; poems by James Schevill and others. And in "Who Listens to Him Today?" (pp. 10–12, 36–38) Harold Blodgett directly explores the "relevance" of Whitman to our own time, concluding that he is less heard in the academy (students with superficial knowledge of Whitman are likely to take his belief in "the good, the true, and the beautiful" as "an affront . . . in these days of existential anguish") than by "the great company of amateurs," of all parts of society, who are attracted especially by "the poet's redemptive power, his role as inspirer and quickener," and who find in Whitman "an aesthetic vision of timeless vitality."

Finally, there is a small, attractive collection of poems to Whitman by Spanish writers: *Homage to Walt Whitman* (Homenaje a Walt Whitman), translated and annotated by Didier Tisdel Jaén, with a foreword by Jorge Luis Borges (University, Univ. of Ala. Press). It includes works of nine poets (among them Lugones, Lorca, Neruda), with facing Spanish and English texts; helpful notes on the poets and their interest in Whitman; and, in an appendix, a translation of the 1887 essay on Whitman by the Cuban writer José Martí. The brief foreword is memorable not because of new ideas but because of Borges, who somehow manages to say everything memorably. He speaks of the hero of *Leaves of Grass* as threefold: the writer of the book, "the splendid shadow projected by him" (the imagined hero), and the reader himself. This complex creation Borges calls "the divine vagabond of *Leaves of Grass*."

### *ii*. Dickinson

*a*. **Bibliography, editions, collections.** The wayward riches of Emily Dickinson's 1775 poems, as registered in the Thomas H. Johnson edition, are still being sorted out and reordered. For example, a note by Carl A. Adkins ("Emily Dickinson's 'Would You Like Summer? Taste of Our's': A Note on the Composition Date," *ELN* 7:53–55) uses both circumstantial and internal evidence to correct the date of the poem to 1861 from 1863, as first conjectured by Johnson.

And while the complete Dickinson canon continues to be formulated, it is most useful to have made available in one volume a facsimile reproduction of the first three Dickinson collections of 1890, 1891, and 1896: *Poems, 1890–1896*, with an introduction by George Monteiro (Gainesville, Fla., SF&R, 1967). This volume includes of course the facsimile manuscript pages of "Renunciation" printed in the 1890 collection and the prefaces by Thomas Wentworth Higginson (first series) and Mabel Loomis Todd (second and third series). Those who have not read these prefaces recently, or at all, may find a certain exhilaration in Higginson's linking of Emily to "Undine or Mignon or Thekla" and Mrs. Todd's comparisons of the poems, in their absence of conventional form, to "Wagner's rugged music." George Monteiro's introduction to the facsimile edition is a judicious review of the circumstances of Dickinson's first publication, noting that as a matter of literary history these first editions are important, even with their alterations of poems, for perhaps only in that way could they have been published at all. Another reason to be grateful for this edition is William White's comment (in a review of Dickinson publications, "Nostalgia Revisited: The Emily Dickinson Industry," *ABC* 19,v:27–28) that a copy of *Poems: Third Series 1896* which cost five dollars in 1950 was priced at fifty dollars in 1968.

In "Giving Emily Dickinson to the World" (*PULC* 31:47–54) John S. van E. Kohn gives information on the Dickinson collection assembled by Mrs. John Pershing and presented to the Princeton University Library on 7 June 1969. Kohn reviews the history of

Dickinson manuscripts and publication and describes generally its extent in books and a miscellany of related items. The collection is described in the pamphlet *The Margaret Jane Pershing Collection of Emily Dickinson*, compiled by Robert W. Fraser, introduction by Richard M. Ludwig (Princeton, N.J.: Princeton Univ. Library).

*b.* **Biography.**   While not strictly biographical, two articles focus on Emily Dickinson's relationship with her father. In "Psychoanalytic Remarks on a Poem by Emily Dickinson" (*PsyR* 56:247–64), M. D. Faber analyzes "My Life Closed Twice Before Its Close" in Freudian terms. The poem as a whole, he says, deals with past and future attachments to older, "forbidden men," and expresses "on the level of secondary process . . . its author's lack of fulfillment, her death-in-life brought about by her failure to know the men to whom she was attracted, and her simultaneous desire for and dread of such knowledge." In terms of primary process, "it is the attachment to the father that ultimately brings about the death-in-life . . . . The real closing of Miss Dickinson's life . . . may be traced to her early attachment to her father." The language of the poem is also analyzed with some Freudian extensions ("event" leads to "vent," or "opening"). In "Father and Daughter: Edward and Emily Dickinson" (*AL* 40:510–23), Owen Thomas shows the influence of Edward on Emily in terms of her predilection for the language of law, finance, and politics—her father's life of the "market-place." In her early period, between 1858 and 1861, images of finance are frequent; in the later periods, images of law predominate. The implications are not only that Emily Dickinson's father was a strong presence, but that her own "poetic wit" and her frequent use of such terms in a metaphysical way suggest a mind alive to the intellectual atmosphere, that "she was well aware of the world outside of her little room" and used its language to create much of her best poetry.

*c.* **Criticism: general.**   Four books on Emily Dickinson were reviewed in *ALS 1968*. No books were published in 1969, though a number of articles try to define her and the way she saw.

   First in interest seem to be matters of the spirit—religion, mysticism, transcendentalism. Her protest against the conventionalities of religion is noted, though there are also arguments for a "conversion" and a continued reliance on Christian imagery. In a perceptive essay,

"Compound Vision: Emily Dickinson" (*NASRC* 11:28–35), M. G. Capoor of the University of Rajasthan suggests that her faith in immortality, best expressed by doubts and questions, was only an undercurrent, and that she was held back by "her Lockeian belief that the senses were the only reliable doors to reality." Even in her poems on death she did not attempt to go beyond her experience. But with her startling discovery that she could find infinity in the human mind, she moved from "a metaphysical Infinity to a simple mathematical infinity." Her poetic technique was thus developed "to impart infinity to finite objects" (illustrated by "There's a Certain Slant of Light"). In a way, suggests the author, she had resolved the old conflict between Locke and Kant: "It was mind, an active agent, which could free matter of its finiteness and impart meaning to it."

In a somewhat rambling essay, "Sorting Out: The Case of Dickinson" (*SoR* 5:436–46), J. V. Cunningham deals with our attitudes affecting pro and con our reading of Dickinson (distrust of the striking phrase, disapproval of the finished thing), with her prosody, with problems of biographical relevance, and finally with her attitudes toward religion. He finds many attitudes and no clear sequence of development. This is not a very clear discussion. In contrast, "Emily Dickinson and Transcendentalism," by Hisashi Noda (*KAL* 11 [1968]:44–58), is a well-ordered, economical discussion, first summarizing Dickinson's intellectual milieu and concluding that, although Transcendental echoes would be inevitable in her poems and letters, "most of the poems that have established Emily Dickinson as one of the greatest poets in the English language are those that show in one way or another aspects of deviation and break from the transcendental influences of her formative years." The ultimate significance of Transcendentalism for her was that it triggered a lifelong quest for meaning in existence, her poems being the result of that "lone quest for a personal revelation." She went beyond Transcendentalism but would not have done so without its initial influence.

Perhaps the most extended and satisfying of recent short studies on Dickinson is Hyatt Waggoner's chapter "Proud Ephemeral" in *American Poets* (pp. 181–222). The theme is primarily Emerson's powerful influence on her work but the drama of the counterinfluence of the Bible is clearly drawn. Her inconsistency in separate poems is corrected by a whole view of them as a body of work in which no single part attempts to present "the whole Truth" or to construct a philosophy. In the end, it is the "sophistication of the thinking of this secluded and tortured woman" as she transcends uncertainty with "surmise" and wills "commitment to the Possible" that creates the most moving drama of all. (See also a good review of the Waggoner book by F. L. Morey, "Placing Dickinson in a School," *Markham Rev* [1],v:[18–20].)

Several points of view are considered. Theodore Holmes, in a review article, "The Voice of a Poet: The Art of Emily Dickinson" (*DR* 48[1968–69]:551–55), takes the attractive but possibly controversial stand that criticism concerned only with her mind overlooks the basic fact of Dickinson's womanhood, and "Woman is the genius of the physical." Her transcendence is "thus rooted in her sensuality, as is perhaps the case with all saints . . . . Her subjects are all her own emotions, the universe her home." Here, says Mr. Holmes, "is the fullest expression of woman in art that I know." William Bysshe Stein, in "Emily Dickinson's Parodic Masks" (*UR* 36:49–55), reads a number of poems as satires in which the speaker is "the local historian and critic of a stagnant Calvinistic community." The idea is worth considering, but the poems here seem a bit overexplicated. The sky-riding poem "I Taste a Liquor Never Brewed" is shot down with theology ("inns of Molten Blue" is an echo of the birth of Christ in the stable of a tavern, with "a sly reference to the symbolic color of the Virgin Mary"). A similar view on satire is in M. G. Towheed's "The Wit of Emily Dickinson" (*BP* 4[1968],ii:20–30), though with a lighter tone (her satire is "playful" or "irreverent"). Some good details in her "bold, humorously and defiantly experimental language" are observed. Another article from the same issue of *Banasthali Patrika* (pp. 83–85) is N. Sahal's "Emily Dickinson on Renown," a general appreciation. And J. Normand, in a spirited essay, "Emily Dickinson: une aventure poétique" (*EA* 21[1968]:152–59), writes of the vibrant, questioning poet who was at home in the universe, transforming confinement into freedom. In her "vagabondage" between earth and heaven, "the coming of a new month was as much of an event as the arrival of a flesh-and-blood guest."

Three articles survey language and imagery in the poems. "Alcoholic Beverage Imagery in the Poems of Emily Dickinson" by Scott Garrow (*Markham Rev* 2,i:[11–15]) is a fairly elementary counting and cataloguing job (though it is interesting to see how pervasive is drink, and especially wine, in the poems). "Emily Dickinson's Geography: Latin America" by Rebecca Patterson (*PLL* 5:441–57) is a detailed and informative study of geographical references and their probable sources in Dickinson's reading (Prescott's *Mexico* and *Peru*, for example) and in the general public knowledge of her time. She used few local names, for she needed something exotic, removed, before she could raise it to a symbol, says the author, and she may have been drawn to her frequently used Latin American images by a kind of "hemispheric patriotism." J. K. Packard, S.J., in "The Christ Figure in Dickinson's Poetry" (*Renascence* 22:26–33) differs with those who say that Dickinson in effect "lost" Christ during a conversion crisis in the late 1840's. There was, he thinks, a spiritual transformation of the Christ figure in her subconscious mind, and she later identified with Him not as a divine but as a mythic figure who is savior and mediator. Some representative poems are cited and explicated.

In other attempts to place or define Emily Dickinson, David P. Drew writes of "Emily Brontë and Emily Dickinson as Mystic Poets" (*BST* 15[1968]:227–32). Dickinson, he says, is "more clinical, more precise, more analytical"; she tries to interpret her experience. To her the "happening" was "a search for ultimate Truth"; for Brontë it was "ecstasy for its own sake." In "The Poetry of Emily Dickinson and Henriqueta Lisboa" (*Proceedings: Pacific Northwest Conference on Foreign Languages* [Victoria, B.C., Univ. of Victoria], 20:103–12), Blanca Lobo Filho shows numerous likenesses between Dickinson and the modern Brazilian poet in their lives, their themes, and their attitudes. One interesting discussion is "Emily Dickinson's 'Test of Trouble'" by Robert F. Higgs (*Essays*, pp. 129–37). Higgs describes Emily Dickinson's preoccupation with psychological time, her "inner clock" being never "synchronized with the motions in the world." Extending J. B. Priestley's distinction (*Men and Time*, 1964) of two kinds of psychological time—Great Time (of the myths and the gods) and passing time, he notes that, although both appear in Dickinson, passing time is predominant. She could not free herself from it. As contrast, Walt Whitman "lived only in Great Time."

*d.* **Criticism: individual poems.** A dozen brief explications probe into the language and suggest implications of single poems. Two of them discuss "The Soul Selects Her Own Society," though not in entirely new terms. Simon Tugwell (*Expl* 27:item 37) shows the ambivalence in the poem: the surface seems to be "trite, comfortable truth," but the imagery of incarceration, death, and stone pulls in the opposite direction. *Shutting out* is also *being shut in*. Virtually the same point is made by Paul Witherington in "The Neighborhood Humor of Dickinson's 'The Soul Selects Her Own Society'" (*CP* 2,ii:5–9), but he expands a view to see something of "the humor of Emily's larger drama, a personality observing its own dissenting parts." The Soul may be seen as the withdrawing artist; the "I" is then Society as caustic observer. Another example of ambivalence is found in "Death Is a Dialogue Between," as Virginia H. Adair (*Expl* 27:item 52) notes that Death is both "a Dialogue" and Dust—both the imminent separation of the Dust and Spirit which have been joined in life, and Dust itself, for Death "Argues from the Ground."

Writing on "The Lamp Burns Sure—Within" and "The Poets Light But Lamps," Stuart Lewis (*Expl* 28:item 4) makes the sensible point that one poem can sometimes be understood best in conjunction with another use of the same symbols. These two poems together establish "Lamp" as poetry, the poet as "serf" or servant; their theme is "the permanence of poetry contrasted to the brevity of human life." The first poem emphasizes art as more important than the poet who serves it; the second deals with the independence of the work of art, subsequent ages interpreting it with their own lenses. Connotations of the language support James S. Mullican's note on the "bitterly sarcastic" tone of "Praise It—'Tis Dead" (*Expl* 27:item 62) and, perhaps less obviously, the point made by Ted-Larry Pebworth and Jay C. Summers (*Expl* 27:item 76) on the "traditional, undoubting approach to Christianity" in "The Feet of People Walking Home." Nancy Lenz Harvey (*Expl* 28:item 17) calls "What Soft—Cherubic Creatures" a "stinging denunciation of the hypocrisy embodied in gentlewomen" who by alienating themselves from both God and man turn to brittle creatures, more mineral than human. In a substantial analysis of "The Tint I Cannot Take—Is Best," Sister Ellen Fitzgerald (*Expl* 28:item 29) emphasizes the separation of the self from the "tint" of her surroundings; the poet "remains the consciousness who creates, never taking on the tints of her own artifact." Nature is separate, and also, in a higher sense, unknowable until death. On the other hand, Sister Victoria Marie Forde, S.C., notes (*Expl* 27:item

41) that the Jay in "No Brigadier Throughout the Year" is linked to man, viewed lightheartedly, but as one with the family of the Universe.

Pierre Michel, in "The Last Stanza of Emily Dickinson's 'One dignity delays for all—'" (*ES* 50:98–100), identifies "One dignity" as a funeral procession, the speaker changing from the position of observer to that of the dead person himself. Disagreeing with other interpretations, he suggests that the "meek escutcheon" of the dead is, like a coat of arms on a shield, "an ensign armorial, granted in memory of some achievement or distinguished feat"—here as a sort of epitaph, on hearse or tombstone, recognizing a meek or humble life. Ronald Beck extends previous interpretations of "I Heard a Fly Buzz—When I Died" (*Expl* 26[1967]:item 31). The company around the deathbed waits for Death in the guise of a king, but only an unpleasant fly arrives, thus contrasting the ironic reality of private dying with the presumed nobility of death as a public event. In a somewhat longer piece, "Emily Dickinson's 'A Clock Stopped'" (*MSE* 1[1967]:52–54), R. A. Sheffler argues that the poem does not, as Charles Anderson interprets it in *Emily Dickinson's Poetry* (1960), *border* on blasphemy: it *is* blasphemous. The "Dial life" of the stopped clock is equated with the puppet life of the victim or man, and for none of them does a "Great Artificer" come to put life together again.

*University of Nebraska*

# 5. Mark Twain

## Hamlin Hill

In 1969 the Mark Twain Industry continued churning, though much of the output appeared fragile and of dubious workmanship. If nothing as spectacular as the Edmund Wilson controversy sparked the year, there were the second three volumes of The Mark Twain Papers to keep interest stirring, several important volumes, a few valuable articles, and even hopeful progress for that eternal bridesmaid, the *Works of Mark Twain.*

### i. Textual and Bibliographical

In "Mark Twain's Unpublished Letter to Tom Taylor—an Enigma" (*MTJ* 14,i:8–9), James R. Sturdevant prints a short letter of 5 January 1874 which may suggest that Mark Twain wished to discuss the possibilities of dramatizing *The Gilded Age* with Taylor, a dramatist and editor of *Punch*. In one of the handsomest books of Mark Twain material since the Book Club of California published *Ah Sin* and *Concerning Cats*, Edgar M. Branch has collected *Clemens of the "Call," Mark Twain in San Francisco* (Berkeley, Univ. of Calif. Press). Branch has attributed 471 items from the *Call* between June and October 1864 to Clemens, 198 of which he reprints here with expert annotation and a full textual apparatus. Felicitously, Branch has chosen to group his selections topically rather than chronologically. Part I deals with local reporting, Part II with "Crime and Court Reporting," and Part III with judicial and political matters. As Branch is the first to admit, Clemens rather than Mark Twain is the proper name for the author of the *Call* material. It is bread-and-butter work in which the comic shines through occasionally in a ridiculous pun or word play—but, alas, not frequently enough. Still, enhanced by contemporary illustrations and imposing design, *Clemens of the "Call"* fills in a significant blank spot in the Mark Twain canon.

In the second installment of *The Mark Twain Papers*, the University of California Press has issued three volumes of major importance. Lewis Leary's edition of *Mark Twain's Correspondence with Henry Huttleston Rogers, 1893–1909* prints "complete texts of all known correspondence between Clemens and Rogers, as well as relevant letters to and from their wives and secretaries," six publishing agreements between the Clemenses, Harper & Brothers, and the American Publishing Company, all engineered by Rogers, and Twain's 1902 "A Tribute to Henry H. Rogers." The collection is thoroughly annotated and provides a colossal 768-page record of Clemens's business activities in the last sixteen years of his life. The intricate and interminable bankruptcy proceedings, the Plasmon investment and other financial schemes, the complete negotiations involved with transferring Mark Twain's copyrights from the American Publishing Company to Harper & Brothers, and undoubtedly the clearest and most lucid explanation of that Gordian knot, the Paige Typesetter companies and affiliates—all are here in imposing detail. The bulk of the 464 letters were written by Mark Twain; less than a hundred are by Rogers, Olivia Clemens, or Katherine Harrison, Rogers's secretary. Until after his wife's death, Mark Twain's share of the correspondence was concerned almost entirely with business matters and high finance (a decent month out for Susy's death, however). After about 1904 the letters become mellower, more intimate, calmer. Rogers too begins to show charm, affability, and even a surprising sense of humor in the later letters, which counters the formidable, iron-clad-battleship exterior portrayed in most of the photographs of him in the volume. Leary has assembled an imposing body of material for future biographers.

Walter Blair's edition of *Mark Twain's Hannibal, Huck and Tom* collects ten manuscripts, from "Tupperville-Dobbsville" in the late 1870's to "Doughface" in 1902. These represent the surplus building materials of the Matter of Hannibal. In addition to these ten manuscripts, Blair's exhaustive notes and introductions provide virtually a complete collection of notebook and correspondence references to Hannibal, Huck Finn, and Tom Sawyer. The textual apparatus is formidable, including not only the insertions and deletions in manuscripts and descriptions of paper types upon which the dating is based, but even the identification of which of two typewriters—felicitously named *A* and *B*—transcribed which lines of the mawkish *Tom Sawyer: A Play*. The most interesting documents in the collection are *Villagers of 1840–3* (1897), in which Twain provides thumb-nail "characters" for 168 inhabitants of Hannibal, 120 of whom Blair has amazingly been able to identify and most of whom, he points out, are the forebears of the "inhabitants of Spoon River, Winesburg, and Peyton Place," not to mention Yoknapatawpha County; *Huck Finn and Tom Sawyer Among the Indians*, the sequel to *Adventures of Huckleberry Finn*, which falters and fails when a Sioux mass-rape of the heroine appears to be the only way out of the corner into which Twain had written himself; and *Tom Sawyer's Conspiracy*, an almost complete novella in the form of a detective story with the Duke and King as the villains, which is interesting philosophically because of Tom's, Huck's, and Jim's debates over Providence and predestina-tion. This valuable book finally gives us the complete spectrum of the Hannibal setting, characters, and recurrent incidents and motifs. Let us hope that the University of California Press will reissue it in paperback for classroom adoption in the near future.

Already out in paperback as well as hard cover is William M. Gibson's edition of *Mark Twain's "Mysterious Stranger" Manuscripts*, among the most important volumes of Mark Twain's writings pub-lished since the *Autobiography*. By now everyone must know that Albert Bigelow Paine and Frederick A. Duneka sophisticated a text of *The Mysterious Stranger*, omitting a villain priest, adding an astrologer, writing transitional material, and perpetrating what Gib-son calls "an editorial fraud." The original texts are reproduced here for the first time, accompanied by full textual apparatus and a skillful introduction. The earliest fragment, *Chronicle of Young Satan*, is the basis for most of what is known as *The Mysterious Stranger*, set in Austria in 1702. The second is *Schoolhouse Hill*, in which young 44 appears magically in Petersburg, stays with the Hotchkiss family, and performs miracles. The third is *No. 44, The Mysterious Stranger*, formerly called the "Printshop Version." In it, the version on which Twain worked last (1902–04, 1905, 1908), August Feldner befriends No. 44 in a castle which houses a printing shop in Austria in 1490. Forty-four bedevils a magician, settles a strike by creating Dupli-cates of the printers, and enlightens August on the miserable nature of the human race. The famous concluding chapter, written discretely in 1904, is added to this final version in Gibson's text. Each of the three versions is unfinished, each flawed to some extent by Mark Twain's inability to resist putting the miraculous powers of his

"stranger" to burlesque and low-comic uses; but the three texts together constitute an amazingly powerful and vivid testament. Mark
Twain's obsession with the structure and form of the *Stranger* manuscripts during a decade and more, his forceful indictment of the
moral sense, his ability to generalize from specific contemporary incidents about the meanness and cruelty of the human race, all combine to overcome the obvious imperfections and blemishes in the
fragments.

Frederick Anderson in "Team Proofreading: Some Problems"
(*CEAAN* 2:15) recounts some difficulties in the oral proofreading
for the Mark Twain editions in progress—in particular the inability to
distinguish between some singular and plural possessives, as well as
between numbers written as numbers and numbers written out
(*twelve* versus *12*, for example). Robert A. Rees and Richard D.
Rust have examined several manuscript versions—holograph and
typescript—at Berkeley and Wisconsin and have reported their collation of "Mark Twain's 'The Turning Point of My Life'" (*AL*
40:524–35). The omission of "The Parable of the Two Apples" from
the published version, the revision of burlesque jokes, and the
strengthening of serious deterministic elements improved the story
during the process of revision, in line with the humorist's mechanistic
philosophy.

Chandler (San Francisco) has issued a revised edition of Hamlin
Hill and Walter Blair's *The Art of Huckleberry Finn*, adding five
critical selections to the casebook from post-1962 writings.

## ii. Biography

Justin Kaplan's "On Mark Twain: 'Never Quite Sane in the Night'"
(*PsyR* 56,i:113–27) merely reprints chapter 16 of *Mr. Clemens and
Mark Twain*. Charles Vandersee in "The Mutual Awareness of Mark
Twain and Henry Adams" (*ELN* 5[1968]:285–92) reproduces a comment by Joseph B. Gilder showing that—contrary to prior assumptions—Mark Twain and Adams had indeed met. On the evening of
28 January 1886 Gilder and Clemens, looking for John Hay next
door, called upon Adams. "Mark Twain," by Gilder's account (originally published in *The Critic* in 1905), "was as droll as usual, if not
more so; and Mr. Adams, though not in particularly good spirits

[Clover Adams had recently committed suicide], easily lived up to his reputation as a graceful and pregnant talker."

Malcolm Bradbury's "Mark Twain in the Gilded Age" (*CritQ* 11:65–73) is one of those English-style review articles which says more on its own than it does about the books under discussion—in this case ostensibly Justin Kaplan's *Mr. Clemens and Mark Twain* and James M. Cox's *Mark Twain: The Fate of Humor*. Bradbury argues that the tension between vernacular Western and genteel Eastern values defined Mark Twain's art; that he was one of a group of writers "bewildered by the remarkable changes of the last part of the nineteenth century and equally bewildered by the inheritance, moral and social, of the past, which seemed likewise to deny them access to a sense of social meaning." Such summarizing generalizations are of very little value in defining Mark Twain's relationship to his culture—or to the various cultures to which he paid allegiance.

A too long and too dull phrenological report of Mark Twain's head, originally published in Fowler and Wells's *Phrenological Journal and Science of Health* in April 1901, is reprinted in Madeline B. Stern, "Mark Twain Had His Head Examined" (*AL* 41:207–18). Even sillier is Marjory H. Odessky's "The Impartial Friend: The Death of Mark Twain" (*JHS* 2:156–60), a collection of facts and dates culled from Paine and Kaplan, without a redeeming insight or new information.

Arthur L. Scott's *Mark Twain at Large* (Chicago, Regnery) is a comprehensive blend of biographical information about Mark Twain's trips and residences abroad and critical assessment of his travel writings. Scott charts Twain's progress from "Westerner" in *Innocents Abroad* (valuing most highly "such things as progress, utilitarianism, fair play, and material well-being") to "Easterner" in *A Tramp Abroad* ("Twelve years of associating almost exclusively with people of culture in the East and abroad had cost him much of the charming innocence which had animated his first travel book"). Successive chapters deal with the "Nationalist," "Ambassador-at-Large," "Internationalist," and "Oracle," and trace the humorist's anti-imperialism and despair. The volume is encyclopedic in its description of major, minor, and unpublished works and in cataloguing Mark Twain's opinions on international affairs. Much less comprehensive but dealing with the same material and ideas is Helen E.

Ellis's "Mark Twain: The Influence of Europe" (*MTJ* 14,iii:14–18),
which suggests that between *Innocents Abroad* and *A Tramp Abroad*
Mark Twain's increasingly mature attitude allowed him to criticize
Americans and commend Europeans and European culture; finally,
in *A Connecticut Yankee*, he universalized the basic weaknesses of
all humanity.

A single biographically oriented dissertation was completed during the year: Herbert C. Feinstein's "Mark Twain's Lawsuits" (*DA*
29:4484A).

### *iii.* General Criticism

In "Platform Manner in the Novel: A View from the Pit" (*MASJ*
10,ii:49–59) John A. Barsness applies the theories of "How to Tell a
Story" to Mark Twain's written work. Barsness concludes that in
earlier works ("The Jumping Frog," *Innocents Abroad*) the humorist
embodies attributes of the lecture pose (ostensibly didactic in intent) and the lecture method (deadpan first-person narrator). By
the time of *Huckleberry Finn*, Twain "is now aware that he must
divorce himself from the lecturer role"; but Huck fails to recognize
human absurdity, as do other later characters who embody an
evolved version of the humorless, myopic, deadpan technique.

In a comprehensively researched and engagingly written article
(engagingly written articles are rare; in *PMLA* they are positively
unnerving) Joseph H. Gardner has traced the relationship of "Mark
Twain and Dickens" (*PMLA* 84:90–101). Gardner amasses great
detail to show which works of Dickens Twain definitely read or
probably read. He suggests that Twain's reading of and enthusiasm
for Dickens waned in the 1890's after a high point in the seventies
and eighties. The enthusiasm was concealed by deprecatory public
statements about Dickens, however, and Gardner speculates that
Mark Twain was uncomfortable in the role of literary critic, was
posing as a self-made anti-intellectual, and was suspiciously jealous
of other literary idols.

Allison Ensor's book *Mark Twain and the Bible* (Lexington, Univ.
Press of Ky.) discusses the humorist's use of the Bible from his early
Western journalism to *Letters from the Earth*, though in 103 pages
it has been necessary for Ensor to be highly selective. He examines
allusions, puns, burlesque incongruities in early writings; he isolates

three themes which fascinated Twain—the Prodigal Son, Adam and Eve and the Fall, and Noah and the Flood—and traces their recurrent use throughout Twain's writings. Finally, Ensor looks at "The Attack on the Bible" in Twain's writings, predominantly the later works. *Mark Twain and the Bible* is a helpful book in spite of its selectivity and brevity; hopefully, Mr. Ensor will expand it into a fuller study when the later unpublished works are all available for commentary.

Three dissertations of a general nature were completed during 1969: Don W. Harrell, Jr., "Patterns of Escape in Mark Twain's Fiction" (*DA* 29:3140A); Charles M. Kerlin, Jr., "Life in Motion: Genteel and Vernacular Attitudes in the Works of the Southwestern American Humorists, Mark Twain, and William Faulkner" (*DA* 29:4492A); and Harold H. Kolb, Jr., "The Illusion of Life: American Realism as a Literary Form in the Writings of Mark Twain, Henry James, and W. D. Howells in the Mid-1880's" (*DA* 29:3102A).

### iv. Earlier Works

Only two items dealt with works before *Huckleberry Finn* in 1969, both discussing *The Adventures of Tom Sawyer*. L. Moffitt Cecil in "Tom Sawyer: Missouri Robin Hood" (*WAL* 4:125–31) proposes that Tom's game of "Robin Hood" has a serious undercurrent, because Tom, like Robin Hood, is oppressed by Church and State, is the leader of a small band of discontents, and is a champion of outcasts and underdogs. Louis D. Rubin, Jr., has undertaken a major evaluation of the novel in "Mark Twain: *The Adventures of Tom Sawyer*" in *Landmarks* (pp. 157–71). Rubin, who nominates *Tom Sawyer* as Twain's second-best novel, examines the distancing achieved by omniscient point of view and authorial intrusions, resulting in humor and irony. Rubin also discusses the question of Tom's ultimate identification with and allegiance to the society represented by St. Petersburg; Rubin argues that Tom's triumph is his ability to gain society's approval, but by asocial exploits and methods—"instead of conforming to the adult values, he has made the adult community conform to his."

### v. Huckleberry Finn

Among the comments on *Huck* are three source studies. Pap's speech castigating Huck for learning to read (chapter 5) is based on Gaffer

Hexam's similar tirade against Charley in Book I, chapter 6, of Dickens's *Our Mutual Friend*, according to Joseph H. Gardner ("Gaffer Hexam and Pap Finn," *MP* 66[1968]:155–56). In Loren K. Davidson's "The Darnell-Watson Feud" (*DuR* 13[1968]:76–95) there is a thorough historical account of that feud, upon which the Grangerford-Shepherdson one was based. A shooting at Compromise on 4 September 1859 was the incident Mark Twain almost witnessed; but H. M. Darnall continued his feuding over an impressive span of time, taking lives as indiscriminately as Huck took watermelons. E. Bruce Kirkham, "Huck and Hamlet. . ." (*MTJ* 14,iv:17–19) identifies all the fractured quotations in the soliloquy—all are from *Hamlet*, *Macbeth*, or *Richard III*—and then provides a "reading" of the garbled Mark Twain version which debates action versus inaction and is appropriate to Huck's own indecision.

Two articles consider the language of the novel. In a study drawn from his dissertation (see *ALS 1968*, pp. 80–81) Curt M. Rulon has looked at the various dialects represented in *Huck*. In "Geographical Delimitation of the Dialect Areas in *The Adventures of Huckleberry Finn*" (*MTJ* 14,i:9–12) he concludes that there are "basically only two dialects represented, namely, a mixture of Caucasian (South) Midland and Southern speech on the one hand, and a mixture of Negro (South) Midland and Southern speech on the other hand." Rulon attempts to establish the location of the Phelps Farm in northern Arkansas, but unfortunately a set of figures referred to in the text is not printed. Rulon concludes that "there is no evidence. . . that Twain was serious when he spoke of four modified varieties of Pike-County speech" in *Huck*. When Huck sweated over a poem in imitation of Emmeline Grangerford but gave it up as too difficult, he was being too modest, according to Robert Coard, "Huck Finn and Mr. Mark Twain Rhyme" (*MQ* 10:317–29). Coard catalogs double and triple rhymes, alliteration, assonance, near rhymes, and other poetic techniques in *Huck* and other works of Mark Twain and decides that Huck's speech patterns are more poetic than Mark Twain's. He suggests that the humorist pulled out all the stops when he wrote "in the breezy speech of a sharp but functionally illiterate boy."

Five short articles discuss and explicate minor passages or incidents in *Huck*. W. Keith Krause ("'Huckleberry Finn': A Final Irony," *MTJ* 14,i:18–19) argues that the second pair of Wilks brothers are also fakes, because of their speech and their description of the tattoo, which is not apparent on the corpse. Allison Ensor replies in "The 'Opposition Line' to The King and The Duke in *Huckleberry Finn*" (*MTJ* 14,iii:6–7) that it is not likely the second set of brothers are imposters, but rather that Huck's reporting of events is faulty. Ensor has also contemplated "The Location of the Phelps Farm in *Huckleberry Finn*" (*SAB* 34,iii:7). Unlike Rulon (above) Ensor believes the farm is in southeastern (rather than northern) Arkansas, from the evidence of the working notes for the novel, statements in the *Autobiography* and *Tom Sawyer, Detective,* and inferences from the novel itself.

Wallace Graves has provided the solution for the mystery of the Burning Shame. The king's nude performance, originally called the Burning Shame but changed to the Royal Nonesuch at Mrs. Clemens's insistence, was a skit Mark Twain saw or heard in his Western mining days. According to Graves, who heard a telling of the story of the "outrageous" act in Seattle in the 1930's, the king's "costume" included a lighted candle in his rectum—a burning shame which Huck refused to describe. By bringing it to print in "Mark Twain's 'Burning Shame'" (*NCF* 23[1968]:93–98) Graves has plugged a hole, so to speak, in Mark Twain scholarship. It is also a curious footnote to the usual image of Mrs. Clemens that she must have known the complete version of the story to have reacted so violently to the mere name.

In a reading of the Solomon dialogue in chapter 14, Manuel Schonhorn argues that Jim is more than a minstrel-show straight man. "Mark Twain's Jim: Solomon on the Mississippi" (*MTJ* 14,iii:9–11) argues that Jim shows charity and an inability to cope with abstract logic. The scene somehow foreshadows a brief paragraph in chapter 18 in which Jim acts "Solomon-like" in regaining the lost raft.

Two comparative studies of *Huck* and other works appeared in 1969. Daniel J. Casey in "Universality in *Huckleberry Finn*: A Comparison of Twain and Kivi" (*MTJ* 14,i:13–18) makes a strained comparison with Aleksis Kivi's *Seven Brothers,* a Finnish novel. Much more interesting—indeed, one of the most thoughtful articles of the year—is Martha Banta's "Rebirth or Revenge: The Endings of *Huckleberry Finn* and *The American*" (*MFS* 15:191–207). Miss Banta works astutely with a broad range of cultural dichotomies which Twain and James embodied in their characters: revenge and passivity, morality and pleasure seeking, "flexible adaptability or rigid resistance." She concludes that Mark Twain did not "cheat" with the ending of *Huckleberry Finn*, because Huck has consistently sought "the free, the easy, and the comfortable life."

Somewhat similar is Michael Hoffman's interpretation of the novel. In "Huck's Ironic Circle" (*GaR* 23:307–22), Hoffman suggests that Huck is controlled by his social morality throughout the book. We *hope* that he has transcended the values of his culture on the raft trip, but Mark Twain actually says that there is no escape. According to Hoffman, Huck "has never condemned society, never condemned slavery, has always admired Tom Sawyer disproportionally, has always patronized Negroes (even Jim on the raft), and has not really been changed by his experience on the river." Thus the evasion brings the novel full circle: "escape is only temporary, . . . sooner or later one must return and make his peace with the established social order." Finally, in a very brief and summarizing article, Herbert L. Carson traces "Mark Twain's Misanthropy" (*Cresset* 33,ii:13–15), predominantly in *Huckleberry Finn*, especially as Tom's restrictions on Huck's freedom in the evasion chapters constitute a philosophical pessimism.

### *vi.* Later Works

In a provocative essay, "Mark Twain on War and Peace: The Missouri Rebel and 'The Campaign That Failed'" (*AQ* 20[1968]:783–94), J. Stanley Mattson has joined the growing group of commentators on "The Private History of a Campaign That Failed." Mattson points out that the original series, Battles and Leaders of the Civil War, which ran in *The Century*, included romantic and chauvinistic reminiscences of generals. Mark Twain, on the contrary, desired to counter the traditional approach and launch an assault on "the entire concept of the glory of war." By emphasizing the ineptness of the "organization" which he joined, the capriciousness of its members, and the ludicrousness of its uniforms, Mark Twain successfully deflated, Mattson argues, that concept—and was the sole contribution to the series omitted from the book publication of Battles and Leaders.

*A Connecticut Yankee in King Arthur's Court* received two commentaries in 1969. Philip Butcher, in "'The Godfathership' of *A Connecticut Yankee*" (*CLAJ* 12:189–98), amasses a great deal of evidence from letters, notebook entries, and comments by both Mark

Twain and Cable—more evidence than necessary—to suggest that Mark Twain's interest in medieval settings and mysterious strangers antedated George Washington Cable's introduction of the humorist to Malory's *Morte d'Arthur.* Thus, Butcher says, Cable is not the godfather of *A Yankee.* Reid Maynard, in "Mark Twain's Ambivalent Yankee" (*MTJ* 14,iii:1–5), summarizes three "schools" of *Yankee* critics: those who consider the book a denunciation of medieval and Romantic England; those who see the book as ambivalent, praising technology but also regretting the loss of Romantic values and innocence; and those who claim the book's major condemnation is of "Yankeedom" and major affirmation is of "lost ideals that were prevalent in an age of innocence." Maynard argues for the "ambivalent" school, which leaves us just about back where we started.

Michael Orth nominates Mayne Reid's *The Quadroon; or, a Lover's Adventures in Louisiana* as a probable source for *Pudd'nhead Wilson.* In "*Pudd'nhead Wilson* Reconsidered or The Octoroon in the Villa Viviani" (*MTJ* 14,iv:11–15) he points out the popularity of the octoroon theme in popular nineteenth-century literature and suggests specifically that Reid's work parallels the plot of *Pudd'nhead* in several ways, notably with an ingenious Yankee whose experiments with a camera uncover a murderer. Barbara A. Chellis traces a number of ironies implicit in *Pudd'nhead* which arise from heredity versus environment as controlling and motivating factors in the novel. "Those Extraordinary Twins: Negroes and Whites" (*AQ* 21:100–12) is especially interesting on the point that Roxy, as Tom's nurse, is responsible for his upbringing and for those personality traits which make him despicable even in Roxy's own eyes.

Henry B. Rule carries his reading of "The Man That Corrupted Hadleyburg" to an unfortunate extreme: "The Role of Satan in 'The Man That Corrupted Hadleyburg'" (*SSF* 6:619–29) suggests that the stranger is Satan, Goodson (Good Son) is Christ, Hadleyburg is Eden, and Mrs. Richards is Eve (in a postmenopausal condition, I presume). While the motif works sensibly in the story, Rule places too heavy stress on the meanings of names to support the reading: Goodson's sweetheart's name, Nancy Hewitt, "reveals the spiritual or heavenly quality of Goodson's love" only if Mark Twain knew *Nancy* came from Hebrew *Hannah, grace,* and Hewitt from Teutonic, *for spirit.* D. S. Bertolotti points out in "Structural Unity in 'The Man That Corrupted Hadleyburg'" (*MTJ* 14,i:19–20) that each section of the story begins with a letter which Stephenson writes: "a letter is introduced and an episode containing action based on the content of the letter follows."

In a major examination of *The Mysterious Stranger*, Wendell Glick ignores and dismisses the solipsistic concluding chapter. "The Epistemological Theme of *The Mysterious Stranger*" (*Themes and Directions*, pp. 130–47) examines how the first ten chapters achieve their form through a dialectic between characters who argue a "Christian absolutism" in their morality versus Satan's "prudential utilitarian morality." Thus the basis for the form resides in Lecky's *History of European Morals*. And, additionally, the dialectic is ironic because the inhabitants of Eseldorf actually practice a pragmatic morality while they pay lip service to the absolutist moral sense. Glick points out that a number of flaws remain in the fragment; the tone is too strident and the censure of man too severe, since man cannot foresee the consequences of his moral options, as Satan can. Margaret N. Sipple's dissertation deals with "Mark Twain and the Mysterious Stranger" (*DA* 29:3110A).

It was a year of increasing attention to later works, then, from *Huckleberry Finn* on, while some earlier pieces ("The Facts Concerning the Recent Carnival of Crime in Connecticut" and "The Great Revolution in Pitcairn," for example) still need thorough explication. John Gerber's suggestion in this space last year, that "what we need are essays that are more comprehensive in scope, that dig deeper into Mark Twain's intellectual habits and are more concerned with his assumptions, conscious or unconscious," remains substantially unheeded.

*University of Chicago*

# 6. Henry James

## William T. Stafford

The big news in Jamesian scholarship during 1969 was the publication of the fourth and still not final segment of Leon Edel's now long-appearing life. The method of this volume is his most psychological to date; its facts are probably his most sensational ones. Also important, however, in a totally different kind of way, is H. Montgomery Hyde's *Henry James at Home*. Other scholarship of the year was more or less Jamesiana as usual: a book-length study of his fictional children, nine dissertations (not otherwise noted here), a plethora of comparative and source studies, and about the normal number of explications of individual novels and tales. Probably worthy of special notice are William Hoffa's fine study of the *Autobiography*, Nina Baym's view of *The Spoils of Poynton*, and Strother B. Purdy's analysis of James's uses of the word *sacred*. The last two in particular may well be indicative of new directions to come: Mrs. Baym's demonstration of the disparity between what James was doing and what he thought he was doing, and Mr. Purdy's representation of a growing number of linguistic approaches to the novelist.

### i. Biography and Bibliography

The publication within a few months of both H. Montgomery Hyde's *Henry James at Home* (New York, Farrar, Straus & Giroux) and Leon Edel's *Henry James: The Treacherous Years, 1895–1901* (Philadelphia, Lippincott) would appear to demand at least some kind of comparative judgment about their respective worths. In fact, however, their views on the art of biography are so different, their respective intentions and coverages so disparate, their relations to their subject so unlike, the contexts in which they have worked so radically unmatched as to make any comparison between the two gratuitous and probably fruitless, their acrimonious exchange of letters about the rights to source material on James in the pages of the *Times Literary Supplement* during 1968 notwithstanding (see *ALS 1968*, pp. 87–88).

*Henry James at Home* is an old-fashioned biography, a good old-fashioned biography, let me hasten to add. It is marked by copious quotations from diaries, letters, and memoirs; an almost total indifference to what James was writing during the years covered (roughly 1876, when the novelist moved to London, until his death); no centrally articulated thesis about its subject; a graceful style; thorough documentation; and even, in its old-fashioned way, a familial relationship between the biographer and the novelist (Mr. Hyde is a distant cousin of Henry James). Its organizing principle, as its title indicates, is place, James's various "homes" in England during his long stay there. Four of its seven chapters use place names indicating the novelist's respective residences (Mayfair, Kensington, Rye, and Chelsea), with the Rye chapter followed by longish accounts, in two additional chapters, of James's servants and secretaries, his visits and visitors. The last chapter is devoted to the war and his death.

The book makes only a few original revelations. The nine pages or so he devotes to James's prurient interest in sex, maintaining that "there was . . . a Rabelaisian side to Henry's character, which none of his previous biographers nor the discreet editor of his Letters has hinted at," is documented well enough through James's correspondence, especially as it relates to Gosse and J. A. Symonds, to James's exploration with John Buchan of some then-unpublished Byron papers, to an off-color anecdote about a visit Maupassant made with James, and, of course, to the Wilde case. But nothing new is added in Hyde's account of the dramatic years and the *Guy Domville* fiasco, and he passes over James's relation with Constance Fenimore Woolson in less than a page.

James's whole *factual* relation to Rye is thoroughly explored (Hyde himself lived in Lamb House for a while), and his chapter on the Lamb Household, James's various cooks, butlers, houseboys, maids, and gardeners is fascinating, especially when buttressed by the diaries of two of the novelist's three amanuenses, those of Mary Weld and Theodora Bosanquet (the Scot, Macalpine, apparently left very little). The total result here is probably the most intimate on record of James's domestic habits, what he customarily ate and drank, how he worked, how he "ran" his Lamb House "family." Also good, for me, is Hyde's elaborate account of the events surrounding the Sargent portrait given to James by his friends in commemoration of his seventieth birthday.

I found less revealing James's well-known relations with fellow writers, his concern about and involvement with the war effort, the break with Wells, the adoption of British citizenship, the presentation of the Order of Merit, and his death and funeral, although the last has a certain vividness of detail I do not remember seeing elsewhere. An appendix reprints Hyde's little pamphlet, "The Lamb House Library." In total, however, *Henry James at Home* is a very readable book. And one somehow leaves it with a strange sense of the man— not of the writer, or of the critic, or of the Master—that is occasionally memorable and vivid.

*The Treacherous Years*, in contrast, is a very modern biography, in almost every sense of the word. It has a complex but clearly articulated thesis about the man *and* his fiction; it is audaciously psychological; it is the most dramatic to date, as the fourth of Edel's now projected five-volume life of the Master. Edel's decision to have culled this fourth volume from his originally projected final one strikes this reader as a happy one, for the period between the dramatic failure with *Guy Domville* in 1895 and the magisterial accomplishment of his great international "trilogy" soon after the turn of the century is probably the most crucial, the most troubled, and in some ways perhaps the most brilliantly productive in James's entire literary development.

Edel's thesis begins with the contention that James may be said to have suffered a kind of "nervous breakdown" following the popular and critical failures of his attempts at drama. "It was," Edel continues,

in part a failure of confidence, although his belief in his art never seems to have faltered. Yet while living through his depression and mourning for the "death of childhood," James kept before him an ideal of the invincibility of his craft. He was to "function" so long as he kept to his belief. And in returning to earlier, to earliest experience, he re-discovered the means by which he had long before armed himself for life. He healed his wounds, and recovered his strength, finding new sources of

power within himself. The steps by which this occurred, and
the heroic effort required, constitute not only a fascinating
chapter of literary history, but a striking "case" of literary
psychology [pp. 15–16].

That "chapter," that "case" are precisely the burden of this volume.

The literary chapter and the psychological case join, according to
Edel, in a revealing sequence. The novels of the late nineties are thus
read as "a series of parables, an extensive personal allegory of the
growing up of Henry James," who "was intuitively questioning his
unconscious experience, reliving the long-ago 'education' of his emotions." It begins with the murder of Effie (from *The Other House*,
1896), which Edel associates with "the brutality of the audience of
*Guy Domville*"; it ends with the emergence of Little Aggie and
Nanda (both from *The Awkward Age*, 1899), "a projection of two
sides of the Henry of late adolescence," one side reading forbidden
French novels, the other an emerging "young literary novice." In
between, says Edel, the parable is developed through Maisie, Flora,
and the unnamed girl of "In the Cage." The "disguise of a female
child" had been "the protective disguise of . . . [James's] early years."
With it, "James performed imaginative self-therapy." These tales of
the treacherous years, therefore, reveal "the unconscious revisiting of
perceptions and feelings, to minister to adult hurts. . . . they now
served as aid against the new brutalities" (p. 264).

This thesis is nowhere so simply put in the study itself. And Edel
is nowhere blind to the literary worth of these tales outside the
biographical possibilities, to the influence of the dramatic years on
their form and structure, to their experimental innovations with
"modes of indirect narration and the refining of the novelist's om-
niscience," or to their pointing the way to the later achievement of
writers such as Joyce or Virginia Woolf. Nor does he fail to remind
us that James's explorations were being paralleled at almost exactly
the same time with unconscious but analogous explorations by Freud
and Proust.

Other aspects of the biography are more traditional. James's com-
ings and goings, his dinings in and out, his travels, his editorial labors
and negotiations, his various domestic arrangements, his move to
Rye, his first amanuensis and the "fierce legibility" of his first type-

writer, his earliest dictations—all are chronicled and arranged and given with that clarity and order and strong "story line" that earlier volumes of the life have led us to expect.

Also given are James's multitudinous relations with others, with family and cousins, with fellow writers, with painters and sculptors, with actors and actresses, with critics, editors, and publishers, with old friends and new. And among the new, Edel here reveals for the first time, is a young American sculptor, Hendrik Andersen, whom James first met in Rome in 1899 and whose apparent relationship with the novelist will surely strike some as little less than sensational.

The facts Edel gives about this relationship are meager: a meeting in Rome in the apartment of Maud Elliott; the purchase by James of a bust by young Andersen; the placing of the bust in James's dining room in Lamb House "where it would stand . . . for years"; a three-day visit to Lamb House at James's invitation in 1899; a return, "only after much pleading on James's part," two years later; another return, some months following; a meeting in America in 1905; another in Rome in 1907. The sources Edel cites are excerpts from a series of previously unpublished letters from James to Andersen, beginning in July of 1899 and running through August of 1911.

These letters from James to Andersen are, for Edel, "the saddest and strangest perhaps in his entire *epistolarium.*" He cites two significant elements. "The first is the quantity of physical, tactile language"—language, any reader, I think, would have to describe as homoerotic. The second is "James's unusual and reiterated cry for the absent one." Both contentions are amply supported. Edel's conclusions are perhaps more problematical: first, his stated inability to know "whether the use of the term 'lover' and the verbal passion of the letters was 'acted out'; second, his contention that James's experience with Andersen "inspired feelings . . . akin to love"—a love Edel equates with Fenimore Woolson's love for James as Edel rendered it in the preceding volume. Hendrik Andersen, incidentally, is not mentioned in Hyde's book.

More about Andersen's relationship with James will surely be forthcoming in Edel's final volume, but not only that. For the Henry James we see on the last page of *The Treacherous Years* is a new Henry James, clean shaven for the first time in years, "a new face for the new century" (he writes Grace Norton), and busily at work, "in the brightening summer that heralded the twentieth century," daily giving shape to *The Ambassadors*.[1]

Two additional biographical items by Hyde and Edel are perhaps worthy of brief comment. Edel's "Henry James and Sir Sydney Waterlow: The Unpublished Diary of a British Diplomat" (*TLS*, 8 Aug 1968: 844–45) publishes excerpts from what he describes as the best of the Rye diarists, a diary Mr. Hyde uses extensively in *Henry James at Home*, where he describes initially having discovered it. The entry in it that every Jamesian should know, however, appears in the *TLS* account: a report of the Master once having killed a cat on his lawn at Rye and then having vomited and collapsed at having done so! Mr. Hyde's *TLS* entry (15 May: 525) denigrates a published account (in a recent book on Wilde) about some compromising James letters reported to be circulating in London, asserting that the "idea of the circumspect Master having had a homosexual affair . . ." is ridiculous.

Two other biographical notes are Robert K. Martin's "Henry James and the Harvard College Library" (*AL* 41:95–103) and William White's "Unpublished Henry James on Whitman" (*RES* 20:321–22). Martin's is a model presentation of books James may well have checked out (for himself or for other members of his family) from the Harvard College Library between 10 September 1862 and 12 May 1871. White's is an unimportant letter from James to a Dr. John Johnston (dated 9 November 1898), thanking him for a copy of Johnston's *Diary Notes of a Visit to Walt Whitman and Some of His Friends in 1890*.

Finally, mention should probably be made here of Jan W. Dietrichson's "The Image of Money in the Works of Henry James" (in his *The Image of Money in the American Novel of the Gilded Age* [Oslo, Universitetsforlaget; New York, Humanities Press], pp. 24–164) for its comprehensive coverage of the financial circumstances of the James family and of James himself, as well as the development of the novelist's attitude toward it. Although not new information, it is gathered here by Dietrichson in a very useful way.

The one bibliographical item of the year is George Monteiro's "Addendum to Edel and Laurence: Henry James's 'Future of the Novel'" (*PBSA* 63:130), which points out that James's essay was

1. This account of *The Treacherous Years* is a somewhat briefer version of that written by this writer for *VQR*, 45:526–30.

first printed in the *Saturday Review of Books and Arts,* a weekly supplement to the *New York Times,* on 11 August 1900, p. 541.

## ii. Drama and Criticism

Rudolf Kossmann's *Henry James, Dramatist* (Groningen, Wolters-Noordhoff N.V.) has very slight reasons for existence. Its plodding accounts of the plots of each of the plays, its reports on the reception of each by the critics, its dogged incorporation of the scholarship on the subject—all lead to conclusions already long established by others. A final chapter on James's dramatic criticism perhaps does a little more than most with James's complex attitude toward Ibsen, but the novelist's equally complex attitude toward Shakespeare is hardly touched at all. The book should never have been printed.

Two additional notices about James's drama appeared during the year in *TLS.* "Commentary" (11 Sept:1000) is an anonymous editorial on the contretemps that developed between Robert Manson Myers, the author, and Basil Ashmore, the director, over a dramatic adaptation of James's *The Spoils of Poynton.* Charges and countercharges followed by others (see *TLS* 18 Sept:1027; 9 Oct:1158; and 16 Oct:1211). Edward D. McDougal's "Henry James" (*TLS* 13 Nov:1313) notes that Julian Field's one-act farce, *Too happy by half,* which preceded the premiere of James's *Guy Domville* as a curtain raiser, was, unlike James's play, roundly applauded, the author coming forward, and received favorable mention in the press by such critics as Shaw, Wells, and the writer from the *Athenaeum.*

An exceptionally good article in this nonfictional category is William Hoffa's "The Final Preface: Henry James's *Autobiography*" (*SR* 77:277–93), a beautifully perceptive, close analysis of the motivation, the composition, and, finally, the achievement of James's three autobiographical volumes. For Hoffa, the autobiography served for James as an "act of life," for "the process of writing . . . [it] is itself an experience of the same nature as the process of growing into manhood." Its themes and methods are seen as precisely those of the major phase, "poetic dramas" concerned with "modes of perception, reflection, and resolution." Thus, the process of rendering his "life" is seen as much more important than the subject per se, and the volumes consequently as a kind of "final Preface," doing "for his life what his 'Prefaces' had tried to do for his fiction: to uncover certain 'formative' principles." Finally, in sharing many of the themes and techniques with his late novels, the autobiography becomes, in a sense, the " 'American novel' he had hoped to write after his trip to the United States in 1904–05."

Also good is Walter R. McDonald's "The Inconsistencies in Henry James's Aesthetics" (*TSLL* 10:585–97), which sees in the novelist's total criticism contradictory attitudes toward the relation of art to life, of the novel to the romance, of story to novel, and of mimetic representation to organic, ideal growth. His appeals to various critical schools have thus depended upon what part of his criticism spokesmen for each school happened to have read. His problem, concludes McDonald, is perhaps his "metaphorical method," his "tendency to overstate, to formulate abstractions." Perhaps it should have ended instead with a statement to the effect that James was too devoted a writer of fiction, ultimately too indifferent a critic, to allow theory to interfere with the living, complex, sometimes contradictory practice of his art, a practice which instinctively demanded shifts from time to time, as first he emphasized one thing, then another.

Finally, mention should be made here of Donald Emerson's "The Relation of Henry James's Art Criticism to His Literary Standards" (*TWA* 57:9–19) for its comprehensive, well-documented view of the limitations of James's art criticism as it related to his developing literary criticism.

### iii. Sources, Influences, Parallels

Alfred Habegger's " 'The Siege of London':Henry James and the *Pièce Bien Faite*" (*MFS* 15:219–30) is probably the most important of the three articles of the year concerned with James's French sources. Habegger closely examines how James's admitted sources for the story, Emile Augier's *L'aventurière* and *Le demi-monde* by Alexandre Dumas *fils*, are transformed. He may go a little far in positing the tale as a prime example of the "modern temper, with its ambivalences, uncertainties, and suspended beliefs," but few would dispute, I believe, that the story does indeed reveal those "features that we associate most closely with his art—reduced external action, a central problem of judgment, and a point of view that admits us to the minds of the characters"—features notably absent in his sources. P. R. Grover's "Mérimée's Influence on Henry James" (*MLR* 63 [1968]:810–17) cites "the construction of a well-conducted action, the conveying of emotion through significant detail, [and] the presence of strong passions" as "the principal elements in the early lessons" James drew from the French novelist. He also sees ties between "The Last of the Valerii" and *La Vénus d'Ille* and between "Madame de Mauves" and *La double méprise*. And in "Henry James and George Sand" (*RLC* 43:47–55), David A. Leeming surveys James's various reviews of Sand's work to conclude "that James used Sand . . . as a means of clarifying his own aesthetic and as a means of demonstrating that morality in art must be derived from within the world of art—that art has its own standards just as the 'world' has its."

Seven critics contrast or compare James with American writers. In "The Central Problem of James's Fictional Thought: From *The Scarlet Letter* to *Roderick Hudson*" (*ELH* 36:416–39), Quentin G. Kraft sees life vs. form as a central problem of both novels; and the unresolvable dilemma of freedom vs. morality (in *The Scarlet Letter*) he sees precisely as the problem James was centrally concerned with in his first novel. That James refused "to contrive a solution, his willingness to leave a dialectical stalemate in the novel" is the exact mark "of integrity and maturity on this early work." This stance is then related backward to Hawthorne's novel and forward to the later James. In "Life in a Picture Gallery: Things in *The Portrait of a Lady* and *The Marble Faun*" (*TSLL* 11:761–77) Jay Bochner compares and contrasts the ways old country houses, cathedrals, museums, and pictures are rendered by these two American writers, concluding, predictably, that for James (unlike Hawthorne) "symbolic meaning . . . is particular and human, a matter of personal, not of social or religious, morality."

In "Cognitive Apparatus in *Daisy Miller, The Ambassadors*, and Two Works by Howells [*A Chance Acquaintance* and *The Son of Royal Langbrith*]: A Comparative Study of the Epistemology of Henry James" (*Lang&S* 2:207–25) Michael Shriber presents a highly special study of the literary representation of "cognition" as it reveals itself in early and later works of the two novelists. In so far as I can understand it, he maintains that the later Howells was "even less interested in . . . representing cognitive mental process" than he had been earlier, whereas the later James produced in Strether, in contrast to Winterbourne, "a kind of cognitive hero."

These two American writers are joined in their relation to James in Robert E. Long's "*The Ambassadors* and the Genteel Tradition:

James's Correction of Hawthorne and Howells" (*NEQ* 42:44–64),
a fine essay tying Strether to Colville (of *Indian Summer*) and to
Coverdale (of *The Blithedale Romance*). For Long, James's corrections of the "type" are numerous, but he is especially expert, in
contradistinction to his two predecessors, by rendering Strether "as
a *social* manifestation of the Puritan inheritance" and by squarely
facing the ties of the artistic life to sexuality. Twain and James are
joined in Martha Banta's "Rebirth or Revenge: The Endings of
*Huckleberry Finn* and *The American*" (*MFS* 15:191–207) wherein
Huck and Newman are seen as operating under similar "codes of
pleasure while proving the . . . truth that the American must recognize the limitations of *human* nature even as he refuses to be diminished by self-destroying forces of *social* codes of revenge."

Two studies are comparisons with modern American writers.
Miroslav Beker's "T. S. Eliot's Theory of Impersonality and Henry
James: A Note" (*SRAZ* 27–28:163–67) points to how James's
"thoughts [in the Prefaces] on the depersonalization of the artist"
parallel those of the poet. And Daniel Russell Brown's "The Cosmopolitan Novel: James and Lewis" (*SLN* 1,i:6–9) sees ties between
*The Ambassadors* and *Dodsworth*, "for both treat of the question of
how best to live, the elemental philosophical question, and both
embody this . . . theme within the dramatic conflicts of the Old and
New Worlds."

In "James's 'Maud-Evelyn': Source, Allusion, and Meaning" (*IEY*
13[1968]:24–33) Mario L. D'Avanzo examines Browning's "Evelyn
Hope" as a major source of James's story, seeing him turn "the
forward-looking idealism of . . . [it] completely around and face it
into the past." He also sees in the tale allusions to the Romantic poets
and to Hawthorne, maintaining that they play "a central role in expressing his themes, coloring his ironies, shading his tone, and suggesting his esthetic principle of story telling."

Abigail A. Hamblen, in "The Inheritance of the Meek: Two
Novels by Agatha Christie and Henry James" (*Discourse* 12:409–
13), fortuitously links *Endless Night* with *The Wings of the Dove*.

### iv. Criticism: General

A splendid virtue of Muriel G. Shine's *The Fictional Children of
Henry James* (Chapel Hill, Univ. of N.C. Press) is her responsible

recognition of the need for placing James in some kind of historical context. She meets that responsibility beautifully in the opening chapter of this study of James's many fictional children in one of the most concise accounts I know of the various roles of children in the imaginative literature of English and American literature. That she makes a little less than I would have made of the pervasive attention to the young in American literature in particular (both before *and* after James) is not necessarily to fault the really admirable and broader kind of context she does provide. Moreover, she is especially good with the Jamesian context, his views, memoirs, letters, and travel literature.

Her central attention, of course, is to those remarkable Jamesian children of the 1890's—Morgan Moreen, Effie, Maisie, Miles and Flora, and Nanda Brookenham. However, James's earlier children and adolescents are also carefully analyzed, Nora of the early *Watch and Ward*, Randolph Miller, Pansy Osmond, Dolcino Ambient, and Hyacinth Robinson, to name only some of the most prominent. There is some categorization, chapters on the spoiled child, on children as victims, and on educational theory and the *jeune fille*, for example; but in general Miss Shine stays close to the text and renders clearly the highly individualized nature of each fictional child. Some readers will surely quarrel with her particular literary readings of Morgan, of Maisie, and of Nanda, but few, I think, would argue with her conclusions about how "the intuition" of James "led him to discover truths that psychologists were later to corroborate in their investigations of behavior in the young." And perhaps even fewer would dispute the central role children play in James's fiction and his pervasive thematic concerns (in both his fiction and nonfictional writings) with American vs. European educational theories about how properly to educate them. I find myself in agreement with the more general claim that we "owe a debt of gratitude to Henry James for his active role . . . to establish the child in literature as a worthy object of complete and honest investigation."[2] *The Fictional Children of Henry James* is a model dissertation and a useful book.

Of three ambitious books with chapters on James, the most elaborate is Peter K. Garrett's "The Creations of Consciousness" (in his *Scene and Symbol from George Eliot to James Joyce: Studies in*

2. A more extensive account of this book by this writer appeared in *NCF* 25(1970):241–42.

*Changing Fictional Mode*, New Haven, Yale Univ. Press, pp. 76–
159). Garrett gives over the whole center of his study to James, whose
work is seen as occupying "a central position in the transition from
traditional to modern fictional modes." His analyses of several works,
especially the elaborate ones of *The Portrait of a Lady* and the novels
of the late trilogy, serve to demonstrate how, for James, "the creations
of consciousness constitute the essence" of his meaning, how "the
actual and symbolic" are therefore one. Thus the "creative vision of
his central characters" permits them to "become not only the agents
but the counterparts of the artist." This is hardly a new view of
James, but I have never before seen it so nicely placed historically as
here, between the works of George Eliot and Conrad.

Joel Porte's chapter on James (in his *The Romance in America*,
Middletown, Conn., Wesleyan Univ. Press, pp. 193–226) examines
early, middle, and late examples of what he considers to be James's
most characteristic contributions to the form, *The American*, *The
Turn of the Screw*, and *The Golden Bowl*. James's "place" in this
American "genre" is established clearly enough (as Chase, Lewis,
and others have previously demonstrated), but the discussions of the
works themselves leave us with little we had not known before.
Porte's most elaborate attention is given to *The American*, but his
most provocative goes to *The Golden Bowl* and its ties to Poe (even
if they in fact constitute no more than "a flicker of recognition") and
to the multiplicity of meanings Porte sees symbolically radiating from
the bowl itself.

John T. Frederick, in his chapter on James in *The Darkened Sky:
Nineteenth-Century American Novelists and Religion* (Notre Dame,
Ind., Univ. of Notre Dame Press, pp. 229–53), sees the novelist as
"the most religious" of the six nineteenth-century American novelists
he examines, "if," he says, "we make our definition of religion broad
enough." The disparate materials he gathers methodically to support
this thesis may be more impressive than the conclusions he reaches.
He surveys the elder James's Swedenborgian beliefs, some of the
few men of the cloth who appear as characters in the novelist's
fiction, his early reviews of books on religion, his religious observations in his travel sketches, and his late essay, "Is There A Life After
Death?" All this is given in addition to a cursory survey of the major
fiction, wherein Frederick sees as a religious concept what he calls
"a central conflict in all of James's mature fiction": that "between the

impulse to dominate, to exploit or control others . . . and the will and power to give, to renounce, to live and love unselfishly."

Lyall H. Powers's *Merrill Guide to Henry James* (Columbus, Ohio, Merrill) is thirty-nine narrow pages of an encyclopedia-like essay on James's life and writings. There is nothing in it for the scholar, with the one possible exception of Powers's brief provocative attention to the symbolic uses of Maggie Verver's hands in his short discussion of *The Golden Bowl*.

Two of the most provocative essays to appear during the year give broad coverage to James's fiction, but through a narrow, narrow perspective. Leo Bersani's "The Jamesian Lie" (*PR* 36:53–79) is brilliantly concerned with the ultimate self-sufficiency of James's formal unities. James's "deceptively banal position that only execution matters," observes Bersani, "means most profoundly that verisimilitude, profoundly considered, is the grace and the truth of a formal unity." He is especially good with *The Golden Bowl* (although in fact he moves all over the canon), seeing in that novel an "artistic passion so intense that it works, most deeply, to destroy the very manifestations . . . of its designs." In the last line of that novel "passion can dispense with the fiction." Strother B. Purdy's "Henry James and the Sacred Thrill" (*PQ* 48:247–60) is equally profound in examining the variety of ways James uses the word *sacred* in his later works, demonstrating the impossibility of understanding it in any of the normal ways and the necessity of close study of its multiple contextual uses in almost all of the works after about 1895.

Both Ronald M. Meldrum and Gerald Fiderer use three of James's novels to make their respective points. In "Three of Henry James' Dark Ladies" (*RS* 37:54–60) it is Olive (of *The Bostonians*), the governess (of "The Turn of the Screw"), and Kate (of *The Wings of the Dove*) whom Meldrum examines in conflict with fair-haired virgins in each work. In "Henry James's 'Discriminated Occasion'" (*Crit* 11,ii:56–69) Fiderer makes a not very persuasive defense of Fleda Vetch (of *The Spoils of Poynton*) by way of associating her with Strether (of *The Ambassadors*) and with Densher (of *The Wings of the Dove*).

John V. Antush's "simple sketch," as he himself calls his "Money as Myth and Reality in the World of Henry James" (*ArQ* 25:125–33), traces some ways James uses money "to move his plots, to motivate and expose his characters . . . [and] to create a human condition in which his characters . . . [are free to] find an Eden-like freedom to explore the potentials of human growth." The complexity and extensiveness of this subject in James, as Antush demonstrates it, would seem to be justification enough for Jan W. Dietrichson's extended treatment of this subject in his "The Image of Money in the Works of Henry James," already mentioned in section *i* above. In fact, however, Dietrichson's chapters on the *literary* aspects of this subject— its relation to manners, to morals, and to its "figurative" uses in his fiction—are somewhat disappointing; for the treatment there is more often turgid and pedantic than imaginative or audacious. Of the 140 pages devoted to the total subject, for example, Dietrichson gives only 8 to what should be the very center of his subject, the metaphorical and imagistic uses of money in James's fiction. His survey of the criticism and scholarship on his subject, also a brief chapter, is much better.

Raymond Thorberg's little note, "Henry James and the 'New England Conscience'" (*N&Q* 16:222–23), is a recording of James's first use of the phrase in 1879.

### *v.* Criticism: Individual Tales

The early "De Grey: A Romance" is pointed to by John Tytell in "Henry James and the Romance" (*Markham Rev* [1]v:[1–2] as representing an "important example of a young writer assimilating the lessons of two earlier masters, Hawthorne and Poe, and then veering off in his own direction.

H. Vandermoer's "Baroness Münster's Failure" (*ES* 50:47–57) depicts Eugenia as being as limited as Robert Acton (in *The Europeans*) and thus as subject as he to "suspicion, fastidiousness, egoism, [and] self-sufficiency." Together they represent a Europe and an America that can never meet.

Of the three studies of the year on *Daisy Miller*, Motley F. Deaken's "Daisy Miller, Tradition, and the European Heroine" (*CLS* 6:45–59) is probably the most important. In a nice corrective, he shows that the literary heroines of Turgenev, Cherbuliez, George Sand, and Mme de Staël are as much the source of James's conception as real American girls he may have observed. Thus, Daisy's death is due as much to an "essentially traditional, European resolution" as it is to a view of her as "the champion of and martyr to freedom."

R. P. Draper, in "Death of a Hero? Winterbourne and Daisy Miller" (*SSF* 6:602–08), contends, after nods to Shakespeare and D. H. Lawrence, that Winterbourne is the true center of interest in the tale. It is "his slow, lingering, and almost comically *un*-dramatic death that is the main theme, and his ironically distanced, but unavailing struggle for life that provides the material for the slender plot." And Donald E. Houghton, in "Attitude and Illness in James's *Daisy Miller*" (*L&P* 19:51–60), presents a not very persuasive Freudian reading of the tale that sees defiance of European society metaphorically rendered in various kinds of illnesses.

Anna S. Brylowski's "In Defense of the First Person Narrator in *The Aspern Papers*" (*CentR* 13:215–40) is probably the longest, most learned, and most dogged reading on record of this famous tale. Her approach to the narrator is to one as he might have functioned in a poetic dramatic monologue. In fact, it is John Lehman's treatment of the genre in his *The Poetry of Experience* that provides her with a method—and a conclusion: "a subjective narrator" who has largely replaced the author, and an "ironic tone," largely supplied by the reader himself. The result: a great dramatic poem, "suggesting [quoting Lehman] a number of different meanings at different levels simultaneously." Samuel Hux, in "Irony in *The Aspern Papers*: The Unreliable Symbolist" (*BSUF* 10,i:60–65), sees the papers themselves embodying "a controlling moral corruption" that in turn is revealed to us as the narrator, all unconsciously, to be sure, verifies it in *his* growing corruption.

In "'The Lesson of the Master': An Interpretive Note" (*SSF* 6:654–58) Charles R. Smith repeats a good deal of well-known biographical and critical material to support a reading that clearly "accepts" the last line of the tale: to wit, "the Master was essentially right ... nature had dedicated him [Paul Overt] to intellectual, not to personal passion."

Juliet McMaster, in "'The Full Image of a Repetition' in *The Turn of the Screw*" (*SSF* 6:377–82), gives us an unbelievably revealing analysis of this much overanalyzed tale by examining the series of times the governess replaces the ghosts to "recreate the 'full image' of her own perception." This is true technique as discovery, for how the governess *becomes* the ghosts parallels the two ways one may look at the story: "Just as we may choose to look through the glass *with* the governess or *at* her, so we may choose to listen with the ladies, and

hear a ghost story, or with [James], and hear a psychological novel."
Robert L. Berner's "Douglas in *The Turn of the Screw*" (*EN* 3[1968–
69]:3–6) is simply another defense of the "non-apparitionist" reading,
emphasizing here the importance of the introductory comments by
Douglas to support that well-known view.

Eddy Dow, in "James' 'Brooksmith' [Paragraphs 4 and 5]" (*Expl*
27:item 35) sees the butler cogently named as one who, unlike women,
is able "to direct through a smiling land, between suggestive shores, a
sinuous stream of talk."

"The Beast in the Jungle" is the subject of Courtney Johnson's
"John Marcher and the Paradox of the 'Unfortunate' Fall" (*SSF*
6:121–35), an elaborate and lengthy and somewhat pretentious autobiographical, psychological, and mythical reading of the story. Its
purpose is to pinpoint the nature of Marcher's limitations.

Strother B. Purdy's "Conversation and Awareness in Henry James's
'A Round of Visits' " (*SSF* 6:421–32) is a somewhat strange linguistic
examination of the dialogue in this rarely-discussed story that sees its
"strangely un-dramatic and unanalytical conversation" managing
somehow both "a dramatic scene and . . . a psychological analysis."

The studies of individual tales, as well as those of individual novels
discussed in section *vi* below, should of course be supplemented by
the rather numerous studies of both cited above, especially in section *iii*.

### vi. Criticism: Individual Novels

John Scherting's "*Roderick Hudson*: A Re-Evaluation" (*ArQ* 25:101–
19) is an extensive, persuasive argument in support of the view that
the novel's central character is Rowland Mallet rather than Roderick,
that its central theme is "intimately bound up with Rowland's character, motives, and deeds," and that the novel, finally, "is primarily a
subtle but persistent attack on those who seek to direct the destiny of
others by imposing absolute standards of conduct on the lives of their
fellow human beings."

In "Henry James's *The American* Simplified (*KN* 16:61–64) Szala
Alina examines a Polish version of the novel (*Amerykanin*, Lwów,
1879, trans. A. Callier) and speculates about the liberties the translator took, probably as a result of then-current stereotyped views of
what "the American" should be.

Abigail Ann Hamblen, in *"Confidence*: The Surprising Shadow of Genius" (*UR* 36:151–54), makes a brief, unconvincing case for finding an instance of modern "situation ethics" in this early Jamesian novel.

It was, as usual, however, *The Portrait of a Lady* that received the most extended attention during the year. And of the six studies of it that I was able to examine, I think I like best Marjorie Perloff's "Cinderella Becomes the Wicked Stepmother: *The Portrait of a Lady* as Ironic Fairy Tale" (*NCF* 23:413–33), an extensive, provocative view of Isabel's egoistic limitations, especially as they are revealed in her relations with Pansy. Seymour Kleinberg, in "Ambivalence: The Psychology of Sexuality in Henry James's *The Portrait of a Lady*" (*Markham Rev* [1],v:[2–7]), may well have penned the best line of the year in his description of Goodwood as "a character so flat and unbelievable that one sees him as a metonomy [*sic*], a walking erection." How sexuality defines all the characters is his main subject, however, especially Isabel's final discovery "that her entire life had been a colossal denial of eros." Courtney Johnson would not be in disagreement with this in his "Adam and Eve and Isabel Archer" (*Renascence* 21:134–44) and its often-made point that at the end she is on her way to a kind of redemption by first seeing herself for what she is. And Charles Feidelson, in "The Moment of *The Portrait of a Lady*" (*Ventures* 8, ii[1968]:47–55), finds in the novel James's initial awareness of the uses of the inward life, his discovery of the dramatic uses of consciousness.

Two studies are concerned with particular parts of the novel. In "The Conclusion to *The Portrait of a Lady* Re-examined" (*AL* 41:55–63) Dominic J. Bazzanella surveys the contradictory critical attention, including that of the reviews, devoted to the novel's ending and sees the revisions of 1908 in part as a reaction to this criticism. And John T. Frederick's "Patterns of Imagery in Chapter XLII of Henry James's *The Portrait of a Lady*" (*ArQ* 25:150–56) is a close, close analysis of the imagery of Isabel's famous "meditative vigil," seeing the central image to be that of a prison, with contrasting ones of space and freedom. Images of darkness and light, of cold and heat, and many other subordinate and ancillary ones "play their parts in sharpening the reader's participation in Isabel's reflections."

Graham Burns's "*The Bostonians*" (*CR* 12:45–60) is the only interpretive view among the three studies of the novel that appeared during the year. Burns is perceptive in seeing the feminist movement as metaphor, in seeing James's sympathetic portrayal of Olive "as she loses connection with the outside world and her own sustaining illusion," and in seeing that the novel as a whole "is saturated with an awareness of the egoistic forms the moral life may take when the natural is subverted." Herbert F. Smith and Michael Petnovich's "*The Bostonians*: Creation and Revision" (*BNYPL* 73:298–308) is an informative history of the serial publication of the novel in the *Century*, its account of how Richard Watson Gilder persuaded James to write for him, the indifference of the *Century*'s readers to the work, and the nature of James's revisions for the first book version. Clare R. Goldfarb's "Names in *The Bostonians*" (*IEY* 13[1968]:18–23) is a somewhat silly account of the symbolic possibilities in the names of Verena Tarrant, Olive Chancellor, and Basil Ransom.

Mildred E. Hartsock's "*The Princess Casamassima*: The Politics of Power" (*SNNTS* 1:297–309) contains a nice correction in not confusing Hyacinth's dilemma about "the dichotomy of past and present, tradition and change," with James's view. Hyacinth, says Miss Hartsock, is a "non-hero," whereas James was perfectly aware "that any social meliorism must be human, humane, and tentative; and it must fall within the context of the politics of necessity."

An important instance of the recently increasing number of studies that question James's true awareness of what he was doing in his fiction is Nina Baym's "Fleda Vetch and the Plot of *The Spoils of Poynton*" (*PMLA* 84:102–11). The case here is a persuasive one in seeing that the Fleda *realized* in the novel is radically different not only from the Fleda of the extended *Notebook* entries but also from the Fleda that James described in his Preface. James in fact, she says, "wrote a better novel than he planned," and many more studies are needed to "help us distinguish the artist James was from the artist he imagined himself to be." Mildred E. Hartsock, in "A Light Lamp: *The Spoils of Poynton* as Comedy" (*ES*[Anglo-Amer. supp.]:xxix–xxxviii) would also question previous readings of the novel which do not see clearly its comedy, its mock-epic form, its satiric style, its indifference to deep psychological probing, its clear emphasis upon irony.

Albert E. Stone, Jr.'s "Introduction" to *Twentieth Century Interpretations of "The Ambassadors"* (Englewood Cliffs, N. J., Prentice-Hall) is much better than those in some of the volumes in this series of reprinted criticism for his meticulously careful survey of the conception and the writing of the novel, of the critical responses to it, and for its recognition of the ultimate necessity of linking it to *The Wings of the Dove* and to *The Golden Bowl* for a full understanding of its meaning. J. A. Ward's "*The Ambassadors* as a Conversion Experience" (*SoR* 5:350–74) is also an excellent essay, especially in placing Strether in a context that also includes the thinking of William James, Emerson, and Thoreau, a context that both "confines" and "releases" meaning. It is beautifully written and developed. And if Ward sees in the end no more than a "modifying irony" in Strether's "dogged demand 'To be right,' " an irony I would see as much more powerful, he is convincing enough in seeing that Strether's final conversion is into something "quite incompatible with a relation within the strict human order." James N. Wise, in "The Floating World of Lambert Strether" (*ArlQ* 2,i:80–110), is predictable enough, seeing that "the fermentation, the sense of being launched, the hesitancy, the changing of 'boats' indicate the far-reaching unities of the novel." It is of course a "dry" Woolett that Strether leaves, and it is "with . . . new knowledge [that] Strether [goes] . . . floating off again at the novel's end."

Finally, we have in Millicent Bell's "The Dream of Being Possessed and Possessing: Henry James's *The Wings of the Dove*" (*MR* 10:97–114) a not very original but nonetheless startlingly thorough reading of the novel in her delineation of such aspects as the "deterministic" context that makes Kate and Densher what they are, the way materialistic *things* are never out of the vision of what we are "seeing" in the novel, and, ultimately, the way James saw that "all of our cultural contradictions, is manifest in the personal life at its most personal, in sexual behavior."

*Purdue University*

# 7. Faulkner

## Michael Millgate

It is perhaps significant that the most important recent work on Faulkner is of a largely retrospective kind. Heinrich Straumann's comprehensive study and James B. Meriwether's magisterial survey make it at once possible and necessary to take stock of the Faulkner field, to assess the value of what has been done, and to chart the directions that future work might most profitably take. Much, clearly, has been achieved by Faulkner criticism: the major novels, at least, are immensely more accessible, more readily and richly comprehensible, than they were only a decade ago. Faulkner scholarship has, perhaps, made less spectacular advances, but important bibliographical and biographical work has already been done and the academic air has for some time now been electric with the imminence of biographies, editions of letters, and new editions of some of the works themselves. In the interval before Faulkner studies take their next major step forward it seems clear that the most useful contributions will be made not by fresh critical surveys of the whole Faulkner canon or of arbitrarily selected features of works within it, but by close, detailed studies of particular books or of particular aspects of Faulkner's career. Most of the better pieces published in 1969 certainly fall into this category: it is distressing to note how few of the doctoral dissertations on Faulkner appear to do so.

## i. Bibliography, Editions, and Manuscripts

James B. Meriwether's section on Faulkner (pp. 175–210) in Jackson R. Bryer, ed., *Fifteen Modern American Authors: A Survey of Research and Criticism* (Durham, N.C., Duke Univ. Press) is, quite simply, indispensable. The survey, carried out with meticulous thoroughness and discriminating shrewdness, does not of course mention everything that has ever been published on Faulkner; its great value, indeed, is precisely that it confines itself to the orderly listing and careful assessment of work likely to be useful to the serious Faulkner student. An admirable feature is the coverage given to studies published outside North America and to doctoral theses, some of which (e.g., George R. Sidney's on Faulkner's Hollywood career and Sylvan Schendler's on *A Fable*) are properly identified as the fullest treatments of their particular subjects yet to have appeared. James B. Meriwether also contributes a much briefer listing of work about Faulkner to Louis D. Rubin, Jr., ed., *A Bibliographical Guide to the Study of Southern Literature* (Baton Rouge, La. State Univ. Press). Of some bibliographical relevance is the review article by Mikhail Landor, "William Faulkner: New Translations and Studies" (*SovL* 8 [1968]:180–85): interest in Faulkner in the Soviet Union apparently runs high, even though few of his works have as yet been translated there.

A new edition of Faulkner's *New Orleans Sketches*, first published by Rutgers University Press in 1958, was published in 1968 by Random House; the editor, Carvel Collins, has added a new preface, enlarged and revised his introduction, and included for the first time Faulkner's 1925 essay on Sherwood Anderson. James A. Winn's "Faulkner's Revisions: A Stylist at Work" (*AL* 41:231–50) contains original material of great interest—quotations from prepublication versions of *Absalom, Absalom!*, *As I Lay Dying*, *The Sound and the Fury*, *Wild Palms*, and *The Hamlet*—but the value of his own commentary is severely limited by the decision to discuss Faulkner's revisions under the separate and somewhat arbitrary headings of "expansion, concentration, substitution, and reorganization."

## *ii.* Biography

H. Edward Richardson's *William Faulkner: The Journey to Self-Discovery* (Columbia, Univ. of Mo. Press), offered as a critical biography of Faulkner up to the publication of *Sartoris*, focuses chiefly on Faulkner's childhood, on the New Orleans period, and on the recurrence of particular themes and images in the verse and the early prose. As biography, the book advances sweeping generalizations and large psychological speculations upon the basis of what is for the most part an uncritical compilation from familiar published sources which are themselves often of doubtful authority. As criticism, it is undistinguished.

Other recent contributions have also concentrated upon the early stages of Faulkner's career. Phil Stone's widow, responding to a series of very general questions put by William R. Ferris, Jr. ("William Faulkner and Phil Stone: An Interview with Emily Stone," *SAQ* 68:536–42), covers what is now well-worn factual and apocryphal ground, stressing in particular Faulkner's early familiarity with Joyce under Stone's guidance. Fresher perspectives are opened up by James E. Kibler, Jr. ("William Faulkner and Provincetown Drama, 1920–1922," *MissQ* 22:226–36), who argues—largely on the basis of circumstantial evidence—that Faulkner, through his friendship with Stark Young, must have seen some of the plays performed by the Provincetown Players in 1920–21; Kibler particularly discusses Faulkner's acquaintance with O'Neill's work and the influence of Edna St. Vincent Millay's one-act play, *Aria da Capo*, upon Faulkner's own *Marionettes*. Carvel Collins's revised introduction to *New Orleans Sketches* (see section *i* above) incorporates important new information about the inception and subsequent course of Faulkner's relationship with Sherwood Anderson: it seems to have been Faulkner's friend Ben Wasson who urged him to see Anderson in New Orleans in the fall of 1924. An earlier piece only now listed in the MLA bibliography, Elmo Howell's "William Faulkner's New Orleans" (*La Hist* 7[1966]:229–39), offers no new information.

### *iii.* Criticism: General

*a.* **Books.** In his *William Faulkner* (Frankfurt, Athenäum, 1968) Heinrich Straumann has performed a valuable service for German readers by making available to them, in an orderly and highly responsible manner, the conclusions of the best work in Faulkner scholarship and criticism. Straumann summarizes Faulkner's career and the history of the reception of his work in England, France, Italy, and Germany before developing extended analyses of each of the novels and of the *Collected Stories* volume. He has no hesitation in tackling difficult critical issues (e.g., the question of the "contrapuntal" unity of *Collected Stories*), and if his book breaks relatively little new ground, every chapter bears nonetheless the mark of independent and perceptive reading (see the review by John V. Hagopian, *AL* 41:451–53).

The declared aim of Elizabeth M. Kerr's *Yoknapatawpha: Faulk-*

ner's *"Little Postage Stamp of Native Soil"* (New York, Fordham
Univ. Press) is to provide a "comprehensive view" of Yoknapatawpha County both as a fictional creation and as a reflection of the
world of Lafayette County, Mississippi (no mention is made of
the possibility that Faulkner may once have had somewhere other
than Oxford in mind as the "original" of Jefferson); its tendency,
however, is so persistently towards the sociological that attention is
constantly shifted away from Faulkner's work to the actual world it
is assumed to "represent." Since she is a literary critic and not a
social historian, Professor Kerr thus puts herself somewhat at a dis-
advantage and severely diminishes the value of an approach that
had seemed unusually promising. Given the approach, it seems a
pity that so little use should have been made of Faulkner's own statements outside his fiction.

*b.* Articles and dissertations.   In "Faulkner's Use of the Past: A
Comment" (*Renascence* 20[1968]:198–207,214) Terry Otten suggests, in an analysis of four works, the ways in which Faulkner may
use the past either to dramatize or to universalize his moral themes.
No new ground is broken by Jewell H. Gresham's "Narrative Techniques of Faulkner's Form" (*Nassau Rev* 1,iii[1966]:103–19) or by
Leonard I. Kulseth's "Cincinnatus Among the Snopeses: The Role
of Gavin Stevens" (*BSUF* 10,i:28–34), while in "Spring Paradigm:
Faulkner's Living Legacy" (*ForumH* 6,ii[1968]:4–7) Melvin E. Bradford says nothing that he does not say in more specific terms elsewhere. The remaining items which fall under this "general" heading
are—somewhat alarmingly—all dissertations. Two confine themselves
to the initial stages of Faulkner's career: Frank F. Carnes, "On the
Aesthetics of Faulkner's Fiction" (*DA* 29:894A–95A), and Kenneth W. Hepburn, "*Soldier's Pay* to *The Sound and the Fury*: Development of Poetic in the Early Novels of William Faulkner"
(*DA* 29:2263A). Several deal primarily with aspects of characterization: Charles T. Gregory, "Darkness to Appall: Destructive Designs
and Patterns in Some Characters of William Faulkner" (*DA* 30:
1565A–66A), David W. Mascitelli, "Faulkner's Characters of Sensibility" (*DA* 29:608A–09A), Fran J. Polek, "Time and Identity in the
Novels of William Faulkner" (*DA* 29:3151A), and Joseph F. Trimmer, "A Portrait of the Artist in Motion: A Study of the Artist-
Surrogates in the Novels of William Faulkner" (*DA* 29:3623A).
Others range more widely: Melvin E. Bradford, "Faulkner's Doctrine

of Nature: A Study of the 'Endurance' Theme in the Yoknapatawpha Fiction" (*DA* 29:3999A), Rosemary F. Franklin, "Clairvoyance, Vision, and Imagination in the Fiction of William Faulkner" (*DA* 29:3135A), and William J. Schultz, "Motion in Yoknapatawpha County: Theme and Point of View in the Novels of William Faulkner" (*DA* 29:3154A).

*c.* **Ideas, influences, intellectual background.** One item listed under Faulkner in the MLA bibliography—William J. Swanson's "Notes on Religion" (*CimR* 7:45–52)—in fact touches only briefly on *The Sound and the Fury* as a point of departure for a discussion of the religious themes in Styron's *Lie Down in Darkness*. Thomas Merton, however, does deal primarily, though not exclusively, with Faulkner in " 'Baptism in the Forest': Wisdom and Initiation in William Faulkner," published as the introductory essay to *Mansions of the Spirit: Essays in Literature and Religion*, edited by George A. Panichas (New York, Hawthorn, 1967), pp. 19–44. In a discussion interesting for its ideas but perhaps too unspecific to be really helpful as criticism, *The Wild Palms* and *Go Down, Moses* are considered as contrasted examples of Faulkner's concern for the "old verities" in terms of myths and symbols which, while not necessarily Christian, are nonetheless "of a kind that man has always spontaneously recognized to be 'religious' in a sense that is not confessional but sapiental." Although Elmo Howell's "William Faulkner: The Substance of Faith" (*BYUS* 9:453–62) does not lack specificity, it sustains inadequately its contention that Faulkner, temperamentally "buoyant and cheerful," had a profound faith in the South, its people, and its values.

In "Dickens and Faulkner: The Uses of Influence" (*DR* 49:69–79) Joseph Gold links Dickens and Faulkner as representatives of "the central humanist tradition of the English novel," points to broad similarities between their writings and suggests that direct influences can be detected in some Faulkner novels (e.g., *Intruder in the Dust* may be indebted to *Great Expectations*). Jean Weisgerber, on the other hand, draws no significant conclusions for Faulkner criticism from the argument, in "Faulkner's Monomaniacs: Their Indebtedness to Raskolnikov" (*CLS* 5[1968]:181–93), that Faulkner was profoundly influenced by Dostoievski and that the figure of Raskolnikov can be detected behind such Faulknerian "monomaniacs" as young Bayard, Quentin Compson, Joe Christmas, Thomas Sutpen, and

Mink Snopes. A dissertation by Sister Joan M. Serafin, F.S.E., is entitled "Faulkner's Uses of the Classics" (*DA* 29:3155A–56A).

Examples of Faulkner's use of tall tales, local superstitions, dialect speech, etc., are recounted by John T. Flanagan, "Folklore in
Faulkner's Fiction," included in *Studies in American Literature*, pp.
119–44.

*d.* **Language and style.** The most important contribution under
this heading is Richard P. Adams's "Some Key Words in Faulkner"
(*TSE* 16[1968]:135–48), which points out that the contexts within
which Faulkner uses such words as "doom," "terrific," "terrible," etc.,
result in their taking on meanings quite distinct from those of everyday speech. Three other articles are of minor interest: neither Calvin
S. Brown's "Faulkner's Use of the Oral Tradition" (*GaR* 22[1968]:
160–69) nor the late Frederick J. Hoffman's discussion of Faulkner's
rhetoric ("William Faulkner," in *American Winners of the Nobel
Literary Prize*, edited by Warren G. French and Walter E. Kidd
[Norman, Univ. of Okla. Press, 1968], pp. 138–57) confronts its subject in any very substantial way, while James F. Farnham ("A Note
on One Aspect of Faulkner's Style," *Lang&S* 2:190–92) offers only
very limited evidence for his suggestion that Faulkner uses the "not
. . . but . . ." structure to reflect confusion and uncertainty on the part
of his characters. Some mention should perhaps be made, however,
of Richard Gunter's sensible essay review (*MissQ* 22:264–79) of
Irene Kaluza's *The Functioning of Sentence Structure in the Stream-
of-Consciousness Technique of William Faulkner's "The Sound and
the Fury": a Study in Stylistic Linguistics* (Krakow, 1967).

#### iv. Individual Works, to 1929

*a.* **Poetry and early prose.** H. Edward Richardson's study (see section *ii* above) gives extended treatment to the poetry and especially
to the nature and sources of its imagery. His reading of *The Marble
Faun* as an intensely regional work is usefully corrected by Cleanth
Brooks's remarks in "Faulkner as Poet" (*SLJ* 1,i[1968]:5–19) upon
the excessively "literary landscape" of the volume. Brooks does not,
perhaps, greatly advance our understanding of the poetry itself, but
he argues very suggestively that, although Faulkner thought of himself as a "failed poet," what brought his "poetry" to fruition was pre-

cisely fiction's greater amplitude and more realistic contexts: "Most of all [Faulkner] needed the kind of context which would allow him to set up a real tension between his more purely 'literary' tendencies and his sense of a solid and believable world." Michel Gresset's review of Maurice Coindreau's translation of *The Wishing Tree* ("Un Faulkner féerique," *NRF* 17[Sept]:437–40) is of particular importance in that it draws upon manuscript evidence in discussing the history of the story and in speculating upon its relationship to such works as *The Sound and the Fury* and "That Evening Sun." The new edition of *New Orleans Sketches* has been mentioned earlier: see section *i* above.

*b.* **Novels.** *Soldier's Pay.*    H. Edward Richardson's "The Decadence in Faulkner's First Novel: The Faun, The Worm, and the Tower" (*EA* 21[1968]:225–35) has been incorporated, with minor modifications, in his book (discussed in section *ii* above).

*Mosquitoes.* Two companion pieces in the special Faulkner issue of *Mississippi Quarterly* (Summer, 1969) contribute substantially to our understanding of a minor yet difficult work: Mary M. Dunlap ("Sex and the Artist in *Mosquitoes*," *MissQ* 22:190–206) demonstrates how the sexual sterility or abnormality of particular characters is specifically correlated with the quantity and quality of their artistic productivity or of their interest in the arts; Phyllis Franklin ("The Influence of Joseph Hergesheimer Upon *Mosquitoes*," *MissQ* 22:207–13) points to Faulkner's early review of three Hergesheimer novels and suggests ways in which Faulkner may have drawn upon them, and especially upon *Linda Condon*, in the composition of his own novel.

*Sartoris.* Two articles make minor points: in " 'Some Homer of the Cotton Fields': Faulkner's Use of the Mule Early and Late (*Sartoris* and *The Reivers*)" (*PLL* 5:190–96) William T. Stafford sees the famous eulogy of the mule as clearly related to the central themes of the novels; while in "Structure in William Faulkner's *Sartoris*: The Contrast Between Psychological and Natural Time" (*ArQ* 25:263–70) Dale A. Sorenson offers little of substance beyond the familiar perception that young Bayard, though surrounded by a vital present, can live only in the past. In a third article, "*Sartoris*: Germ of the Apocalypse" (*DR* 49:80–87), Lauren R. Stevens bases a comprehensive misreading of the novel upon a highly forced comparison with Shakespeare's *Hamlet*.

*The Sound and the Fury.* Although the book itself carries a somewhat ambitious title, the chapter on Faulkner in Martha O'Nan's *The Role of Mind in Hugo, Faulkner, Beckett, and Grass* (New York, Philosophical Library), pp. 13–22, is simply headed "William Faulkner's Benjy: Hysteria." Despite an occasional suggestive comment, the discussion of Benjy as a victim of hysteria is wholly unconvincing. Beverly Gross's "Form and Fulfillment in *The Sound and the Fury*" (*MLQ* 29[1968]:439–49) is, on the other hand, an interesting essay which closely examines the conclusion of the novel in order to demonstrate that the resolution it offers is not narrative or dramatic but "poetic," constituting a kind of epitomization of the novel's whole experience and relating back specifically to Benjy's earlier ride to the cemetery in the first section. Not so successful is James M. Mellard's attempt ("Jason Compson: Humor, Hostility and the Rhetoric of Aggression," *SHR* 3:259–67) to distinguish between "humor," "wit," and "the comic" in Jason's section and to determine the contribution made by each to a "rhetoric of aggression" which at once expresses Jason's vision of the world and serves to develop Faulkner's characterization of him. Three briefer pieces make useful contributions: William W. Cobau ("Jason Compson and the Costs of Speculation," *MissQ* 22:257–61) investigates Jason's cotton speculations on 6 April 1929 and shows that although the details are technically improbable and historically inaccurate, Faulkner has skillfully used the general principles of cotton speculation to dramatize important aspects of Jason's character; Thomas L. McHaney ("Robinson Jeffers' 'Tamar' and *The Sound and the Fury*," *MissQ* 22:261–63) points persuasively to thematic and verbal similarities between the story of incest treated in Jeffers's poem and the relationship of Quentin and Caddy; Willard Pate ("Benjy's Names in the Compson Household," *FurmS* 15,iv[1968]:37–38) suggests that the names used by other characters in referring to Benjy serve as an index of their degree of compassion for him. Rather less convincing are Charles D. Peavy's questioning of the existence of a "suicide pact" between Quentin and Caddy ("A Note on the 'Suicide Pact' in *The Sound and the Fury*," *ELN* 5[1968]:207–09) and Weldon Thornton's identification of the Jason in II Maccabees as a possible source for the naming of Jason Compson ("A Note on the Source of Faulkner's Jason," *SNNTS* 1:370–72).

### v. Individual Works, 1930–39

*As I Lay Dying.* In "Doing the Best They Can" (*GaR* 23:292–306) Thornton H. Parsons very helpfully points to the skill with which Faulkner controls our changing response to the various members of the Bundren family, allowing us finally to see Anse as "one of Faulkner's shabby heroes of endurance" and the maintenance of Bundren family unity as "another commonplace miracle of existence." Barbara Lanati, who finds this Faulkner's most exciting novel, makes a number of suggestive stylistic comments in the course of a long appreciative article, "Il primo Faulkner: *As I Lay Dying*" (*Sigma* 19 [1968]:83–119). Two other discussions of the novel—Robert R. Sanderlin's "*As I Lay Dying*: Christian Symbols and Thematic Implications" (*SoQ* 7:155–66) and Peter G. Beidler's "Faulkner's Techniques of Characterization: Jewel in *As I Lay Dying*" (*EA* 21[1968]:236–42) —fail to come seriously to grips with the problems they address.

*Sanctuary.* T. Frederick Keefer ("William Faulkner's *Sanctuary*: A Myth Examined," *TCL* 15:97–104) may well be right in demanding a high ranking for *Sanctuary* among Faulkner's novels, but he is unwise to do so in total disregard of recent Faulkner criticism.

*Light in August.* Apart from André Bleikasten's "L'espace dans *Lumière d'août*" (*BFLS* 46[1967]:406–20), which interestingly explores the figurative functions of locations, spatial relationships, and patterns of movement in the novel, there are no new contributions other than three notes in the *Explicator*: Frederick Asals (*Expl* 26 [1968]:item 74) discusses the complex relationship between Joe Christmas and Joanna Burden and suggests analogies with the account of the temptations of Christ in Matthew 4; William G. Clark (*Expl* 26[1968]:item 54) speaks of Joe's need for reassurance as to the meaningfulness of the distinction between being black and being white, and in a more recent comment (*Expl* 28:item 19) he relates Joe's compulsion to sleep in a stable before Joanna's murder to the earlier use of McEachern's stable as a setting for ritualized punishment. A useful selection of previously published material has been brought together in *Twentieth Century Interpretations of* Light in

August: *A Collection of Critical Essays*, edited by David L. Minter
(Englewood Cliffs, N.J., Prentice-Hall).

*Absalom, Absalom!*. No articles of importance appeared during
1969. Anselm Atkins ("The Matched Halves of *Absalom, Absalom!*,"
*MFS* 15:264–65) draws no significant critical conclusions from his
argument, itself overstated, that there are close parallels between the
opening narrative by Rosa Coldfield and the closing narrative by
Quentin and Shreve. In "'New Men' in Mississippi: *Absalom, Absalom!* and *Dollar Cotton*" (*NMW* 2:55–66) Melvin E. Bradford conducts a rather unfruitful exploration of points of similarity between
Faulkner's novel of 1936 and John Falkner's novel of 1942. *Absalom,
Absalom!* is one of the works treated in a dissertation by Mitchell A.
Leaska, "The Rhetoric of Multiple Points of View in Selected Contemporary Novels" (*DA* 29:3145A–46A).

*The Unvanquished.* Joseph F. Trimmer's "*The Unvanquished*:
The Teller and the Tale" (*BSUF* 10,i:35–42) takes the view that the
romanticized quality of the "tales" in *The Unvanquished* is deliberately designed to reflect the narrator's (Bayard's) inability to view
reality in other than romantic terms. An insubstantial item by Matthew C. O'Brien ("A Note on Faulkner's Civil War Women," *NMW*
1[1968]:56–63) is also chiefly concerned with *The Unvanquished*.

### vi. Individual Works, 1940–49

*The Hamlet.* Carey Wall ("Drama and Technique in Faulkner's *The
Hamlet*," *TCL* 14[1968]:17–23) very interestingly discusses the structural and stylistic features of the novel in relation to Faulkner's
presentation of the fundamental struggles of the human spirit as a
kind of "ritualistic game" in which, despite inevitable defeat, brief
moments of fulfillment (e.g., Ike and the cow) may yet be achieved.
Linda T. Prior ("Theme, Imagery, and Structure in *The Hamlet*,"
*MissQ* 22:237–56) offers pertinent comments about Eula, Ike, and
the failure of love; she sees the novel as a tragedy and the imagery
and structure as richly embodying the central themes of waste, emotional impotence, and greed. In a rather less firmly focused article
in the same Faulkner issue of the *Mississippi Quarterly*—now, and
for some years past, the leading journal in the Faulkner field—Pan-
thea R. Broughton ("Masculinity and Menfolk in *The Hamlet*,"

*MissQ* 22:181–89) argues that the male characters can conceive of
masculinity only in terms of crude sexual subjugation or of mas-
ochistic suppression. Less persuasive is Allen Gates's "The Old
Frenchman Place: Symbol of a Lost Civilization" (*IEY* 13[1968]:44–
50), in which the old Frenchman Place is seen as functioning in the
novel as a central symbol of the South.

Some attention has been given to the Snopes trilogy as a whole.
Ladell Payne ("The Trilogy: Faulkner's Comic Epic in Prose,"
*SNNTS* 1,i:27–37) usefully draws out the epic and mock-epic elements in the trilogy, which is seen as a version (perhaps deliberate)
of the Fieldingesque "comic epic poem in prose." For Joseph J.
Arpad ("William Faulkner's Legendary Novels: The Snopes Tril-
ogy," *MissQ* 22:214–25) the trilogy is a work in which "truth" is never
established; his article traces the process by which Flem becomes a
legendary figure, a creation of the popular imagination and, technically, of the contradictions between the narrators in *The Town* and
*The Mansion*. There are also two dissertations: James Gray Watson's
"'The Snopes Dilemma': Morality and Amorality in Faulkner's
Snopes Trilogy" (*DA* 29:1237A–38A), and Donald A. Petesch's
"Theme and Characterization in Faulkner's Snopes Trilogy" (*DA*
29:3618A–19A).

*Go Down, Moses* is discussed most rewardingly by Edwin M.
Eigner in "Faulkner's Isaac and the American Ishmael" (*JA* 14:107–
15). Eigner compares Ike McCaslin to Melville's Pierre and other so-
called Ishmael figures (the term, he thinks, has been too loosely employed) and suggests that Ike's disastrous renunciation of his heritage
closely corresponds to his failure to shoot Old Ben: "He is as unwilling to come into his wilderness kingdom as into his plantation patri-
mony, because he is unwilling to commit the act of blood and guilt
which is the requirement." On a somewhat similar topic, Gloria R.
Dussinger ("Faulkner's Isaac McCaslin as Romantic Hero *Manqué*,"
*SAQ* 68:377–85) argues that Faulkner deliberately presented Ike as
a failed Romantic hero, divided and incomplete because of his incapacity to see nature as other than good or society as other than
evil. Melvin E. Bradford ("All the Daughters of Eve: 'Was' and the
Unity of *Go Down, Moses*," *ArlQ* 1,i[1967]:28–37) comments sensibly on the role of "Was" within the overall pattern of the novel and
on the significance of Miss Sophonsiba's capture of Buck McCaslin.
Daniel Hoffman's "William Faulkner: 'The Bear'" (*Landmarks*,

pp. 341–52) is an eloquent restatement of a view of "The Bear" (as independent tale) and of Ike (as "spiritual hero") which was once standard but which recent Faulkner criticism has tended more and more to reject. Although Blanche H. Gelfant ("Faulkner and Keats: The Ideality of Art in 'The Bear,'" *SLJ* 2,i:43–65) also sees "The Bear" in isolation, her article does usefully emphasize the allusive potential of Cass McCaslin's invocation of the "Ode on a Grecian Urn" and especially the way in which Keats's poem answers to Ike's obsession with moments of arrested time and motion, to his essentially "Romantic desire to escape from the human condition." A sadly misconceived article by Joyce W. Warren ("The Role of Lion in Faulkner's 'The Bear': Key to a Better Understanding," *ArQ* 24[1968]: 252–60) links Lion and Old Ben together as "two mighty forces of nature" whose struggle teaches Ike that the spirit of nature can never die.

*Intruder in the Dust.* Mary Anne G. DeVillier ("Faulkner's Young Man: As Reflected in the Character of Charles Mallison," *LauR* 9,ii:42–49) writes of Charles Mallison's achievement of maturity in *Intruder* and compares him with other young men in Faulkner's fiction. In Clifford L. Lewis's "William Faulkner: The Artist as Historian" (*MASJ* 10,ii:36–48) *Intruder* is set alongside James W. Silver's *Mississippi: The Closed Society* and praised for its "penetration into the mind of a racist society"; the article fails, however, to do justice to Faulkner's subtlety as a novelist or to the complexity of his views on the racial issue.

*Knight's Gambit.* In "The Thematic Unity of *Knight's Gambit*" (*Crit* 11,ii:81–100) Jerome F. Klinkowitz argues, with admirable independence, that *Knight's Gambit* has been misunderstood and misrepresented even by those few critics who have paid attention to it; he sees the volume as possessing an underlying unity derived not so much from the figure of Gavin Stevens as from the recurrence of the theme of the outsider in his relationship to the community.

### *vii.* Individual Works, 1950–62

*Requiem for a Nun.* In a comparison of Camus's stage adaptation of *Requiem* with Faulkner's original, John G. Blair ("Camus' Faulkner: *Requiem for a Nun*," *BFLS* 47:249–57) observes that, while Camus is "remarkably faithful" to Faulkner, his own position as a "moral absolutist" emerges clearly in contrast to Faulkner's moral meliorism. None of the three articles on the novel itself is of particular importance. James R. Giermanski ("William Faulkner's Use of the Confessional," *Renascence* 21:119–23,166) evolves from a highly selective reading the conclusion that "Faulkner by his use of the confessional, uniquely transports the reader through Christian sacramental expiation"; Elmo Howell speculates, in "A Name for Faulkner's City" (*Names* 16[1968]:415–21), as to whether Faulkner's account of the naming of Jefferson reflects his own changing attitude to Jeffersonian ideas; John K. Crane ("The Jefferson Courthouse: An *Axis Exsecrabilis Mundi*," *TCL* 15:19–23) portentously discusses the origins of Jefferson in terms of Mircea Eliade's theory of civilization.

*A Fable.* In "A Source for Faulkner's *A Fable*" (*AL* 40[1968]: 394–97) Julian Smith succeeds in establishing that Humphrey Cobb's *Paths of Glory* (1935), a book which Faulkner had in his library, was almost certainly a source for *A Fable*.

*The Town* and *The Mansion.* See the discussions of the Snopes trilogy listed under *The Hamlet* above. Joel A. Hunt ("William Faulkner and Rabelais: The Dog Story," *ConL* 10:383–88) finds in *Pantagruel* a plausible (though perhaps unnecessarily exotic) source for the device by which Ratliff, in *The Mansion*, ends the political career of Senator Clarence Egglestone Snopes.

*The Reivers.* Ben M. Vorpahl's "Moonlight at Ballenbaugh's: Time and Imagination in *The Reivers*" (*SLJ* 1,ii:3–26) takes Mark Twain's "How to Tell a Story" as the starting point for a suggestive though somewhat overingenious discussion of Lucius Priest as both narrator and victim of a "humorous tale"; it also relates certain aspects of the novel to historical and geographical "originals." Comments on *The Reivers* are included in the article by William T. Stafford mentioned under *Sartoris* (above), while Lois Muehl's "Faulkner's Humor in Three Novels and One 'Play'" (*LC* 34[1968]:78–93) conveys, with breezy unsophistication, the author's pleasure in the comedy of *The Reivers*—the "play" of her title—and of other Faulkner novels.

### viii. The Stories

As suggested in section *iii* (*a*) above, Heinrich Straumann's chapter on the stories is of particular interest. Among the articles, the most useful is Melvin E. Bradford's "Certain Ladies of Quality: Faulkner's

View of Women and the Evidence of 'There Was a Queen'" (*ArlQ* 1,ii[1967–68]:106–39), a sound but overextended discussion of "There Was a Queen" and of Miss Jenny as a type of Faulkner's "natural" women. In "Apotheosis and Apocalypse in Faulkner's 'Wash'" (*SSF* 6:586–600) Jack F. Stewart sees the story as a kind of concentrated fable of Southern society's decadence and defeat; Wash Jones himself is described—a little extravagantly—as "the Apocalyptic figure of the man with scythe, the silent, self-destroying prophet of social revolution." In a brief note ("Faulkner's 'Wash,'" *Expl* 27[1968]: item 17) Joseph F. Tuso comments on the apposite naming (Griselda, Penelope) of Sutpen's mare, faithful producer of a male foal, in "Wash" and in *Absalom, Absalom!*. Charles C. Clark writes unconvincingly of "'Mistral': A Study in Human Tempering" (*MissQ* 21[1968]:195–204); T. J. Stafford advances interesting but perhaps excessive claims for "Tobe's Significance in 'A Rose for Emily'" (*MFS* 14[1968]:451–53); while in "The Chronology of 'A Rose for Emily'" (*SSF* 6:461–62) Paul D. McGlynn's conclusion that Emily dies in 1938 seems to overlook the fact that the story was first published in 1930. There is a dissertation by Anthony P. Libby ("Chronicles of Children: William Faulkner's Short Fiction," *DA* 30:1568A).

*University College, University of Toronto*

# 8. Hemingway and Fitzgerald

## William White

On the basis of entries in the *1969 MLA International Bibliography*, it is evident that there is a marked increase of scholarly attention to Scott Fitzgerald and Ernest Hemingway over that of the previous year. Fitzgerald, whose 1968 showing of thirteen items (plus one for Zelda) was the lowest since 1957, had a respectable thirty-three under his name; but Hemingway soared from forty-seven to eighty-four for 1969, making him the fifth most "popular" American author—after Henry James, Hawthorne, Melville, and Faulkner—in the academic fraternity. To quote statistics once more, for whatever they are worth, we find one book, four dissertations (there were none in 1968), and four chapters in festschriften among the Fitzgerald listings; and for Hemingway eight books, six theses, and twelve festschriften. It might also be mentioned that a few of the entries are for earlier years.

It has often been Fitzgerald's lot to be bracketed with, yet subordinate to, Hemingway. For example, in the *Encyclopedia of World Literature in the 20th Century*, edited by Wolfgang B. Fleischmann (2 vols., New York, Ungar, 1967–69), Fitzgerald is given two and a half columns, Hemingway more than five. Of the former, Melvin J. Friedman notes that "Fitzgerald is certainly not as widely known in Europe as Faulkner or Hemingway, but his position in England is probably more secure. He enjoyed considerable prestige among his fellow writers as attested by Gertrude Stein's remark in *The Autobiography of Alice B. Toklas:* 'She thinks Fitzgerald will be read when many of his well known contemporaries are forgotten'" (1:388). In the able discussion of Hemingway, Robert W. Lewis, Jr., says that "Along with Faulkner, Hemingway is often considered the major writer of fiction in American literature of the twentieth century" (2:99). These judgments are borne out by citations in the MLA Bibliography, where Fitzgerald has only four items by foreign scholars, to Hemingway's twenty-seven. In George Wickes's *Americans in Paris* (Garden City, N.Y., Doubleday), one of the six sections is devoted to Hemingway (pp. 149–187), whereas Fitzgerald, who finished *The Great Gatsby* on the Riviera in 1924 and began *Tender Is the Night* there, is mentioned a mere half-dozen times, and the mentions are only passing references. The pages devoted to Hemingway and Gertrude Stein, especially on their eventual quarrel, are perhaps the most valuable observations. Wickes says that Gertrude Stein, more original than Hemingway, "wrote indiscriminately . . . and lazily, never revising," but "with rigorous discipline, his painstaking revision . . . made his work immediate and lucid as hers was not" (p. 164). Their quarrel, after he outgrew her and made her "jealous of his sudden success while she continued to struggle for recognition," followed her attack in the *Autobiography* on him. The dispute may have been caused more by Hemingway's parody of her friend Sherwood Anderson in *The Torrents of Spring* than by parodies of her, confirmed by *A Moveable Feast*. A minor "comment" on the Hemingway-Fitzgerald relationship is David Levine's caricature in his *Pen and Needles* (Boston, Gambit), p. 16, of the two authors in bow ties and straw hats doing a soft-shoe dance behind footlights: each carries a pen in his arm, but the point of Hemingway's is sticking into Fitzgerald's breast.

### *i.* Bibliographies and Texts

Both Hemingway and Fitzgerald are well represented in *Fifteen Modern American Authors: A Survey of Research and Criticism*, edited by Jackson R. Bryer (Durham, N.C., Duke Univ. Press): Fitzgerald (pp. 211–38) by the editor, and Hemingway (pp. 275–300) by the man to whom the book is dedicated, the late Frederick J. Hoffman. There are no two better surveys among the fifteen, and they are models of their kind; no one concerned with the literary reputations of Hemingway and Fitzgerald through 1967 can afford to neglect these chapters. As surveys by two acknowledged experts of editions, manuscripts, letters, biography, and criticism they are invaluable.

Roderick S. Speer's "The Bibliography of Fitzgerald's Magazine 'Essays'" (*FHA* 1969:43–46) is not itself a bibliography, but corrects some errors in Jackson R. Bryer's *The Critical Reputation of F. Scott Fitzgerald: A Bibliographical Study* (Hamden, Conn., Archon, 1967). Addenda to Audre Hanneman's *Ernest Hemingway: A Com-*

*prehensive Bibliography* (Princeton, Princeton Univ. Press, 1967) appeared in a few reviews, but a more complete list is promised in future issues of the *Fitzgerald-Hemingway Annual*, where yearly bibliographies of both writers, similar to those in the old *Fitzgerald Newsletter*, will be published.

An unknown Hemingway piece, a review of Sherwood Anderson's *A Story-Teller's Story*, from *Ex Libris* (2[March 1925]:176–77), discovered by Matthew J. Bruccoli (*FHA 1969:71–74*) praises Anderson but distrusts his literary friends. There is a companion review of the same book by Gertrude Stein. This new *Fitzgerald-Hemingway Annual*—well edited and well designed and printed in hard covers—also contains "Dearly Beloved" (pp. 1–3), a Fitzgerald short story, his only serious fiction about a Negro[1] found among his papers at Princeton. This 900-word tale is reprinted in the *New York Times*, 20 August, with an appraisal by Arthur Mizener, who calls it "the least successful of [Fitzgerald's] unpublished stories . . . , though it does suggest that black—at least bronze—is beautiful, in an unfashionable Thoreauvian way."

Although printed in a section called "Documentary," Fitzgerald's translation of Rimbaud's "Voyelles" (*Delos* 2[1968]:100–04) includes the original French text as well as the English on opposite pages and also has notes by Paul Schmidt, who quotes part of a slightly different translation Fitzgerald made for Sheila Graham, turning the sonnet into a love poem—"the *her* is explained, and O equals sex, after all."

An example of Russian interest in Hemingway is seen in *A Farewell to Arms* (Moscow, Progress), an English text, with the novelist's 1948 introduction (also in English); in addition there is a Russian introduction, by M. Mendel'son, plus thirty-four pages of notes for students (in English) on words, places, and people in the story.

Of particular value to collectors and to those who see prices of manuscripts and first editions as an indication of an author's reputation is C. E. Fraser Clark, Jr.'s "Hemingway at Auction" (*FHA 1969:105–24*).[2]

1. Those interested in this subject should see Gerald R. Griffin, "Hemingway's Fictive Use of the Negro: 'the curious quality of incompleteness,'" *HussonRev* 1(1968):104–11.
2. For comments on Philip Young and Charles W. Mann, *The Hemingway Manuscripts: An Inventory* (University Park, Pa. State Univ. Press), see *ALS 1968*, p. 109.

### ii. Memoirs and Biography

Carlos Baker's *Ernest Hemingway: A Life Story* (New York, Scribner's), certainly the most important book of the year on this author and likely to be the best source of biographical details about him, was reviewed in *ALS 1968*, pp. 109–10. Far shorter and far less valuable—if it contributes anything at all—is William Seward's *My Friend, Ernest Hemingway: An Affectionate Reminiscence* (South Brunswick, N.J., A. S. Barnes), which could be a candidate for the worst book on Hemingway, except that it does tell us how kind the novelist could be if he chose—which we knew already. Too, it shows once more how wrong generalizations can be on small evidence.

The *Connecticut Review* for October has a section entitled "Hemingway: Views and Reviews," consisting of five pieces. The first, by Donald St.John, "Interview with Hemingway's 'Bill Gorton' (Part II)" (3,i:5–23), continues a discussion of Bill Smith (see *ALS 1968*, p. 110), on whom the character was largely modeled and who turns up five and possibly six times in Hemingway's fiction. Smith's sister Kate, who married John Dos Passos, introduced Hemingway to Hadley Richardson, and in the Chicago apartment of Y. K. Smith, his brother, Hemingway met Sherwood Anderson, who not only talked Hemingway into going to Paris but gave him a letter of introduction to Gertrude Stein. The second article in the group, Bertram D. Sarason's "Hemingway in Havana: Two Interviews [with Armando Chardiet and Robert T. E. Schuyler]" (3,i:24–31), deal with Hemingway at the Floridita bar and are slight—both report that the writer could really drink. The third and fourth items are reviews of Baker's biography by Claude Simpson, Jr., and Donald St.John (3,i:32–42), the former favorable, the latter unfavorable though for rather personal reasons. And the fifth article in the magazine, by Arthur H. Moss, "More Ways of Hemingway" (3,i:43–44) adds an unflattering brief reminiscence to his previous "The Many Ways of Hemingway" (*ConnR* 2,ii:14–16).

Lillian Hellman's *An Unfinished Woman: A Memoir* (Boston, Little, Brown), while it adds little new to what is generally known and felt about Hemingway and Fitzgerald in their relationships with contemporaries (pp. 66–72, 76–80, 101–03), does record sensitive first-hand impressions of their behavior by one who knew them both; she recalls briefly the "famous first meeting [at Gerald Murphy's] where Ernest told Fitzgerald that Zelda was crazy" (p. 77), and what comes through Miss Hellman's few pages on them is Hemingway the bully and braggart and Fitzgerald's fear of him.

Robert E. Long's "Fitzgerald and Hemingway on Stage" (*FHA* 1969:143–44) is a review of an unsuccessful 1968 play, "Before I Wake," in which the two writers, the only characters in the drama, use dialogue, 95 percent of it taken from their letters to each other.

The one biographical article on Fitzgerald, "Hollywood—It Wasn't All That Bad," by R. L. Samsell (*FHA* 1969:15–19) makes light of the notion of Fitzgerald's "suffering" in the movie capital: "Try to see him [instead] in the light of hard work, of good times, friends of his own selection, places of his own liking, moments that were probably among his best."

### *iii.* Criticism

Of the books of criticism dealing with Hemingway published in 1969, the best one, Jackson J. Benson's *Hemingway: The Writer's Art of Self-Defense* (Minneapolis, Univ. of Minn. Press) was noticed in *ALS 1968*, pp. 111–12. One is in Hungarian, Mihály Sükösd's *Hemingway világa* (Budapest, Európa K.); and another is published by a European house, *Hemingway: Direct and Oblique*, by Richard K. Peterson (The Hague, Mouton). Peterson's study tries to relate Hemingway's ideas, themes, and attitudes to his style, imagery, and technique; and, the critic says, an analysis of the Hemingway manner and mannerism reflects his feeling toward words and writing rather than toward life. The understatement and indirection of Hemingway's early work, before *Death in the Afternoon* (1932), are contrasted with the expansiveness (and exaggeration) and directness of the later writing, as Peterson shows how words and images reveal the novelist's value system. The last chapter in the book, "Phonies and Heroes," on the Hemingway "code," is concerned so much more with ideas than technique that it seems to be tacked on to the volume. Although this is the most extensive discussion we have of Hemingway's rhetoric, it is unfortunately too discursive and inconclusive to be the final word on the "meaning" of his style.

My own *Merrill Guide to Ernest Hemingway* (Columbus, Ohio,

Merrill) is a relatively straightforward introduction to the man and his works, the novels and several of the important and representative short stories. A companion volume, *Studies in "The Sun Also Rises"* is analyzed in *ALS 1968*, p. 113.

The single volume devoted to Fitzgerald, Marvin J. LaHood's edition of *"Tender Is the Night": Essays in Criticism* (Bloomington, Ind. Univ. Press) is a collection of fifteen studies of the novel, all of them previously published between 1955 and 1967. Now that *Tender Is the Night* has achieved a place of importance beside *The Great Gatsby* and Fitzgerald's own life, and as its author's most ambitious and profound work, LaHood has brought together these pieces because the novel "cannot be elucidated by a single method or from any single perspective." Making his choices at approximately the same time that Jackson R. Bryer was writing his chapter in *Fifteen American Authors*, LaHood has included among his fifteen no fewer than twelve essays that Mr. Bryer singled out for praise or as worthy of mention. Although some of the articles are more specialized, and some briefer, than others, there is not a weak or dull one in the collection.

Among the Hemingway dissertations are a variety of subjects: Lawrence R. Broer, "The Effects of Ernest Hemingway's Identification with Certain Aspects of Spanish Thinking on His Rendering of Character" (*DA* 29:3606A); Naomi M. Grant, "The Role of Women in the Fiction of Ernest Hemingway" (*DA* 29:4456A); Thomas N. Hagood, "Elements of Humor in Ernest Hemingway" (*DA* 29:3139A); Wayne E. Kvam, "The Critical Reaction to Hemingway in Germany, 1945–1965" (*DA* 30:1139A–40A); Joseph C. Nucci, "The Poetry of Time and Place in the Fiction of Ernest Hemingway" (*DA* 30:733A–34A); and Delbert E. Wylder, "Faces of the Hero: A Study of the Novels of Ernest Hemingway" (*DA* 29:4029A–30A). Only Wylder's has been announced as being published.

Of the four Fitzgerald dissertations, only one has to do specifically with *Gatsby*, a good indication of the ever-increasing interest in all of Fitzgerald's work: Albert E. Elmore, "An Interpretation of *The Great Gatsby*" (*DA* 29:2706A); Nina N. Kenyon, "Self-Hatred as a Basis for Criticism of American Society" (*DA* 29:2713A); Robert Emmet Long, "The Hero and Society in the Earlier Novels of F. Scott Fitzgerald: A Study in Literary Milieu" (*DA* 29:2715A–16A); and Sister Mary E. Millani, "Irony and Symbolism: An Examination of the Longer Fiction of F. Scott Fitzgerald" (*DA* 29:2718A). One of these eleven dissertation writers, R. E. Long, has written several articles on Fitzgerald (see below).

Scholarship on the two novelists published in India, Japan, and Germany attests to foreign interest in them. *Variation*, published in New Delhi, contains three essays in English: S. P. Das's "The World and Experience of [the] Hemingway Hero" (pp. 76–85), Jai S. Gahlot's "*The Old Man and the Sea*: A Reading" (pp. 89–92), and Vishaw M. Kapoor's "The Style of Ernest Hemingway" (pp. 86–88). The importance is not so much in what they say as that Indian scholars are seriously discussing Hemingway. Two essays in Japanese indicate the continuing interest in that country. In *Maekawa* Muneyoshi Kato contributes "Macomber and Lion and Theme" (pp. 165–76) and Tadashi Watanaba writes on "The Style of Hemingway's Short Stories" (pp. 229–39). In a German collection, *Amerikanische Erzählungen*, there are two studies of Hemingway (Peter Nicolaisen, "Hemingways 'My Old Man' und Faulkners 'Barn Burning': Ein Vergleich," pp. 187–223; and Paul G. Buchloh, "Bedeutungsschichten in Ernest Hemingways *The Old Man and the Sea*," pp. 224–41). In the same publication Horst Kruse's article ("F. Scott Fitzgerald: *The Pat Hobby Stories*," pp. 155–86) is worth noting because it is a full treatment of a minor work, another indication of Fitzgerald's rising stature in Europe.

David L. Minter's academic and complex *The Interpreted Design as a Structural Principle in American Prose* (New Haven, Yale Univ. Press) uses the concept of interpreted design "as a metaphor for works structured by the juxtaposition of two characters: a man of design or designed activity, who dominates the action of his world, and a man of interpretation through whose mind and voice the story of the man of design is transmitted." He uses works by Edwards, Franklin, Thoreau, Henry Adams, Hawthorne, Henry James, Faulkner, and Fitzgerald; and Jay Gatsby and Nick Carraway fit ideally into Minter's theories, as seen in his discussion of *The Great Gatsby* (pp. 181–90). Unfortunately, the novel that Minter is treating illuminates his theory more fully than the theory illuminates the novel.

*The Great Gatsby*, as might be expected and as was the case in 1968, continues to interest critics more than all the other Fitzgerald writings combined, with nine entries in the MLA list specifically devoted to it, eight of them articles. These may best be discussed in alphabetical order. Thomas E. Boyle's "Unreliable Narration in *The Great Gatsby*" (*BRMMLA* 23:21–26) is a relatively minor piece; William F. Hall's "T. J. Eckleburg: 'un dieu à l'américaine'" (*FHA* 1969:35–39) shows the links between the eyes of the spectacled God in *Gatsby* and the Goncourt Journals for 1861, Lothrop Stoddard's *The Rising Tide of Color Against White Supremacy*, and Crèvecoeur's *Letters from an American Farmer*. Harold Hurwitz, in *"The Great Gatsby* and *Heart of Darkness*: The Confrontation Scenes" (*FHA* 1969: 27–34), adds to several previous studies of Conrad's influence on Fitzgerald, commenting in detail on the similarities between the interviews at the end of the two novels. Hurwitz says the borrowing was not accidental but conscious, and the comparison shows what Fitzgerald was attempting and how and why he used an important episode from the earlier English story to do it. Josephine Z. Kopf's "Meyer Wolfsheim and Robert Cohn: A Study of a Jewish Type and Stereotype" (*Tradition* 10,iii:93–104), obviously about *Gatsby* as well as *The Sun Also Rises*, regards both characters as inauthentic and their Jewishness as not central to the novels in which they appear; their "meanness, corruption, and weakness are somehow closely bound-up with Jewishness. It was undoubtedly the way in which they [Fitzgerald and Hemingway] felt they could most effectively achieve the character portraits they sought."

Robert Emmet Long ("The Vogue of Gatsby's Guest List," *FHA* 1969:23–25) shows how William Styron's *Lie Down in Darkness* and James Baldwin's *Tell Me How Long the Train's Been Gone* are indebted to Fitzgerald for the guest list device to summarize a place and an era. Paul McCarthy examines in detail "Daisy's Voice in *The Great Gatsby*" (*LHR* 11:51–56), a voice which suggests the nature of Gatsby's dream, "love and romance," and the weaknesses of that dream and is the gauge of Daisy's basic insincerity. Peter Rodda's *"The Great Gatsby"* (*ESA* 11[1968]:95–126) is a general study introducing the Fitzgerald novel to African students and serious readers. The last item on Fitzgerald's best known novel, Alexander R. Tamke's "The 'Gat' in *Gatsby*: Neglected Aspect of a Novel" (*MFS* 14[1968]:443–45), is a note in which its writer perhaps overstates his case that "Jay Gatsby's perfect name should at last be recognized for the exquisite irony it is." Mr. Tamke similarly takes up minor aspects of Hemingway in "Jacob Barnes' 'Biblical Name': Central Irony in *The Sun Also Rises*" (*ER* 18,ii[1967]:2–7).

That major attention is paid *Gatsby* and that the Fitzgerald book of the year on *Tender Is the Night*—such things are natural and understandable. What is quite welcome in Fitzgerald criticism is that two articles are devoted to each of his earlier and less appreciated novels, whether we agree with the findings or not. The studies of the first novel are Clinton S. Burhans's "Structure and Theme in *This Side of Paradise*" (*JEGP* 68:605–24) and Barry Gross's "*This Side of Paradise*: The Dominating Intention" (*SNNTS* 1,i:51–59). In a style that sometimes hampers his cause, Burhans says, "Recognizing and tracing the structural patterns in *This Side of Paradise* illuminates Fitzgerald's struggles with a complex and significant thematic development equally obscured by the novel's chaotic materials and techniques." Nevertheless Burhans does show how Fitzgerald handled these matters, how they are related to the rest of his work, and his triumph with them in *The Great Gatsby*. "The dream and disillusion thread in *This Side of Paradise*," Burhans concludes, "informs much of Fitzgerald's subsequent writing" and is "central to his essentially tragic vision of the human condition." Barry Gross has a somewhat different approach: he sees Fitzgerald as always a moralist, concerned with "the need to impose order on a chaotic world, the seductive destructiveness of aristocracy, the foredoomed attempt to guide and control life, love as both a unifying and divisive force, [and] personal responsibility as a moral good." He says *This Side of Paradise* is about the realization that "life is essentially a cheat and its conditions are those of defeat, and . . . the redeeming things are not 'happiness and pleasure' but the deeper satisfactions that come out of the struggle." Though the "dominating intention" of this first novel is the same as in Fitzgerald's four other major works, Gross thinks "it is not necessary to go outside [*This Side of Paradise*] to find it worthy."

Barry Gross also writes about Fitzgerald's second novel, "The Dark Side of Twenty-five: Fitzgerald and *The Beautiful and Damned*" (*BuR* 16,iii[1968]:40–52); as does Richard Astro, "*Vandover and the Brute* and *The Beautiful and Damned*: A Search for Thematic and Stylistic Reinterpretations" (*MFS* 14[1968]:397–413). The richness in this novel, for Gross, "resides in its confusions—not in ambiguities but in a twenty-five year old's confusions"; and he also finds it "as convincing a study in disintegration as *Sister Carrie*." Instead of autobiography, Fitzgerald is "trying to explain and justify things before they occur"; his decade also "foresaw and foretold the crack-up over and over again but was powerless to prevent it." Gross's rhapsodic conclusion is that in *The Beautiful and Damned* we "are in the presence of an imagination that could not really substantiate what it envisioned yet could not deny the truth of what it saw. We catch the rich confusion of a twenty-five-year-old golden boy who had it made in the moment he acted out his three-o'clock-in-the-morning dark night of the soul long before he could know it would happen." Richard Astro takes an entirely different tack: he says "the most practical manner in which to understand and appraise the motivating force in *The Beautiful and Damned* is through a study of Fitzgerald's literary sources in this novel," and that means Frank Norris's *Vandover and the Brute*; thus with a fresh insight we may measure the Fitzgerald novel "in terms of a new and more satisfying perspective." Both novels, Astro tells us, are criticisms of the American social scene, have similar characters, themes, and stylistic devices; Fitzgerald's novel, he finds, is a "didactic tract against self-indulgence," and "has as its merits a successful attempt to probe new fictional depths." Thus "it must be regarded as a unique achievement in the catalogue of Fitzgerald's fiction." This is stronger on rhetoric than evidence.

Clinton S. Burhans, whose piece on *This Side of Paradise* is noticed above, has another essay, "'Magnificently Attune to Life': The Value of 'Winter Dreams'" (*SSF* 6:401–12). More than a sort of first draft of the Gatsby idea, this short story is an "early reflection of the themes that characterize most of [Fitzgerald's] significant writing," the dream and disillusion motif, the striving for dreams rather than their fulfillment, and the view that man is "a creature whose imagination creates dreams and goals his nature and circumstances combine to doom."

Richard Foster's "Mailer and the Fitzgerald Tradition" (*Novel* 1[1968]:219–30) is more on the younger writer than on Fitzgerald. Constance Drake's "Josephine and Emotional Bankruptcy" (*FHA* 1969:5–13) shows how the Josephine stories, though artistically weak, thoroughly examine the causes and course of emotional bankruptcy ("drawing on resources which one does not possess"); and if we understand Josephine we can best understand the other and better Fitzgerald novels and stories. More important than these articles is James Gindin's "Gods and Fathers in F. Scott Fitzgerald's Novels" (*MLQ* 30:64–85), in which he demonstrates how the novelist's concern for his characters—Blaine, Patch, Gatsby, Diver, and Stahr—increased at the same time "as did his sympathy for their human struggles and relationships, for all the questions they could not answer. And the romantic hero, still doomed, was doomed less by moral order or original sin than by accident. Still unable to control his own destiny as he so powerfully wanted to, [he] turned his attention to the very human relationships that contributed to his doom." Gindin labels Fitzgerald's form "always that of the parable . . ." [but] *Tender* and *Tycoon* "explode from the tidiness of judgment and evaluation of the 'American experience,' into deeper questions, as well as richer and less systematic understandings about the perplexities of man."

Two European essays are worth citing to show the nature of the work being done there: Michael Hoenisch, "Die Werke F. Scott Fitzgeralds: Entwurf einer Chronologie der Entstehungsdaten" (*JA* 14:185–218), and R. Rougé, "F. Scott Fitzgerald: la femme et la mort" (*EA* 21 [1968]:160–67). "A Comparative Statistical Analysis of the Prose Styles of Fitzgerald and Hemingway," by Elizabeth Wells (*FHA 1969*:47–67), is written with authority, conviction, and understanding about Fitzgerald's "The Rich Boy," Parts I through V, and Hemingway's "Big Two-Hearted River: Part I." Hemingway seems to come out better in this limited sampling. Perhaps one day, as Miss Wells suggests, a computer will take over such analyses, with a larger sampling and more valid results.

Of the shorter pieces of Hemingway criticism one may profitably begin with Earl H. Rovit's chapter, "Ernest Hemingway: *The Sun Also Rises*," in *Landmarks*, pp. 304–14.

Articles dealing with Hemingway, in European publications, either in English or in foreign languages, present an interesting picture, though few American scholars can read all of the Russian, Slavic, Italian, Swedish, German, and French studies. Ten countries or languages are represented, and the fifteen essays appear in fourteen different periodicals. Three are in German: Herbert von Borch, "Hemingway" (*Univ* [Stuttgart] 24:801–07); W. Damp, "Individuum and Gesellschaft in Hemingways Romanen" (*WZUG* 16[1967]:189–92); and Wolfgang Wittkowski, "Gekreuzigt im Ring: Zu Hemingways 'The Old Man and the Sea,'" (*DVLG* 41[1967]:258–82). Two are in Italian: Mario Corona, "Considerazioni sull'ordine di successione dei racconti di Hemingway" (*SA* 13[1967]:325–37); and Giuseppe Gadda

Conti, "Hemingway e la pace dei nostri giorni" (*VeP* 52:3–20). There
are also two in Russian journals published in Moscow: I. Finkel'štejn,
"Sovetskaja kritika o Xeminguèe" (*VLit* 11,viii(1967):174–90); and
E. Solov'ev, "Cvet tragedii: o tvorčestve E. Xemingueja," *NovM*
44,ix(1968):206–35.

The two from Denmark are in a Copenhagen periodical, written
in English: Gerald Gillespie, "Hemingway and the Happy Few" (*OL*
23[1968]:287–99); and Rafael Koskimies, "Notes on Ernest Hemingway's *For Whom the Bell Tolls*" (*OL* 23[1968]:276–86). Gillespie
says the "happy few" (from *Henry V*, act IV, scene iii) are trying to
be true to themselves in a "world of hypocrisy and moral ugliness";
they are "modern versions of the older cult of Beautiful Souls, the
self-electing aristocracy of inward values who crave sincerity and thus
experience sublime joy in meeting their fellows." Hemingway's heroes, such as Jake Barnes, "challenge us with a profound question in
the midst of dislocating changes, wars, tawdriness, hypocrisy: Do we
believe that a man can be beautiful, inside and outside?" Hemingway's answer is yes. Koskimies's notes are on (i) the Communist leaders, (ii) the Matador Finito [de Palencia], Pilar's lover, and (iii)
Robert Jordan and Maria: she and Hemingway's women, the Finnish
critic says, "have all been created by a powerful poetic imagination"
as the "eternally feminine," none of which tells us very much.

Peter Egri begins a long study, written in English, in a Hungarian
journal, "The Relationship Between the Short Story and the Novel:
Realism and Naturalism in Hemingway's Art. Part I. 1923–1929"
(*HSE* 4:105–26). Another English-language article, appearing in a
Dutch magazine, Nicholas Joost's "Ernest Hemingway and *The Dial*"
(*Neophil* 52 [1968]:180–90,304–13), was largely covered in his book,
*Ernest Hemingway and the Little Magazines: The Paris Years* (Barre,
Mass., Barre Publishers, 1968), reviewed in *ALS* 1967, pp. 98–99. Also
in English, this time in a Paris organ, is Helmut Liedloff's "Two War
Novels: A Critical Comparison" (*RLC* 42[1968]:390–406), on *A Fare-
well to Arms* and Erich Maria Remarque's *Im Westen nichts Neues*.[3]
Three other foreign items are in their authors' native Rumanian,
Slavic, and Swedish: Fănica N. Gheorghe, "Hemingway si sentimen-

3. Richard K. Peterson, in *Hemingway: Direct and Oblique* (p. 60), which
I review above, compares Paul Bäumer, in *All Quiet on the Western Front*, with
Krebs, in Hemingway's "Soldier's Home."

tul tragic al existentei" (*Contemporanul* 12 Sept:9); V. A. Kuxarenko,
"E. Xemingguèj v perevode A. Voznesenskogo" (*FN* 11, vi[1968]:40–
49), on Voznesenskogo's translation of Hemingway; and Hilding
Sallnäs, "Studie i Hemingway" (*Studiekamraten* 51:23–26).

As for Hemingway criticism in American periodicals, Matthew J.
Bruccoli's new publication has three: Donald Torchiana's "*The Sun
Also Rises:* A Reconsideration" (*FHA* 1969:77–103), one of the best
pieces of the year; Bruccoli's " 'The Light of the World': Stan Ketchel
as 'My Sweet Christ' " (*FHA* 1969:125–30); and John Unrue's "Hemingway and the *New Masses*" (*FHA* 1969:131–40). With considerable
insight and appreciation, Torchiana makes a full and plausible case
that Hemingway's first novel is not an offshoot of T. S. Eliot's *Waste
Land*, not a "journey to nowhere, a study in futility, and a picture of the Lost Generation"; in showing how Hemingway was con-
temptuous of Eliot and did not agree with Gertrude Stein's view of
the age, the critic says the tragedy of the novel "belongs to those who
truly love the earth and share its death, though they endure in our
minds for their love of it and turn the tragedy into a joyful, affectionate
thing." And, he reiterates, "the earth does endure forever." Bruccoli's
point that "The Light of the World" is first-class Hemingway hinges
on our knowing about the flamboyant middleweight champion Stan
Ketchel, through whom the 350-pound whore Alice is both lost and
saved. Unrue tells us what we may not have known in detail but surely
knew in general: the critics of the radical Left did not exert a dam-
aging influence on Hemingway, for the artist in him would simply
never permit it.

Mario D'Avanzo ("The Motif of Corruption in *A Farewell to
Arms*," *LHR* 11:57–62) says little that is new in treating Hemingway's dark and tragic world, whose hero and victim must, as in *Hamlet*
and *King Lear*, face death stoically and endure; Lieutenant Henry's
farewell, he writes, "comes with a rather extensive knowledge of the
ripeness and rottenness at life's core." Michael J. Hoffman's interesting thesis, in "From Cohn to Herzog" (*YR* 58:342–58), is that Robert
Cohn has won a major battle, for, "humiliated and dismissed before
the end of *The Sun Also Rises*," he is resurrected as Moses Herzog and
assumes "the center of the literary stage denied him by Ernest Hemingway and now usurped by Saul Bellow." Believing that the "code"
fails, Hoffman concludes that "life may be hell and the self terrible,

but if a man has dignity and style he can still be ten feet tall. . . . Herzog would not be Herzog for long if he were not fouling up something. Nor would the rest of us be what we are. But this is a comic note, not a tragic one. To be human is to be absurd. This is why we respond to Moses Herzog." In the same issue of *Yale Review*, Alan Lebowitz ("Hemingway in Our Time," *YR* 58:321–41) has produced an excellent piece of prose on Hemingway's "discovery that life is harsh and dull, that God—if He exists—is not on our side, and that man, under sentence of annihilation, is while he lives only a human punching bag." But Hemingway was writing of *his* time, not ours, and we can now look back on what he left as "a body of work as worthy of serious attention as the personality of the man himself," whose "fruitless search for a place in some community, for new roots to replace rejected ones, is a primary theme through most of [his] fiction after *In Our Time*." As one who lived "his exotic fantasies" and wrote "his real nightmares . . . the self-heroics continually illuminate the fiction." Calling Hemingway an "Oak Park existentialist . . . in a hard, dull, Godless world," Lebowitz feels that the novelist "did manage to make of himself something at least of the exotic, almost undefeated, foreign hero," and "although art may have more truth than real life, it is something less exciting."

After this high point in Hemingway criticism, the many remaining pieces—such as explications by William Aiken (*Expl* 28:item 31), Mario L. D'Avanzo (*Expl* 27:item 39), and George D. Murphy (*Expl* 28:item 23)—contribute small matter; and Martin Light, in "Of Wasteful Deaths: Hemingway's Stories About the Spanish War" (*WHR* 23:29–42), for example, merely remarks that Hemingway was searching "for a true way to recreate the Spanish experience," out of which came *For Whom the Bell Tolls*; and it needs no saying that these stories express "his major preoccupation and his perennial themes." Along with the spate of Hemingway books, there were also a few review articles in 1969—by Robert M. Davis (*SHR* 3:382–95), Richard W. Noland (*HSL* 5:540–45), and William Wasserstrom (*VQR* 45:531–37). The last is perhaps the best; in it the reviewer poses the "Hemingway problem: how to avoid treating this extraordinary man as just a painful case or merely an inviting target"; and Wasserstrom's summing-up: "Sometimes merely a very bold man, at other times a brave man, Hemingway was also at times just a virtuoso and at other times a man of genius. Obviously he lacked either taste or equipment for the long haul. I think he knew this and chose therefore to transcend himself."[4]


### iv. Conclusion

Hemingway and Fitzgerald enthusiasts and specialists, as we can see from this review of research and criticism for 1969, plus a few from earlier years, are almost being drowned in a sea of academic ink. Much of the writing, if not most of it, is of a fairly high quality, though some of the work is in the area of esoterica, a little of it is pedantic, and some professorial mountains bring forth scholarly mice. Those who have followed Hemingway's reputation from the time, even before his death in 1961, when many wondered how long he would survive on the American literary scene, cannot but be surprised—and some of us pleased—at the high position he now occupies. The same thing may be said of Fitzgerald, whose climb upward has been longer and slower.

In the case of both of these twentieth century giants of our native fiction, more full-length studies are certain to be written, at home and abroad; and there is no sign that the flood of shorter critiques, evaluations, notes, and reviews will abate—certainly not soon. At the moment it is not likely that much, if any, material "by F. Scott Fitzgerald," surely little work of any substance, will turn up. Of Hemingway, the opposite is true: Philip Young and Charles W. Mann's *The Hemingway Manuscripts: An Inventory* promises that we may expect at least a few short or long imaginative pieces "by Ernest Hemingway" in the near future. No one is predicting its quality; however, we can all be assured that it will be discussed endlessly.

*Wayne State University*

---

4. In *ALS 1968*, p. 111, I misquoted Richard B. Hovey (*Hemingway: The Inward Terrain*, p. 208): "at least half a dozen of the stories will last as long as people read the English language." Apologies are due for the misquotation. Hovey actually wrote, "a generous dozen"—not "half a dozen."

*Part II*

# 9. Literature to 1800

## Richard Beale Davis

Studies and editions of literature before 1800 increased by at least ten percent over 1968. The sorely needed modern reprintings of early authors and collections appeared in considerable numbers. Although there was no complete or authoritative biography of a major figure, several minor writers were satisfactorily delineated at length, and several significant details or elements in the lives of major authors were presented. Criticism and cultural and literary history were overwhelmingly concerned with Puritans and Puritanism, too often repetitious or trivial, but there was some stirring of activity in studies of Southern and Middle Colony writing.

### i. Bibliography, Libraries, and Publishing History

Checklists and bibliographical catalogues appearing during the year were of considerable usefulness. Distinctive among them is Louis D. Rubin, Jr.'s *A Bibliographical Guide to the Study of Southern Literature* (Baton Rouge, La. State Univ. Press), a comprehensive yet selective listing of critical writings on general topics and individual authors by various scholars. Sections on the Colonial Period and the Early National Period and entries under Beverley, Byrd, Davies, Hansford, Jefferson, Lewis, Sandys, Smith, and Tucker are among those offering interesting proof that a number of early Southern writers have received critical attention. Perhaps even more intriguing is J. A. Leo Lemay's appendix listing eighty-six additional writers of the Colonial South and indicating the lack of commentary concerning them, with the obvious and strong suggestion that herein lies a fertile field for investigation. Vital to any study of eighteenth-century religious literature is Leonard J. Trinterud's *A Bibliography of American Presbyterianism During the Colonial Period* (Philadelphia, Presbyterian Historical Society, 1968), a work keyed to Charles Evans's *American Bibliography*, but adding many items not in Evans. Included are authors known for their work in other than religious areas, such as H. H. Brackenridge, William Livingston, David Ramsay, and Hermon Husband. Poems, theological essays, reports, sermons, histories, and religiopolitical polemics are among the entries. Richard Beale Davis's *American Literature Through Bryant* (New York, Appleton-Century-Crofts, Goldentree Bibliographies) is a convenient listing of background, general reference, and individual author material, all together more than two thousand items principally Colonial for the use of graduate student or advanced researcher.

Perhaps most exciting and novel among checklists of the year is the first installment of J. A. Leo Lemay's "A Calendar of American Poetry in the Colonial Newspapers and Magazines and in the Major English Magazines Through 1765" (*PAAS* 79,pt.2:291–392). A clarification of criteria for inclusion, indication that *all* known eighteenth-century poets and many hitherto unknown turn up in periodicals, and a discussion of abbreviations and genres in introductions and notes make this an extremely useful work, already suggesting many possibilities for investigation. The inherent and unavoidable weakness of the calendar must be in attributions of authorship for anonymous or pseudonymous verse. Undoubtedly some of Professor Lemay's fairly bold determinations, often on internal evidence, may prove to be wrong, but his suggestions and method of procedure are generally sound. One may predict that when this census is complete and published in book form it will be one of the most useful tools of colonial scholarship and will accelerate the pace of investigation a great deal. A much narrower field is covered in Jane Donahue's "Colonial Shipwreck Narratives: A Theological Study" (*BBr* 23:101–34), a discussion and "complete" listing of all such narratives of the seventeenth and eighteenth centuries. Included are epistles, sermons, theological tracts, and other forms. This is hardly as "complete" as the compiler suggests, for the relatively rigid criteria set up by Miss Donahue may exclude such narratives as those of Henry Norwood and William Strachey, though both have theological overtones and undertones. And surely there are others that may be included even under the imposed criteria. More generally interesting is Roger E. Stoddard's "A Catalogue of Books and Pamphlets Unrecorded in Oscar Wegelin's *Early American Poetry, 1650–1820*" (*BBr* 23:1–84), a list including hymns, moral verse, orations, voyages, and other form-themes and such interesting writers as H. H. Brackenridge, Samuel Byles, John

Davis, John Fox, David Humphreys, John Leland, and Susanna
Rowson among dozens of others better known as poets. One predicts
that the Rubin and Lemay lists noted above may or could add many
more entries to this valuable supplementary list. Certainly this addendum indicates how outdated Wegelin now is, another evidence of the
enormous recent activity in studies of early literature. Directly related to this literature too is James C. Wheat and Christian F. Brun,
*Maps and Charts Published in America Before 1800: A Bibliography*
(New Haven, Yale Univ. Press), for many items were originally included in the histories and other literary productions of the period,
and others throw light on literary biography and criticism. In several
instances the cartographers were also writers of distinction.

At least two Puritan worthies are represented in checklists. They
are useful for both primary and secondary items: Richard W. Etulain,
"John Cotton: A Checklist of Relevant Materials" (*EAL* 4,i:64–69)
and Mary Jane Elkins, "Edward Taylor: A Checklist" (*EAL* 4,i:56–
63). Related to such catalogues is Malcolm Freiberg's "The Winthrops
and Their Papers" (*PMHS* 80:55–70), a survey of this vital collection
as to contents, members of family contributing, vicissitudes of the
collectors, and the publications from the papers.

In "The New Franklin Texts" (*CEAAN* 2:6–8), J. A. Leo Lemay
complains that the edition of the *Papers of Benjamin Franklin* is not
including many newspaper pieces which may be identified as Franklin's, perhaps because the editors are weak on literary and intellectual
history. Lemay's own weakness is that his evidence of authorship is
principally internal, a by no means always reliable criterion, as he
himself is aware. But the warning that the history-oriented editors
of the papers of Franklin, Jefferson, and Madison, among others, may
omit significant documents because of insufficient investigation of
periodical sources may well be worth these editors' serious consideration. Harrison T. Meserole, in "Notes on Editing Seventeenth-
Century Poetry" (*CEAAN* 2:11–14), offers some judicious advice
springing from his own experience as to sources, contradictions in
external data, attributions of authorship, and the matter of text. In
"Rubrication in American Books of the Eighteenth Century" (*PAAS*
79:29–43) Frederick R. Goff points out interesting examples of red-
ink (in whole or in part) titlepages in early books printed from Boston
to Charleston, indications of artistic aim and product in a number of
distinguished volumes on law, religion, and belles-lettres.

John Melville Jennings (*The Library of the College of William
and Mary in Virginia, 1693–1793*, Charlottesville, Univ. Press of Virginia) traces the history of books in the first century of our second-
oldest college. Despite fires and depredations in time of war, William
and Mary in 1781 had the second-largest university library in English
America or the United States. Fascinating for the intellectual historian is C. Malcolm Watkins's *The Cultural History of Marlborough,
Virginia: An Archaeological and Historical Investigation of the Port
Town for Stafford County and the Plantation of John Mercer. . . .*
(Washington, Smithsonian Institution Press, 1968), a study in depth
of one plantation microcosm, including information on the remains of
an architectural gem among mansions owned by a leading lawyer-
writer of the eighteenth century. Two appendixes, on Mercer's reading and on his library, are based on surviving ledgers and other manuscripts. They reveal tastes and interests almost as broad as William
Byrd's, with a naturally greater emphasis on legal literature but
including belles-lettres ancient and modern, sermons, religious tracts,
and history—all together an impressive list.

### ii. Texts

Formidable indeed is the list of reprintings, some in facsimile with
good introductions, some completely edited and of course reset, of
colonial and early national volumes now quite hard to come by. They
include six volumes by Puritans, three novels, a number of journals
and travels, histories political and natural, and some little-known
plays. In addition there are several new volumes of collected works,
anthologies, and a rare history of early poetry.

Two of the Puritan volumes were not actually written in America
but were a part of New England thinking and were almost universally
present in the region's libraries. One is William Ames's *The Marrow
of Theology*, edited by John D. Eusden, from the 3d Latin edition of
1629 (Boston, Pilgrim Press, 1968). The editor stresses the popularity
and pervasiveness of the thought expressed in this work, declaring it
one of the two most influential books from the time of the Pilgrims
to the American Revolution. Certainly this modern translation is
the clearest exposition and outline of New England theology in existence. Samuel Mather, uncle of Cotton, wrote and printed in Dublin
his *Figures or Types of the Old Testament, Opened and Explained,*

introduction and bibliography by Mason I. Lowance, Jr., and text of the 2d ed., 1705 (New York, Johnson Reprint). The editor suggests that this is the seminal account of "types" and is crucial to an understanding of the tradition of American symbolism, especially to an understanding of Edward Taylor and Increase and Cotton Mather. Both introduction and text (in sermon form) will be basic for students of Puritan literature. Another significant work is the imposing folio *A Compleat Body of Divinity ... by Samuel Willard*, introduction by Edward M. Griffin and text of the 1726 edition (New York, Johnson Reprint). It includes 250 expository lectures. A good facsimile reproduction, the folio presents what Perry Miller called the "summa of New England doctrine," a long commentary on the Westminster Assembly's *Shorter Catechism*. The introduction sets the volume in its proper frame of Boston in the later seventeenth century. Marjorie W. McCune has edited all the extant poems by Samuel, Samuel, Jr., and John Danforth in "The Danforths: Puritan Poets" (*DA* 29: 4498A–99A).

Three other New England writings are less orthodox, either in form or doctrine or subject. Thomas Lechford's *Plain Dealing: or News from England* (1642), introduction by Darrett B. Rutman, and text of 1867 (New York, Johnson Reprint), is an exposition of disillusionment with New World Puritanism by a moderate who arrived in Boston in 1638. Opposed to the Laudians in old England, Lechford soon found he could not stomach New England's extreme congregationalism. Though considered a polemic in its time, and labeled by Thomas Dudley as "hereticall," it will seem to most modern readers dispassionately analytical. It has long been rare, despite several reprintings generations ago. Samuel Sewall's *The Selling of Joseph: A Memorial*, edited by Sidney Kaplan (Amherst, Univ. of Mass. Press), is not quite so rare and is polemical in a quite different way from Lechford's book. This classic little antislavery pamphlet is printed from the only known copy of the 1700 complete text, and includes notes as well as a useful introduction which discusses among other things details of the John Saffin–Sewall controversy on slavery. One hopes that some day the Saffin reply will be printed in its entirety as a matter of record and comparison or contrast. Nathaniel Ward's *The Simple Cobler of Aggawam in America*, edited by P. M. Zall (Lincoln, Univ. of Nebr. Press), is controversial more in style and detail than doctrine, but it is well to have a completely edited text available with explanatory introduction and notes. The text, based on the fourth edition in the Huntington Library, has sprung from a collation of four editions in that institution. A list of textual variants among the four editions is included.

Three Southern Colonial classics were reprinted in facsimile with illuminating introductions, in two instances in unusually legible photo-offset reproduction. William Stith's *The History of the First Discovery and Settlement of Virginia* (1747), introduction by Darrett B. Rutman (New York, Johnson Reprint), has been published for the second time in four years (see *ALS 1965*, p. 113), this time in more legible format and with a more critical introduction, but lacking the useful index and bibliographical note appended to the 1965 printing. Here and in other reprints, incidentally, the Johnson Reprint Corporation must make absolutely clear what edition and issue is being reproduced. John Brickell's *The Natural History of Carolina* (1737), introduction by Carol Urness (New York, Johnson Reprint), though in large part highly derivative, contains an appreciable percentage of original observation and thus will be useful to students of intellectual history. William Strachey's version of Sir Thomas Dale's *Lawes Divine, Morall and Martiall, etc.*, edited by David H. Flaherty (Charlottesville, Univ. Press of Va.), contains a perceptive and comprehensive introduction to a remarkable document of Colonial legal literature. Some eloquent writing, including Strachey's preface and the daily prayer of the Watch, is included. The little book is a fine example of Jacobean prose instigated by and at least in part composed in the Virginia colony. This edition is an accurate resetting in letterpress.

James Adair's *The History of the North American Indians Particularly those Nations adjoining to the Mississippi, East and West Florida, Georgia, South and North Carolina, and Virginia*, introduction by Robert F. Berkhofer, Jr., and text of 1775 (New York, Johnson Reprint), is not only a great descriptive account of the tribes of southern redmen but also a significant sociological and philosophical work remarkably free of moral judgments. The author was a trader who spent most of his time among the aborigines. The purpose avowed in the preface is to give "the Literati proper and good materials for tracing the origin of the American Indians" and to promote the best interests of the colonies and mother country. A handsome facsimile, this is still not as useful an edition as that of Judge Williams of a generation ago, which gave much more background on author and subject. Yet we must welcome the renewed availability of what is probably the most distinguished book written on the Indian during the whole colonial period.

Four rare Southern Colonial documents were edited or reprinted with introductions and notes, and there was a collection of Southern verse. Bibulous statesman-letterwriter-litterateur John Pory's *Proceedings of the General Assembly of Virginia July 30–August 4, 1619* . . . , edited by William J. Van Schreeven and George H. Reese (Jamestown, Va., Jamestown Foundation), has been reproduced in parallel-page facsimile–modern letterpress in handsome format. This legislative record of the first representative assembly of the English New World contains letters, petitions, and laws in beautiful and stately English well worth studying. A monumental work is Philip L. Barbour's *The Jamestown Voyages Under the First Charter, 1606–1609* (2 vols.; Cambridge, Cambridge Univ. Press, Hakluyt Society). The editor gives new and authoritative texts of miscellaneous letters and official papers, and of Smith's *True Relation* and *A Map of Virginia*, among other things, and a thoughtful commentary based on his enormous knowledge of the period and facility in many languages, including the Renaissance Spanish from which he re-translates some of his material. Richard Beale Davis, "Three Poems from Colonial North Carolina" (*NCHR* 46:33–41), published from manuscript or early newspaper text the three earliest known poems of that colony.

Three early novels are of significance for various reasons. Jeremy Belknap's *The Foresters, an American Tale* (1792), edited by Lewis A. Turlish (Gainesville, Fla., SF&R), is one of our earliest fictions to draw on the matter of American Colonial and Revolutionary history. Epistolary in form and whimsical in tone, this delightful satiric allegory of our early history from the beginnings to Washington's administration is well worth reading. The first edition in many years of our first sentimental novel, William H. Brown's *The Power of Sympathy*, edited by William S. Kable, (Columbus, Ohio State Univ. Press), is a textually authoritative printing based on a collation of ten copies and following modern bibliographical practice. The general introduction weighs the evidence for Brown as author, concluding that the probability is strong that he composed the work. The third novel, William Williams's *Mr. Penrose:The Journal of Penrose, Seaman*, edited by David H. Dickason (Bloomington, Ind. Univ.

Press), will prove a delightful surprise to most readers. Though an abbreviated and bowdlerized edition under another title was published early in the nineteenth century, this is the first printing from the manuscript, discovered in Great Britain by the editor. In genre and theme somewhere between Defoe's *Robinson Crusoe* and Melville's *Typee* and *Moby Dick*, this rapid-paced narrative of a castaway among primitive American tribes is historically as well as intrinsically significant, for it was written before 1783 by a painter then living in New York. Accurate natural history and real humor are among its attributes. It is among the claimants for preeminence as the first American novel.

The travel journals, most of them written by European observers or men who lived at most only for a short period in America, are all of some value. Francis Bailey's *Journal of a Tour in Unsettled Parts of North America in 1796 and 1797*, edited by John F. McDermott, (Carbondale, Southern Ill. Univ. Press), is a complete edition of travel notebooks edited from original manuscripts. An intelligent traveler who perhaps had planned to remain in the United States, Bailey is our prime observer among those who traversed the western waters of the late eighteenth century. Arriving at Norfolk, Virginia, Bailey made a grand tour of inland America down the Ohio and Mississippi and return via the Natchez Trace, his account ending abruptly as he reached Knoxville, Tennessee. Good story telling, including detailed description and droll humor, mark this revealing journal. For the years 1783–84 an Italian count left a thinner journal and letters describing his experiences in the eastern states. *Seeing America and Its Great Men: The Journal and Letters of Count Francesco dal Verme* (Charlottesville, Univ. Press of Virginia) has been beautifully translated and edited by Elizabeth Cometti. This is a useful addition, from a new point of view, to the British and European journals of travels after the Revolution. Less interesting, and less well edited, is William Eddis's *Letters from America*, edited by Aubrey C. Land (Cambridge, Mass., Harvard Univ. Press, Belknap Press), a series of comments between 1769 and 1776, during which period Eddis was a Maryland customs official. It is worth noting that Eddis published bits of verse and prose in the *Maryland Gazette* during his stay in America and was a member of Jonathan Boucher's Homony Club. The *Letters* are useful as a firsthand Loyalist account of Maryland during the first year of the Revolution. *George White-field's Journals* (*1737–1741*) *to Which Is Prefixed His "Short Account"* (*1746*) *and "Further Account"* (*1747*), edited by William V. Davis (Gainesville, Fla., SF&R), covers only the evangelist's first two visits to America, but shows both man and mind in the New World's first Great Awakening. Fascinating as cultural, art, and literary historian as well as folklorist is *Lewis Miller: Sketches and Chronicles: The Reflections of a Nineteenth Century Pennsylvania German Folk Artist*, introduction by Donald A. Shelley (York, Pa., Historical Society of York County, 1966), a humorous, picturesque, minutely detailed panorama of rural and small-town Pennsylvania in the late eighteenth and early nineteenth centuries. The drawings are fascinating, but equally so are the English and German bits of verse and prose which explain the water-color illustrations. Virginia, Maryland, New York, and even Europe are also represented in this colorful portfolio of our first national period.

Timothy Dwight received attention in two good editions. *The Major Poems . . . (1752–1817) with a Dissertation on the History, Eloquence, and Poetry of the Bible*, edited by William J. McTaggart and William K. Bottorff (Gainesville, Fla., SF&R), may not add much to the Yale poet's stature, but it gives us a reliable and readily accessible collection of his verse. The critical introduction explains the primary topics for Dwight's theories of verse and his growing critical attitude toward other parts of America. Explicit and implicit in Dwight's *Travels in New England and New York*, edited by Barbara M. Solomon and Patricia M. King (4 vols.; Cambridge, Mass., Harvard Univ. Press, Belknap Press), is the author's regional chauvinism and yet patriotic Americanism. Dwight regarded his well-nigh interminable and frequently dull but always informative record as a defense of his countrymen, as a correction to misguided opinions of foreign observers. Within his narrow geographical (and mental) self-imposed restrictions he gives the first encyclopedic defense of America from many points of view. More comprehensive in most ways than Jefferson's *Notes on the State of Virginia*, to which it should be compared, it is not nearly so interesting or well-written. Beautifully edited, this should stand as the authoritative edition of a useful book. One other Yale poet, Dwight's contemporary Joel Barlow, is now represented by an edited, hitherto unpublished poem. Its structure is based upon mystical signs of the zodiac, and it is concerned with natural religion as Volney saw it: Kenneth R. Ball, "Joel Barlow's 'Canal' and Natural Religion" (*ECS* 2:225–39).

Early drama is well represented in Walter J. Meserve and William R. Reardon's edition of *Satiric Comedies*, vol. 21 of *America's Lost Plays* (Bloomington, Ind. Univ. Press). Four of the five included fall within our period: Governor Hunter's *Androboros* (1714), the anonymous *The Trial of Atticus* (1771), *The Battle of Brooklyn* (1776), and *Darley's Return* (1789). *Androboros* has the distinction of being the first play printed in the present United States. An early critical history of Colonial verse is included in James L. Onderdonk's *History of American Verse* (published 1901; New York, Johnson Reprint), still relevant; and Harrison T. Meserole's fine *Seventeenth-Century American Poetry* (New York, N. Y. Univ. Press) is now available in a new edition in cloth binding.

Finally, among texts should be noted two series volumes. *The Papers of Benjamin Franklin, Volume XIII. January 1, 1776 through December 31, 1766* (New Haven, Yale Univ. Press), edited by Leonard W. Labaree et al., contains more of Franklin's trenchant pamphlets, significant scientific letters, and much correspondence on the printing trade. *The Papers of James Madison, Volume 6. 1 January 1783–30 April 1783*, edited by William T. Hutchinson and William M. E. Rachal (Chicago, Univ. of Chicago Press), has much of political interest but for our purposes is most valuable for the annotated list of books Madison drew up for a future library for Congress.

### *iii.* Biography, Critical and Narrative

This was not a year of notable biographies. Twelve items, only four of them complete volumes, make up the lot. The essays add a few details or sum up some aspect of a single figure, or occasionally provide a capsule of a career.

The only extensive work on a major figure is Robert Douthat Meade's *Patrick Henry, Practical Revolutionary* (Philadelphia, Lippincott), the second and concluding volume of what is considered the standard life. The thesis suggested in the title is thoroughly proved, but the book is unsatisfying as a portrait of Henry's private life and disappointing in that there is no real critical-rhetorical analysis of the subject's oratorical style. The other major biography is of a minor figure, at least literarily speaking. For Edmund and Dorothy Berkeley's *Dr. Alexander Garden of Charles Town* (Chapel Hill, Univ. of N.C. Press) is concerned with an able, indefatigable, and widely known colonial scientist who is somewhat incidentally a literary man and whose principal contributions were to the Royal Society's *Philosophical Transactions* and to books edited or authored by European botanists. As a letter writer Dr. Garden of South Carolina does have some place in literary history, for he gives vivid accounts of the cultural climate of the South at mid-eighteenth century.

Grace Steele Woodward's *Pocahontas* (Norman, Univ. of Okla. Press) is an unassuming, semipopular account of the Indian princess and employs most of the contemporary writing about the myth goddess. More useful is the reprint, with a new introduction by Alexander Cowie, of Karl P. Harrington's *Richard Alsop, "A Hartford Wit"* (Middletown, Conn., Wesleyan Univ. Press), a volume originally published in only 300 copies and long unobtainable. Allen Hatch's *The Byrds of Virginia: An American Dynasty, 1670 to the Present* (New York, Holt, Rinehart, and Winston) devotes more space to William Byrd II than to other illustrious members of the family. It is a well-written account of the master of Westover which should make a good introduction for beginners in Colonial literature, though it is a little marred by misspellings and a few factual errors.

Winton Calhoun's "Jeremiah Dummer: The 'First American'?" (*WMQ* 26:105–08) defends his subject's Americanness by surveying Dummer's actions at home and abroad, partly through and partly outside the recently published diary. Philip E. Diser, in "The Historical Ebenezer Cooke" (*Crit* 10,iii[1968]:48–59), summarizes and analyzes all the factual data he can find, primarily to show how John Barth used the real person, and the poet, in his novel *The Sot-Weed Factor.* All this causes the reader to reevaluate both poem and novel. William G. Belser, Jr.'s "John Smith, Admiral of New England" (*Nassau Rev,* 1,v:1–7) in a relatively popular account surveys Smith's relations with New England from 1614, implying or stating that Smith was more favorable to the northeastern colony, by any account a mistaken assumption.

More personal is Clayton H. Chapman's "Benjamin Colman and Philomela" (*NEQ* 42:214–31), the story of the New Englander's "love affair" in England with Elizabeth Singer of Somersetshire. Equally personal, though in another way, is James A. Sappenfield's

"The Bizarre Death of Daniel Rees and the Continuity of Franklin Criticism" ( *EAL* 4,ii:73–85), which cites an episode early in Franklin's career as marking the beginning of the abuse of his character. Sappenfield concludes that Benjamin's strong personality then and later frequently incited the wrath of his neighbors. Jerry W. Knudson in "The Rage Around Tom Paine: Newspaper Reaction to His Homecoming in 1802" ( *NYHSQ* 53:34–63) fills a gap in Paine biography by tracing the newspaper attacks on the patriot-deist when he returned to America. Finally, a minor figure of the end of our period is reassessed, though here only briefly, in Robert R. Sanderlin, "Alexander Graydon: The Life and Literary Career of an American Patriot" ( *DA* 29:2280A).

### *iv.* Criticism and Literary and Cultural History

This was a prolific though not especially distinguished year for criticism and literary history. More than a dozen books in several languages, two score essays on the Puritans, a respectable number on the major figures of the Revolution and early national period, and a handful on Southern and Middle Colony authors and works make up most of the tally. Many of the essays are mere notes, a number of them dissertation abstracts.

Puritans and Puritanism were conspicuous in quantity, but only rarely in quality. Jean Béranger's *Nathaniel Ward (ca. 1578–1652)* (Bordeaux, Société bordelaise de diffusion de travaux des lettres et sciences humaines) is a thorough, careful, and complete (in that it covers all sides) study of Ward and his writings, with sometimes fresh and original emphases on his *Body of Liberties* and works other than *The Simple Cobler.* Béranger has utilized an enormous amount of critical opinion back to Moses Coit Tyler, though he appears to rely entirely too much on two recent American dissertations for both facts and critical ideas. His full-length study stresses Ward, however, as few if any previously have done, as a significant builder of the city set upon a hill. Concerned with the Puritans but centered on a non-Puritan is Donald F. Connors's *Thomas Morton* (TUSAS 146), a study designed to evaluate Morton's place among New England and American authors. The focus is on the *New English Canaan* and its picture of the enchanted wilderness of New England. The author appears not to take sides, but suggests that there was more than half-truth in Morton's comments on Pilgrim-Puritanism. Connors emphasizes Morton's significance as the beginning of the anti-Puritan tradition in America, which coincided with the beginning of the Puritan-Pilgrim tradition. This is one of the fresher volumes in the TUSAS series, for its subject—man and book—has not before been treated at length in perspective. A third book on a colonial New Englander, *Jonathan Edwards: A Profile*, edited by David Levin (New York, Hill and Wang), is anything but fresh in one sense, for it is a gathering of essays on Edwards beginning with Samuel Hopkins's biography, which is almost a third of the whole. Admittedly a favorable picture, it is hardly a complete or even a balanced one. A curious little volume concerned with New England worthies is Phyllis Franklin's *Show Thyself a Man: A Comparison of Benjamin Franklin and Cotton Mather* (The Hague, Mouton), a study motivated by the belief that Franklin was more and Mather less of a Puritan than has presumably been thought. Half the work is pretty obvious truth, half misleading conclusion because it does not take into consideration elements of environment other than Puritanism as shaping forces in both men.

Perhaps the most ambitious book of the year on the northeastern colonials is Peter N. Carroll's *Puritanism and the Wilderness: The Intellectual Significance of the New England Frontier, 1629–1700* (New York, Columbia Univ. Press), an analysis of Puritan attitude toward the forest and the influence of the wilderness on Puritan social thought. Sermons, letters, tracts, histories, and official records form the basis for the study. Much too much space and emphasis is devoted to the first generation. And the idea of a concept, or a series of concepts, never comes into focus. Hawthorne in *The Scarlet Letter* and Cooper in *The Wept of Wish-ton-Wish* caught artistically more of the spirit of the Puritan attitudes than the historian here does. Chadwick Hansen's *Witchcraft at Salem* (New York, Braziller) was written avowedly "to set the record straight," a rather presumptuous aim, yet in one sense fairly well carried out. The explanation and analysis of the New England frame of mind at the time is good enough, but Hansen fails to explain why similar trials in Maryland, Virginia, and South Carolina did not result in executions, why juries or judges did not convict. One interesting possible implication of what he does say is that the average Southern juror-jurist was better educated and/or better balanced mentally (though he also believed in the *existence*

of witches) than his New England contemporary. The Japanese study
by Naoichi Ōshita, *Pyuritanizumu to Amerika: dentō to dentō e no
hangyaku* [Puritanism and America; tradition and revolt against
tradition] (Tokyo, Nan'undo), is made up of ten essays on phases
of Puritan literature and individuals such as Edwards, Emerson,
Hawthorne, and Melville, much of it with a strong emphasis on
Puritanism as religion. The preface states that the origins and nature
of New England Puritanism need to be explained to the Japanese
student of modern America. Apparently this Japanese scholar, like
most other Asiatics, has a distorted, overmagnified view of the significance of Puritanism in American literature and culture. It is
hardly his fault; he is merely taking our one-sided criticism (at least
up to the last decade) as truth.

    The shorter studies of Colonial New England differ widely in
quality. Norman Grabo's "Puritan Devotion and American Literary
Theory" (*Themes and Directions*, pp. 6–21) demonstrates New
England Colonial belief in the power of art and its beauty in devotion. Grabo's point, which he acknowledges to be tentative, is that
it is possible to talk about early American writing as literature in
a way that makes this writing continuous with later American literary
development. Grabo's "William Bradford: *Of Plymouth Plantation*
(*Landmarks*, pp. 3–19) is perhaps a little too sympathetic, but as is
usual with this scholar's work it is replete with insights and straight-
to-the-mark critical analysis. An interesting juxtaposition is made in
Alfred Habegger, "Preparing the Soul for Christ: The Contrasting
Sermon Forms of John Cotton and Thomas Hooker" (*AL* 41:342–54).
Cotton's sermon is seen as merely a bridge to convey grace to the
elect, Hooker's as an instrument efficacious in itself and thus to be
made as powerful and rhetorical as possible. In other words, Cotton's
is a deliberately plainer style. Three essays on Cotton Mather consider both man and his writings. Mason I. Lowance, Jr., in "Typology
and the New England Way: Cotton Mather and the Exegesis of
Biblical Types" (*EAL* 4,i:15–37), shows the two ways in which
Mather used the Old Testament in the *Magnalia*, his foremost objective being to show that New England was under continuous
Providential guidance. In "Cotton Mather's *Manuductio ad Theo-
logiam*: The 'More Quiet and Hopeful Way'" (*EAL* 4,ii:3–48) Ken-
nerly M. Woody traces Mather's maxims for ministers through various
works up to and including the *Manuductio*. William M. Richardson

("Cotton Mather: The Man and the Myth," *Arl Q* 1,ii[1967–68]:281–94), sees his subject's career as a study in irony, with emphasis on misreadings of the *Diary* and other works as primarily egocentric, and concluding that Mather was a good man by the standards of any time.

Besides the profile noted above, consideration was given Jonathan Edwards in two thoughtful essays. Much of what Roland A. Delattre has to say in "Beauty and Theology: A Reappraisal of Jonathan Edwards" (*Soundings* 51[1968]:60–79) was covered in the same author's book noted in *ALS 1968*, p. 132, though naturally the conclusions as to the nature and modern relevance of Edwards's concept of beauty are more succinctly stated here. George Rupp ("The 'Idealism' of Jonathan Edwards," *HTR* 62:209–26) contends that if one is to put this idealist in proper perspective, one must examine the early essays "Of Being," "The Mind," and "Notes on Natural Science." Thus one may understand Edwards's reconciliation of apparent opposites and his conviction that every being and event is directly dependent upon the Deity.

Ursula Brumm, in "Edward Johnson's *Wonder-Working Providence* and the Puritan Conception of History" (*JA* 14:140–51), gives a fairly good analysis, perhaps overpraising and certainly overemphasizing Puritan expression and experience in the founding of the nation. She explains that Johnson's apparently awkward structure is a frame which provides for religious interpretation and that the key to departure, crossing, and resettling stages of experience is the necessity of suffering. "Deodat Lawson's *Christ's Fidelity* and Hawthorne's 'Young Goodman Brown'" (*EIHC* 104[1968]:349–70), by B. Bernard Cohen, suggests that the little-known 1692 volume dedicated to Judge Hathorne was a major source for the story. Paola Cabibbo ("Mary Rowlandson, prigioniera degli indiani," (*SA* 13 [1967]:7–36) examines the captivity account for realism and symbolic discovery and stresses the importance of the appearance of symbol (especially biblical) as a means of interpretation of a "determined" reality. In "Richard Sadler's Account of the Massachusetts Churches" (*NEQ* 42:411–25), by Richard C. Simmons, we have a study and first printing of an anti-Puritan observer's manuscript highly critical of New England church government. With the books by Lechford and Morton noted above, Sadler's is another proof that not all emigrants to the Massachusetts Bay region saw eye to eye with the Saints. Anecdotal in style, Sadler's account really fails to convince the reader of the deleterious effects of the congregational way. Two brief and more general Puritan studies should be noted. Michael G. Hall, in "Renaissance Science in Puritan New England" (*Aspects of the Renaissance*, pp. 123–36), shows how scientific ideas at first lagged behind some theological and social ideas. Bradstreet, Danforth, and Increase Mather were originally Aristotelian in their science but gradually, like people in old England, brought themselves up to date in scientific developments. Cecelia Tichi ("Thespis and the 'Carnall Hipocrite': A Puritan Motive for Aversion to Drama," *EAL* 4,ii:86–103) argues not very convincingly that the Puritans treated hypocrisy in terms of Thespian figures and saw drama as imagination run wild.

A whole issue of *Early American Literature* devoted to Edward Taylor and a number of other essays again make the Westfield pastor-poet the most popular subject of the year. Alexis T. Gerhart ("A Keen Nose for Taylor's Syntax," *EAL* 4,iii:97–101) emphasizes the necessity for discovery of meaning through syntax, using as example the eighth stanza of "Christ's Reply" in the second of the two sections of *God's Determinations*. Robert D. Arner, in "Edward Taylor's Gaming Imagery: 'Meditation 1.40'" (*EAL* 4,i:38–40), using the same Meditation as did Calvin Israel in his "Barley-breaks" essay, carries on interpretation of multiple meaning in imagery, with the suggestion of sexual innuendos in the gaming figures. Kenneth R. Ball ("Rhetoric in Edward Taylor's *Preparatory Meditations*," *EAL* 4,iii:79–88) stresses the not entirely new idea that Taylor composed his imagery according to the rhetorical rules as given in books he had at his disposal. Kin to this is Sargent Bush, Jr.'s "Paradox, Puritanism, and Taylor's *God's Determinations*" (*EAL* 4,iii:89–96), which sees structure and imagery representative of the essential paradox of man's position in creation. James T. Callow ("Edward Taylor Obeys Saint Paul," *EAL* 4,iii:89–96) analyzes a sub-sequence of the *Meditations* and finds all inspired by the same chapter and verse (Phillipians 2:9), one example that the reader should look behind motto into the Bible for new leads as to the meaning of this and other work. "Edward Taylor and the Tradition of Puritan Typology" (*EAL* 4,iii:27–47), by Thomas M. Davis, suggests examining Taylor's twenty-two extant sermons to ascertain his knowledge of typology. Donald Junkins also looks at the sermons in "Edward Taylor's Creative Process" (*EAL* 4,iii:67–78), asserting that the poems can be understood only by examination of the sermons and making close sermon-to-poem studies. One of the most thoughtful of the essays is Karl Keller's "The Example of Edward Taylor" (*EAL* 4,iii:5–26), in which the author addresses himself to the question why Taylor suppressed his poetry. Among other reasons Keller sees the characteristic American obsession with process rather than product. The answers are not completely satisfactory, for the author admits that Taylor may have intended publication. Charles W. Mignon's "A Principle of Order in Taylor's *Preparatory Meditations*" (*EAL* 4,iii:110–16), George Monteiro's "Taylor's 'Meditation Eight'" (*Expl* 27: item 45), and Gene Russell's "Taylor's 'Upon Wedlock, and Death of Children'" (*Expl* 27: item 71) elucidate method, explicate individual poems, and explain the uses of imagery, among other things.

In India, M. G. Krishamurthi ("Edward Taylor: A Note on the American Literary Tradition," *Indian Essays*, pp. 27–39), prefers "metaphysical" to "baroque" as a descriptive adjective for the Colonial poet's work and analyzes a few poems to support his contention. Though the contention is hardly new, the outside view is refreshing. A German scholar, Fritz W. Schulze ("Strophe, Vers und Reim in Edward Taylors 'Meditations,'" *Literatur und Sprache*, pp. 11–33) gives an interesting study of Taylor's rhyme schemes as integral to his stanza forms, and the use of assonance and other rhetorical sound devices to bind together the whole.

Abstracts of dissertations suggest the variety of work now being done in the Colonial area, ranging from critical lives through critical editions to imagery and a number of other matters. Characteristic are these: Thomas E. Johnston, Jr., "American Puritan Poetic Voices: Essays on Anne Bradstreet, Edward Taylor, Roger Williams, and Philip Pain" (*DA* 29:3141A–42A); Diane M. Darrow, "Thomas Hooker and the Puritan Art of Preaching" (*DA* 29[1968]:1535A); John E. Trimpey, "The Poetry of Four American Puritans: Edward Johnson, Peter Bulkeley II, Nicholas Noyes, and John Danforth" (*DA* 29:3112A); Albert E. Millar, Jr., "Spiritual Autobiography in Selected Writings of Sewall, Edwards, Byrd, Woolman, and Franklin: A Comparison of Technique and Content" (*DA* 29[1968]:1873A–74A); Bonnie L. Strother, "The Imagery in the Sermons of Thomas Shepard" (*DA* 29[1968]:1548A); Cecelia Halbert, "The Art of the Lord's Remembrances: A Study of New England Puritan Histories" (*DA*

29:2211A–12A); Thomas M. Davis, "The Traditions of Puritan Typology" (*DA* 29:3094A); Alan B. Howard, "The Web in the Loom: An Introduction to the Puritan Histories of New England" (*DA* 29:2214A–15A); and Jack D. Wages, "Southern Colonial Elegiac Verse" (*DA* 29:2331A–32A), a promising description of an unknown or neglected Southern form and tradition, and a collection to represent it.

For the eighteenth century, early and late, there was an unusually large number of books and essays. Edwards has already been mentioned. But most scholarly studies of the second Colonial century concerned persons and writings outside New England, though some more general or comprehensive studies included that region.

"The Elegies of Ebenezer Cooke" (*EAL* 4,ii:49–72), by Edward H. Cohen, considers these poems as representative of their genre and as clues to the identity of the author. More might have been said of the poems' relation to a Southern elegiac tradition. Renate Schmidt-von Bardeleben examines another Southern writer in "Das Tagebuch des kolonialen Südens: William Byrd of Westover, *The Secret Diary*" (*Literatur und Sprache*, pp. 34–46), an analysis of the diary and its relation to other writings. Schmidt–von Bardeleben sees in Byrd's longer and better-known works the essential stylistic-content traits of the three known segments of the diary. Byrd emerges from this somewhat loaded comparison with Sewall and Pepys as a finer artist than even his greatest admirers have in general been willing to admit. "Epicurus at Monticello" (*Classical Studies*, pp. 80–87), by Henry C. Montgomery, examines Jefferson's personal philosophy and finds a specific bent toward Epicureanism but not a literal interpretation of the creed.

Bernard W. Sheehan's "Paradise and the Noble Savage in Jeffersonian Thought" (*WMQ* 26:327–59) presents the paradox of the early republican axioms that the noble savage lived in paradise and that paradise might be improved. Again paradoxically, what seemed a condition of perfection laid the basis for a dynamic augmentation of the virtues of the American land and its savage inhabitants. These paradoxes are shown to be present in the thinking of Thomas Jefferson, William Bartram, Daniel Boone, St. Jean de Crèvecoeur, Philip Freneau, and others. This perceptive analysis explains some of the literature of the era, and more of the era's failure with the Indian. That in Logan's Speech Jefferson recognized the failure and the guilt is not here mentioned. Another side of the American paradise is considered in Peter A. Fritzell's "The Wilderness and the Garden: Metaphors of the American Landscape" (*FH* 12[1968]:16–22), a significant study of the use of the terms "paradise" or "garden of Eden" to describe Southern regions, and "wilderness" or "howling wilderness" to characterize New England, and the extrapolations of the terms and thinking behind them into philosophical and religious concepts. Fritzell argues that New England gained much more from the wilderness concept—in unified thinking and acting—than did Virginia with its vaguer paradisiac image. Actually Fritzell shows little knowledge of Southern writing, especially that immediately after 1700 reflecting or representing earlier thought, for he sees no natural adjustments to environment which that writing suggests.

One book and a few essays are directly concerned with writers of the Middle Colonies. C. Webster Wheelock gives us more (see *ALS 1968*, pp. 123–24) of "The Poet Benjamin Prime, 1733–1791" (*AL* 40: 459–71), of the nature of his poetry, and generous samples from it. Howard Miller ("The 'Frown of Heaven' and 'Degenerate America': A Note on the Princeton Presidency," *PULC* 31:38–46) considers the form and significance of funeral sermons on four presidents (including Samuel Davies) who died within the decade of the great war for empire. Miller finds the Presbyterian clergy bewailed in classic examples "of the traditional jeremiad infused with an apocalyptic note of peculiar urgency." The frown of heaven was on society, not the deceased clergy. Ella Cassaigne ("L'anti-esclavagisme de John Woolman," *EA* 21[1968]:142–51) considers the Quaker's writings and concludes that he is one of the four great American champions of antislavery, no very startling proof or conclusion. A longer and more ambitious study is Paul Rosenblatt's *John Woolman* (TUSAS 147). It is not a bad appraisal, but in its choppy sections it insists too much and too frequently that this and that in Woolman is still relevant. It drags in comparisons of various ideas with those of Thoreau and Emerson, Whitman, Cooper, and Dreiser. It is more than possible to suggest Woolman's relevancy for our time, and his influence in his own, without the too obvious intrusion upon the study of the Quaker mind. In his book Edwin Cady (see *ALS 1965*, p. 122) confines such comparisons to a final section; Rosenblatt spoils continuity and emphasis by constant reference to them throughout his book.

Pennsylvanians other than Woolman received attention. Frieder

Busch's "William Bartrams bewegter Stil" (*Literatur und Sprache*, pp. 47–61) presents an analysis of word order, new syntax for words, sentence structure, and sources in rococo and in earlier eighteenth-century models combined with strong originality. Busch confutes contentions that Bartram was humorless or oversentimental. Two dissertations and a note are concerned with Brackenridge. Joseph H. Harkey ("Captain Farrago's Letter on Duelling and Judge John Breckinridge of Kentucky," *WPHM* 52:251–53) demonstrates that the noted Kentuckian in the 1790's appropriated a letter from *Modern Chivalry* as a satirical reply when challenged by a British officer, interesting evidence of the popularity of the book even on the contemporary frontier. Frances H. Kuliasha ("Form and Patterning in *Modern Chivalry* by Hugh Henry Brackenridge," *DA* 29:4494A) and Wendy Martin ("The Chevalier and the Charlatan: A Critical Study of Hugh Henry Brackenridge's *Modern Chivalry*," *DA* 29:2220A) suggest extended examination of structure and characterization in this major work. Carl F. Kaestle, in "The Public Reaction to John Dickinson's *Farmer's Letters*" (*PAAS* 78[1968]:323–53), compares the content of the letters with the myriad statements praising them and then examines the publication history of both letters and response, altogether an impressive record of this political tract's enormous influence. Franklin's best-known work again received attention in Ralph L. Ketcham's "Benjamin Franklin: *Autobiography*" (*Landmarks*, pp. 20–31), a brief critique, seeing the work as a reminder that "personal qualities, the character of a people, must somehow underlie the more conscious aspects of nation-building."

One book, two dissertations, and one brief essay were concerned with Freneau. Philip L. Marsh (*The Works of Philip Freneau: A Critical Study*, Metuchen, N.J., Scarecrow Press, 1968) employs wide knowledge of the Poet of the Revolution to produce what is actually a manual for the student who may later plunge more deeply into Freneau's works. It is mostly descriptive, with generous selections from prose and poetry. Kenneth T. Reed ("Philip Freneau as a Political Satirist," *AN&Q* 7:147–49) gives a useful though hardly original survey of Freneau's sources and techniques as a satirist. Reed apparently did a more extensive study in "Philip Freneau and the Art of Political Satire" (*DA* 30:1571A–72A). Mary A. Weatherspoon's "The Political Activities of Philip Freneau and Washington Irving" (*DA* 29:3591A) also involves Freneau's use of satire. G.

Ferris Cronkhite ("Freneau's 'The House of Night,'" *CLJ* 8:3–19) compares the 1779 and 1786 versions of the poem named and indicates their significance in Freneau's changing philosophical and religious views. Russel B. Nye gives a fine brief evaluation of a Freneau contemporary in "Michel-Guillaume St.Jean de Crèvecoeur: *Letters from an American Farmer*" (*Landmarks*, pp. 32–45), seeing the book as the beginning of several American literary traditions and employing several characteristic American themes. In the same volume as Nye's study is Melvin K. Whiteleather's "*The Federalist*" (pp. 46–55), emphasizing these papers as the great American contribution to the literature of constitutional government and federalism, a classic of Western political thought.

Kenneth Silverman's *Timothy Dwight* (TUSAS 145) is easily one of the best critiques in the series in which it appears. Fair, coolly and rightly critical, Silverman shows Dwight for what he was, a Calvinist Connecticut Yankee so parochial, so limited in perception or lacking in breadth, and so static in mind that he deserves to be relegated to an even lower place than he has held. Charles Brockden Brown was the subject of two dissertations and one brief article. James E. Mulqueen in "The Plea for a Deistic Education in Charles Brockden Brown's *Wieland*" (*BSUF* 10,ii:70–77) offers not too convincing an argument that the novelist meant to say that "if Wieland had been educated to believe in a benevolent and non-interfering deity, he would not have been attracted to the idea of an awful Jehovah." Frederick S. Frank's "Perverse Pilgrimage: The Role of the Gothic in the Works of Charles Brockden Brown, Edgar Allan Poe, and Nathaniel Hawthorne" (*DA* 29[1968]:1866A–67A) has more original implications than the title may indicate. And R. J. Ullmer ("The Quaker Influence in the Novels of Charles Brockden Brown," *DA* 30:1577A–78A) expatiates on a subject which has hitherto only been treated lightly. Robert B. Kettler ("The Eighteenth-Century American Novel: The Beginning of a Fictional Tradition," *DA* 29: 3975A–76A) attempts to prove that the Americanness of our novel was present from the beginning, that Brown is not a radical departure from earlier writers, and that characteristic traits recognized by Fiedler and Chase may be seen in many early works.

Eugene L. Huddleston in two essays, "Depictions of New York in Early American Poetry" (*NYFQ* 24[1968]:275–93) and "Poetical Descriptions of Pennsylvania in the Early National Period" (*PMHB*

93:487–509) presents useful names of authors and places, and modes of description, and the significance of both as evidence of early literary nationalism. Robert E. Spiller ("The American Literary Declaration of Independence," *Literatur und Sprache*, pp. 62–73) sees Emerson's "American Scholar" address as the end and not the beginning of slow development into literary independence, with Freneau, Barlow, Tyler, and C. B. Brown among those marking the gradual evolution. In "Images of the Negro in Early American Fiction" (*MissQ* 22:47–57) Jack B. Moore points out that in the 1790's this image appeared in Northern magazines, was determined by hatred of slavery, and was expressed primarily in sentimental terms. "God and Man in Baptist Hymnals, 1784–1844," by David Singer (*MASJ* 9,ii[1968]:14–25), traces the gradual disintegration of the doctrine of limited atonement and its replacement by concepts of universal atonement—in other words, an evolution from a kind of Calvinism to a form of Arminianism within this period, all of it involved with the evangelical movements of the time. "The Streaks of the Tulip: The Literary Aspects of Eighteenth-Century American Natural Philosophy," by David S. Wilson (*DA* 29:2689A–90A), argues strongly and convincingly for the inclusion of the early literature of science in humane studies. William L. Hedges ("Towards a Theory of American Literature: 1765–1800," *EAL* 4,i:5–14) suggests that before we form a viable theory, we must develop a more comprehensive view of life and society in the late eighteenth century. Hedges sees the literature of the period as largely a public expression with strong affinities to pulpit, courtroom, and legislative assembly. A peculiar pastoralism and millennialism, idyllic and inverted, the latter intertwined with the theme of ruins, are among the elements of the early federal writing which must be considered as we become conscious that the later pervasive "power of blackness" is already present.

Four book-length studies of the eighteenth century conclude this survey of 1969 scholarship. Martin Christadler's *Der amerikanische Essay, 1720–1820* (*BzJA* 25[1968]) is a detailed survey, including suggestions of sources and models in Europe, forms used, principal writers, and theories of purpose and form in the essay. The letter form with its variants occupies a great deal of attention. Neglected is the chief glory of the eighteenth-century essay in American literature, the political, especially Madison's. Though the Southern

*Gazettes* are referred to occasionally, their great feature, the politico-
economic essay—as of Landon Carter, Richard Bland, James Maury,
and a score of others—is barely mentioned or ignored entirely. So
with the essay sermons and tracts of Davies, Cradock, Josiah Smith,
Bacon, and Stith. William J. Free, in *The Columbian Magazine and
American Literary Nationalism* (The Hague, Mouton, 1968), employs one periodical to document the pressures that shaped American literary nationalism. He chose the *Columbian* for several reasons,
primarily because it was the longest-lived, with the largest circulation among the journals of the eighteenth century. He surveys all
features of the journal, including its use of American land, Indian,
and glorious past. The book is disappointing, for there is little new
here. Actually the examples show a "development" as nothing more
than a conflict between English standards and American ideas and
themes, with the gradual ascendancy of the native.

Donald H. Stewart's *The Opposition Press of the Federalist Period* (Albany, State Univ. of N.Y. Press) shows that much of the
credit for Jeffersonian achievements at the polls may be attributed
to the skillful presentation and use of propaganda. In other words,
Stewart's principal object for examination is the kind of essay Christadler largely ignored, though verses and editorials, not merely political essays, are included in the survey. This is a remarkable coverage
of newspapers from New England to Georgia and west to Knoxville,
Tennessee. Useful and apparently thorough, this book is in some
ways a continuation of Philip Davidson's *Propaganda and the American Revolution* and recent studies of the British press during the
Revolution.

Finally one must look at Paul M. Spurlin's *Rousseau in America,
1760–1809* (University, Univ. of Ala. Press), a study that may upset
some popular notions of the French philosopher's influence on the
early American mind. For the fifty-year period indicated in its title,
Spurlin tries to reconstruct the literary fortunes of Rousseau. He
examines book sales of writings, their presence in public and private
libraries, and the individual popularity of certain books, such as *The
New Eloisa* and *The Social Contract*. He concludes that it is obvious that Rousseau had a vogue but little influence on thinking in
eighteenth-century America. For example, he sees little if any effect
of *The Social Contract* on governmental theory. This admittedly se-

lective survey is not as satisfying nor are its conclusions as obvious as the author avers. It is a useful preliminary reconnoiter, but any reader will suspect that direct and indirect influences on education and pastoral ideals, mostly intangibles, are far greater than is here allowed.

*University of Tennessee*

# 10. Nineteenth-Century Fiction

## J. V. Ridgely

Though publicly wounded in its dignity last year by the attacks of Edmund Wilson and others, the MLA Center for Editions of American Authors (CEAA) maintained its stately and measured course in 1969, releasing the first volumes in the Irving, Simms, and Crane editions and adding to the Howells and other collections. It is apparent, however, that some further disenchantment has set in over the need for an editor's applying *all* of its rigorous standards to *all* the works of a relatively minor author in order to obtain its seal of approval. Thus, Lewis Leary, reviewing Simms's previously unreprinted *Voltmeier* (*AL* 42[1970]:100–02), comments: "To patch and therefore mangle, even with textual commentary keyed to page and line, an already mangled text represents clerical good will stretched to an extreme." William Randel, in the same periodical (pp. 109–10), is much more sympathetic toward the editors of the Virginia edition of Crane: "The general student uninitiated in the mysteries of advanced bibliographical methods cannot but be impressed—and grateful that a few scholars have been willing and able to master and use them." But he also enters a cavil: "Some of [Crane's] admirers, however, may question whether 'every known piece of his creative writing and journalism,' to quote from the foreword to Volume I, deserves the meticulous attention required for the CEAA seal." Something further may follow of this fusillade.

Meanwhile, scholarship in the field ranged as usual from the puerile to the perceptive. The relatively elevated reputations of Irving, Cooper, Howells, and Crane have not been successfully challenged; no other aspirant among nineteenth-century fiction writers has yet made it to this modest mountaintop.

### i. General Topics

The contents of four ambitiously conceived books deliver somewhat less than their titles promise; all are focused on the era's major figures, but they do provide commentary on such contemporaries as Cooper, Howells, and Crane. Joel Porte's *The Romance in America* (Middletown, Conn., Wesleyan Univ. Press) derives much of its concept of the romance as genre from the studies of Charles Feidelson, Richard Chase, Leslie Fiedler, and others. Porte's prefatory statement is thus familiar: the rise and growth of our fiction "is dominated by our authors' conscious adherence to a tradition of non-realistic romance sharply at variance with the broadly novelistic mainstream of English writing." "Our authors," however, turn out to be—as the subtitle acknowledges—limited to Cooper, Poe, Hawthorne, Melville, and James. Relevant here is the fifty-page section on Cooper, which draws together under topical rubrics selected themes from the Leatherstocking Tales: e.g., the question of race, the dark and the fair lady and the American Adam, the pictorial element, and the nature of romance as New World epic. On this last topic Porte is particularly provocative; but the chapter as a whole presents too restricted a view of Cooper as romancer. John T. Frederick's *The Darkened Sky: Nineteenth Century American Novelists and Religion* (Notre Dame, Ind., Univ. of Notre Dame Press) is much too limited to justify its sweeping title. Religion here means Christianity, and the only novelists examined at length are Cooper, Hawthorne, Melville, Twain, Howells, and James. Within the limits he has set for himself, though, Frederick presents a useful examination of the range of conflicts of doubt and faith. Jan W. Dietrichson proclaims that he will investigate *The Image of Money in the American Novel of the Gilded Age* (Oslo, Universitetsforlaget; New York, Humanities Press), but he restricts himself almost entirely to Howells and James. The sometimes ambivalent attitudes of both authors toward wealth are well worth the close analyses of content which Dietrichson presents, but many readers will feel that he slights equally important motifs in his tracking of a single theme. Noted here last year in its version as a dissertation, Gordon O. Taylor's *The Passages of Thought: Psychological Representation in the American Novel, 1870–1900* (New York, Oxford Univ. Press) now appears in book version. Taylor's range of authors is broader—from James through Dreiser—and his readings of individual passages are often fresh and penetrating. But this rather short, 172-page study of the ways in which his chosen authors gradually altered techniques in representing "thought" is more a tantalizing introduction than a fully developed investigation of a complex subject. A fifth book of the year is bibliographical rather than critical. Lyle H. Wright has issued a second revised edition of his standard *American Fiction 1774–1850* (San Marino, Calif., Huntington Library), first published in 1939. This reset "Wright I" adds 143 new titles and lists several hundred new editions of previously recorded titles, swelling the total to about 3,500 entries.

The crop of dissertations on general topics recorded this year reveals commendable ambition not always matched by thoroughness of performance. (One should complain, parenthetically, that the summations in *Dissertation Abstracts* are sometimes carelessly prepared, badly printed, and condensed beyond the point of usefulness.) The following are the most relevant studies. In "The American Historical Novel from Cooper to Crane" (*DA* 29:3973A) Harry B. Henderson III undertakes "the search for imaginative structures which are common to both narrative history and the historical novel," drawing on historians like Prescott and Bancroft and novelists like Cooper and Hawthorne. John C. Gerlach's "The Kingdom of God and Nineteenth Century American Fiction" (*DA* 30:1524A–25A) analyzes a number of novels in pursuing the notion that America has often considered itself the chosen nation for the site of a "kingdom of God" or the means of its growth. "Industrial progress and social justice were interpreted as signs of the imminent kingdom," though writers like Melville, Twain, and Howells "were more critical of the role of this messianic pattern in human events." Wayne C. Miller, in "The American Military Novel: A Critical and Social History" (*DA* 30:730A–31A), makes a charge through fiction from Cooper to novels of the nuclear age, evaluating the ways in which these novels reflect (among other things) "changing American attitudes toward war." Assuming that popular literature "offers clues to the culture which produces it and gives it a market," Joan M. Mooney focuses on "The American Detective Story: A Study in Popular Fiction" (*DA* 29:2680A–81A). Her main conclusion is that the genre, though a "frankly escapist literature, is extremely critical in its presentation of society." Joseph L. Cady, Jr., reveals his subject in his comprehensively titled thesis "The Containment of Chaos: The Representation of Poverty in Fiction by Authors Associated with the Dominant Literary Culture in Late Nineteenth Century America" (*DA* 29:4450A–51A). Aware that social observers were implying that "to be poor was equivalent to existing in a state of chaos," conventional and "re-

spectable" fiction writers "reverted to standard strategies to keep
their chaotic subject within safe and fixed limits and to shield their
audience from a disturbing psychological experience."

Two excellent articles on general themes warrant mention. Drawing from a wide range of Southern fiction, Guy A. Cardwell seizes on
a provocative topic in "The Plantation House: An Analogical Image"
(*SLJ* 2,i:3–21). The article resists brief summation, but a central
statement is the author's view that "The plantation house may be at
once image, metaphor, sign, allegorical equation, and symbol." The
article also supplies valuable correction of the notion of William R.
Taylor, in his influential *Cavalier and Yankee* (1961), that novelists
of the Old South used ruined plantation houses "to symbolize the
decline of the tidewater aristocracy." Frederick R. Karl's "Picaresque
and the American Experience" (*YR* 57[1968]:196–212) finds the
peculiarities of the American experience expressed not in the structured novel of the Jamesian tradition but in the picaresque form.
Tracing differences between the European and the American picaro,
Karl asserts that the native type denies the past and other limitations
and believes in American invincibility. But because he denies all
limitations, he cannot know existential despair; he deludes himself
with visions of what might be.

Because eventually they will provide both a commentary on and
a substantial library of the works of many minor authors, several
publishers' projects are mentioned under this rubric. All of the texts
appearing in these series furnish competent critical introductions and
other editorial apparatus; but, except in a few cases of exceptional
interest, they will not be discussed singly. Under the general editorship of C. Hugh Holman and Louis D. Rubin, Jr., the University of
North Carolina Press has issued the first four volumes in its Southern
Literary Classics series. The Steck-Vaughan Company of Austin,
Texas, has produced a substantial pamphlet series on Southwestern
writers and has inaugurated another on Southern figures. The Chandler Publishing Company includes Crane's *Maggie* in its inexpensive
paperback series of facsimile first editions. Garrett Press is offering
two new collections: an American Authors series (the first group
under the direction of Donald Pizer), which is to include facsimile
first editions of the works of about fifty authors; and American Fiction, 1774–1860, under the general editorship of J. V. Ridgely, facsimile reprints of first editions of forty-seven significant but scarce

titles. The Charles E. Merrill Program in American Literature (Columbus, Ohio, Merrill), with Matthew J. Bruccoli and Joseph Katz at its head, will include bibliographical checklists, critical pamphlets, casebooks, and standard editions.

## *ii.* Irving, Cooper, and Their Contemporaries

The long-needed edition of Irving's *Complete Works* begins with the admirably introduced, annotated, and produced *Journals and Notebooks, Volume I. 1803–1806*, edited by Nathalia Wright (Madison, Univ. of Wis. Press). Henry A. Pochmann is the general editor of this edition, which bears the CEAA seal. Haskell S. Springer's "Washington Irving's *Sketch Book*: A Critical Edition" (*DA* 29:3621A) also follows CEAA principles in presenting "a corrected, unmodernized version of *The Sketch Book*, embodying, insofar as the surviving documents permit, Washington Irving's intentions." The edition also includes historical and textual essays. Ben H. McClary's *Washington Irving and the House of Murray: Geoffrey Crayon Charms the British, 1817–1856* (Knoxville, Univ. of Tenn. Press) is a carefully edited and annotated presentation of sixty-eight letters from Irving to John Murray II and his son. The letters, fifty-eight of which are first printed here, not only trace Irving's growing estrangement from his early British publisher but also illuminate British-American literary relationships during the period.

A number of articles this year show a growing respect for Irving as historian and craftsman. In "The Satiric Use of Names in Irving's *History of New York*" (*Names* 16[1968]:380–89), Wayne R. Kime finds both serious onomastic discussion and employment of names for comic ends. By including "burlesque etymologies, insulting sobriquets, and fanciful interpretations of topographical, generic, and family names, Irving utilized his own interest in name study." Martin Roth also calls on the *History* for further elucidation of "Rip Van Winkle." In "The Final Chapter of Knickerbocker's New York" (*MP* 66:248–55) he finds that both history and tale dramatize the same central issue: a mythic struggle between the Yankee and the Dutch as symbols of opposed views of history and culture. Making a case for the improvement of Irving's reputation as a careful historian, Wayne R. Kime, in "Washington Irving's Revision of the *Tonquin* Episode in *Astoria*" (*WAL* 4:51–59), compares an early draft of a crucial incident with the later version. His conclusion is that Irving managed to heighten the drama while remaining true to the information he received. In "Washington Irving: A Grace Note on 'The Pride of the Village'" (*RS* 36[1968]:347–50), George Monteiro attempts with some success to rescue a neglected *Sketch Book* piece from the estimate of "sickly pathos." The narrator's sentiments are in conflict; the maiden is the vessel for the worldly pride of the village but she is also a girl whose early death is to be deplored. Charles G. Zug III suggests that Irving's use of folklore has also been misapprehended. In "The Construction of 'The Devil and Tom Walker': A Study of Washington Irving's Later Use of Folklore" (*NYFQ* 24[1968]:243–60) Zug argues that Irving shifted from the rewriting of whole folktales discovered in his reading to the incorporating of oral sources and varied folk motifs in the creation of new and harmonious forms.

Though the MLA bibliography lists a number of items, the scholarship on Cooper this year is not particularly notable. In "Ossian, Scott and Cooper's Indians" (*JAmS* 3:73–87) Barrie Hayne notes that apologists for the grandiosity of Cooper's Indian speech have sought for sources in Byron or Ossian or have argued for his following of transcriptions of Indian orations, whether faithful or not. Hayne finds that the two views share the truth between them, and he concludes that what Ossian, Scott's Highland romances, and Cooper's Leatherstocking Tales have in common is the elegizing of a past full of glory, the sense of its loss, and the intent of evoking through that loss the existence of a national past. Writers of dissertations on Cooper continue to hunt for new footprints in well-trodden territory. Beverly G. Seaton centers on "James Fenimore Cooper's Historical Novels: A Study of His Practice as Historical Novelist" (*DA* 29:3155A). The historical novel is defined simply as one which has the past as a subject; it has four "problem areas": characterization, plot, style, and theme. Twenty-five of Cooper's novels are then explicated in accordance with these terms. Thomas J. Steele's "Literate and Illiterate Space: The Moral Geography of Cooper's Major American Fiction" (*DA* 29:4507A) argues that since Cooper saw the land as a source of aesthetic and moral value, a character is good or bad depending on whether his relationship to land is suitable to his type. Types are engendered, says Steele, by race (white or nonwhite) and culture (literate or illiterate).

Two contemporaries of Cooper—William Gilmore Simms and Harriet Beecher Stowe—are on the verge of achieving "major minor" status. Simms took the lead with the appearance of *Voltmeier; or The Mountain Men,* Volume I of *The Writings of William Gilmore Simms: The Centennial Edition,* under the editorship of John C. Guilds (Columbia, Univ. of S.C. Press). Another CEAA "approved text," it flaunts the full panoply of contemporary scholarship: an introduction and explanatory notes by Donald Davidson and Mary C. Simms Oliphant and a text established by James Meriwether. Unfortunately, however, the introduction overrates the tale as a work of art; and the editorial effort expended in transferring to book form the original serial publication in 1869 far exceeds the literary worth (and price) of the text. *Voltmeier* is a potpourri of long-outmoded ingredients stirred together by an aging, sick, and harried author; its appearance as the initial item in a series which is to include other scarce Simms items (as well as the apparently inevitable *The Yemassee*) can hardly enhance the author's reputation. Meanwhile, Elmo Howell turns to earlier tales in "The Concept of Character in Simms's Border Romances" (*MissQ* 22:303–12); his conclusion, though, is hardly new: "Simms's achievement in the border novels is to give expression to a people striving towards nationhood." John C. Guilds completes his study of Simms's connection with a prominent periodical in "The 'Lost' Number of the *Southern Literary Gazette*" (*SB* 22:266–73). The most important find in this rediscovered issue is evidence that Simms—as he had said—derived his *Martin Faber* not from F. M. Reynolds's *Miserrimus* but from his own earlier "Confessions of a Murderer." Two foreign studies show a widening of interest in Simms. Francesca C. Gozzini, in "W. G. Simms e *The Yemassee*" (*SA* 13[1967]:101–27), examines and defends Simms's concept of romance as a genre. Simone Vauthier, in a long and ambitious article, deals with the "Légende du Sud: présentation de William Gilmore Simms" (*BFLS* 47:259–90); this is a solid recapitulation and critique of the thesis of Simms as maker of Southern legend. Another foreign article is concerned with a rival of Simms in the use of Southern material: Donnatella A. Badin's "La narrativa di John Pendleton Kennedy" (*SA* 13[1967]:129–68) is a well-informed discussion of Kennedy's major works of fiction.

Mrs. Stowe as creative writer is the concern of Alice C. Crozier's *The Novels of Harriet Beecher Stowe* (New York, Oxford Univ.

Press). The study takes as its point of departure two main features of
her work which can be seen as typifying "what was generally expected and accepted in the fiction of her time." These, Mrs. Crozier
says, were that her novels were historical, in the school of Scott, and
that Byron was a factor of paramount importance, particularly as he
influenced her Byronic heroes. The analyses may make the reader
think again about some of the lesser novels, which are elucidated
with skill; but the book as a whole seems thin, composed without
much reference to the recent revaluations of Mrs. Stowe as a writer.
Cushing Strout's "*Uncle Tom's Cabin* and the Portent of Millennium"
(*YR* 57[1968]:375–85) is an effective rebuttal to James Baldwin's
1949 critique "Everybody's Protest Novel." Strout perceives in *Uncle
Tom's Cabin* that "its confused anxieties and emotional power, as
well as its intellectual limitations, stem not from racial prejudice but
from the ambivalent encounter of the American Protestant imagination with history." The major novel is also the subject of E. Bruce
Kirkham's "Harriet Beecher Stowe and the Genesis, Composition, and
Revision of *Uncle Tom's Cabin*" (*DA* 29:4492A–93A). According to
Kirkham, his most significant conclusion is that she is "more of a
literary craftsman than earlier critics . . . have stated." John R.
Adams's "Harriet Beecher Stowe (1811–1896)" (*ALR* 2:160–64) is
a bibliographical essay which also suggests areas worthy of further
study.

### iii. Local Color, Humor, and Popular Fiction

Critical interest continues to run high in that group of disparate
writers whom we still lazily lump together as local colorists; our
humorists and fabricators of popular fiction lag far behind. Robert
L. Russell's "The Background of the New England Local Color
Movement" (*DA* 29:4468A–69A) examines the formative period
before the Civil War; it seeks sources in humorists like Seba Smith,
in popular writers like Lydia Maria Child, in the pioneer work of
Mrs. Stowe and Rose Terry Cooke, and in the major periodicals of
the 1850's. Susan E. Toth, in "More Than Local Color: A Reappraisal of Rose Terry Cooke, Mary Wilkins Freeman and Alice
Brown" (*DA* 30:1577A), argues that these three New Englanders
deserve to be better known for their general contributions to the development of the short story. Mrs. Freeman is also the subject of a
useful bibliographical essay by Perry D. Westbrook (*ALR* 2:139–

42). Clayton L. Eichelberger is the compiler of "Sarah Orne Jewett (1849–1909): A Critical Bibliography of Secondary Comment" (*ALR* 2:189–262), an invaluable annotated checklist. In the same issue Richard Cary's "The Other Face of Jewett's Coin" (pp. 263–70) discusses the portrait of the artist which emerges from her letters and reveals some of his problems in editing her correspondence. Mary C. Fultz's "The Narrative Art of Sarah Orne Jewett" (*DA* 29:3135A) is the latest of several dissertations making high claims for her artistry.

The South was a particularly stimulating subject this year. Louis D. Rubin, Jr., in *George Washington Cable: The Life and Times of a Southern Heretic* (New York, Pegasus) concentrates on those aspects of Cable which have made him seem peculiarly relevant recently: his work for the cause of the Negro and his "heretical" view of post-bellum Southern society. The book complements the studies of Arlin Turner, Guy Cardwell, and Philip Butcher in offering acute and often fresh analyses of Cable's novels and nonfiction. Cable's stature as social critic is also the concern of Herman P. Sandford's "The Moral Vision of George Washington Cable" (*DA* 30:696A–97A); Sandford cites three moral principles as the foundation of Cable's ethical system: the supernatural authoritarianism of his church, the standard of rationality, and a type of utilitarianism. Cable's fellow writer on Louisiana, Kate Chopin, is the subject of a biography which may as well at once be labeled standard. Per Seyersted's *Kate Chopin: A Critical Biography* (Baton Rouge, La. State Univ. Press) deals with the facts of her life and with her artistry as local colorist and realist and then devotes several chapters to analyses of specific works. The study is made doubly useful by Seyersted's edition of the *Complete Works of Kate Chopin,* issued by the same press; the two-volume collection contains much scarce and some new material. The inevitable revival of critical interest has already begun with Lewis Leary's "Kate Chopin's Other Novel" (*SLJ* 1,i[1968]:60–74). A close reading of *At Fault,* it concludes that in *The Awakening* "a master handles her tools with expert skill in analysis of a single character—nothing is wasted, the focus remains sharp; in *At Fault* she is experimenting, producing rough first designs of what later would be fashioned to art." Finally, Darwin T. Turner's "Daddy Joel Harris and His Old-Time Darkies" (*SLJ* 1,i[1968]:20–41) is a critical gloss on Harris's fictional treatment of the Negro. Turner pointedly summarizes:

Harris "molded actual Negroes into the old-time slaves essential to the romantic myth of a utopian plantation, governed by a kingly and paternal master. All too soon, this Anglo-Saxon myth became more popular than the African tales. . . . Thus, Joel Chandler Harris, the collector of tales became 'Daddy Joe,' the father of a myth."

The man usually credited with initiating the local color movement, Bret Harte, is the subject of one dissertation. Dominic V. O'Brien, in "Bret Harte: A Survey of the Criticism of His Work, 1863–1968" (*DA* 30:1534A), decides that most of the criticism "has been invalid; it is either imitative or uninformed or both"—a surprisingly definitive indictment. D. M. McKeithan fights against a strong current in "Bret Harte's Yuba Bill Meets the Ingenue" (*MTJ* 14,i:1–7), arguing that in Harte's last ten years he produced a few stories which "can compare in quality with his earlier successes." The main body of the article is given to an analysis of "An Ingénue of the Sierras." Charles W. Foster's dissertation is on "The Representation of Negro Dialect in Charles W. Chesnutt's *The Conjure Woman*" (*DA* 29:3596A–97A); he finds it "remarkably accurate." The University of Michigan Press adds to its reissues of Chesnutt's works *The Marrow of Tradition*, with an introduction by Robert M. Farnsworth.

One dissertation deals with frontier humorists; Margaret M. Gooch's "Point of View and the Frontier Spirit in the Old Southwestern Tales of Baldwin, Longstreet, Hooper, and G. W. Harris" (*DA* 29:2261A–62A). Focusing on the technique of point of view, she concludes, "When a gentlemanly teller was prominent, the author's ultimate allegiance was to traditional ideals; when a rustic protagonist commanded the limelight, frontier attitudes wielded significant control."

Writers of popular literature continue to be the preserve chiefly of bibliographers and Ph.D. candidates. A brief bibliographical essay on James Lane Allen is contributed by William K. Bottorff (*ALR* 2:121–24) and a similar one on Helen Hunt Jackson by John R. Byers, Jr. (*ALR* 2:143–48). Raymond C. Phillips, Jr., chooses to examine "F. Marion Crawford: The Theory and Practice of Fiction" (*DA* 29:3619A). Crawford emerges not as a "crass businessman of letters" but as "a romancer intent on coming to grips with the problems and tensions of his age." Another late writer of romances is reassessed in John M. Solensten's "The Fiction of Richard Harding Davis: The Legacy of a Romancer and Defender of Ideality" (*DA*

29:3983A–84A); the legacy is "a colorful total impression of a bois-
terous, restless era by a man who was its living apotheosis and one of
its most popular writers." Bernard Baum's "God of Hosts and Hostess-
es" (*SHR* 3:126–37) discovers unexpected interest in Henry van
Dyke's *The Story of the Other Wise Man* by treating it as a forerunner of our own "confounding of optimistic formulas with faith,
the evasion of existential truth. The lines from Henry van Dyke to
Norman Vincent Peale and Billy Graham are continuous."

### iv. Howells, Realism, and Post–Civil War Fiction

With *William Dean Howells: The Friendly Eye* (New York, Oxford
Univ. Press) Edward Wagenknecht has produced his seventh "psy-
chograph" of an American author within a nine-year span. Like earlier volumes in the series, this is a highly idiosyncratic reading of the
writer's life and works in order to get at his "character and personality." As always, Wagenknecht is informative and stimulating;
but the many sides of Howells have forced him to adopt an odd
organization under the occasionally misleading headings of "Mr.
Twelvemough," "Mr. Dean," "Mr. Papa," "Mr. American," and "Mr.
Homos." For all its expressed warmth of feeling toward its subject,
this remains a curiously detached portrait which never quite allows
us to see very deeply into Howells. The most useful scholarly tool to
appear this year is "A Bibliography of Writing About William Dean
Howells," prepared by James Woodress and Stanley P. Anderson
(*ALR* spec.no.:1–139); the period surveyed is from 1860 to the
present. Note should also be taken of the appearance of another
volume in the Selected Edition of W. D. Howells. This is *The Al-
trurian Romances*, with introduction and notes by Clara and Rudolf
Kirk and a text established by Scott Bennett (Bloomington, Ind.
Univ. Press, 1968).

Several excellent scholarly articles support a generally increasing
awareness of depths in works long ignored. Marion W. Cumpiano's
"The Dark Side of *Their Wedding Journey*" (*AL* 40:472–86) draws
attention to the darker picture of the perils of modern life which
shadow the more pleasant scenes of the honeymoon trip. Similar insights are found by David L. Frazier in his more extensive study,
"*Their Wedding Journey*: Howells' Fictional Craft" (*NEQ* 42:323–
49). Noting that Howells "seems to have intended it as a new kind of

literature involving a mixture of generic modes [travel sketch and novel]," Frazier finds that the book "follows the progress of its couple in a journey which is generally made to be the course of their understanding of the world and of themselves. Its interpretation of their external and internal conditions is the predominant meaning, and the result is essentially an artistic interpretation of life." G. Thomas Tanselle's "The Boston Seasons of Silas Lapham" (*SNNTS* 1,i:60–66) offers the not particularly startling observation that Howells makes seasonal references carry heavy weight in both the structure and meaning of the novel. Jack H. Wilson's "Howells' Use of George Eliot's *Romola* in *April Hopes*" (*PMLA* 84:1620–27) is a thorough study of the character relationship between Tito Melema and Alice Pasmer. The article by Tom H. Towers, "Savagery and Civilization: The Moral Dimensions of Howells's *A Boy's Town*" (*AL* 40:499–509), is an incisive treatment of the growth of "my boy" in the book from a state of "savagery" (innocence and moral ignorance) to the stage of being equipped for a man's responsibilities in the community of civilization. Two other articles are of primarily biographical interest. Richard Cary's "William Dean Howells to Thomas Sergeant Perry" (*CLQ* 7[1968]:157–215) prints for the first time quotations from 123 letters; they relate largely to Howells's own writing and to comments on other writers and miscellaneous subjects. Clara and Rudolf Kirk's "William Dean Howells, George William Curtis, and the 'Haymarket Affair'" (*AL* 40:487–98) is the first publication of parts of an exchange between Howells and Curtis; the quotations clarify the stages in Howells's growing activism in this notorious case.

Dissertations on Howells also mount steadily. Marion W. Cumpiano's "Howells' Bridges: A Study of Literary Techniques in the Early Novels Exemplified by *Their Wedding Journey* and *Indian Summer*" (*DA* 30:1558A–59A) discusses "the dialectic of extremes bridged by a perfect mean." Thus, in *Indian Summer*, "the bridge between the Old World and the New, symbolized by the lovely woman the hero finally marries, is the ideal reconciling of the innocent freedom and moral virtues of the earlier, more natural America with the mellowness of Italian civilization." Harold D. Fox's "William Dean Howells: The Literary Theories in *Criticism and Fiction* and Their Application in the Novels of 1886 and 1887" (*DA* 30:1560A–61A) deals with *Indian Summer, The Minister's Charge,* and *April Hopes* as an expression of the creed of realism developed in the book of essays. David L. Frazier, in "Love and Self-Realization in the Fiction of William Dean Howells" (*DA* 29:4484A–85A), finds that "Ideal self-realization in love is possible only temporarily; it is doomed by the internal and external changes time inevitably brings." James L. Dean's "Howells' Travel Writing: Theory and Practice" (*DA* 29:4481A) concludes that Howells "makes a significant contribution to the field of travel writing, both as critic and artist."

Four issues of *American Literary Realism, 1870–1910* appeared in 1969. One was the special Howells issue, noted above. Volume 2, number 1 contains critical bibliographies of secondary comment on the works of Edgar W. Howe and Joseph Kirkland, together with brief notes on their lives and works. Howe is also the subject of Calder M. Pickett's *Ed Howe: Country Town Philosopher* (Lawrence, Univ. Press of Kan., 1968), a book which is strongest on Howe's association with the *Atchison Globe*. Number 2 contains brief bibliographical essays on nine authors ranging alphabetically from Henry Adams to Harriet Beecher Stowe; an article by Harold H. Kolb, Jr., "In Search of Definition: American Literary Realism and the Clichés" (pp. 165–73) concludes that "while the realists do not achieve or even attempt to achieve absolute objectivity, they do strive for the illusion of objectivity. . . . Fiction is still a puppet show. The difference, largely introduced by the realists, is that there has been a frame and covering built around the fictional stage." Number 3, in addition to the Jewett bibliography listed above, contains four brief papers drawn from the continuing seminar at annual MLA meetings on the nature of realism. These are Sanford E. Marovitz's "*Yekl*: The Ghetto Realism of Abraham Cahan" (pp. 271–73); Harvey M. Sessler's "A Test for Realism in De Forest's *Kate Beaumont*" (pp. 274–76); David E. E. Sloan's "John Hay's *The Bread-Winners* as Literary Realism" (pp. 276–79); and Robert H. Woodward's "Illusion and Moral Ambivalence in *Seth's Brother's Wife*" (pp. 279–82). The debate may not be approaching definitive conclusions, but some easy assumptions have been challenged. Moreover, we are getting provocative analyses, particularly of novels not often surveyed so rigorously.

### v. Stephen Crane

Like Irving and Simms, Crane has won the accolade of an edition approved by the CEAA. The University of Virginia Edition of the

Works of Stephen Crane (Charlottesville, Univ. Press of Va.), under the editorship of Fredson Bowers, presents its first two installments: Volume I, *Bowery Tales*, with an introduction by James B. Colvert; and Volume VII, *Tales of Whilomville*, introduced by J. C. Levenson. Bowers also contributes a general introductory essay on the text and textual notes for each of the tales. A good deal of this is top-drawer Crane and worth such editorial and critical attention; the fact remains, however, that no substantive variants of any significance have been turned up. (A negative finding, of course, is still a service to Crane scholars.) The Virginia edition ultimately is to include "every known piece"; meanwhile stray works are being reprinted elsewhere with surprising frequency. "Stephen Crane: A Portfolio" (*PrS* 43:174–204) contains "San Antonio," a newly discovered article in the *Omaha Daily Bee*; "Apache Crossing," the text of an unfinished story with notes by R. W. Stallman; two critical "Notes on 'The Blue Hotel'" by Robert Narveson and Bernice Slote; and "Stephen Crane in Havana," a biographical sketch by Otto Carmichael first printed in the *Omaha Daily Bee*. A later issue (*PrS* 44:287–96) adds "Two Uncollected Articles": "Filibustering" and "The War Correspondents," initially printed in the *Pittsburgh Leader*.

No new books on Crane were reported this year, but Jean Cazemajou's pamphlet *Stephen Crane* (UMPAW 76) is an authoritative introduction which puts much stress on Crane as a moralist who works through ironic counterpoint. A fair number of articles also display a breadth of scholarship and a depth of insight to which few others among our lesser writers are treated. Three studies are concerned with *Maggie*. Malcolm Bradbury's "Romance and Reality in *Maggie*" (*JAmS* 3:111–21), building a bridge between sociological and literary studies, finds in it "a new world of style, one that leads us away from the familiar linear structures of fiction, from plots humanistic in character. We call it realism or naturalism, but it is realism as a metaphor for the situation of modern man in his way of making and shaping his own awareness." Milne Holton, in "The Sparrow's Fall and the Sparrow's Eye: Crane's *Maggie*" (*SN* 41:115–29) discusses various views of the book as a work of naturalism before summing up: *Maggie* "is about an incapacity of vision, about the fear or ignorance or confusion which brings about that incapacity, about the escapes available in avoiding clear seeing and the consequences of those escapes. *Maggie* is about the fall of a Bowery sparrow, but it is also about the failure of her eye." C. B. Ives brings *Maggie* into an article which also includes comment on *George's Mother, The Red Badge of Courage,* and "The Monster." His "Symmetrical Design in Four of Stephen Crane's Stories" (*BSUF* 10,i:17–26) discovers a meticulous craftsman at work; each of these tales shows a turning point at the mathematical center and the halves are contrasted. Criticism on *The Red Badge of Courage* continues the argument over the extent of Henry Fleming's maturation. In John J. McDermott's reading, "Symbolism and Psychological Realism in *The Red Badge of Courage*" (*NCF* 23[1968]:324–31), Henry at the close of the tale "remains a person of mixed motives and partial insights. But the fundamental thrust of his character has been set: he has discovered and developed within himself a capacity for a detached spirit of self-sacrifice based on an imperfect but nonetheless profound self-knowledge." John W. Rathbun focuses on form in "Structure and Meaning in *The Red Badge of Courage*" (*BSUF* 10,i:8–16); he finds the book made up of four major blocks of action and a coda. When this structure is examined for a pattern of meaning, he argues, it confirms that Henry has matured—but his maturation is based on instinctive behavior rather than on reason or ethical choice.

Joseph X. Brennan ranges across several of Crane's better known works in a penetrating examination of "Stephen Crane and the Limits of Irony" (*Criticism* 11:183–200). He notes that several critics, in discussing Crane as ironist, have "generally taken for granted a clear line of demarcation between the limited viewpoint of the involved character and the cosmic viewpoint of the detached, ironic narrator." His own study, though, says Brennan, makes clear that the narrator is "not in fact content to function only as a detached commentator, but in a variety of ways both fuses the two perspectives into one and directly intrudes his ironic perspective into the very thoughts and words of his characters." Several other articles listed this year are of relatively minor biographical and bibliographical interest.

Two dissertations focus on Crane himself; two others draw him into comparisons with other writers. John H. Sieglen's "The Metonymous World of the Child in Stephen Crane's *Whilomville Stories*" (*DA* 29:4504A) argues that Crane "had in mind unified themes that attack the adult world and use the child world as a microcosm of society." Bernard Weinstein examines "The Journalism of Stephen

Crane: Its History and Significance" (*DA* 30:345A–46A); his contention is that "one may see, through a complete study of his journalism,
how Crane's philosophical views changed." Mark L. Krupnick, in
"Stephen Crane and Edith Wharton: Two Essays in the Literature
of Disinheritance" (*DA* 30:1567A–68A), finds similarities in the ways
their work "reflects a vivid sense of loss—of religious certainty, social
community, cultural standards." Anastasia C. Hoffmann's "Outer and
Inner Perspectives in the Impressionist Novels of Crane, Conrad and
Ford" (*DA* 29:2711A–12A) is a comparative study which includes a
review of Crane's views on impressionism and their effect upon *The
Red Badge of Courage*.

The year's issues of the *Stephen Crane Newsletter* continue an
established pattern: informative brief critical, biographical, and bibliographical notes; minor items on the level of a fan club journal;
and authoritative but often truculent reviews.

### vi. Naturalism and the Late Nineteenth Century

Without directly referring to Charles C. Walcutt's *American Literary
Naturalism: A Divided Stream* (1956), Stanley R. Harrison opens his
"Hamlin Garland and the Double Vision of Naturalism" (*SSF* 6:548–
56) with similar observations: "It is strange that the compelling fascination of literary naturalism resides in its somber tone and its non-
exit circumstance when, in fact, it is excitation of hope and the potential for escape that create the naturalistic vibration." Harrison's
article is largely a summation of his impression of Garland's work in
the 1890's; the conclusion places his achievement high: Garland
"presents the vibrations of hope and despair, naturalism's double
vision of life and death, in possibly the most complex fashion of all."
In the midst of his world of destructive economic and natural forces,
Garland offers three havens of liberation for his prairie characters:
"they find respite and transcendent wonder in the physical beauty
indigenous to the landscape, spiritual satisfaction in their tragic
anger and in their own humanity, and hope in the possibility of
eventual escape." In editing *Hamlin Garland's Diaries* (San Marino,
Calif., Huntington Library) Donald Pizer draws selections from the
forty-three volumes of diaries which Garland kept from 1898 to 1940
and arranges them thematically. As Pizer remarks, the entries are
"neither intimate nor philosophical"; rather, their interest lies "in the

range of his activities as an American man of letters and in the depth of his response to the conditions of his life." Pizer is also the editor of a welcome reprint, *Rose of Dutcher's Coolly* (Lincoln, Univ. of Nebr. Press).

Only two other contemporaries of Garland were studied with any thoroughness this year—Harold Frederic and Frank Norris. Austin Briggs, Jr., in *The Novels of Harold Frederic* (Ithaca, N.Y., Cornell Univ. Press), offers the first book-length study of his fiction. In the face of those critics who see Frederic chiefly as a pioneer realist (and occasionally as a naturalist), Briggs puts emphasis on his "comic" inventiveness. The comments on *The Damnation of Theron Ware* illustrate the thesis; so long as critics treat Frederic primarily as a figure within the realistic movement, the novel "will probably never attract the kind of reader who would most appreciate its fine and subtle ironies, its complex and original treatment of the most American of themes—the ambiguous relationship between innocence and experience." Two articles assess other virtues in Frederic's major novel. Elmer F. Suderman, in *"The Damnation of Theron Ware* as a Criticism of American Religious Thought" (*HLQ* 33:61–75) shows how Frederic transformed and inverted a stock situation in the pietistic novel—"the conversion of a skeptic by the evangelistic prowess of a beautiful young woman." The result in the novel was an incisive criticism of "the premises implicit in the convention." In a lesser study, David Williams ("The Nature of the Damnation of Theron Ware," *MSE* 2:41–48) concludes that "Theron is damned to dream the dream. A part of everyman's damnation (if Theron is Everyman) is his inability to live without the dream." Theron continues, "in spite of his experience, to cling to his illusive world of glory, honor, and the applause of men." The *Frederic Herald* continues in its annual issues to supply its readers with brief biographical, bibliographical and critical comments; a few new letters are printed.

Frank Norris was also the subject of one book, William B. Dillingham's *Frank Norris: Instinct and Art* (Lincoln, Univ. of Nebr. Press). As a general introduction it is quite adequate, but it is comparatively short (179 pages) and lacks the scope and depth of other recent work on Norris.

One other late-nineteenth-century writer was the subject of a dissertation. John R. Bovee's "Ignatius Donnelly as a Man of Letters"

(*DA* 29:3126A) sees Donnelly's literary career as largely an extension of his political activities. Bovee concludes that, while he had real literary ability, "his books will be mostly read for their presentation of fascinating ideas; ideas which are often well ahead of their time." At least one reviewer could wish, in conclusion, that this last phrase were applicable to more of the works of scholarship on nineteenth-century fiction surveyed this year.

*Columbia University*

# 11. Poe and Nineteenth-Century Poetry

*Patrick F. Quinn*

The title of this chapter implies that there will be some parity between the two areas of its subject matter, even though "nineteenth-
century poetry" is to be understood as not including the work of
Whitman and Dickinson. But the disparity is even more pronounced
this year than it was last. The chapter is, perforce, almost entirely
concerned with the work of Poe. To judge by the published results in 1969, interest in Bryant, Whittier, Longfellow, Lowell, and
Holmes seems far from lively; nor are writers of dissertations giving
them much attention. On the other hand the work of Poe remains
as attractive as ever. His fiction continues to evoke most discussion.
But *Eureka* is more and more being thought of as perhaps the primal
Poe text, indispensable to a comprehension of both his imaginative
and critical writings.

## i. Poe

*a.* **Bibliography.** The January number of the *Poe Newsletter* is concerned with bibliographical matters. G. Thomas Tanselle, after an
authoritative review of "The State of Poe Bibliography" (2:1–3),
concludes that insofar as *secondary* bibliography is concerned the
situation is good and promises to improve, but that we are no better
off now than we were thirty-five years ago, when the expert opinion
was: "There is a very pressing need for a definitive bibliography of
Poe." How good the secondary bibliography situation is may be seen
in Richard P. Benton's "Edgar Allan Poe: Current Bibliography"
(2:4–12). Each item in this long list is commented on by Benton.
The same helpful practice is employed by Robert L. Marrs in his
"Fugitive Poe References: A Bibliography" (2:12–18). This is something of a bibliographical bonus, consisting mainly of "brief items

buried in longer works under different headings," but screened to
include only items of some significance. Also in this issue are Hensley
C. Woodbridge's bibliographical account of Poe's fame in South
America (2:18–19) and Claude Richard's critique of some instances
of recent French work on Poe (2:20–23).

J. Albert Robbins's *Merrill Checklist of Edgar Allan Poe* (Columbus, Ohio, Merrill) catalogues Poe's major book publications, old and
new editions of his writings, and the important biographies and memoirs; but it is chiefly a selective inventory of scholarship and criticism
having to do with Poe's more memorable poems and critical essays,
forty-five of his stories, and *Eureka*. The list is up to date, with several 1969 items mentioned. Inevitably, though, what with the attention now being paid to Poe, some revisions are already in order. This
handbook would be made more useful if there were a few blank
pages in it for adding supplementary entries.

In Louis Broussard's *The Measure of Poe* (Norman, Univ. of
Okla. Press) disproportionate space is given to a bibliography which
"presumes to include all the books written about Poe, in whole or
in part, since his death in 1849, and all the periodical essays published since 1925." Is such all-inclusiveness necessarily of value?
Despite its length the Broussard bibliography omits a number of
important items, and because of its length it includes many unimportant ones.

Mainly of bibliographical interest is the dissertation of Esther F.
Hyneman, "The Contemporaneous Reputation of Edgar Allan Poe
with Annotated Bibliography of Poe Criticism: 1827–1967" (*DA*
30:686A). One conclusion reached is that though Poe had some
powerful professional enemies, especially George Gaylord Clark,
who kept his work from being widely noticed, he was in his lifetime
better known as a creative writer than has usually been assumed.

***b*. Texts.**    In a bibliographical note at the end of his *Edgar Allan
Poe* (1965) Geoffrey Rans remarked about editions: "Those who will
later enjoy the fruit of Mabbott's labours are to be envied." His death
in 1968 prevented Thomas Ollive Mabbott from bringing his labors
to the fruition that would have been represented by the appearance
of his *Collected Works of Edgar Allan Poe*. Of the volumes projected
Mabbott was able to give the finishing touches only to Volume I,
*Poems* (Cambridge, Mass., Harvard Univ. Press, Belknap Press).

But the indications are that his editorial work on two other volumes, of *Tales and Sketches*, was well along and that they will in time be published. What Mabbott had in mind was, in his word, an "unabridged" edition. The volume of *Poems* is just that. In a comment on this matter elsewhere (*SLJ* 2:114–15) I called Mabbott's work a model of editorial practice. I withdraw that cliché. In its commitment to plenitude Mabbott's editing is *sui generis*. He did choose to be selective about the examples of "purely aesthetic criticism" to be included in his notes. But otherwise the edition seems to have everything, and in abundance. Usual matters, like the background, publishing history, and sources of each poem are of course discussed. It is the numerous extras that are so unexpected: a listing of the serious rhymes occurring in Poe's prose, an appendix dealing with verses written by Poe's relatives, a biographical essay, an account of a nonextant Poe poem, and what not. This edition of the *Poems*, reflecting the devotion and work of a lifetime, is a kind of monstrous cabinet in which one could rummage almost indefinitely.

A new arrival in the Merrill series of Standard Editions is *Tales* and *The Raven and Other Poems* (Columbus, Ohio, Merrill). The text in each case is a facsimile of the first impression, first edition, published by Wiley and Putnam in 1845. It is interesting to see how Poe's pages looked to those who were reading them in this format in that year, but otherwise the rationale for this republication is not obvious. The introduction by Jay B. Hubbell moves along conventional textbook lines.

***c.* Biography.**    Four articles of varying degrees of pertinence to the biography of Poe appeared in 1969. Most peripheral is Alvin H. Rosenfeld's "The Poe-Chivers Controversy" (*BBr* 23:89–93), in which a footnote is added, via a newly discovered Chivers letter, to the record of the uneasy friendship that existed between the two men. Sidney P. Moss in "Duyckinck Defends Mr. Poe Against New York's Penny-a-Liners" (*Studies in American Literature*, pp. 74–81) brings to light a brief article by Evert Duyckinck that appeared unsigned in the *Home Journal* of 9 January 1847. At this point in his life Poe's psychological and professional fortunes were probably at their lowest ebb. But at this point, too, he heard rumors about his increasing fame in France, and he described this development to Duyckinck, who took the hint and wrote a perceptive appraisal of Poe, one theme of which is that "our most neglected and best [*sic*] abused authors are generally our best authors." Poe's relationship to the *Broadway Journal* and its founding editor, C. F. Briggs, is the subject of an absorbing account by Heyward Ehrlich, "The *Broadway Journal* (1): Briggs's Dilemma and Poe's Strategy" (*BNYPL* 73:74–93). How did Poe come to be full editor and half-owner of a magazine he was not much interested in? And why did he? The explanation involves many wheels within wheels, but what chiefly seems to have motivated Poe was the possibility of using the *Broadway Journal* as a tool in promoting his two dominant interests: acquiring a magazine of his own and arranging, with Wiley and Putnam, for book publication of his tales and poems. Also of interest is the associated article by Bette S. Weidman, "The *Broadway Journal* (2): A Casualty of Abolition Politics" (*BNYPL* 73:94–113). The Poe-Briggs relationship is succinctly treated, but the article is mostly about the kind of paper Briggs wanted the *Journal* to be and about the way in which Abolitionist hostility, more than financial difficulties, forced it to go under.

*d.* **General studies.**    An English scholar, Michael Allen, prefaces his study of *Poe and the British Magazine Tradition* (New York, Oxford Univ. Press) by distinguishing between the two main lines that commentators on Poe have followed and defining his own stand, different from both. On the one side there is the Baudelaire–Hervey Allen orientation, in which Poe is seen as a great writer who was relatively independent of his place and time. On the other side are those who, while agreeing about Poe's importance, insist on his American roots and the American reality in which he did his professional work as a journalist. A. H. Quinn's biography is the monumental presentation of this view. In Allen's estimation, Poe's greatness is less on the order of Goethe's than of Bulwer's or De Quincey's, and his work as a writer can be most clearly defined when seen in the context of his awareness of and relationship to such British periodicals as *Blackwood's* and the *New Monthly*. It does not at first seem an especially original idea or one that need be dealt with at book length. But Allen shows how an apparently narrow topic can be opened into a widely illuminating discussion if its full range of implications can be discerned. His general conclusion is that Poe in his own distinctive way followed a number of the conventions of contemporary British journalism. Allen suggests, however, that in doing this Poe fell more and more out of step with American popular culture. The "American-ist" commentators have argued that Poe, a hard-working journalist, knew what the reading public wanted and wrote his fiction accordingly. A major theme of Allen's book is that this view should be revised.

Something over one-third of Broussard's *The Measure of Poe* consists of bibliography, on which comment has been made. Similar inefficient use of space is evident in Part I of the book, "The Critical Estimate of Poe." This is mostly a routine survey of various opinions, from Emerson and Griswold to Eliot and Tate. The point the author is interested in making is that there has been no steady growth in critical understanding and appreciation of Poe's work. The point is made, but not with much dispatch. Meantime, clarification of what might be meant by "the measure of Poe" is delayed until Part II. Here Broussard attempts to see Poe's work "whole," his thesis being that it is the expression of a unified philosophy the final word of which is *Eureka.* "Before *Eureka,*" he writes, "the emphasis in the poetry and the best fiction is all on decay, disintegration, death. . . . The longer Poe lived, the more experience intensified his impression of life as a process of loss and decomposition." But in the end he resolved his despair "into the romantic conclusion which is *Eureka.*" In that work disintegration, dissolution, and death are seen positively, as phases in a process that culminates in a kind of apotheosis. *Eureka* was indeed Poe's final word; but did it evolve from Poe's earlier thinking or was it, in sudden reversal, a last-gasp effort at affirmation? Poe's measure is not adequately taken if this question is left hanging.

In a long chapter, "The Death of the Present," in John F. Lynen's *The Design of the Present: Essays on Time and Form in American Literature* (New Haven, Yale Univ. Press, pp. 205–271), this question is faced and decisively answered. Lynen's theory is that Poe was preoccupied in all his work with one universal process, the movement toward unity. *Eureka* happens to be the document which expresses this preoccupation most fully and most emphatically, but evidence of it abounds elsewhere in Poe's writings. Lynen gives special stress to *Eureka* and its implications by way of showing "that what readers consider perverse, grotesque, or compulsively destructive in Poe's poems and tales has its source not in the phantasies of a diseased mind but in a metaphysical system reasoned with great subtlety and precision" (p. 223). This last phrase is close to the "unified philosophy of thought" which Broussard is concerned with in his book, and close to the "singularly self-consistent vision" which Joseph J. Moldenhauer examined in an important article (see *ALS 1968*, pp. 159–60). Others also have put a similarly heavy accent on *Eureka*. What distinguishes Lynen's treatment is the fecundity of its insights, not bobbing up here and there as occasional *aperçus* but sustained and expanded so as to constitute almost his entire discussion.

For example, on Poe's use of the motif of destructiveness Lynen makes this comment. It "tends to seem even more irrational than the poet intended. One is much less frightened by the obvious terrors . . . and far less moved by the proclaimed sorrows . . . than by the odd angle of vision from which they are seen. The typical qualities of Poe's horror are sickliness, not pain; lethargy, not violence; and stupefaction, not grief" (pp. 207–08). This is an acute observation, valuable per se. But instead of occurring as merely an isolated insight it becomes the starting point for an extended analysis of Poe's intensively paradoxical procedure and outlook. Opposites do not cancel each other out. The effort to live is a movement toward self-destruction, and what might be called a death wish is in its way a striving for life. Lynen concludes:

> For Poe the final catastrophe [as described in *Eureka*] is implicit in all experience: the more an experience is understood, the more closely it is seen in relation to universal history, the more, in consequence, emotion crystallizes into the terror of death, and the more the percipient's view approximates a vision of annihilation. This movement of mind is the essential drama Poe's poems and tales reenact [p. 222].

The rest of the chapter brings this thesis to bear on a number of poems and tales, especially "The City in the Sea," "The Raven," "The Fall of the House of Usher," and "The Gold Bug." Occasionally in these commentaries Lynen seems as obsessed as he says Poe was with "the movement toward unity." He crams everything under that rubric, asserting at one point that in Poe's conception of things no object, and therefore no image, "can avoid being a symbol . . . for to be mentioned in the poem an object must be known to consciousness, and since awareness of it relates it to other objects, it is already representative of things beyond itself and already united in some degree to them." This seems strained. But an occasional extravagance does not diminish the brilliance of Lynen's commentaries.

In working out his own definition of what Poe was doing Lynen explains his reasons for disagreeing with other interpreters, notably Wilbur, who find psychological allegories in the stories and poems. This orientation, recommended long ago by John M. Daniel in this country and by Baudelaire in France, is given fresh statement by Joel Porte in the Poe chapter of his book, *The Romance in America* (Middletown, Conn., Wesleyan Univ. Press, pp. 53–94). Not annihilating unity but something no less mysterious, the secret soul of man—this, according to Porte, was Poe's lifelong obsession. Thus what Roderick Usher apprehended and what the visitor to his house refused to see was "the realm of the submerged—the underside of human consciousness," and specifically its illicit sexual component. A similar approach is made to "Ligeia," but the guidance here is less reliable. In his reading of what he calls a dark, erotic fantasy Porte harps on a word Poe uses only once to describe Ligeia, *voluptuous*; and he ignores the possible significance of both her name and the detail Poe gave maximum stress to, her eyes. With apparently a straight face he responds to "The Conqueror Worm" as if it were a Women's Lib manifesto: "From Ligeia's point of view, the play is the tragedy 'Woman' and its hero the conquering male organ." On "Berenice," however, we are given a persuasive as well as provocative commentary. I know of none better, although, to be sure, discussion of this story is in rather short supply. *Arthur Gordon Pym* is a work that *has* been a frequent subject for exegesis, but Porte's pages on this subject are probably his best. To mention one detail: I had never imagined that Poe's boring account of South Pacific rookeries in chapter 14 could be seen as thematically significant, but I see this possibility now.

John Seelye comments on some aspects of Poe's fiction, and, more generally, on his career and intellectual milieu, in "Edgar Allan Poe: *Tales of the Grotesque and Arabesque*" (*Landmarks*, pp. 101–10). With a fair amount of ground to cover in a restricted space, Seelye's essay is somewhat superficial, but within its limits quite professional: a poetic essay, a flourish of impressions and insights, colorfully written. "Poe's universe" (for instance) "could have been bounded by a nutshell were it not for his bad dreams, whose whirling spirals of terror provided the only reality he could depend upon" (p. 110). Seelye points out that for Poe's literary contemporaries space connoted expansiveness, breadth, infinity. Poe responded oppositely, as evidenced by the ocean he presents in "MS. Found in a Bottle": a gigantic helix, leading to a maelstrom. In *Eureka* he tried to come to terms with the concept of pure space, and in that work—built on the pairings of attraction and repulsion, the one and the many, matter and spirit, body and soul—Seelye finds the basic clue to Poe's outlook and mode of expressing it: the rule of two. Retroactively, *Eureka* illuminates, among other tales, "William Wilson": "The reuniting of the pairs, body and soul, matter and spirit, result in annihilation for both, for duality is but oneness exemplified and oneness is death. . . . Only by keeping the pairs diffused can life go on. Togetherness is annihilation" (p. 107).

The fear of inevitable annihilation, which is implicit in the stories and explicit in *Eureka*, and the lack of a moral center are the two symptoms by which Allen Tate diagnosed the peculiar modernity of Poe's work. Basically the same metaphysical despair and moral vacuity characterize the hollow men of T. S. Eliot. This is the theme examined by Victor Strandberg in "Poe's Hollow Men" ( *UR* 35:203–12). A number of stories, especially those involving the motif of perverseness, are discussed from this point of view. "It is typical of Poe's own perversity," Strandberg writes, "that, unlike Eliot or Hawthorne, he was interested only in the psychological, not the moral situation of his protagonist." Of all his protagonists those who ring hollowest are William Wilson and the narrator in "The Man of the Crowd." A secondary theme of this essay is the relationship between Poe and Eliot, a matter also alluded to by Broussard and Lynen. Strandberg, who seems a bit cross with Eliot, adopts this perspective: "In his core of serious writing, Poe's intellect was no less developed than Eliot's own, no less mature, consistent, and skeptical . . . concerning the large and permanent issues of human nature and man's fate."

Poe's treatment of those issues is examined from the point of view of Christian orthodoxy by Jean S. Stromberg in "The Relationship of Christian Concepts to Poe's 'Grotesque' Tales" ( *GorR* 11[1968]: 144–58). As might be expected, the evidence shows that Poe was well aware of the traditions of the Christian faith, and, giving them his own special inflection, made use of them in his tales. The argument is more interesting when the author seeks to show how by "rejecting the Son," ignoring the significance of the Incarnation, Poe's vision necessarily focused on the dehumanization of man. But if one adopts existentialist sympathies, Poe's vision can be interpreted as affirmative of human power, or at least of the strength of the human reason and will. This is the thesis of J. E. Miranda in "Edgar Allan Poe o la existencia amenazada" (*CHA* 76[1968]:775–80). In a phrase that translates poorly Baudelaire called Poe *un écrivain des nerfs*. Miranda would agree, if it be understood that it is not nervous despair as such but triumph over it that interested Poe. The discussion would be more substantial if more attention had been paid to specific texts. Miranda comments too briefly on too few stories and then turns to survey "the lineage of Poe," other American writers—including Willa Cather and especially Ray Bradbury—who have dealt with the theme of "threatened existence." The title of another article in Spanish, Juan-Eduardo Cirlot's "El pensamiento d'Edgar Poe" (*PSA* 52:239–44), promises a good deal more than is in fact given. It is not Poe's thought that is dealt with but only one aspect of it, Poe's fascination with death, and the treatment this gets is tantalizingly diffuse and subjective.

It is a relief, then, to turn to so precise and thoughtful an article as Doris V. Falk's "Poe and the Power of Animal Magnetism" (*PMLA* 84:536–46). We tend to be vague about what was actually meant by the cluster of dated terms, mesmerism, hypnosis, animal magnetism. It is useful to be instructed about how those terms were used and to learn in particular of the significance that the concept of animal magnetism had for Poe. The stories in which this concept is put to use—"Valdemar," "Ragged Mountains," "Mesmeric Revelation"—are not intrinsically of interest as examples of Poe's fiction; but they are indispensable in investigating the continuities that exist in Poe's work as a whole. Although hypotheses about it differ, there does seem to be some figure in the carpet. This article, which might have had a narrowly antiquarian focus, is a contribution to the reading of that figure.

The legend that Poe was a dope addict is now, one trusts, on its last legs. It is almost toppled over—but not quite—in Alethea Hayter's chapter on Poe (pp. 132–50) in her *Opium and the Romantic Imagination* (Berkeley, Univ. of Calif. Press, 1968). There is, she says, only slight and ambiguous evidence that Poe was addicted to opium.

He certainly was not victimized by the drug, as were Coleridge, De Quincey, and Francis Thompson, but he may well have been an occasional opium taker or laudanum drinker. On the other hand, Baudelaire and Thompson, both familiar with the effects of the drug, saw Poe's world as, in Thompson's phrase, "the world of an opium-dream." And although Miss Hayter doubts that recognizable opium-inspired patterns can be discerned in imaginative literature, she thinks it likely that Poe's halls and chambers—long and lofty, and yet claustrophobic—come out of an opium world.

*e.* **Fiction.**   An important essay that should have been noticed before now is Donald B. Stauffer's "The Two Styles of Poe's 'Ms. Found in a Bottle'" (*Style* 2[1967]:107–20). Stauffer calls the two styles "plausible" and "arabesque," the one dominant at the beginning of the story, when an air of authenticity is evoked, and the other at the end, when the effect sought is that of heightened emotion. Stauffer grants that there may be some satirical elements in the story, but what he emphasizes is its imaginative dimension, its rendering of a voyage of the mind. That this is the right emphasis is borne out by his analysis of the story's structure and imagery, as well as style.

A story similar in some ways but ending in triumph rather than in apparent disintegration and oblivion is the Maelström story. Margaret J. Yonce examines it in "The Spiritual Descent into the Maelström: A Debt to 'The Rime of the Ancient Mariner'" (*PN* 2:26–29). For some reason, literary debts, so called, do not usually lend themselves to interesting treatment. Here is an exception. Similarities between Coleridge's poem and Poe's story are not immediately obvious, and so in following this discussion one tends to keep withholding assent. But the evidence adduced—thematic and imagistic parallels—makes it difficult to dismiss this critic's contention that the sea journeys in poem and story are archetypal voyages both, and that the experience of spiritual transcendence is what the two authors are writing about.

Two new articles, of unequal merit, can be added to the lengthening list of *Pym* studies. Of less interest is Peter J. Sheehan's "Dirk Peters: A New Look at Poe's *Pym*" (*LauR* 9,ii:60–67). The theory here is that the story is a kind of allegory about the growth of man's consciousness. Pym and Peters are parts of a whole (as Pym and Augustus were earlier in the story). Pym may be seen as the imaginative faculty, the creative force; Peters is man's rational side, his conscience. Intellect is shared by both. These distinctions seem overly programmatic. A reading of the story that shows greater literary sophistication is that of Richard A. Levine in "The Downard Journey of Purgation: Notes on an Imagistic Leitmotif in *The Narrative of Arthur Gordon Pym*" (*PN* 2:29–31). Levine sees as the story's main-spring a tension between the rational and the irrational, between the conscious and the unconscious. What the *Narrative* is symbolically about is man's journey of purgation. This is not very different from Sheehan's theory, but Levine's exposition is more expert. He brings out in considerable detail an aspect of the story previously over-looked, the pervasive imagery of above-and-below, as above and be-low the waterline, ground level, the equator, and so on. Also lending support to this low-keyed Jungian reading is an imagistic pattern of light and dark.

In Kathryn M. Harris's brief note "Ironic Revenge in Poe's 'Cask of Amontillado'" (*SSF* 6:333–35) the suggestion is made that the story's central conflict is one between Catholicism and Freemasonry. It is not an implausible idea, but one would like the inquiry to take in some supplementary considerations. Is it likely that Poe would make the Catholic side (Montresor) victorious? In a more searching examination, "Poe's 'Cask of Amontillado': A Tale of Effect" (*JA* 13[1968]:134–42), John Freehafer considers and rejects the sugges-tion that the long-standing insult resented by Montresor was For-tunato's Freemasonry. Some other hypotheses about the main drift of the story are also weighed. What Freehafer stresses is its irony, exemplified in numerous details, and, above all, its success in em-bodying a single, preconceived effect. But as defined, the effect hardly seems single: "the ultimate horror story of a perfect crime of revenge, in which the revenger enjoys the mastery and impunity of the god-dess Nemesis and demands admiration for the artistry and sangfroid with which he has sacrificed his victim."

There seems to be increasing agreement that beneath its overt interest as a horror tale in the Gothic tradition there is an under-current of serious meaning in "The Pit and the Pendulum." In James Lundquist's article "The Moral of Averted Descent: The Failure of Sanity in 'The Pit and the Pendulum'" (*PN* 2:25–26) the story is read as a Kafka-esque parable: "The anonymous hero condemned for an unknown, or at least unstated, crime by a merciless Inquisition apparently represents mankind condemned by a vindictive power for an almost forgotten sin."

One of Poe's more unreliable narrators is a mild way of describing the madman who tells the story of "The Tell-Tale Heart." He is a victim, probably, of paranoid schizophrenia, one symptom of which is (as Poe understood the matter) the phenomenon of hyperacute perception. Above all was this man's hearing acute, and what he heard after he had buried his victim was the sound made by the "lesser," as distinguished from the "greater," death-watch. Such are the essentials in John E. Reilly's "The Lesser Death-Watch and 'The Tell-Tale Heart'" (*ATQ* 2:3–9). This may seem rather prosaic, and indeed there is in the article too full a display of entomological lore. But Reilly moves on to more imaginative levels and interprets the sound of the insect as a metaphor of human mortality and the story as a whole as registering the Romantic complaint against time.

It is the opinion of G. R. Thompson that "the hoaxer, the puzzle-solver, the parodist, and the ironist comprise the quintessence of Poe —especially in his most flawed works." One such work is examined from this point of view in Thompson's "Is Poe's 'A Tale of the Ragged Mountains' a Hoax?" (*SSF* 6:454–60). Another story that more loudly calls for this kind of reading is the one discussed by Gerald E. Gerber in "Poe's Odd Angel" (*NCF* 23[1968]:88–93). His basic finding is that "the narrator's nightmarish dream of accidents and oddities . . . burlesques the spirit of reform." Claude Richard, who specializes in this side of Poe, disagrees with the Gerber interpretation. For him the key to the satire is found in the list of books mentioned at the beginning of the story. He develops this hunch in "Arrant Bubbles: Poe's 'The Angel of the Odd'" (*PN* 2:46–48).

A different area of Poe's work is represented by his sketches "Silence" and "Shadow." These are customarily referred to as prose poems, commended as such, and dismissed. Two new articles attempt more responsive treatment. In "What Has Poe's 'Silence' to Say?" (*BSUF* 10,i:66–70) Alice Claudel proposes that this sketch has to do with "the death of poetry in a kind of wasteland under the aegis of a controlling élite [probably the Transcendentalists]." It is good to be reminded that this strange scenario, which Poe subtitled "A Fable," does deserve some interpretation. The one offered here is rather thin. "Shadow" is more interestingly treated by Joseph M. DeFalco in "The Source of Terror in Poe's 'Shadow—A Parable'" (*SSF* 6:643–48).

His thesis is that the sketch is concerned with what Poe wrote about thirteen years later in *Eureka*: loss of individual identity after death. In that work the theme is managed with a certain forced optimism; here it is felt as a metaphysical horror.

The least popular of the detective tales is discussed by Richard P. Benton in "'The Mystery of Marie Rogêt'—A Defense" (*SSF* 6:144–51). Benton concurs with Dorothy Sayers in finding it the most interesting of Dupin's three cases, "a masterpiece of detective fiction"; but seen more technically it is also, in Frye's term, a "colloquy," and includes elements of tale, essay, and satire.

What is probably the most popular and the most discussed of Poe's gothic tales is the subject of a collection of critical essays, edited by Thomas Woodson, *Twentieth Century Interpretations of "The Fall of the House of Usher"* (Englewood Cliffs, N.J., Prentice-Hall). Part I lines up six different viewpoints on the story. Part II contains more extended pieces, interpretations by D. H. Lawrence, Darrel Abel, Leo Spitzer, Charles Feidelson, Jr., Patrick F. Quinn, Edward H. Davidson, Lyle H. Kendall, Jr., Georges Poulet, and James M. Cox. Additional articles are cited in a bibliography briefly annotated. Faced with the large amount of commentary on "Usher" now available—most of it written during the past twenty years—Woodson must have had a hard time making his selections. For example, why reprint Kendall's examination of the vampire motif instead of J. O. Bailey's? Woodson does not try to explain his choices; he lets his editing stand on its evident merits. The book would probably be more useful if it contained the text of "Usher." But if I had to choose between that bonus and Woodson's excellent introduction I would retain the latter. It is a good preface to a reading not only of this story but also of Poe's other major works of fiction.

*f.* **Poetry.** Disconcertingly high-flown in diction and effusive in approach is the discussion of Poe's "amorous verse" in Haldeen Braddy's "Edgar Allan Poe's Princess of Long Ago" (*LauR* 9,ii:23–31). That admiration of Poe's poetry does not necessarily preclude reasoned discussion of it is made evident on many pages of Floyd Stovall's *Edgar Poe the Poet: Essays New and Old on the Man and His Work* (Charlottesville, Univ. Press of Va.). There are nine essays in the book, some of them required reading for all students of Poe, viz., "An Interpretation of 'Al Aaraaf'" (1929) and "Poe's Debt to

Coleridge" (1930). But there are others, "Poe as a Poet of Ideas"
(1932) and "The Conscious Art of Edgar Poe" (1963) which do
hardly more than riffle through some of the germane considerations.
For Stovall it is the poetry and the poetic theory that constitute Poe's
major achievement, but he does not ignore Poe's other work. One of
the new essays, "The Poetic Principle in Prose" (1968), looks first
into what is poetic about *Eureka* and then inquires into how a (if not
the) poetic principle operates in a wide range of stories. Whether
Stovall's generally "sensible" readings are quite in the spirit of the
author is a discussible point. But though there may be more imaginative critics of "Ligeia," does any of them notice, as he does, the
import of "shrinking from my touch" in the final scene? On balance,
though, Stovall's scholarly investigations seem of more durable interest than the essays that are mainly critical and interpretive.

*g. Eureka* **and criticism.**    In discussing Poe's work as a whole or in
part it is becoming increasingly *de rigueur* to take *Eureka* into account. Another relatively new development is an emphasis on Poe
as a satirist. These two lines intersect in Harriet R. Holman's impressive article "Hog, Bacon, Ram and Other 'Savans' in *Eureka*: Notes
Toward Decoding Poe's Encyclopedic Satire" (*PN* 2:49–55).

The most famous partisan of *Eureka*, Paul Valéry, was unaware
of a satirical intention significantly present in that work. He valued
it for its demonstration that the same basic faculties are employed
by poet, artist, and scientist. Valéry's interest in Poe's "abstract in-
telligence" began in youth, fluctuated throughout his middle years,
but remained strong from 1937 until his death in 1945. The history
of this interest is traced by Reino Virtanen in "Allusions to Poe's
Poetic Theory in Valéry's *Cahiers*" (*Poetic Theory/Poetic Practice*,
pp.113–20). A similar survey of the interest Poe had for another poet
is made by B. R. McElderry, Jr., in "T. S. Eliot on Poe" (*PN* 2:32–33).
The conversion factor for Eliot was the high regard in which Poe
was held by the French Symbolist poets.

In the practice of French Symbolism *la suggestion* was the key
concept for the reason that transcendental reality cannot be expressed directly in words; it can only be suggested by symbols that
embody correspondences between the spiritual and phenomenal
universes. Krishna Rayan in "Edgar Allan Poe and Suggestiveness"
(*BJA* 9:73–79) shows how in this and other ways Poe made a con-

tribution of continuing importance when, in his review of Moore's
*Alciphron,* he brought *suggestiveness* as a technical term into the
vocabulary of literary criticism.

   Robert D. Jacobs's *Poe: Journalist and Critic* (Baton Rouge, La.
State Univ. Press) is, with the Mabbott edition of the poems, one of
the two most important contributions made to Poe studies in recent
years. In this massive and yet never ponderous volume, and in a
style that remains energetic and alert, Jacobs makes a very detailed
survey of Poe's transactions with literature. We have here as full
an account as we could want of Poe's career as reviewer, editor, and
literary theoretician. But the scope of the book is even wider than this.

> In his practice of criticism Poe was a rhetorician whose rules
> were as strict as those of one of his sources, the Reverend Hugh
> Blair; but as a theorist who sought to analyze the nature of
> beauty and to ascribe a final cause for the hedonic value of
> art, Poe eventually went beyond all rules and rested his apology
> for poetry in the imagined nature of an artist-God whose great-
> est pleasure came from the contemplation of his own perfec-
> tion, but who had to experience the pain of phenomenal
> existence before he could fully enjoy his own being [p. x].

Here is a condensed statement of the thesis which the book elab-
orates. Poe was not a major literary critic. But through his work as a
reviewer, and overcoming a certain Enlightenment cast of mind and
a tendency toward what Jacobs calls "reductionism," Poe's thought
never ceased to develop. Hence his intellectual legacy is not so much
in the texts of his reviews and critical essays as it is in the larger
whole which they point to and imply: an imaginative-philosophical
theory of nature, man, and God.

   One of the major contentions advanced and defended by Jacobs
is that the mind of Poe was much less disposed towards the Romantic
outlook of Coleridge and A. W. Schlegel than it was toward the intellectual method of eighteenth-century rationalism. Indirectly this
view is supported in two articles by J. Lasley Dameron: "Poe and
*Blackwood's* Thomas Doubleday on the Art of Poetry" (*ES* 49[1968]:
540–42) and "Poe and *Blackwood's* Alexander Smith on Truth and
Poetry" (*MissQ* 22:355–59). Both clearly of Enlightenment persuasion, Doubleday and Smith philosophized about literature in a way
that clearly anticipates Poe's more famous formulations.

*h.* **Sources.**   Perhaps the most important example of recent work in this category is Michael Hinden's "Poe's Debt to Wordsworth: A Reading of 'Stanzas'" (*SIR* 8:109–20). The article develops a suggestion made years ago by Killis Campbell, that in structure and imagery the poem is indebted to the "Intimations" ode. Taking note of Wilbur's characterization of "Stanzas" as largely incoherent, Hinden's inquiry leads him to conclude that it is this particular poem which "most perfectly embodies what Wilbur himself . . . describes as Poe's most prevalent recurring allegory, the myth of the poet's life." Thus Poe's debt to Wordsworth may include this myth.

After reading two articles by Burton J. Pollin—"Victor Hugo and Poe" (*RLC* 42[1968]:494–519) and "*Notre-Dame de Paris* in Two of Poe's Tales" (*RLV* 34[1968]:354–65)—it is hard to believe that the Hugo-Poe relationship was for so long ignored. Perhaps, as Pollin suggests, the connections between *Hernani* and "The Masque of the Red Death" are so obvious that they discourage discussion. He brings to light several less obvious connections, as for instance that between the trial and punishment of Esmeralda in *Notre-Dame* and the events described in "The Pit and the Pendulum."

Another of Pollin's suggestions is that Poe's terms *grotesque* and *arabesque* derive from Hugo's Preface to *Cromwell* rather than, as is usually assumed, from Scott's essay "On the Supernatural in Fictitious Composition." In Paul A. Newlin's article "Scott's Influence on Poe's Grotesque and Arabesque Tales" (*ATQ* 2:9–12) the usual assumption is made, but what Newlin mainly wants to show is that the ways in which Poe defined the new fictional modes in his important letter to White may also have been inspired by Scott's essay.

Given the interest of the story concerned, Richard P. Benton's article "'The Masque of the Red Death'—The Primary Source" (*ATQ* 1:12–13) should be mentioned. The source Benton nominates is Letter XVI of Willis's *Pencillings by the Way*, in which occurs a description of a macabre masked ball in Paris.

## *ii.* Bryant, Lowell, Willis, Lanier, and Others

Bryant's lectures on poetry are appraised as "the first significant, unified theory of poetry to appear in America" by William J. Free in "William Cullen Bryant on Nationalism, Imitation, and Originality in Poetry" (*SP* 66:672–87). In working out that theory Bryant avoided the extremes of both the colonialist position, which urged the imitation of approved transatlantic models, and the nationalist position, dedicated to making all things new. Bryant saw for what they were the half-truths which these two positions represented. The position he himself took is not very different from Eliot's in "Tradition and the Individual Talent."

A sane view of the relationship between tradition and originality was also taken by Lowell, and this is one point scored in his favor by Herbert F. Smith in the introduction to his *Literary Criticism of James Russell Lowell* (Lincoln, Univ. of Nebr. Press). This is an intelligently conceived edition. Essays, lectures, and reviews are set up under headings, such as Defense of Poetry, Principles of Criticism; and each item is prefaced by a concise headnote. In his introductory essay Smith tries to be even-handed about Lowell's strengths and weaknesses. He sees his theoretical work as clearly superior to his ventures in practical criticism. But Smith shares the normal editorial impulse to make a case and he does this in part by suggesting some affinities between Lowell's views and more recent modes of critical thought. The names of Eliot, R. S. Crane, and even Susan Sontag are brought into play. But the final praise sounds faint: "Thus we see that Lowell is not entirely dead as a critic."

A partisan stance is taken by Cortland P. Auser in *Nathaniel P. Willis* (TUSAS 132): "If past literary historians have stressed only the ephemerality of many of his productions, this present work has attempted to strike a balance by highlighting his accomplishments." But just as Willis in his fiction could deal with his characters in only a superficial way, so with Auser's treatment of Willis in this biography. We are left with only a dim sense of the man. And his literary accomplishments are not in fact "highlighted." Auser speaks, rather, of Willis's "potential ability as a teller of tales," says that "he was not able to handle structurally the longer short story," that his essays "are not without merit," and that the only poems of Willis "which still retain some degrees of liveliness" are those about life in New York City.

An unpretentious piece which does its job with speed and authority is Donald A. Ringe's "Sound Imagery in Whittier's *Snow-Bound*" (*PLL* 5:139–44). Ringe's point is that though visual images are the dominant ones, there is a subsidiary pattern of sound imagery, used with restraint and skill, which enhances the theme of the poem and further defines its structure. The dissertation of Charles R. Tegan on "The Religious Poetry of John Greenleaf Whittier" (*DA* 29:4471A–72A) is less concerned with analysis and evaluation than with inventory and cataloguing.

A dissertation by Linda Jane Rookwood Robinson—"Henry W. Longfellow's *Hiawatha*: An American Epic" (*DA* 29:3107A–08A)— proposes that we see the poem in a new light, not as an "Indian Edda," as Longfellow himself described it, but as having to do with the promises and dangers of white American civilization. Seen in this way, the poem is thematically related to *The Waste Land*.

That Lanier is "one of our most vital and most interesting minor poets" is the generalization with which the late Edd Winfield Parks concluded the middle chapter in his *Sidney Lanier: The Man, the Poet, the Critic* (Athens, Univ. of Ga. Press, 1968). But in just what ways Lanier as a poet remains vital and interesting is not adequately discussed. Similarly in the biographical chapter Parks confines himself to a recital of facts. Interpretative comment is not risked. Nor does the chapter on Lanier's critical endeavors amount to much more than objectively annotated bibliography. An excessive emphasis on summary and paraphrase restricts this book to only elementary usefulness. Parks does not discuss *Tiger-Lilies*. In a new edition of this novel, in the Southern Literary Classics series (Chapel Hill, Univ. of N.C. Press) there is an introductory essay by Richard Harwell, who tells us much about the circumstances involved in the novel's composition, but in an evaluative comment says only that it "has no great merit as a novel." *Tiger-Lilies* is used as exhibit A in Jack de Bellis's interesting article "Sidney Lanier and German Romanticism: An Important Qualification" (*CLS* 5[1968]:145–55). The basic argument is that, contrary to received opinion, Lanier's acquaintance with German Romantic literature was almost entirely second-hand, via Carlyle, and that Richter and Novalis were much less important in his literary culture than was Goethe. By way of making this particular point De Bellis underscores another, of wider application: "how scholarly investigation may be misled when unprovable assertions are relied upon through sixty years of criticism." An account of Lanier's other career—as musician and composer—is given by John S. Edwards in "Sidney Lanier: Musical Pioneer" (*GaR* 22[1968]: 473–81). It seems that Lanier was not musically innovative nor was he especially productive. Nonetheless, Edwards contends, he played a role of some importance in the history of American musical life.

The 1905 edition of Stickney's *Poems* is now a rare item, and so Stickney is known on the basis of anthology selections which do not do him justice. This situation has led to a dissertation by Amberys R. Whittle, "The Poetry of Trumbull Stickney" (*DA* 30:346A–47A). Besides reproducing all of Stickney's extant verse, plus variants, the edition includes four chapters of introduction, an account of the literary situation in the 1880's and 90's, and a discussion of Stickney's prose writings, his poetic style, and his characteristic themes.

Stickney is one of the poets whose work is studied in the dissertation of Robert J. Scholnick, "The Children of the Night: The Situation for Poetry in the American 1890's" (*DA* 30:1574A). Particular attention is given to the early writings of Moody and Robinson and to how they defined for themselves their vocations as poets independently of the genteel leadership offered by E. C. Stedman.

*Wellesley College*

# 12. Fiction: 1900 to the 1930's

## Warren French

### i. General Studies

Three important books published in 1969 focused on the "iconoclasts" of the 1920's and 1930's—Anderson, Fitzgerald, and Lewis—as central figures in different groups made from different viewpoints by perceptive and highly readable critics.

The only strictly "literary" study of the three is Anthony C. Hilfer's *The Revolt from the Village, 1915–1930* (Chapel Hill, Univ. of N.C. Press), which takes its title from an article that Carl Van Doren wrote in 1921 for the *Nation*, pointing out that American novelists were attacking the cherished belief in the small town as a refuge from the evil city. Hilfer believes that this much-discussed "revolt" has frequently been viewed too simplistically, because all participants have actually had ambivalent attitudes toward small towns. Until 1930, revolt was stronger than nostalgia in their writings, but thereafter the village was once again idealized by some of the very leaders of the earlier attack. Hilfer examines the growth of the "village myth" from Oliver Goldsmith to Thornton Wilder and then traces the history of the countermovement, advancing the provocative idea that no later writers made more telling attacks upon the village than Stephen Crane and Mark Twain did during the "first revolt" between 1871 and 1899. Hilfer treats Sinclair Lewis and his contemporaries less condescendingly than some recent critics have. He defends the continuing value of Lewis's work in understanding the conformity and emotional suffocation of American life, observing "it is unnecessary to write another Babbitt, because he has not changed that much" and further that the "anti-village" writers would have been less interesting if they had been more sophisticated (and inclined probably, like Henry James, simply to ignore the whole distasteful business). Little of Hilfer's material is new, but his book is distinguished by his willingness to make and defend sharply critical judgments of many respected writers, so that his compact account provides an admirable introduction to a long and central movement in American letters.

The two other books use literary materials to explore historical themes. Nelson M. Blake's *Novelists' America: Fiction as History, 1910–1940* (Syracuse, N.Y., Syracuse Univ. Press) argues that novelist and historian must have some of each other's quality because "the historian who is mere grubber for facts and has no imagination is seriously handicapped," and "the novelist who has nothing but information will be a mere spinner of tales." Blake then goes on to point out what the historian can learn from novels by Wolfe, Lewis, Fitzgerald, Faulkner, Steinbeck, Dos Passos, Farrell, and Wright to give life and meaning to bare statistics. Throughout the study he is careful to stress, however, that novels are "not history, but material for history." His material will be familiar to literary critics of the period, but may alert other academicians to the value of fiction outside the literature classroom.

Walter Allen's *The Urgent West: The American Dream and Modern Man* (New York, Dutton) covers a wide range of materials from colonial times to the present to point out the relationship between the development of American literature and a unique "American Dream." He draws generously, however, from novels published between 1900 and 1940; and in the second section of his book, "American Spokesman," he makes extensive analyses of Cather, Farrell, Henry Roth, Dreiser, Anderson, Lewis, Hemingway, Fitzgerald, Wilder, Wolfe, Steinbeck, and Dos Passos. The study is especially helpful to Americans in illuminating the difference between their native literature and that of western Europe and the way in which American novelists have made the American dream the property of the whole world.

### ii. The Inheritors of the Genteel Tradition

As the 1960's end, interest lags in those who sought to uphold the tradition of Howells and James, indicating—in conjunction with a parallel rise of interest in rowdy writers—a general shift in critical tastes that reflects a widespread increase in dissent in academic circles. A rash of dissertations suggests, however, that we may soon be hearing more about the more polite artists.

Bernice Slote continues her devoted efforts to Willa Cather by contributing a survey of Cather scholarship to *Fifteen Modern American Authors* (pp. 23–62) and "Willa Cather Reports Chautauqua, 1894" to the University of Nebraska Centennial issue of *Prairie Schooner* (43:117–28). The latter article draws upon nine feature articles that Miss Cather contributed to the Lincoln *Evening News* to re-create one of the most important annual cultural events in the state. Sister Lucy Schneider continues mining her dissertation on Willa Cather's "Land-philosophy"; "'Land' Relevance in 'Neighbor Rosicky'" (*KanQ* 1,i[1968]:105–10) illustrates that while Willa Cather's early works suggest "a desire for transcendence in art and living," the later works show that we cannot become isolated from humanity, but must find values "incarnate in human living," as in the love and goodness of the title character of the story.

A stimulating new approach to Willa Cather's work is suggested by one of the year's finest articles, Terence Martin's "The Drama of Memory in *My Ántonia*" (*PMLA* 84:304–11), which answers previous objections to the novel as either the story of Ántonia herself or of Jim and Ántonia; he points out that it is Jim's image of Ántonia that provides a unity that "takes the special form of a dream of memory" that is not only resolved but fulfilled by Jim's becoming reconciled to the present by discovering the enduring values of the past. A similar thesis about the relationship between the past and present in Miss Cather's work is developed in Maynard Fox's "Proponents of Order: Tom Outland and Bishop Latour" (*WAL* 4:107–15), which advances the thesis that in both "Tom Outland's Story" and *Death Comes for the Archbishop* "the symbols having the dominating position are nature-oriented," the chief one of a garden, "an Eden or an Arcadia of nostalgic and mythic memory."

Ellen Glasgow is discussed this year only in a rather unfavorable light in an article to be mentioned among others about James Branch Cabell. Edith Wharton fares better. E. M. and S. B. Puknat's "Edith Wharton and Gottfried Keller" (*CL* 21:245–54) points out detailed thematic and technical parallels between *Ethan Frome* and the Swiss author's *Romeo und Julia auf dem Dorfe*. In a more lively article, "Edith Wharton and the Twilight of the International Novel" (*SoR* 5:398–418), Christof Wegelin observes that Mrs. Wharton's novels acquired a new tone as she began to satirize the crudeness of modern Europeans as well as Americans.

Only scattered references appear to Mrs. Wharton's male successors. Abigail A. Hamblen works hard in "Booth Tarkington's Classic of Adolescence" (*SHR* 3:225–31) to prove that because the world of *Seventeen* is different from ours, the novel allows us "to see our own day in perspective" and to gain a little in understanding. French and Italian journalist-scholars are beginning to discover H. P. Lovecraft, whose macabre fantasies represent the ultimate collapse of gentility into aberration.

Two new books in the Twayne series provided the first extended critical introductions to popular writers whose conservative values ally them to the genteel tradition. Clarence K. Sandelin's *Robert Nathan* (TUSAS 148), published last year, points out that "Nathan's didactic emphasis, subjective exposition, mystical argument, familiar premises, nostalgic moods, and folkloristic story motifs" seemed old-fashioned even in the 1920's. Sandelin discusses Nathan's many works fully and sympathetically, but fails to arrive at any synthesis except the observation that Nathan—like many contemporaries—has had a deep and growing sense of alienation from American society. Leedice M. Kissane's *Ruth Suckow* (TUSAS 142) presses harder the claims of its subject, to whom "beauty was all-important." Miss Suckow's writings, her celebrator proclaims, protested the "cultural barrenness" of country people, who live in the midst of natural beauty. Neither book is likely to stimulate interest in its subjects. Both are—as the writings of the novelists appear to be from the long descriptions provided—affectionately and thoughtfully written, but unexciting. When Sandelin says that Nathan "creates no Ahabs," he puts into a few words why minor authors remain minor.

### *iii.* "The Redskins"—Ungenteel Voices of Protest

A colleague who predicts that we are moving into a neoproletarian period finds ample support in the attention being lavished on the principal saboteurs of the genteel tradition. A turning point has surely been reached in Dreiser studies: three long bibliographical accounts of his work and writings about him appeared in 1969—Robert H. Elias's essay in *Fifteen Modern American Authors* (pp. 101–38), Jack Salzman's similar essay in *American Literary Realism* (2:132–38), and Hugh C. Atkinson's *Merrill Checklist of Theodore Dreiser* (Columbus, Ohio, Merrill). (The same publisher also provided Charles

Shapiro's *Merrill Guide to Theodore Dreiser.*) Surpassing even these
useful tools, however, is Richard Lehan's *Theodore Dreiser: His
World and His Novels* (Carbondale, Southern Ill. Univ. Press), an
indispensable starting point for future studies of Dreiser as an artist.

A trouble with much writing about Dreiser has been that the
authors themselves have come from the wrong side of the tracks and
have treated their subject as culture hero rather than as craftsman.
Lehan's study shows that an objective, sophisticated scholar-critic
can treat familiar books in a fresh way. Maintaining that Dreiser's
"literary concerns and emphases" never changed radically, Lehan
finds that Dreiser's characters were the victims of a "romantic dilemma," yearning "after the infinite while they were restrained by the
physical." Out of this dilemma emerged "the displaced hero: the
man who has a place in the world but cannot find it." He is a victim of
his temperament, time, "a society that he cannot fully accept or totally
reject," but most of all of "his own romantic illusions" (pp. 52–53).
Lehan traces this concept through Dreiser's novels, observing that at
last in *The Stoic* Dreiser created for Berenice Fleming a transcendent
world "wherein an idealized self could find fulfillment."

Jonas Spatz in *The Forties* also focuses on one of Dreiser's last
novels and finds that in *The Bulwark*, the novelist "manages, despite
its primitive style, to achieve an authenticity that transcends current
conventions of language, characterization, and narrative technique"
("Dreiser's *Bulwark*: An Archaic Masterpiece," pp. 155–62).

Most critics continue, however, to concentrate upon *Sister Carrie*.
Two articles by Jack Salzman help dispel myths about the publication of Dreiser's first novel. From "The Critical Recognition of *Sister
Carrie*, 1900–1907" (*JAmS* 3:123–33) we learn that although major
American journals ignored the book when it appeared, early reviewers were generally favorable and that the even friendlier reviews
of the British edition led, ironically, to a yet more favorable attention
when the 1907 reprint appeared in the United States. "Dreiser and
Ade: A Note on the Text of *Sister Carrie*" (*AL* 40:544–48) points out
that the only substantial revision by Dreiser in this 1907 reprint was
in the initial description of the traveling salesman, Drouet, making
the account less like a similar description in one of George Ade's
*Fables in Slang* than the original passage had been.

Christopher G. Katope's "*Sister Carrie* and Spencer's *First Principles*" (*AL* 41:64–75) analyzes the philosopher's influence upon the

novel and demonstrates that Carrie's rise illustrates Spencer's idea that evolution is a process during which matter passes from "indefinite, incoherent homogeneity" to "definite, coherent heterogeneity," while Hurstwood's fall illustrates the dissolution that Spencer says occurs when the evolutionary process has run its course. In *The Passages of Thought: Psychological Representation in the American Novel, 1870–1900* (New York, Oxford Univ. Press) Gordon O. Taylor is also much concerned with Dreiser's use of "process" in creating a fiction that breaks with nineteenth-century tradition. Taylor uses *Sister Carrie* as the terminal point in a study that begins with *Uncle Tom's Cabin* to illustrate that "roughly between 1870 and 1900 fictive psychology in the American novel undergoes a fundamental shift . . . away from a notion of static, discrete mental states requiring representational emphasis on the conventional nature of particular states, toward a concept of organically linked mental states requiring emphasis on the nature of the sequential process itself" (p. 5). In this short book that every student of American fiction should read with extreme care, Taylor singles out *Sister Carrie* because a conventional attitude no longer suffices to account for the protagonist's actions, so that "careful consideration of the process underlying those actions becomes [the] primary thematic concern and representational resource" (p. 145).

Charles Child Walcutt's "*Sister Carrie*: Naturalism or Novel of Manners" (*Genre* 1[1968]:76–85) looks at the novel from quite a different viewpoint, reasoning that it is not so much "naturalistic" as a novel of manners. Although Dreiser's characters are "impelled *not* by values concerned and held in the intellect but by animal impulses of desire and self-preservation," since people without cultivation could rise much higher in the United States in the 1890's than they could in Europe, *Sister Carrie* is really a perfect novel of manners, depicting people not in revolt, but responding in the only way they can to the values of a society in which luck counts more than ability.

Donald Pizer's "Theodore Dreiser's 'Nigger Jeff': The Development of an Aesthetic" (*AL* 41:331–41) examines the three major extant versions of the short story—each associated with an important phase of Dreiser's career—to show that they "incorporate Dreiser's principal beliefs about the nature of art," from the "inspired sentimentality" of the first to the "moral polemicism and incipient philosophizing" of the last. Charles L. Campbell's "*An American Tragedy*: Or, Death in the Woods" (*MFS* 15:251–59) maintains that to understand Dreiser's novel we must understand Thoreau, because Dreiser uses imagery transposed from *Walden* to counter Thoreau's optimism with an antithetical vision resulting from the feeling that while American society encourages dreams like Clyde's, "it makes them all but impossible of realization."

Two articles attempt comprehensive surveys of aspects of Dreiser's work. J. D. Thomas's thesis in "Epimetheus Bound: Theodore Dreiser and the Novel of Thought" (*SHR* 3:346–57) is that Dreiser's eight novels "are the fictional expression of Man Thinking." Epimetheus comes in because he is the one around whose head the denizens of Pandora's box flew; but, whereas the gleaming treasure at the bottom of his box was hope, in Dreiser's it is beauty. H. Alan Wycherley's "Mechanism and Vitalism in Dreiser's Nonfiction" (*TSLL* 11:1039–49) takes a close look at the less frequently contemplated biographical works to show the persistence in them of a mechanist-vitalist ambivalence and an underlying mysticism also characteristic of the novels. Robert Palmer Saalbach calls attention to some even less frequently regarded works with his edition of *Selected Poems (from Moods) by Theodore Dreiser* (New York, Exposition Press), maintaining in his introduction that these affected pieces of "uneven merit" exhibit the "passionate compassion" that H. L. Mencken thought made Dreiser's spirit essentially poetic.

Enthusiasm for Jack London continues to grow with the semiannual *Jack London Newsletter* providing a repository for tidbits about the author. Most of the contents are of more interest to buffs than scholars. The first issue of 1969 was largely devoted to bibliographical items and a tribute translated from Danish. Some short notes in the second issue, however, should stimulate controversy. Sue Findley's "Naturalism in 'To Build a Fire'" (2,ii:45–48) maintains that, although London usually saw nature as the same indifferent force that Stephen Crane did, in this story he pictures it as actively and consciously evil, as Conrad and Hardy did. Steven T. Dhondt's "Jack London's *When God Laughs*: Overman, Underdog and Satire" (2,ii:51–57) argues that although London preferred the title story of the collection, "The Chinango" is actually best, because it deals with a proletarian class of characters that London understood better than the middle-class figures in the other story.

James R. Giles strains to find things to write about London: "Thematic Significance of the Jim Hall Episode in *White Fang*" (*JLN*

2,ii:49–50) sees the episode as stressing the vulnerability of men as well as animals to environmental pressure; "Jack London 'Down and Out' in England: The Relevance of the Sociological Study *People of the Abyss* to London's Fiction" (*JLN* 2,iii:79–83) quotes extensively to show the relationship of London's nonfictional view of the city of London to the social views in his fiction; "Beneficial Atavism in Frank Norris and Jack London" (*WAL* 4:15–27) discusses the presence in London's early Yukon tales of the same concept of "beneficial atavism"—"the healthful influence of a life of violence" and an uncritical acceptance of Anglo-Saxon racism—that underlies Frank Norris's preposterous novel, *Moran of the Lady Letty*.

Other London criticism is of equally dubious utility. Earl J. Wilcox's "Jack London's Naturalism: The Example of *The Call of the Wild*" (*JLN* 2,ii:91–101) points out that the "naturalism" of the story is inconsistent, so that the book is of no help to anyone who expected to use it to illustrate the putting of the ideas of theorists like Spencer into fictional practice. Robert B. Pearsall's "Elizabeth Barrett Meets Wolf Larsen" (*WAL* 4:3–13) sets out to prove that Maud Brewester in *The Sea-Wolf* is modeled on Mrs. Browning. Titles are being added rapidly to the British Fitzroy Edition of London's work, edited by I. O. Evans, but the texts are not attractively presented and the introductions are perfunctory.

Despite all this hubbub over Dreiser and London, little was written in 1969 about their contemporaries. In an issue of the *Jack London Newsletter* there appeared a "Jesse Stuart Newsletter" (2,iii:117–20) —a curious instance of a newsletter within a newsletter. *American Literary Realism* was devoted principally to bibliographical surveys and articles about nineteenth-century writers. Only Sanford E. Marovitz's "*Yekl*: The Ghetto Realism of Abraham Cahan" (*ALR* 2:271–73) falls within the province of this chapter. It is a sound and thoughtful analysis of Cahan's first novel, pointing out that, though the book was praised by Howells, it was not well received by a reading public that demanded "beautiful people" and "happy endings" that life on the lower East Side of New York could not provide. Because of Cahan's unsparing portrayal of the frailties and shortcomings of the ghetto dwellers, however, Marovitz feels that *Yekl*'s characters "rise above their provincial limitations" to become universal heroes of real life.

Bernard De Voto is difficult to categorize, but if the thesis that governs the chapter about his fiction in Orlan Sawey's *Bernard De Voto* (TUSAS 151) is sound, he—and similar twentieth-century regional writers—really should be grouped with the "redskins" of the naturalistic tradition, because Sawey's view is that four of De Voto's five novels deal principally with the influence of the frontier on American civilization and express a preference for the sane and less complex life of the frontier West over that of the effete East.

### iv. The Iconoclasts

Turning to this group that gave much of the color to American writing of the 1920's, one is disturbed again to discover that figures already much discussed are being exploited to a point of diminishing returns, while those little noticed—with the exception of writers associated with the Harlem Renaissance—continue to be ignored.

Sherwood Anderson continues to benefit from Ray Lewis White's scrupulous and sensitive editing of the autobiographical documents that help us understand the novelist's behavior. New editions of both *Sherwood Anderson's Memoirs* (Chapel Hill, Univ. of N.C. Press) and *Tar: A Midwest Childhood: A Critical Text* (Cleveland, Press of Case Western Reserve Univ.) became available in 1969, which also saw the publication of a brilliant article on Anderson by Benjamin T. Spencer, which was awarded the annual Norman Foerster prize for the best contribution to *American Literature*.

In "Sherwood Anderson: American Mythopoeist" (*AL* 41:1–18), Spencer maintains that Anderson and other members of the Chicago group in the 1920's differed from writers like Dreiser because they "wished to divert American literature from what they conceived to be its secondary focus on the socio-political and redirect it to the primary and recurring experiences" to be discovered by individuals "looking deeply into themselves." By probing in this way, however, for "the essence" of experience, Anderson "ran the romantic risk of neglecting the existential substance of the American experience." By stressing Anderson's basic concern with creating a myth rather than a photograph of America, Spencer lifts Anderson out of the context of a particular era and creates awareness of his relationship to the long transcendental tradition in American writing. Michael D. West also explores some far-reaching implications of Anderson's work in "Sherwood Anderson's Triumph: 'The Egg'" (*AQ* 20[1968]:675–93), which arrives at the conclusion that the father's "final futile attack upon the egg is an onslaught upon the process of life itself" by a man "haunted by the sense that somewhere in the past America and life itself have gone drastically wrong."

As befits the style of the life and works of the subject author, the most elegant of the new journals focused on one author continues to be *The Cabellian*, edited by Julius Rothman. One of the busiest contributors has been Dorothy B. Schlegel, whose "A Case of Literary Piracy" appears in the first semiannual issue (1,ii:58–63) and whose "Cabell's Translation of Virginia" (2,i:1–11) graces the second. The earlier article advances an interesting argument that Cabell borrowed many details for *There Were Two Pirates* from E. D. Lambright's little known *The Life and Exploits of Gasparilla* (1936) in order to play a joke on reviewers who had in the past accused him of borrowing and who had consistently misread his works. The second article points out at length the way in which Cabell made the medieval French land of Poictesme a reflection of contemporary Virginia in order to provide him with the proper aesthetic distance for writing humorously about his neighbors. Miss Schlegel is also responsible for "James Branch Cabell: A Latter-Day Enlightener" (*CLAJ* 12:223–36), which maintains that his work is not in the usual Anglo-American tradition, but in that of the eighteenth-century Enlightenment, especially in France, particularly in his ridicule of religion.

Other articles in *The Cabellian* provide information of value to scholars and collectors, but are not primarily critical. One exception is Joseph M. Flora's "Vardis Fisher and James Branch Cabell: An Essay on Influence and Reputation" (2,i:12–16), calling attention to the way in which the Western author constantly supported the Virginian by calling attention to Cabell's merits during the 1930's and 1940's when his reputation was at low ebb. Edgar E. MacDonald also raises in "The Storisende Edition: Some Liabilities" (i,ii:64–67) the important question of whether this rearrangement of Cabell's works into a chronological story-pattern may not have harmed rather than helped the author's reputation by starting with better works and winding up with poorer and also by wasting Cabell's time during his creative maturity. MacDonald also provides elsewhere a thoughtful analysis of "Cabell's Hero: Cosmic Rebel" (*SLJ* 2,i:22–42), which examines the figure as a mixture of Don Juan and Faust and explains that "from a heavy emphasis on donjuanism in the early *Cords of*

*Vanity*, Cabell seems to make his hero progressively more demoniac and speculative in the Faust tradition," marking his transition from "a struggler against fleeting time" to "a rebel against darkness."

Cabell's relationships with fellow Southern artists are also being scrutinized. M. Thomas Inge's "The Unheeding South: Donald Davidson on James Branch Cabell" (*Cabellian* 2,i:17–20) is a slender study that quotes Davidson's articles speaking sarcastically of Cabell because of the latter's refusal to take conspicuous stands on contemporary social and political issues. Edgar E. MacDonald's "The Glasgow-Cabell Entente" (*AL* 41:76–91) is a more detailed analysis of a pleasant social relationship that could not be called "a great literary companionship," because it was "predicated on their being useful to one another," with Cabell's efforts outweighing Miss Glasgow's.

The late John Dos Passos is beginning to rise once again in critical esteem now that his blatant right-wing journalism after World War II has ceased to be a disturbing influence. A beautiful edition of *One Man's Initiation* (Ithaca, N.Y., Cornell Univ. Press), which Dos Passos describes as the first to carry the text as originally written (the first edition was bowdlerized by the printer) contains also reproductions of sketches the author made in Paris in 1918 and a reminiscing foreword in which he explains how his postwar disillusionment drove him toward Marxism, which he also subsequently discovered "hardened into a crusading quasi-religion" worse than the Capitalism it protested. Floyd B. Lawrence compares *One Man's Initiation* with E. E. Cummings's *The Enormous Room* in "Two Novelists of the Great War: Dos Passos and Cummings" (*UR* 36:35–41) and finds Cummings's superior because Dos Passos's paralyzed horror at recalling the experiences he describes makes him virtually unable to say anything relevant outside the historical features of that particular milieu, whereas Cummings, "through his skillful handling of the humor of detachment and compassion, wrote a novel containing the immediacy of the most enduring fiction." (James P. Dougherty also contributes an appreciation of Cummings's novel to *Landmarks*, pp. 288–302.)

E. D. Lowry examines another early Dos Passos work and maintains in "The Lively Art of *Manhattan Transfer*" (*PMLA* 84:1628–38) that this novel must ultimately be understood as "moral act or gesture." Although less personal than the author's early works, it does link "the assertion of human individualism . . . to man's positive engagement with the issues of the time." Lowry illuminates at length Dos Passos's use of such visual art forms as Italian Futurist painting and the cinema.

The most comprehensive study of Dos Passos to appear recently is John D. Brantley's *The Fiction of John Dos Passos* (The Hague, Mouton, 1968). He develops the thesis that the novelist only gradually discovered that what he was attacking was not specific institutions or parties, but "organizational power" at the moment it becomes "a machine," primarily for the purpose of self-perpetuation. The attacks shift objects, Brantley finds, from "a large, impersonal machine" to such "specific and clearly identifiable" objects as the Communist Party.

A *Sinclair Lewis Newsletter* began publication in 1969. Most of the first issue is brief news-notes for specialists, but two discussions of *Dodsworth* provoke general interest. Hilton Anderson's "A Whartonian Woman in *Dodsworth*" (1,i:5–6) suggests that Mrs. Wharton herself is the model for Edith Cortright in the novel; Daniel R. Brown's longer "The Cosmopolitan Novel: James and Lewis" (1,i: 6–9) draws not always convincing parallels between Lewis's novel and *The Ambassadors*. Meanwhile other evidences of his restoration to a position of honor are at hand in studies other than Hilfer's *The Revolt from the Village*. *Babbitt* is examined afresh by Mark Schorer in *Landmarks* (pp. 315–27) and found to endure because people like Babbitt still live throughout the United States: it is not a melodramatic denunciation of evil, but a documented picture of "a crowd of ninnies and buffoons," who if petty and vindictive, are also shown to be absurd and pathetic. From Germany, Wilfried Edener calls also for a revaluation of Lewis in "Zu einigen neuen Studien über Sinclair Lewis" (*NS* 17[1968]:557–61), citing the work of Sheldon Grebstein and other American critics and claiming—like Schorer—that, while the United States may have superficially changed from the one Lewis criticizes, it remains in essence the same. Helen B. Petrullo's "*Babbitt* as Situational Satire" (*KanQ* 1,iii:89–97) is a more formalistic defense and considers the book not as a conventional novel but as a prose satire in the Swiftian tradition which coerces the reader into developing his own moral focus for judging the situation—an undertaking which in Lewis's work, Miss Petrullo wittily finds, resembles the ransacking of hell by Milton's fallen angels to build Pandemonium.

That the condescending attitude to Lewis persists is evident, however, from Martin Bucco's "The Serialized Novels of Sinclair Lewis" (*WAL* 4:29–37), which points out the large differences between the serial versions of novels like *Arrowsmith* and *Ann Vickers*, from which the social commentary is excised, and the book versions. It is a result, Bucco thinks, of a split sensibility that kept Lewis shuttling between the Establishment and the dissidents.

For a balanced judgment of Lewis, one can turn to two more conventional analyses of major novels in the *Ball State University Forum*. James R. Quivey's "George Babbitt's Quest for Masculinity" (10,ii:4–7) sees all of the businessman's efforts to achieve success in business, promiscuity, and outdoor life as attempts to achieve a masculine status that end in abject failure. James D. Barry's "*Dodsworth*: Sinclair Lewis' Novel of Character" (10,ii:8–14) finds this work exceptional among Lewis's because it is a study of character rather than a tale with a thesis. The paired articles present evidence that the two novels can profitably be read comparatively as one author's study of an unsuccessful and of a successful quest.

Enough is beginning to be written about writers associated with the Harlem Renaissance to win them the recognition they deserve as an important subgroup among the iconoclasts of the 1920's. In the most comprehensive recent article, Charles R. Larson examines "Three Harlem Novels of the Jazz Age" (*Crit* 11,iii:66–78) and observes that Claude McKay's *Home to Harlem*, Carl Van Vechten's *Nigger Heaven*, and Countee Cullen's *One Way to Heaven* are all strong on local color and atmosphere, but weak on plot. Richard Kostelanetz's "The Politics of Passing: The Fiction of James Weldon Johnson" (*NALF* 3:22–24,29) points out how *The Autobiography of an Ex-Colored Man* depicts unsentimentally how a black's opportunistic rejection of his heritage to pass as white produces a sense of alienation.

Much attention is being belatedly paid to Jean Toomer, whose biography affords one of the most dramatic examples of the problem of "passing." Arna Bontemps introduces a new edition of *Cane* (New York, Harper & Row) with a brief but helpful account of what is known about Toomer's life. Bontemps maintains, too, that the book has greater overall design than it has been credited with, but a more detailed examination is Todd Lieber's "Design and Movement in *Cane*" (*CLAJ* 13:35–50), one of the finest explications of a modern American novel to appear in 1969. Lieber maintains that *Cane* is more than just thematically unified, as some critics have recognized; that it has a comprehensive design that encompasses its separate parts into a sustained progression. Part I portrays the inherent beauty, mixed with pain, of the black culture that "must be embraced if the black man is to attain spiritual life." Part II presents the consequences of the spiritual death that occurs when the black rejects his heritage, and Part III shows the spiritual rebirth that a return to the South and an acceptance of blackness make possible. Concentrating only on the long story that makes up Part III of *Cane*, William J. Goede maintains in "Jean Toomer's Ralph Kabnis: Portrait of the Negro Artist as a Young Man" (*Phylon* 30:73–85) that in the title character Toomer discovered an appropriate symbol of the Negro writer who hopes to stir "the root-life of a withered people" and to make the first steps up from the underground, "toward a commitment, through art, to the racial experience of Negroes."

### *v.* The Expatriates

Following a flood of writings on Henry Miller in 1968, criticism of the expatriate clan diminished to a trickle. Two articles do make large claims for relatively neglected works. Suzanne C. Ferguson's "Djuna Barnes's Short Stories: An Estrangement of the Heart" (*SoR* 5:26–41) finds that these works "create in a special and powerful way the feeling of disestablishment and disintegration in the society and in the individual," so deeply experienced by the author's generation, but notes further that since "the vision is not so extreme as in *Nightwood*, it comes through with greater clarity and more appeal to the reader." George Knox in "The Great American Novel: Final Chapter" (*AQ* 21:667–82) sees Gertrude Stein's *The Making of Americans* as "the super-spoof" that marks the demise of the cherished nineteenth-century tradition of a "Great American Novel" by parodying the criteria involved in calls for such a work. Donald Shults's "Gertrude Stein and the Problem of Time" (*KAL* 11:[1968]:59–71) is a chatty introduction to the writer that attempts to cover her whole literary career, emphasizing the idea that Miss Stein lived and wrote in a continuous present and felt that "no longer should literature reflect the world, but create it."

The lack hitherto of any focal point for studies of expatriate writers is being remedied by the quarterly publication of *Under the*

*Sign of Pisces: Anaïs Nin and Her Circle*, edited by Richard Centing
of the Ohio State University Libraries, the first issues of which will
be examined in next year's survey.

### vi. The Cosmogonists

We may soon need a separate chapter on Katherine Anne Porter as
explicators increasingly focus their attention on her subtle and artful
stories. Two general works serve to advance Porter studies. Louise
Waldrip and Shirley Ann Bauer's *A Bibliography of the Works of
Katherine Anne Porter* [and] *A Bibliography of the Criticism of the
Works of Katherine Anne Porter* (Metuchen, N.J., Scarecrow Press)
is a competently compiled addition to a useful series; and *Katherine
Anne Porter: A Critical Symposium*, edited by Lodwick Hartley and
George Core (Athens, Univ. of Ga. Press), brings together in a mag-
nificently designed book an interview, a reminiscence by Glenway
Wescott, and fifteen distinguished reprinted critical articles.

Hartley also suggests in "Stephen's Lost World: The Background
of Katherine Anne Porter's 'The Downward Path to Wisdom'" (*SSF*
6:574–79) that the best approach to the story is through Philip
Horton's biography of Miss Porter's friend Hart Crane, whose childhood parallels in many ways that of the little boy in the story. William L. Nance's "Variations on a Dream: Katherine Anne Porter and
Truman Capote" (*SHR* 3:338–45) sees the same story as "the core"
of Porter's fiction, in which there has always been something fixed
and final, as though her early encounter with death "had somehow
short-circuited life's possibilities." Nance sees her work and Truman
Capote's as variations on the "special Neoplatonic paradisal vision"
that is the Southern variant on the American dream. Nance thinks,
however, that Capote has proved more flexible than Miss Porter, by
making each work "a further stage in the campaign to exorcise" the
dream.

"Flowering Judas" has inspired two ponderous metaphysical analyses. Dorothy S. Redden's "'Flowering Judas': Two Voices" (*SSF*
6:194–204) argues that "the paradoxes of Miss Porter's fiction" are
insufficiently illuminated by critics' tacit reliance on the assumption
that the author holds a unitary view of life, when actually the significance of Laura's experience in the story is that "it is impossible to
break the deadlock between inner needs and inculcated precepts" if

the latter are based on conventional Western ideas of moral responsibility. Miss Porter differs from the character, however, Miss Redden goes on to say, in that only the former is aware of the nature of the estrangement that the latter feels. Leon Gottfried's "Death's Other Kingdom: Dantesque and Theological Symbolism in 'Flowering Judas' " (*PMLA* 84:112–24) maintains that Miss Porter differs from traditional religious writers in using their symbolic techniques in a modern secular fashion, in which meaning and value "are created, not given." Because of the absence of any viable faith in "Flowering Judas," it is "a portrayal of a hell without a heaven."

A similar concept of "created values" in "a hell without a heaven" underlies Philip R. Yanella's "The Problems of Dislocation in 'Pale Horse, Pale Rider' " (*SSF* 6:637–42), which uses the story as an example of those concerned with typical Porter characters who are "spatially dislocated" and thus "burdened with the task of moral improvisation to survive." In the story scrutinized, Yanella finds that Miranda gives up her sentimental, nostalgic vision in order to commit herself to the drab reality of the physical world.

Two articles offer quite differing views of "The Jilting of Granny Weatherall." Joseph Wiesenfarth's "Internal Opposition in Porter's 'Granny Weatherall' " (*Crit* 11, ii:47–55) maintains that this is not "a moral tale about forgiveness," but a direction that the reader look at Granny to learn that despite her great efforts she has lived "a less than truly satisfactory life," because at the end she finds that neither marriage nor children nor religion has reconciled her to the inability to love resulting from her jilting sixty years before. Daniel R. and Madeline T. Barnes's "The Secret Sin of Granny Weatherall" (*Renascence* 21:162–65) offers the surprising thesis that Granny has not just suffered from wounded pride, but from fear of "losing her soul," since the story provides evidence that when she was jilted she was pregnant by the man who jilted her and that she has been haunted all these sixty years by "a sense of guilt for her premarital transgression."

William Prater's " 'The Grave': Form and Symbol" (*SSF* 6:336–38) also advances a surprising suggestion—that "the grave" of the title is not one that the narrator knew as a child, but "the burial place" in her mind of an unpleasant experience she has repressed. Joan Givner's "A Re-reading of Katherine Anne Porter's 'Theft' " (*SSF* 6:463–65) leads to the conclusion that the story deals with the same

"self-delusion in the face of evil that is most clearly developed in
*Ship of Fools*." Miss Porter's longest work is focused upon only in
M. M. Liberman's "Some Observations on the Genesis of *Ship of
Fools*: A Letter from Katherine Anne Porter" (*PMLA* 84:136–37),
which describes the unpleasant voyage to Germany in 1931 that
provided the background for the novel.

Study of John Steinbeck is beginning to revolve around the *Steinbeck Quarterly* (formerly the *Steinbeck Newsletter*). Much of the
three issues during 1969 is devoted to memorial tributes by friends,
collectors, and critics of the novelist; but Peter Lisca's "Steinbeck
and Hemingway: Suggestions for a Comparative Study" (*StN* 2,i:9–
17) launches a series of thought-provoking articles that is continued
by John Ditsky's "From Oxford to Salinas: Comparing Faulkner and
Steinbeck" (*StQ* 2,iii:51–55). After pointing out many similarities
and differences between Hemingway and Steinbeck, Lisca concludes
that although they differ in their attraction to violence, "both writers
are notable for the depth of esthetic feeling touched by . . . Nature
and their great ability to express it; and both also present man as
incomplete without intimate contact with that world." Ditsky also
finds that Steinbeck and Faulkner may best be compared with reference to their attitudes toward Nature, though he finds Faulkner's
more clearly defined, since he is "essentially concerned with moral
values" that qualify character, whereas Steinbeck is less successful in
balancing mythic and moral purposes.

The most important event for Steinbeck scholars in 1969, however, was the publication of *Journal of a Novel: The "East of Eden"
Letters* (New York, Viking Press), the transcript of a journal to which
Steinbeck added a note to his editor, Pascal Covici, each day before
he began work on the first draft of the novel. The entries comment
not only on the progress and design of the novel itself, but on Steinbeck's theories about fiction. They will be an enormous aid to scholars
like Henry L. Golemba, who in "Steinbeck's Attempt to Escape the
Literary Fallacy" (*MFS* 15:231–39) attempts to take a comprehensive
view of Steinbeck's fiction that reveals that his "non-teleological"
approach does not achieve the complete objectivity that would enable
him to describe life "as is" without encroaching on the question of
"why" it is. Actually, Golemba concludes, Steinbeck's work portrays
the futility of individual and group effort and the hopelessness of the
future and is colored by "a one-sided philosophy of despair."

Last year I failed to note that Agnes M. Donohue's *A Casebook on "The Grapes of Wrath"* (*ALS 1968*, p. 193) contains besides reprinted material, her own original " 'The Endless Journey to No End': Journey and Eden Symbolism in Hawthorne and Steinbeck" (pp. 257–66), which points out that both authors are concerned with "fallen man and his doomed search for an earthly paradise," as is illustrated by parallels between the corruption of wilderness innocence by the "hell-city" in "My Kinsman, Major Molineux" and Steinbeck's novel.

Turning to other individual works, one finds Hans-Günter Kruppa expressing a generally increasing distaste for purely formalistic criticism by asserting in "John Steinbeck: 'The Debt Shall Be Paid' " (*NS* 18:165–69) that *The Moon Is Down* (which Europeans have always appreciated more than Americans) would be properly valued if the modern pedagogical interest in studying literary structures were directed toward praising structures that illuminated the true nature of people.

The individual stories in *The Long Valley* continue to attract perceptive critics. Elizabeth E. McMahan asserts in " 'The Chrysanthemums': Study of a Woman's Sexuality" (*MFS* 14[1968]:453–58) that critics have not yet adequately explained the sexual basis of Elisa's frustration in the story, and Gerald Noonan adds in "A Note on 'The Chrysanthemums" (*MFS* 15:542) that Elisa overidealizes the tinker's way of life, so that the story illustrates that "nothing is either good or bad, or romantically fulfilling . . . but thinking makes it so." Hilton Anderson perceives an overlooked religious significance in "Steinbeck's 'Flight' " (*Expl* 28:item 12), centered upon suggestions of a kinship between Pepe and the serpent that culminates in the boy's final exorcising of this symbol of evil. Donald E. Houghton's " 'Westering' in 'Leader of the People' " (*WAL* 4:117–24) presents a jaundiced view of the popular story, arguing that "Grandfather's explanation of westering is an unfortunate, confusing, and unnecessary digression which tears at the emotional and thematic unity of the story" and of *The Red Pony* as a whole.

Some respite has occurred in West studies after the intense attention to his small body of work in recent years. Robert I. Edenbaum's "A Surfeit of Shoddy: Nathanael West's *A Cool Million*" (*SHR* 2[1968]:427–39) is valuable for putting the finger on a central weakness in the novel, which Edenbaum sees as not an image of the world at all, but an image of an image—a portrait of William Randolph

Hearst's "self-portrait of the lower middle-class." Edenbaum thinks that the "two-dimensionality" of the novel to which some critics have objected is deliberate and justified, but that the novel is already dated because its violence-oriented vision does not bring to readers' minds today the "smooth, automated public relations fascism of the future." Sanford Pinsker's "Charles Dickens and Nathanael West: Great Expectations Unfulfilled" (*Topic* 18:40–52) finds that the same novel parallels the American chapters of *Martin Chuzzlewit*, since both deal with a naive man seeking in vain to carve out a new life in a wilderness. The article also suggests a parallel between *Miss Lonelyhearts* and *Great Expectations*, since both portray a protagonist with an obsession that is "clearly incompatible and/or impossible with the society surrounding him."

Attention continues to focus on Thornton Wilder's plays. They are responsible really for the one new article on his fiction, K. Riegl's "Max Reinhardt als Vorbild für Thornton Wilders Caesar" (*NS* 17 [1968]:356–58), which suggests that Reinhardt, whom Wilder greatly admired and with whom he worked in 1938 and 1939, is a model for Julius Caesar in *The Ides of March*.

Studies of Thomas Wolfe are reaching a point of diminishing returns, since little new light is shed on the nature or structure of his works by recent criticism. The most ambitious effort, Paschal Reeves's *Thomas Wolfe's Albatross: Race and Nationality in America* (Athens, Univ. of Ga. Press) is an overextended study of Wolfe's incidental references to members of various races. Although Reeves devotes a chapter to Wolfe's treatment of the Negro and produces from the novels examples of such other racial types as Indians and Latin Americans, he fails to prove that Wolfe had any really enduring sociological interest in any racial group except the Jews, whose capacity for abundant living he admired, though he disliked Jewish efforts to conceal racial origin. As for the Negroes, Reeves admits that, although Wolfe struggled to overcome his own environmentally formed prejudices and did condemn the exploitation of the race, he never brought a Negro character into full focus. Reeves deals at length with Wolfe's using the Indian, Nebraska Craven, in *You Can't Go Home Again* as a symbol of what is good and fundamentally American, but fails to demonstrate that Wolfe's treatment of this isolated, symbolic figure suggests any coherent attitude toward his race.

Two criticisms focus on Wolfe's more morbid short works. In a stiffly written analysis, "Thomas Wolfe and the Quest for Language" (*OUR* 11:5–18), Duane Schneider attempts to demonstrate that Wolfe's search for "the word" is a complex metaphor representing his effort to articulate human experience. Elke and Dieter Meinke, on the other hand, in "Thomas Wolfe: Zum Tod in der Groszstadt" (*NS* 18:373–80), find social criticism as well as symbolism in "Death, the Proud Brother" (one of the stories that Schneider bases his argument on). John L. Idol, Jr.'s "The Plays of Thomas Wolfe and Their Links with His Novels" (*MissQ* 22:95–112) locates the elements that were carried over from Wolfe's not very successful plays into his novels.

A fruitful approach for future Wolfe critics appears to be the kind of comparative studies that are beginning to be made of him, as well as of Porter, West, and Steinbeck. Ladell Payne opens his *Thomas Wolfe* (SWS 9) with an intriguing comparison of Wolfe's style and vision to Dickens's, but the rest of the pamphlet is largely plot summary. More successful is Rima Drell Reck's "Céline and Wolfe: Toward a Theory of the Autobiographical Novel" (*MissQ* 22:19–27), which compares and contrasts these two novelists who make extensive use of personal experiences in order to demonstrate that Céline's "tone of *powerless* rage" and Wolfe's tone of "poetic *hindsight*" are their different responses to the essential task of the personal autobiographical novelist, who must create "an objective work of fiction from a subjective insight."

### vii. The Tough Guys and Others

With one exception, the writers that David Madden celebrated last year in his two anthologies on tough guys and proletarians (see *ALS* 1968, pp. 178–79) have not attracted much further attention. James Korges's *Erskine Caldwell* (UMPAW 78) attempts to indicate the subject's neglected achievement, "to prevent if possible another disgrace in American letters of the kind visited on Melville." The pamphlet does a remarkable job of surveying Caldwell's vast output, but it attempts to overwhelm the reader with unsupported assertions of Caldwell's importance rather than to make a convincing case based on clearly discernible critical standards. The same tone that we fight in freshman themes prevails in "Cabalist in the Wrong Season," Harold Billings's introduction to *Edward Dahlberg: American Ish-*

*mael of Letters* (Austin, Texas, Roger Beacham, 1968), a collection of fifteen essays by such erstwhile cronies of Dahlberg as Sir Herbert Read, Allen Tate, and Frank McShane. Billings finds Dahlberg's writings "remarkable reliquaries of feeling and thought" and surveys the ups and downs of the novelist's reputation without providing any significant insight into his tortured personality and his pretentious style. David Bronson's "A Conversation with Henry Roth" (*PR* 36: 265–80) brings out the novelist's feeling that *Call It Sleep* was "too private" for him "to have given much thought to specific social problems." The only piece in this small group that can really be called critical is Scott Donaldson's "Appointment with the Dentist: O'Hara's Naturalistic Novel" (*MFS* 14[1968]:435–42), which examines the argument of early critics of *Appointment in Samarra* that Julian English had no adequate justification for committing suicide and counters that O'Hara constructs his picture of the social ladder in Gibbsville, Pennsylvania, in order to make the point that Julian's tragedy is that "he accepts society's judgment as both inevitable and final" and rejects his own existence rather than slide down the social ladder.

The exception to the general neglect of "depression authors" is Richard Wright. Inspired surely by the recent interest in Black American literature, 1969 brought two-and-one-half books, several magazine issues, and about a half-dozen articles on Wright that may well have doubled the extant criticism of his work.

The books contrast sharply in value. Edward Margolies's *The Art of Richard Wright* (Carbondale, Southern Ill. Univ. Press) is the fullest and most accurate account so far of the meaning and value of the novelist's work. Although some critics see Wright as nothing but a proletarian writer, Margolies, who discussed Wright briefly earlier in *Native Sons* (see *ALS 1968*, p. 177), feels that the novelist "wove his theme of human fear, alienation, guilt, and dread into the overall texture of his work"; but Margolies recognizes that Wright "seldom achieved his fullest measure of artistic promise." This keystone book in Wright studies suffers only from the lack of a unifying thesis that would tie together the perceptive judgments of individual works. Dan McCall's *The Example of Richard Wright* (New York, Harcourt, Brace & World), on the other hand, is simply a piece of bellicose journalism, designed to arouse a new generation's interest in the voice "of a lonely, furious, proud black man from the South, telling us that our culture is crazy." Robert A. Bone's "half-book," *Richard Wright*

( UMPAW 74), provides a far more helpful introduction, but it suffers from awkward organization, as if it had been cut down from a much longer manuscript. The author of *The Negro Novel in America* finds "anguish" to be Wright's "characteristic note" and attributes the novelist's attraction to existentialism to "his tendency to make a virtue out of rootlessness, to conceive of the human condition as a kind of cosmic exile." More debatable is Bone's contention that Wright "must be acknowledged as the major spokesman of contemporary humanism."

Some of the articles in the "Special Richard Wright Number" of *CLA Journal* ( 12,iv) are appropriately discussed in connection with essays about individual works, but some admirably survey Wright's whole achievement. Blyden Jackson's "Richard Wright: Black Boy from America's Black Belt and Urban Ghettos" (pp. 287–309) is a powerful biographical account of the effect of Wright's experiences as a small black boy in Mississippi on his entire career. The aim of George E. Kent's "Richard Wright: Blackness and the Adventure of American Culture" (pp. 322–43) is set forth in his first sentence, "I shall try to focus upon three sources of Wright's power: his double-consciousness, his personal tension, and his dramatic articulation of black and white culture." "Double consciousness," Kent explains in W. E. B. Du Bois's terms, is "the black's sense of being something defined and imprisoned by the myths of white and at war with his consciousness of American citizenship." The "personal tension" results, Kent feels, "from a stubborn self-consciousness of victimization but obsessed with its right" to engage and reap the fruits of universal forces. The "articulation" is achieved by Wright's presentation of the presence or absence in both cultures of rituals that emphasize such positive qualities as "rational drive, curiosity, revolutionary will, individualism, self-consciousness" and such negative ones as "blindness, softness, shrinking from life, escapism, otherworldliness, abjectness, and surrender." Donald B. Gibson's "Richard Wright and the Tyranny of Convention" (pp. 344–57) also examines the way in which Wright, in nearly all his works, shows a concern "with the individual in conflict with social convention," because of his struggle "to know the extent to which, in the face of convention's tyranny, the realization of the individual's human potential is possible." Gibson has also compiled "Richard Wright: A Bibliographical Essay" (pp. 360–65).

The only other effort to survey Wright's entire artistic career is

Warren French's "The Lost Potential of Richard Wright" in *The Black American Writer*, edited by C. W. E. Bigsby (2 vols., Deland, Fla., Everett/Edwards, vol. 1, pp. 125–42), which argues that the novelist's work, like John Steinbeck's, suffered when he turned from vivid re-creations of deeply felt direct experiences to indulge a penchant for allegory. Wright created in *Native Son* a black analogue to Dreiser's *An American Tragedy*, but thereafter he was kept too busy serving as a Black spokesman to enjoy the inconspicuousness needed for the development of his artistic vision.

*Native Son* remains the principal subject of critical scrutiny. Donald B. Gibson argues in "Wright's Invisible Native Son" (*AQ* 21: 728–38) that ironically most critics have missed the point of the novel because they have misinterpreted the "social person" of Bigger Thomas as "the *real* and *essential* person." Trying to get at the essence, Keneth Kinnamon concentrates on early influences on Wright in two articles: "*Native Son*: The Personal, Social, and Political Background" (*Phylon* 30:66–72) traces the personal experiences that are reflected in the novel; "The Pastoral Impulse in Richard Wright" (*MASJ* 10,i:41–47) points out that "a pastoral motif," in the sense of "a retrospective rural nostalgia from the vantage point of the author's present" recurs frequently, especially in Wright's early stories. Kinnamon feels, however, that this motif does not derive from a conscious use of the Theocritan literary tradition, but from the influence of the Book of Genesis. The same author's "Richard Wright's Use of *Othello* in *Native Son*" (*CLAJ* 12:358–59) suggests parallels with the play.

Other critics suggest the complexity of the novel approached as an autonomous work of art rather than a distinctively Black writing. In "Some Basic Ideas and Ideals in Richard Wright's Fiction" (*CLAJ* 13:78–84) Raman K. Singh argues that while Bigger Thomas joins neither the Christian Church nor the Communist Party, he is deeply comforted by his attorney and becomes "essentially, a Christ figure." James Nagel's "Images of 'Vision' in *Native Son*" (*UR* 35:109–15) suggests that the frequency of "vision" images in the novel means that it is best read as "an analysis of perception," which documents the effect that prejudice, alienation, oppression, and isolation have on one's ability to "see" and "be seen" clearly.

The other novels are found less rewarding, and Singh argues, for example, that *The Outsider* led Wright to a dilemma from which he never recovered—that idealistic action to correct injustice can be carried to an extreme that itself causes injustice. Darwin T. Turner's *"The Outsider*: Revision of an Idea" (*CLAJ* 12:310–21) similarly finds that the novel led Wright to a question that he could not answer: What future exists for a man who can find no solution to his problems in any of the dominant ideas of his society? Turner thinks that *The Outsider* is an attempt to rewrite *Native Son* and "by creating a character on a different economic and social level" to emphasize that Wright was not concerned solely with the American Negro, but "with the problem of existence itself" for any oppressed person, although the novelist failed artistically because his middle-class protagonist "does not evoke the sentimentality which can be showered on those judged to be socially and economically inferior"—the same problem that Steven Dhondt found troubling in Jack London's "When God Laughs."

*Indiana University–Purdue University at Indianapolis*

# 13. Fiction: The 1930's to the Present

## James H. Justus

At the end of the decade, scholarship patterns show that Mailer, O'Connor, and Bellow are the favorite contemporary novelists. Steady interest continues in Nabokov, Warren, and Styron; work in Malamud registers a slight gain; and the Salinger industry is bankrupt. The most remarkable changes are in the widespread recognition of Isaac Bashevis Singer and the sudden interest in Thomas Berger. The first promises to remain substantial because that recognition is so belated; time must determine whether the second can be sustained.[1]

### i. General Studies

*a.* **Overviews.** Aside from its essays on relevant individual figures, which will be discussed in appropriate places below, *The Forties*, edited by Warren French, is also conceived of as a profile of a period that is still difficult to assess. In addition to its generic introductions, it offers a selected bibliography of figures who wrote in the 1940's.

A number of synoptic studies have undertaken to tell us where we are in contemporary fiction and where we have just been. The best of these, two essays by Paul Levine, are both descriptive and evaluative. "The Intemperate Zone: The Climate of Contemporary American Fiction" (*MR* 8[1967]:505–23) is an accomplished account of the transition from the early responses to a chaotic society (Bellow and Ellison) to those which encapsulate that chaos in more "extreme" forms such as neorealism (Burroughs, Selby, Rechy) and fantasy

---

1. Because of space limitations, completed dissertations cannot be noted; those on specific figures include Warren (5), Salinger (2), O'Connor (2), and Singer, Barth, Heller, Powers, and Updike (1 each). I agree with one of the contributors to *ALS 1967* that significant work in dissertations will eventually reach print.

(Pynchon, Berger, Barth). A common theme in the early 1950's—the confrontation between ordinary people and extreme experiences—results in stylistic duality in Baldwin (journalism and fiction), Mc-Cullers (social realism and lyricism), Salinger (comic realism and mysticism), and Bellow (claustrophobic realism and picaresque openness). The writers of the next decade resort to "an ironic fusion of historical fact and black fantasy" to close such gaps. In a more informal piece, "The Politics of Alienation" (*Mosaic* 2,i[1968]:3–17), Levine uses some favorite novels of three college generations to show the sociological shift from alienation to rebellion; "crazy" in Holden Caulfield's lexicon is ambivalent, he says, but not in Yossarian's: "the hero's sanity is now questioned by his society but not by his creator."

Richard Ellman clearly feels disturbing impulses in what he sees as "Contemporary Directions in Literature" (*BaratR* 3[1968]:63–68). "All other heroes having failed," the spontaneous artist "remains the only viable hero." The followers of Beckett-like despair produce writing which he describes as "a lofty parallel to rioting, a form of demonstration against received ideas." But, in what seems a response to Ellman, Alfred Kazin disagrees. "Form and Anti-Form in Contemporary Literature" (*BaratR* 4:92–98) stresses the differences between "modern" and "contemporary," mostly to the discredit of Yeats, Joyce, Eliot, and Pound. Opposing an unhealthy "idolatry of form" is the newer "psychological authenticity," and the old idolatry, as he reads it, "has taken a deserved licking in favor of what you might call the school of experience." The writing is crisp and testy.

Alvin Greenberg's ambitious-sounding "Breakable Beginnings: The Fall into Reality in the Modern Novel" (*TSLL* 10:132–42) is a series of specific readings which support generalizations about the "fragility of relationships" in the precarious balance of the individual and his world. D. H. Lawrence's statement on man's plight in a cataclysmic age, "We've got to live, no matter how many skies have fallen," is not sufficient for Kingsley Widmer, who calls his shrill polemic "American Apocalypse: Notes on the Bomb and the Failure of Imagination" (*The Forties*, pp. 141–51). Enraged that the Bomb remains more a "symbol" than a visceral, haunting, day-to-day horror in our literature, Widmer uses the same brush to tar alike pop artists, documentary fictionists, serious novelists, poets both Beat and liberal, hippies, and literary critics.

*b. Genre studies.* Marjorie Ryan, in "Four Contemporary Satires and the Problem of Norms" (*SNL* 6,ii:40–46), offers no surprising conclusions (norms in satire now tend to be more subjective than they once were), but Heller's *Catch-22* and Purdy's *Cabot Wright Begins* especially benefit from analysis according to the formal aspects of satire. (The other novels used are Barth's *The Floating Opera* and Berger's *Reinhart in Love.*)

W. M. Frohock returns to the attack on those who use the term *picaresque* sloppily (see *ALS 1968*, p. 215) in "The Failing Center: Recent Fiction and the Picaresque Tradition" (*Novel* 3:62–69). Formlessness and lack of verisimilitude, he says, may correspond to "contemporary uncertainties about the central values of our culture," but they do not describe the picaresque; "for every novelist to write a new novel there is at least one critic waiting to find something picaresque in it." Frohock at least maintains his good cheer.

Joseph J. Waldmeir, in "Only an Occasional Rutabaga: American Fiction Since 1945" (*MFS* 15:467–81), identifies five trends and illustrates them perceptively, perfectly aware of their overlapping quality: the social critical, the "accommodationist," the "beat-absurd-black humorist," the "quest," and the "neo-social critical." The last is the most elusive, though Waldmeir thinks such authors belong temperamentally to the Civil Rights movement of the 1960's. Though brief, Scott Byrd's "A Separate Peace: Camp and Black Humor in Recent American Fiction" (*LangQ* 7,i-ii[1968]:7–10) makes sprightly and meaningful discriminations. Byrd sees camp as nonsatiric and nonliterary because it must depend on subject rather than method. Black humor, involved in assertive, often hostile expressions of absolute moral judgments, is a method applicable to any subject. What Byrd needs now is more space to examine the relevant authors: Pynchon, Heller, and Vonnegut.

*c.* **Special topics.** Both Joseph J. Waldmeir and Warren French find only traces of excellence in the welter of World War II novels. In *American Novels of the Second World War* (The Hague, Mouton) Waldmeir, though he devotes a single chapter to other kinds, concentrates on those "complex entities" which reexamine and reevaluate war experience in the light of ideology. These authors—angry, indignant, hopeful—are extensions of the social critics of the 1930's and continue the "hyper-realistic, almost naturalistic style" of Dos Passos and Farrell. Waldmeir's survey shows that the greatest concern was not the formal enemy, individual or social, but the Ugly American (racist, materialist, Dachau apologist). A few novelists, notably Herman Wouk and James Gould Cozzens, because they refused to perceive Nazi-like traits in Americans, were forced to make liberals and intellectuals their villains. Waldmeir concludes that though *The Caine Mutiny* and *Guard of Honor* are "two of the best made novels to come out of the war," their creators are "little more than ideological neo-Fascists." Both the praise and condemnation are excessive.

Although Waldmeir's decision to focus so exclusively on ideology limits the usefulness of his book, its thesis is argued convincingly. The relationship between the novelists of World Wars I and II is solidly presented, and the aesthetic judgments of many novels which are really "tracts or sermons" are rigorous. If certain titles keep reappearing in these pages (*The Naked and the Dead, The Young Lions*), their recurrence tells us something about the quality of most of the 250 novels listed in the carefully compiled bibliography.

In "Fiction: A Handful of Survivors" (*The Forties*, pp. 7–32) French is more interested in analysis than in ideological schema, though he comes to some of Waldmeir's conclusions—for example, Cozzens's acquiescence in the status quo in *Guard of Honor* is "sophisticated" despair, and his conservatism is really juiceless misanthropy. He considers James A. Michener's *Tales of the South Pacific* unpretentiously successful, but only two novels merit rereading today: Thomas Heggen's *Mister Roberts* and John Horne Burns's *The Gallery*. French bluntly concludes his lively essay with the judgment that little noteworthy fiction emerged from the war, and that which did "was a cry of pain—largely unheeded."

"Jewish Writing in America: Jewish or American?" (*BSUF* 10,ii: 40–46) is Ronald Weber's attempt to explain the achievement of literary Jews since about 1945. This journalistic piece is inconclusive. More ambitious and rewarding is Max F. Schulz's *Radical Sophistication: Studies in Contemporary Jewish-American Novelists* (Athens, Ohio Univ. Press), which is best seen as a loosely related series of essays. With more than a nod to Ihab Hassan, Schulz defines his key term variously as the "tenuous equipoise of irreconcilables," the "new Pyrrhonism," and the more down-to-earth "suspension of judgment." The Jewish-American writers accept the notion held by others that the growth of the individual is existential rather than social, but they also affirm the traditional notion that such growth must be in the context of the community.

As its title suggests, *Southern Fiction Today: Renascence and Beyond*, edited by George Core (Athens, Univ. of Ga. Press) is concerned with defining the continuity in the first great literary generation and those writers who have matured since about 1946. Walter Sullivan, C. Hugh Holman, and Louis D. Rubin, Jr., gracefully and intelligently face the issues which they gracefully and intelligently have been facing for years now.

Rubin ("Second Thoughts on the Old Gray Mare: The Continuing Relevance of Southern Literary Issues," pp. 33–50), who sees a nonsectarian religious attitude as a common quality among Southern writers, concludes that such values are still valid in works of the postwar period, many of which show that man is capable of tragic stature. But if Rubin sees no drastic decline in the quality of recent Southern fiction, Sullivan not only sees it but also finds a cause for it in "The New Faustus: The Southern Renascence and the Joycean Aesthetic" (pp. 1–15). Reinforcing an opinion voiced earlier (see *ALS 1968*, p. 203), he sees "hopelessness" and a "thrust toward destruction" characteristic of the recent writers, most of whom have been much smitten by the Dedalian postures of Joyce's hero. In the most hortatory of the essays, Sullivan warns that the new crop will remain barren until the faddish notions that "order is bad" and that "technique is all" disappear.

Judging from both his essay, "The View from the Regency-Hyatt: Southern Social Issues and the Outer World" (pp. 16–32), and his part in the symposium, Holman seems interested less in giving grades than in arguing for an enlarged conception of what "South" means. Beyond frontier humor and baronial romance lie poverty, malnutrition, and fundamental Protestantism as backgrounds against which these writers have exercised their consciences; their method has been essentially "critical social realism," which links Wolfe, O'Connor, Erskine Caldwell, and others with Lewis and Mencken.

Nancy M. Tischler's *Black Masks: Negro Characters in Modern Southern Fiction* (University Park, Pa. State Univ. Press) should remain a standard work for many years. Noted briefly last year (see *ALS 1968*, pp. 310–11), the book is a much-needed study of what has happened to the once-prevalent stereotypes categorized in Sterling Brown's 1937 book, *The Negro in American Fiction*.

Jesse Hill Ford's *The Liberation of Lord Byron Jones* comes in for a drubbing by Thomas H. Landess in "The Present Course of Southern Fiction: *Everynegro* and Other Alternatives" (*ArlQ* 1,ii[1967–68]:61–85) because it is an anachronistic morality play without any "true vitality or relevance." Landess argues for greater complexity in treating race relations, citing Marion Montgomery as the kind of innovative novelist he wants.

While most of the novels discussed in Jonas Spatz's *Hollywood in Fiction* (The Hague, Mouton) fall outside this chapter, its general thesis—that Hollywood becomes an appropriate subject and metaphor for novelists who question the assumptions of the Utopian myth—suggests a tradition out of which come the crisis ideology and radical mentality so crucial in contemporary fiction. In addition to perceptive comments on Mailer's *The Deer Park*, there is also an engaging look at Budd Schulberg's *What Makes Sammy Run?* and *The Disenchanted*.

*d.* **Primary materials.** Important primary materials are to be found in "The Uses of History in Fiction" (*SLJ*, 1,ii:57–90), a symposium with Ralph Ellison, William Styron, Robert Penn Warren, and C. Vann Woodward. This transcription, which includes remarks on the relation of fact and truth, distinctions between the novelist and historian, and other related topics, is a valuable piece marred only by audience participation (when Styron is verbally flogged from the floor by what he calls his *"bête noir,"* an anti-*Nat* Turner questioner). And as a collection, not much can be said for *Afterwords: Novelists on Their Novels* (New York, Harper & Row). A trivial introduction by Thomas McCormack and too many sales-boosting statements from second-rate writers outweigh the remarks by serious novelists. Some of the pieces are reprints, as are all the essays collected by Marcus Klein in *The American Novel Since World War II* (Greenwich, Conn., Fawcett), an excellent anthology, with a useful introduction.

### *ii.* Norman Mailer

The better of two books on Mailer this year is a revised dissertation, Barry H. Leeds's *The Structured Vision of Norman Mailer* (New York, N.Y. Univ. Press), a scholarly and clearly reasoned work on the entire canon. Curiously, the chapter on *The Naked and the Dead*, though workmanlike, lacks the verve and authority evident in later chapters, the finest of which is on *An American Dream*. Leeds is not the first to see Rojack's story as a religious pilgrimage, but he is the first to make his reading persuasive; as Mailer's first positive hero, Rojack discovers his own desire "for total commitment to goodness, to productivity, to fertility and love."

Mailer's search has not been ideological, says Leeds, but aesthetic: to forge a nonderivative art to carry the major themes already present in the first novel, the insistence on the reality of social ills and the intensity of the individual's responses to them. We are also offered a cogent statement on Mailerian existentialism and clarifying explications of Mailer's ideas about the interrelationships of sex and God and personal repression and cancer. One minor weakness throughout is a tendency toward an unquestioning acceptance of Mailer's social premises about U.S. "totalitarianism." Leeds refers to the "hypocrisy which Mailer sees in the simplistic American dream of freedom and plenty" without considering cultural or literary history, which would reveal that as fact *or* myth, the American Dream itself has never been simplistic, and only second-raters have chosen to write as if it were.

Donald L. Kaufmann's *Norman Mailer: The Countdown (The First Twenty Years)* (Carbondale, Southern Ill. Univ. Press) is a gimmicky study (the chapters are numbered 10–1, countdown fashion). Like Leeds, Kaufmann explores Mailer's obsessive concern with sex, sensation, and those other "mysteries," death and God. Unlike Leeds, he shows only perfunctory interest in *The Deer Park*, sees some few human values in *The Naked and the Dead* (though he cites only one example), and traces the ambiguous connections between Mailer ("The Jew as Literary Drop-out") and other Jewish writers. Isolated observations are useful and in chapter 7 we get an astute analysis of Mailer's fascination with Marxism, anarchy, and totalitarianism along with an unastute thesis: *An American Dream* "signals an end to a phase in Mailer's career, an obsession with politics in many styles," a prediction which would have been chancy even had this book appeared five years earlier. Deciding to ignore the last three books is disastrous. Before assuming "Mailer's goodbye to politics," Kaufmann might have remembered his earlier observation: "What also makes Mailer a special case is his sheer unpredictability."

Two interesting essays use very different methods and proceed from quite diverse assumptions. Andrew Gordon, in *"The Naked and the Dead:* The Triumph of Impotence" (*L&P* 19,iii–iv:3–13), traces "some of the psychic determinants" in the fiction. All the novels have "impotent murderer heroes who feel they deserve to be castrated," but Gordon devotes most of his energies to the castration-anal anxieties in the first novel. In its lack of subtlety (a patrol marching into a "fecal jungle" becomes a "journey into the anus"), this essay makes explicit what others have implicitly observed in less technical treatments. Raymond A. Schroth, on the other hand, surveys Mailer's career from what he sees as the mellowed perspective of *The Armies of the Night* in "Mailer and His Gods" (*Commonweal* 90:226–29). In his Manichean vision, Mailer sees war as merely a concentration of tensions in civilian life; the hero—gentle and religious—is most likely to come into contact with God by freely plunging into violence.

Grace Witt's thesis in "The Bad Man as Hipster: Norman Mailer's Use of Frontier Metaphor" (*WAL* 4:203–17) is that the myth of frontier individualism accounts for Mailer's idea of unrestrained violence as therapy. Max F. Schulz's "Norman Mailer's Divine Comedy" (*Radical Sophistication*, pp. 69–109) is a fuller version of an essay noted in *ALS 1968* (p. 212). A succinct and perceptive weaving together of the fiction and the nonfiction, it is unfortunately marred by frequent lapses into pedestrian locutions and off-center analogies: Mailer becomes a "gung-ho marine" who takes risks to win large objectives, and in *Why Are We in Vietnam?* he is seen "striking up the Amazon River of the American psyche."

### *iii.* Flannery O'Connor

The posthumous appearance of miscellaneous prose should be an important event, but Flannery O'Connor's *Mystery and Manners: Occasional Prose* (New York, Farrar, Straus, & Giroux) has been edited in an arbitrary, old-fashioned way by Sally and Robert Fitzgerald. Basic decisions were, as the editors admit, personal. The text in several instances is apparently arbitrary: "We cut away most of the repetitions and took interesting arguments in their best available form; where rearrangements and transpositions were necessary and possible, we performed them." It is useful, nevertheless, to have in a single book the familiar published lectures and essays, along with new ones.

Thematic studies continue to dominate. Carter W. Martin's critical method in *The True Country: Themes in the Fiction of Flannery O'Connor* (Nashville, Vanderbilt Univ. Press) cuts across chronology and genre. Some inevitable repetition and a reluctance to see degrees of success are perhaps corollaries of this method. Martin finds O'Connor's subject to be God's grace (both its recognition and its rejection), though her vehicle is not allegory. He argues persuasively for the appropriateness and integrity of her extreme symbols for the soul (a wooden leg) and the function of grace in the phenomenal world (a crude statue). Such symbols are "big and insolent," he says, but their final effect is "serene," a paradoxical quality characteristic of O'Connor's art generally. There are brief chapters on gothicism and grotesquerie, comedic devices, and satire and irony. Martin is the first to explore the dominant place of proper names in O'Connor's humor, and he finds recurring types in the bumpkin, the "fatuous sage," and the monomaniac. While this book breaks little new ground, it gathers up with considerable skill many of the issues discussed by previous critics.

The industrious Marion Montgomery continues his examination of the theological patterns in three essays. "Flannery O'Connor's Territorial Center" (*Crit* 11,iii:5–10) concerns "spiritual displacement" as a theological and fictional given; the spiritual gift of the crucifixion—the intervention of grace in human affairs—is the "central testimony" of O'Connor's work. "A Note on Flannery O'Connor's Terrible and Violent Prophecy of Mercy" (*ForumH* 7,iii:4–7) and "O'Connor and Teilhard de Chardin: The Problem of Evil" (*Renascence* 22:34–42) both deal more precisely with O'Connor's use of Teilhard than previous critics have done. The first is a thin piece on *The Violent Bear It Away*, but the second explicates the scientist's concept of evil (man is incapable of damnation, and evil is not a province of a malign spirit) in order to show the novelist's significant divergence from it.

Thomas M. Carlson, in "Flannery O'Connor: The Manichaean Dilemma" (*SR* 77:254–76), focuses primarily on the later stories as he traces the two basic heresies of traditional Christianity, Ebionitism and Docetism (which deny the union of flesh and spirit) to latter-day puritanism and humanitarianism. Although O'Connor's protagonists fall into these heresies, they sense a loss which gives them "some limited dimension of tragic stature."

David Eggenschwiler and Robert Drake are considerably more general than Montgomery and Carlson in their studies. In "Flannery O'Connor's True and False Prophets" (*Renascence* 21:151–61,167), Eggenschwiler emphasizes the evolution of Tarwater and Motes, both of whom struggle between self-abnegation and pride before accepting their roles; the themes of both novels derive from the conflict of the same set of opposites. Drake sees man's "encounter with Jesus Christ" as the essential story in any plot by O'Connor in "The Paradigm of Flannery O'Connor's True Country" (*SSF* 6:433–42), and he praises her as the model for the aspiring writer, not because of that theme but because to it she had "absolute and unwavering fidelity." Though unduly chatty, Drake's essay says a good bit about not only the integrity of a "major minor figure" but also the problem of the Southern writer generally.

In "The Halt Shall Be Gathered Together: Physical Deformity in the Fiction of Flannery O'Connor" (*WHR* 22[1968]:325–38) Henry Taylor clumsily surveys most of the fiction without adding much that is new—and in a few cases contributing wrong-headed readings. O'Connoresque deformity, he observes, is a tangible manifestation of a spiritual condition which leads its victim to think deeply about himself, and this deep thinking brings him closer to seeing the need for redemption; but this conclusion is almost nullified by the author himself: "no single story contains evidence to support the general statements I have made; some of the stories even contradict these statements." Taylor's analysis of "Parker's Back" is astonishingly simplistic, but a good essay on that story is Preston Browning, Jr.'s " 'Parker's Back': Flannery O'Connor's Iconography of Salvation by Profanity" (*SSF* 6:525–35). Tattooing is an analogue "for that sense of the Other," and this story is, in part, the study of the subconscious search of an insensitive man for an identity "that is his all the while"; Browning ranks the story as one of the author's finest because it maintains the integrity of both the natural and the metaphysical.

In a clear but spun-out essay, Gilbert H. Muller argues in "The City of Woe: Flannery O'Connor's Dantean Vision" (*GaR* 23:206–13) that "The Artificial Nigger" is as allegorical as the *Inferno*, which supplies it with both theme and technique. But in another piece, "*The Violent Bear It Away*: Moral and Dramatic Sense" (*Renascence* 22:17–25), Muller uses Jamesian terms to stress the aesthetic rather than the allegorical bias in O'Connor. Although the twelve chapters of the novel correspond to Matthew 11:1–12, there is "perfect coincidence" of the two "senses."

Stuart L. Burns, in "Structural Patterns in *Wise Blood*" (*XUS* 8, ii:32–43), gives close attention to the "figurative techniques" in O'Connor's first novel; he finds three symbols (water, sex, and coffin) which function cumulatively to dramatize "the cycle of Hazel Motes's fall, his literal death and symbolic rebirth."

Both Burns and Frederick Asals contribute substantial studies of the apprentice fiction. "The Road to *Wise Blood*" (*Renascence* 21: 181–94) is Asals's examination of four published stories which preceded the first novel. In them Asals finds "the uncertain beginnings of the detachment of the authorial voice from the central consciousness," the discovery of irony and uses of the grotesque, and imagistic heightening. What these stories do not foreshadow, says Asals, is the exuberant comedy of *Wise Blood* or its firm control. In "Flannery O'Connor's Literary Apprenticeship" (*Renascence* 22:3–16), Burns concentrates on three stories from the novelist's Iowa thesis, pointing out her early experiments with dialect and comic satire and the first configurations of the pseudo-intellectual and the ineffectual liberal as characters. We need more such attention to style and craft—as Robert E. Reiter also argues in his brief introduction to *Flannery O'Connor* (St. Louis, Herder, 1968), a collection of ten previously published essays.

### *iv.* Isaac Bashevis Singer

Suddenly it's a Singer year, with two collections of critical estimates and several articles. Both anthologies are valuable, and only two critics—with different essays—are represented in both. The eleven essays, commissioned by Marcia Allentuck for *The Achievement of Isaac Bashevis Singer* (Carbondale, Southern Ill. Univ. Press), constitute the most ambitious appraisal of the Yiddish author yet to appear. The four studies which explore general themes and recurring narrative and ethical patterns are the most useful (and in general the most skillfully written). William H. Gass's "The Shut-In" (pp. 1–13), despite its razzle-dazzle, is useful for its close attention to Singer's language.

Eli Katz, in "Isaac Bashevis Singer and the Classical Yiddish Tradition" (pp. 14–25), contrasts the fictional *shtetls* of the older writers with those of Singer, which are not communities at all since they lack cohesion and social controls. Morris Golden's fine essay, "Dr. Fischelson's Miracle: Duality and Vision in Singer's Fiction" (pp. 26–43) concentrates on "The Spinoza of Market Street" as a summary of salient themes crucial to Singer's general vision. Maximillian E. Novak ("Moral Grotesque and Decorative Grotesque in Singer's Fiction," pp. 44–63) finds that the novelist's demonic world is more akin to the art of Bunyan than that of Poe or Kafka and argues that the techniques are more successful in the stories than in the novels.

Most of the major Singer texts are treated in the other essays, most of which contribute pertinent insights, including even a tiresome study by H. R. Wolf ("Singer's Children's Stories and *In My Father's Court*: Universalism and the Rankian Hero," pp. 145–58), who shows considerably more respect for psychological jargon than he does for Singer's prose or his own. Two of the better essays are by Edwin Gittleman ("Singer's Apocalyptic Town: *Satan in Goray*, pp. 64–76) and Paul N. Siegel ("Gimpel and the Archetype of the Wise Fool," pp. 159–73). The first is a reading of the ambivalent salvation in Singer's fascinating novel, but Gittleman's most tantalizing observation occurs as a throwaway last line: his "imagination of disaster" puts Singer in the Poe-Hawthorne-Melville tradition "rather than in the East-European tradition of the Chelmic storytellers." Siegel sees in Gimpel the merging of two figures: the suffering wanderer who attains "ecstatic wisdom" and the fool (especially interesting are the parallels which he finds with Erasmus's allegorical Folly).

Of the fifteen items in *Critical Views of Isaac Bashevis Singer*, edited by Irving Malin (New York, N.Y. Univ. Press), eight are reprints, some of them representing the best of earlier writing on Singer. The most useful items in Malin are a bibliography ("Isaac Bashevis Singer in English," pp. 220–65) compiled by Jackson R. Bryer and Paul E. Rockwell, and perceptive essays by Melvin J. Friedman ("Isaac Bashevis Singer: The Appeal of Numbers," pp. 178–93) and Edwin Gittleman ("Isaac's Nominal Case: *In My Father's Court*," pp. 194–206). The latter is a fine analysis of the novelist's psychological personae formed through the exercise of the imaginative techniques of fiction; and Friedman sees Singer, like Flannery O'Connor, in the apocalyptic tradition, risking Manicheanism and using shock and "literary disproportion" as tactics for dealing with spiritual

themes. Samuel I. Mintz ("Spinoza and Spinozism in Singer's Shorter Fiction," pp. 207–17) believes that Spinoza is more important to
Singer as a personal figure than as a systematic philosopher—as a
"metaphor" for the problems of all Yiddish writers who must recon-
cile the claims of "tradition" and "enlightenment." Linking Singer
and Muriel Spark would seem to be bold and innovative, but Karl
Malkoff's results are disappointingly inconclusive in "Demonology
and Dualism: The Supernatural in Isaac Singer and Muriel Spark"
(pp. 149–68). Jules Chametzky's brief "History in I. B. Singer's
Novels" (pp. 169–77) is preachy and pious and a notch below the
essay by Max F. Schulz, who covers some of the same ground in the
Allentuck volume ("The Family Chronicle as Paradigm of History:
*The Brothers Ashkenazi* and *The Family Moskat*," *Achievement*, pp.
77–92). The latter essay suggests that more comprehensive comparisons of the brothers Singer would be fruitful.

In general, the critics in both collections stress similar aspects of
Singer. Most of them see him simultaneously as ironist, dualist, and
visionary who writes of the archetypal Jewish experience (which
turns out more often than not to be Man's experience). They mention
his great detachment from his characters and the thematic implications of that distance (though not many bother to explore the technical ways in which he achieves it); the tensions which produce
"religious humor"; the single plane on which Singer places the solid
specifics of the world and the mystical apparatus of the sundry supernatural realms; and his sensitivity to what Frederick R. Karl calls
the "tangential linkage" of freedom and slavery ("Jacob Reborn, Zion
Regained: I. B. Singer's *The Slave*," *Achievement*, pp. 112–23): "One
stays in his father's court; the family orbit, despite friction, saves."

Much of what Max F. Schulz does in six pages (and he does
much) in "Isaac Bashevis Singer, Radical Sophistication, and the
Jewish-American Novel" (*SHR* 3[1968]:60–66) forms the rationale
and establishes the terms which he uses throughout *Radical Sophistication.* One of Schulz's interesting speculations is that the *shtetl* is
to the Jewish-American imagination what the American frontier is to
non-Jewish writers.

Linda G. Zatlin examines three of Singer's stories in some detail
in "The Themes of Isaac Bashevis Singer's Short Fiction" (*Crit* 11,ii:
40–46). Because the characters are allegorical figures working out
resolutions to the dilemma of faith, Singer transcends the Yiddishness

of his subject matter. Sanford Pinsker, however, is more concerned with the ideological and historical context of the *shtetl*, in which its "curious combination of rigidity and homogeneous warmth" became the energizing spirit behind Singer's re-creation of his environments ("The Fictive Worlds of Isaac Bashevis Singer," *Crit* 11,ii:26–39). Contributing new interviews with Singer are both Pinsker (*Crit* 11, ii:16–25) and Cyrena N. Pondrom (*ConL* 10:1–38,332–51). Bonnie Jean M. Christensen has compiled "Isaac Bashevis Singer: A Bibliography" (*BB* 26:3–6).

### *v.* Vladimir Nabokov

*Nabokov: The Man and His Work*, edited by L. S. Dembo (Madison, Univ. of Wis. Press, 1967) is a reprint of a special number of *WSCL* (see *ALS 1967*, p. 200) with two new essays, Charles Nicol's "The Mirrors of Sebastian Knight" (pp. 85–94) and Ambrose Gordon, Jr.'s "The Double Pnin" (pp. 144–56). Both are knowledgeable, and Gordon's is excellent. Nichol's thesis is that *Sebastian Knight* is a presentation of methods by which a biography might be written; attention to the works rather than the life leads the would-be biographer to become Knight. Gordon sees *Pnin* as Nabokov's "ritual expunging of the alien in himself," and the conflict in Pnin between the "eternal Alien" and the "eternal Exile" is resolved in typically Nabokovian terms—the Exile is freed and the Alien is purged through unremitting parody. "Vladimir Nabokov's Critical Reputation in English: A Note and a Checklist" (pp. 225–76) is an especially useful compilation by Jackson R. Bryer and Thomas J. Bergin, Jr. It is, however, difficult to agree with Bryer that Nabokov has been ignored by serious critics, a point made unconvincing by the closely packed forty-six-page checklist.

Dabney Stuart's "All the Mind's a Stage" (*UWR* 4,ii:1–24) suggests that *Invitation to a Beheading* is a stage play rather than a novel; the work emphasizes lighting, costumes, make-up, stage directions, even the use of the same actors to play different characters. Susan Fromberg's "The Unwritten Chapters in *The Real Life of Sebastian Knight*" (*MFS* 13[1967]:427–42) is based on the common notion (supported by Nabokov) that artistic creation is in little what God's creation is in large. Thus V. can become Knight because all souls are "ultimately inhabited by an 'ultimate' soul, the soul which created the universe." Strother B. Purdy calls his "Solus Rex: Nabokov and the Chess Novel" (*MFS* 14[1968]:379–95) some "notes on chess" which he feels can add to our appreciation of Nabokovian artistry. This technical essay is not for the casual buff.

### vi. Robert Penn Warren and William Styron

John L. Longley, Jr.'s *Robert Penn Warren* (SWS 2) is stronger on plot summaries than on criticism. There is no treatment of the neglected short fiction, and the coverage of the poetry and nonfiction is inadequate (six pages out of forty). Longley in some cases is still battling the original reviewers, and he is still trying to understand the lack of popularity of *At Heaven's Gate*, which he declared in an excellent 1960 essay to be Warren's best novel after *All the King's Men*. But talk of shifting climates of opinion and generation gaps— student ignorance of "primitive, Holy-Roller religion and rhetoric" —just won't do.

Neil Nakadate's perceptive "Robert Penn Warren and the Confessional Novel" (*Genre* 2:326–40) deals largely with *All the King's Men* and *World Enough and Time*. Confession, Nakadate says, is a means of bringing order to a problematical existence through aesthetic control, picking up threads of a "reproachable life" and weaving them into a justifiable fabric. The inset stories, one of Warren's favorite devices, are seen as miniatures for showing that the ongoing process of confession is the "necessary counterpoise for the fact of sin in human experience" and the first step in moral reclamation of the self. In fine Warrenesque idiom, Nakadate says "the novelistic confession tells us what we don't want to know and what we never bother to tell ourselves." Paul McCarthy's "Sports and Recreation in *All the King's Men*" (*MissQ* 22:113–30) is not merely a listing of the frequent references to swimming, tennis, hunting, football, and the like; McCarthy relates their diverse effects on the narrator's consciousness to Warren's overall theme.

Of the two items by James H. Justus on *All the King's Men*, "A Note on John Crowe Ransom and Robert Penn Warren" (*AL* 41:425–30) suggests that Ransom's poem "Dead Boy" may be a source for Jack Burden's self-description in chapter 7 and points out themes and technical devices shared by the two men. "All the Burdens of Warren's *All the King's Men*" (*The Forties*, pp. 191–201) explores some of the results of the technical decision to use Burden as narrator of

Stark's story. The record of his growth is reflected in the language of his memoir, and the terms of the struggle (seen in image patterns in the novel) are established prior to the narrative to suggest its operable tensions: the nursery rhyme title (factual and deterministic) and the Dantean epigraph (imaginative and hopeful).

David J. Burt's note, "A Folk Reference in Warren's *Flood*" (*MissQ* 22:74–76) shows that the ballad ("Cotton-eye Joe") which Pretty-Boy Rountree sings in prison symbolizes certainty of purpose as contrasted with the protagonist's divided romanticism. Burt has also contributed, with Annette C. Burt, "Robert Penn Warren's Debt to Ibsen in *Night Rider*" (*MissQ* 22:359–61). Peer Gynt's literal use of an onion, peeling off the layers to indicate the emptiness of his life, becomes a metaphor in Warren's first novel used for prefiguring Percy Munn's destructive flaw.

*William Styron* (SWS 7) is an intelligent and often original survey by Cooper R. Mackin. In his discussion of *Lie Down in Darkness*, he becomes the first critic to consider the importance of Maudie, the lame and retarded sister of Peyton whose spiritual defects are not her own but her parents'. Like most critics, Mackin stresses the weaknesses of *Set This House on Fire* and *The Long March*, the novella whose deceptive simplicity has always frustrated analysis. He praises Styron's decision in *The Confessions of Nat Turner* to make the protagonist a conscious stylist who knows the difference between "mental and verbal styles." A minor demurrer: Mackin is needlessly emphatic on the issue of Nat's "insanity" (I count six reminders in the fifteen-page treatment).

The late Frederick J. Hoffman discusses "the problem of believing" in "The Cure of 'Nothing!': The Fiction of William Styron" (*Frontiers*, pp. 69–87). Pathetic situations, he says, have a way of extending beyond merely subjective horror into the world, causing "great cracks in the human landscape," a modern quality which comes paradoxically from Styron's fondness for late Renaissance writers. Marc L. Ratner, in "Styron's Rebel" (*AQ* 21:595–608), demonstrates that the theme of rebellion, the rebel hero, and the confessional techniques can be seen in all of Styron's work, a fact which complicates oversimplified readings of *Nat Turner*. The slave revolt in the recent novel is a means to an end—Nat's "assertion of *self*"— and Nat's powerful sense of defiance before his death has parallels in Camus and Malamud.

For different reasons, Nash K. Burger and Alan Holder are disturbed by *Nat Turner*. "Truth or Consequences: Books and Book Reviewing" (*SAQ* 68:152–66) is Burger's ill-tempered argument that Stark Young's *So Red the Rose* is better and truer than *Nat Turner* because Young never became a full-fledged city dweller (and thus maintained his "Southern-bred understanding") while Styron now bad-mouths the South from his "Eastern Establishment" home in Connecticut. Holder's "Styron's Slave: *The Confessions of Nat Turner*" (*SAQ* 68:167–80) shows the novel poised between an interior frame of reference (Nat's authoritative religious sensibilities) and an external one (in which the author reduces those terms to the psychosexual); the two impulses, Holder says, pull the novel apart.

Melvin J. Friedman and August J. Nigro, editors of *William Styron* (Paris, Minard, 1967)—a special combined number of the *Revue des lettres modernes*—have collected six essays on the novels (excluding *Nat Turner*) written originally in English and translated for French students. English scholars will find Nigro's bibliography the most useful part of the collection.

### *vii.* Saul Bellow, Bernard Malamud, J. D. Salinger

Remarkable unanimity shows up in the first serious assessments of *Herzog*. In "*Herzog*: A Transcendental Solution to an Existential Problem" (*ForumH* 7,ii:32–36), M. Gilbert Porter sees the growth of this "man of feeling" as an earned process; he endures alienation and suffers anguish, rejecting the void because it lacks a center. What Porter calls transcendentalism Anselm Atkins calls affirmation in "The Moderate Optimism of Saul Bellow's *Herzog*" (*Person* 50:117–29). As "post-crisis man," Herzog "integrates and surpasses" the simplicities of Bellow's earlier protagonists.

Although he makes similar points, Dudley Flamm, in "Herzog—Victim and Hero" (*ZAA* 17:174–88), is primarily interested in relating Bellow's character to the general Jewish "adjustment" in America. Unlike the earlier major protagonists, who are either hero or victim, Herzog is a fusion, and the affirmation at the end reflects an historical Jewish response. The essay is much too long for its modest and arguable point—aspects suggested by Peter Lucko in his response, "Herzog—Modell der *acceptance*: Eine Erwiderung" (*ZAA* 17:189–95).

A revisionist view of Hemingway's Robert Cohn is one of the by-products of Michael J. Hoffman's "From Cohn to Herzog" (*YR* 58: 342–58). The peripheral figure of *The Sun Also Rises* is the literary ancestor of Bellow's hero. Both are "*naifs* in the American tradition of the radical innocent," and both are verbalizers and justifiers. Hoffman also presses hard on the origins and properties of the proper names.

With a slight shift in emphasis, Abraham Bezanker would agree. In "The Odyssey of Saul Bellow" (*YR* 58:359–71) he interprets volubility as symptomatic of the painful frustration of the self-aware individual. Each of Bellow's heroes is "something of a fool" out of Yiddish folklore; and Herzog is the *nebbish*—the man of "innocent and cloistered virtue whom we respect and admire for his purity, the man of intellectual wisdom who stumbles grievously through the ways of the world." Pat T. Overbeck also works out some character types in "The Women in *Augie March*" (*TSLL* 10[1968]: 471–84). The women are cast in the familiar roles of "virago" and "victim."

Focusing primarily on *Herzog* and the play *The Last Analysis*, Ronald Weber in "Bellow's Thinkers" (*WHR* 22[1968]:305–13) argues that for Bellow thought is both precious and ambivalent, "as dangerous and deceptive as ennobling," and as capable of leading one away from life as into it. To suit his ambitious title, Weber might better have been more comprehensive, as is Max F. Schulz, who comes to much the same conclusion in "Saul Bellow and the Burden of Selfhood" (*Radical Sophistication*, pp. 110–53). This most cerebral of Jewish-American writers may appeal to intellectuals, says Schulz, but he gives them little comfort, for he shows a marked suspicion of the human mind. Schulz interestingly sees the tradition of Blakean hortatory in Bellow's major themes.

David P. Demarest, Jr., studies two "dialectical" stories in "The Theme of Discontinuity in Saul Bellow's Fiction: 'Looking for Mr. Green' and 'A Father-to-Be'" (*SSF* 6:175–86). These pieces posit a search for intellectual order against an acceptance of life as it is, and both affirm man's often illogical penchant for alternating perspectives. As men who are brought to full self-awareness, these protagonists prefigure the heroes of the longer fiction.

In "The Cost of Henderson's Quest" (*BSUF* 10,ii:37–39) Thomas R. Knipp says that the plot of *Henderson the Rain King* reveals that the fundamental relationships are not the problems of "being and becoming" but of "doing and receiving." It charts an egocentric quest in which Henderson is a "heavy-handed neo-colonialist who leaves desolation in his wake." Jeff H. Campbell, in "Bellow's Intimations of Immortality: *Henderson the Rain King*" (*SNNTS* 1:323–33), theorizes that the motifs associated with Bellow's hero are drawn from Wordsworth's ode. The novel is a mock-epic enriched, in the first five chapters, with "implicit" parodies of other modern writers, whose views of the human heart must be rejected.

In "The Achievement of Bernard Malamud" (*MQ* 10:379–89) Sanford Pinsker plausibly argues, out of the context of recent history, that, more than his Jewish contemporaries, Malamud has undertaken a cultural as well as an aesthetic task. He has long been trying to write a novel of tragedy, "a fictional argument for the value of suffering and the possibility of human transcendence," and *The Fixer* should be read in light of that desire. Pinsker has also contributed "A Note on Bernard Malamud's 'Take Pity'" (*SSF* 6:212–13).

Tony Tanner's thesis in "Bernard Malamud and the New Life" (*CritQ* 10[1968]:151–68) is that all the novels are "fables or parables of the painful process from immaturity to maturity," and since they run counter to the usual American literary view that initiation into manhood is a trauma, Malamud's "Old World allegiances" may have something to do with the difference. Max F. Schulz's "Bernard Malamud's Mythic Proletarians" (*Radical Sophistication*, pp. 56–68) is also concerned with mythic patterns—vegetation rituals and Grail quests—but mainly as they mask Malamud's basic continuations of the proletarian impulses of the 1930's. Edwin M. Eigner, in "Malamud's Use of the Quest Romance" (*Genre* 1[1968]:55–75), sees the "aged rookie" who undertakes a journey with a vision of a new life of freedom as a variation on the Percival myth. Eigner also gives some interesting insights into Malamud's use of the Supernatural Woman.

Peter L. Hays, in "The Complex Pattern of Redemption in *The Assistant*" (*CentR* 13:200–14), sees in Alpine's story an expression of the "perennial realities of psychological and philosophic truth" through a modern parable that is also a naturalistic novel, the ingredients of which are drawn from Buber-like wisdom, standard classical mythology, and fertility myths. And the trouble with Levin of *A New Life* is that he believes in Cascadia College as the new Eden, says John A. Barsness in "*A New Life*: The Frontier Myth in Perspective" (*WAL* 3:297–302). Although his romantic preconceptions violate both tradition and morality, they make the novel a new breed of Western, one capable of moral comment. Rita Nathalie Kosofsky has compiled for the Serif series *Bernard Malamud: An Annotated Checklist* (Kent, Ohio, Kent State Univ. Press), which includes American and British reviews and critiques as well as the primary works in their several editions.

Only two pieces on Salinger merit attention this year. Theodore L. Gross, in "J. D. Salinger: Suicide and Survival in the Modern World" (*SAQ* 68:454–62), sees the Glass family's obsession over the death of Seymour as various searches for a form of compassion that will permit them to survive. The technical difficulties of *Franny and Zooey* and the later "torpid narratives" are a result of Salinger's determination "to love the world even if he cannot understand it." In "J. D. Salinger and the Crisis of Consciousness" (*Radical Sophistication*, pp. 198–217) Max F. Schulz gives the most satisfactory reading of "Seymour: An Introduction" that has yet appeared. The search for ways to present Seymour becomes, for his brother Buddy, the Romantic's "endless, terrifying exploration into himself."

### *viii.* Thomas Berger, John Barth, Walker Percy

Thomas Berger's *Little Big Man* is the subject of four essays, although one, by Frederick W. Turner, III, "Melville and Thomas Berger: The Novelist as Cultural Anthropologist" (*CentR* 13:101–21), is the occasion for venting annoyance as much as it is for explicating fiction. Like *Israel Potter*, *Little Big Man* is concerned with the quality of American culture; both distort history and its heroes "for the purpose of cultural exegesis." Despite his peevish admonitions to literary critics to discover cultural anthropology, Turner himself seems to know only what A. L. Kroeber tells him and in his missionary zeal fails to see very much humor in Berger.

Another overserious reading of the novel is by Delbert E. Wylder, whose title, "Thomas Berger's *Little Big Man* as Literature" (*WAL* 3:273–84), indicates something of his low regard for comedy. In his mixing of diverse narrative voices, tones, and genres, Berger writes a "Barthian Western." But while it exploits absurdity, it is "distinctly Western in its attitudes toward humanity and human values." One wonders about Wylder's dubious norm: what moral values are exclusive to the "Western spirit"?

Brian W. Dippie's "Jack Crabb and the Sole Survivors of Custer's Last Stand" (*WAL* 4:189–202) is a solid study of sources that turns out to be as imaginative as Turner's essay without its superficial conclusions. Dippie examines both the historical accounts and the patterns in the work of earlier "Custer writers," and concludes that Berger is faithful to "both the West of history and the West of myth," and that the remarkable quality of *Little Big Man* stems from the blending of these two kinds of truth. Jay Gurian, in "Style in the Literary Desert: *Little Big Man*" (*WAL* 3:285–96), agrees with Dippie that Berger is accurate in dates, places, and events, but advances the interesting idea that this Midwesterner could not have written this "Western novel" had he been from the West, partly because speech and narrative patterns have so long been pegged to a kind of stylized realism.

Dippie has also written "His Visage Wild; His Form Exotick': Indian Themes and Cultural Guilt in John Barth's *The Sot-Weed Factor*" (*AQ* 21:113–21), in which he demonstrates Barth's skill in showing how the mythic innocence of the New World is riddled by conspiracy and rivalry; it is a fitting companion piece to Alan Holder's earlier essay on a similar topic (see *ALS 1968*, p. 222).

John M. Bradbury manages to be both magisterial and high-spirited in "Absurd Insurrection: The Barth-Percy Affair" (*SAQ* 68:319–29). The Southern Renascence is being subverted by Camusian characters who do not perform their absurdities with the élan of their elders. In the older systems, self-identity is unattainable "without rebirth into a traditional value system"; in Barth and Percy there are no such families.

Lewis A. Lawson has produced an admirable scholarly study of *The Moviegoer* and *The Last Gentleman* in "Walker Percy's Indirect Communications" (*TSLL* 11:867–900), which is concerned with the various strategies deriving from Percy's familiarity with Kierkegaard.

### ix. Eudora Welty, Carson McCullers, Truman Capote

Neil D. Isaacs, in *Eudora Welty* (SWS 8), approaches his subject from two directions—evaluating the "performances" (narratives told by superbly envisioned characters, usually in soliloquies or monologues) and explicating what he sees as the central myth in her fiction (the use of summer king, winter king, and goddess figure). The variation of these figures threatens always to get out of hand (Mr. Petrie of "The Petrified Man," for example, is declared to be both kinds of king), but Isaacs usually manages to preserve clarity in the face of bewildering permutations. He cites *Delta Wedding* to show that the theme of renewal lies at the heart of Welty's myth. This long essay contains, in addition, one of the finest treatments yet of *The Ponder Heart* and the plausible suggestion that the structure of *The Golden Apples* is musical.

Although "Eudora Welty's *A Curtain of Green*" (*The Forties*, pp. 101–10) is more restricted, in it Robert J. Griffin also discusses the way in which the "plaiting" of verbal repetitions suggests musical structures in many of the stories. Poetic textures, as well as mythic echoes and allusions, permit atmosphere to take precedence over narrative fact. Both Isaacs and Griffin indicate the richness which close study of Welty's language can yield.

Charles E. May and Smith Kirkpatrick, in their essays on two Welty stories, discuss the theme of separateness. In "The Difficulty of Loving in 'A Visit of Charity'" (*SSF* 6:338–41), May points out that despite the heroine's failure to learn anything in a context in which she finds herself a stranger, the New Testament message of love is the means for healing such a division. Kirkpatrick's "The Anointed Powerhouse" (*SR* 77:94–108), though it is irritatingly mannered, is a fine analysis of "Powerhouse," Welty's best story on the artist's role. This musician, unlike the mere craftsmen around him, knows that chaos is both inside and outside man, who "must descend to confront the unordered reality"; through incantation, Powerhouse affirms "love's existence" for closing the gap of separateness. Robert W. Cochran discusses Billy Boy's final retort in "The Petrified Man" (*Expl* 27[1968]:item 25).

Dale Edmonds's *Carson McCullers* (SWS 6) is a competent but predictable essay. The necessity of love and its thwarting by narcissism are major themes, and Edmonds rightly warns that there is no simple dichotomy in *Reflections in a Golden Eye* between "healthy, natural creatures and neurotic, unnatural ones"; each of the major characters is unable to move beyond self-love. In discussing the plays, Edmonds seems reluctant to do more than evaluate; his reading of *The Ballad of the Sad Cafe*, however, is perceptive. He sees its kinship both to the genres of the folk ballad and the old French ballade—with the coda as a kind of envoy.

A. S. Knowles, Jr., in "Six Bronze Petals and Two Red: Carson McCullers in the Forties" (*The Forties*, pp. 87–98), suggests that McCullers's early reputation was enhanced by her regional associations, but that within the scope of her "limited and special vision" she handled her themes of love, loneliness, and alienation "with precision and, at her least morbid and most natural, great tenderness." The morbidity which Knowles dislikes is the apparent simplistic linking of sensibility with "either sexual neutrality or transformation."

"Truman Capote: The Novelist as Commodity" (*The Forties*, pp. 261–69) is a well-written essay by Gene W. Ruoff on the merchandizing of *Other Voices, Other Rooms* and the critical excesses which inevitably resulted. Ruoff sees Capote's first book as thoroughly literary (the patterns are gothic not in any "Southern" sense but in the Walpole-Radcliffe way), an example of "art as serious play," but still superior to recent stylish works from Susan Sontag's camp.

George R. Creeger's "Animals in Exile: Criminal and Community in Capote's *In Cold Blood*" (*JA* 14:94–106) is a detailed study of the organic intimacy between the killers and their victims. The way in which a community categorizes the criminal—metaphorizing him in animal terms—is perhaps too obvious a sociological truth to justify Creeger's lengthy exposition, but this essay confirms the fictive richness of this genreless curiosity.

### x. Others

*a.* **James Agee.** Considerable insight into Agee the man and the writer can be found in this year's book and several essays. Kenneth Seib, in *James Agee: Promise and Fulfillment* (Pittsburgh, Univ. of Pittsburgh Press, 1968), emphasizes the "cinematic vision of experience" which can be seen in each genre in which Agee worked. He abandoned poetry, reportage, and fiction in turn because of a growing feeling of the insufficiency of words. Agee's entire career is seen as a search for form.

"The Knoxville of James Agee's *A Death in the Family*" (*TSL* 14: 1–14) is the result of Kenneth Curry's examination of newspapers, city directories, church records, and interviews to verify and illuminate Agee's 1916 setting. Curry finds minimal adaptation of actual names and occupations and little judgments of the city and the quality of life lived there. Though it poses a potential threat to the security of the family circle, the Knoxville of the novel in effect is "independent of space and time, becoming at last a city that exists only in memory."

Samuel Hynes offers the finest, most sensitive reading yet of Agee's second book in "James Agee: *Let Us Now Praise Famous Men*" (*Landmarks*, pp. 328–40). He sees three approaches by which Agee tries to comprehend the tenant families—descriptive, personal, and aesthetic. Each one is set "in a pattern of repetitions, so that one comments on another, and each alone is seen to be inadequate to the whole truth of the subject."

*b.* **J. F. Powers.** Donald Phelps's "Reasonable, Holy and Living" (*MinnR* 9:57–62), a triumph over wretched type and layout, presents Powers as the only writer to have mastered the comedy of manners "within a *specifically* Catholic terrain." Richard Kelly, in "Father Eudex, the Judge and the Judged: An Analysis of J. F. Powers' 'The Forks'" (*UR* 35:316–18), sees this important story as a gloss on the parable of the talents: it satirizes not the worldly monsignor but idealistic Father Eudex, who self-righteously prefers to destroy a "capitalistic" check rather than invest it for the poor.

Charles F. O'Brien regards *Morte D'Urban* as a penetrating, unflattering history of Catholicism in America in "*Morte D'Urban* and the Catholic Church in America" (*Discourse* 12:324–28). Paul J. Dolan, in "God's Crooked Lines: Powers' *Morte D'Urban*" (*Renascence* 21:95–102), agrees, but contends that the novel is far broader than that. Just as it is formally a modernized Arthurian legend, so thematically its burden is the "adaptation of the Divine and the human," and there are no resolutions in the contradictions because of the fuzzy extent to which divinity is always a part of humanity.

*c.* **John Updike.** Since he detects little development in Updike's fiction or verse, Charles Thomas Samuels organizes his *John Updike* (*UMPAW* 79) unchronologically according to "autobiographical" work and work of "wider range." The first is marked by personal nostalgia, the second by "nostalgia for pre-urban America." Samuels urges us not to see Updike as a psychological novelist or a moralist. Establishing his point "is usually less important to him than creating the action," which, if well done, will establish its own point; if not well done, Updike has squandered his notable techniques on trivial action. Samuels's judgments are credible and unsurprising.

John S. Hill concentrates mostly on *The Centaur* and *Couples* in "Quest for Belief: Theme in the Novels of John Updike" (*SHR* 3: 166–75). The question asked here is, Can man find values in a fragmented world? The answer is no—not if we depend upon Updike, for whom "environment" fails and "socially accepted" women and religion suffer badly. H. Petter's "John Updike's Metaphoric Novels" (*ES* 50:197–206), before it degenerates into a fruitless inquiry into Updike's "Americanness," is an impressive analysis of themes and stylistic strategies. The goals of Updike's figures—reliability and solidity—are also the marks of Updike's language. The central order of his novels "is a metaphor for the order which his characters came to discover as a need." Also useful are Alice Hamilton's "Between Innocence and Experience: From Joyce to Updike" (*DR* 49:102–09), and Elmer F. Suderman's "The Right Way and the Good Way in *Rabbit, Run*" (*UR* 36:13–21).

*d.* **Ralph Ellison.** In "On Lower Frequencies: The Buried Men in Wright and Ellison" (*MFS* 15:483–501), William Goede argues that *Invisible Man* owes more (in Ellison's own use of the terms) to his "ancestors" (Hemingway, Faulkner, Eliot) than to his chief "relative" (Wright). When his protagonist rejects the Brotherhood, Ellison is refusing "in art to Yes the white man to death through the Great American Protest Novel."

The usefulness of Edward M. Griffin's "Notes From a Clean, Well-Lighted Place: Ralph Ellison's *Invisible Man* (*TCL* 15:129–44) lies in its comprehensiveness. Deftly placing elements of the blues tradition, Southern oratory, literary allusions, and other ingredients in the book's overall structure, Griffin convincingly shows the functional progression of its mixed styles from the naturalistic to the grotesque to the surrealistic. And Peter L. Hays, in "The Incest Theme in *Invisible Man*" (*WHR* 23:335–39), examines the Trueblood incident and concludes that incest becomes a shaping metaphor in the novel for the "impure, perverted, incestuous" dealings between people both black and white.

*e.* **Miscellaneous.** Charles D. Peavy contributes two items on Hubert Selby. In both "The Sin of Pride and Selby's *Last Exit to Brooklyn*" (*Crit* 11,iii:35–42), which studies the protagonists of three stories, and "Hubert Selby and the Tradition of Moral Satire" (*SNL* 6, ii:35–39) Peavy argues that Selby's brand of Augustinianism is used to counter those philosophies which deny sin and assert a "neo-Pelagian concept of humanity," a position which he links to Pope, Swift, and Brueghel.

Peavy also discusses, in quite another vein, the works of a Western novelist in "Coming of Age in Texas: The Novels of Larry McMurtry" (*WAL* 4:171–88), but the finest novel of this genre is the subject of Kenneth Andersen's "Form in Walter Van Tilburg Clark's *The Ox-Bow Incident*" (*WR* 6,i:19–25). The classic shape of the novel is reinforced by iterated uses of sounds—the "squishing" textures of a participating nature correspond to the elemental quality of the men as they "break down and dissolve into the ooze of their primitive beings."

Robert Bone contributes an excellent essay on an American Negro expatriate. "William Demby's Dance of Life" (*TriQ* 15:127–41) focuses on *Battlecreek* (1950) and *The Catacombs* (1965), the first of which is called Demby's "myth of disaffiliation," and the second his "myth of reconciliation and return." J. L. Parr makes extravagant claims in "Calder Willingham: The Forgotten Novelist" (*Crit* 11, iii:57–65), and he is almost convincing in his discussion of *Eternal Fire*. L. Hugh Moore's "The Undersea World of Robert Stone" (*Crit* 11,iii:43–56) is a study of the winner of the 1968 Faulkner Award, whose novel, *A Hall of Mirrors*, reflects the moral values of slightly older writers: "the immorality of survival, the wickedness of adaptation."

Leo J. Hertzel, in "What's Wrong with the Christians?" (*Crit* 11,iii:11–22), explains the appeal of Robert Coover (*The Universal Baseball Association*). Unlike slightly earlier writers, Coover explores big questions, cosmic themes, even tentative supernatural possibilities out of his thorough knowledge of history, philosophy, and the black arts. Hertzel also contributes "A Coover Checklist" (pp. 23–24) and conducts "An Interview with Robert Coover" (pp. 25–29) in which the novelist reaffirms his belief in the writer's role as "a kind of priestly vocation."

Wright Morris's "*One Day*: November 22, 1963–November 22,

1967" (*Afterwords*, pp. 10–27) is a valuable glimpse at how the novelist manipulates craft to meet certain felt insistencies and suggests that Morris may well be the most Jamesian of our contemporary novelists. William Gass contributes a brilliant statement not only on his *Omensetter's Luck*, but also on that old chestnut, the differences between poetry and fiction, in the form a "A Letter to the Editor" (*Afterwords*, pp. 88–105).

Richard B. Sale records an interview with Peter DeVries (*SNNTS* 1:364–69), but the subject turns out not to have much to say, except for a few tired comments on black humor and an impression of what it is like to be on the staff of the busy *New Yorker*. Clinton S. Burhans, Jr., in "John Cheever and the Grave of Social Coherence" (*TCL* 14:187–98), offers a substantial argument for seeing Cheever, especially in the work of the last decade, as better than the "whimsical *New Yorker* satirist of urban and suburban absurdities."

William Freedman admits that there is a serious lack of drama and complex characterization in Lionel Trilling's only novel, but he argues that it "most nearly succeeds" in its play of ideas. The lesson which the hero must learn is the necessity to resist oversimplification of issues that are riddled by complexities and uncertainty. "*The Middle of the Journey*: Lionel Trilling and the Novel of Ideas" (*The Forties*, pp. 239–48) is a useful essay. Frederick K. Sanders examines one crucial scene in Allen Tate's only novel in "Theme and Structure in *The Fathers*" (*ArlQ* 1,ii[1967–68]:244–56) to show that the essential movement is from an imperfect public world to the "greater imperfections of an exaggerated, unprincipled individualism."

Raney Stanford, in "The Novels of Edward Wallant" (*ColQ* 17:393–405), discusses the way in which Wallant expands "minor mannerism" into "major revelation" through a distinctive and vital realism. Robert N. Hudspeth dips into historians Hermann Rauschning and Hannah Arendt to give "A Definition of Modern Nihilism: Hersey's *The War Lover*" (*UR* 35:243–49). The essay fortunately uses two earlier and better books as well. Peter J. Longleigh, Jr., has assembled his collection of notes toward a satire in "Donald Barthelme's *Snow White*" (*Crit* 11,iii:30–34), and it is happily brief. Its curtsies to Barthelme's Now Generation (breathless, inarticulate slogans) and its bows to an imagined Critical Establishment (a lexicon stuffed with *nexus, continuum-wise,* and *insighted*) are only modestly amusing.

Finally, Redding S. Sugg, Jr., has written on two very minor figures. "John's Yoknapatawpha" (*SAQ* 68:343–62) is a survey of the writing and painting of John Falkner, whom Sugg believes to be more fully in the Southwest humor tradition than his famous brother. And with Helen White, Sugg recounts the career of a little-known Tennessee writer in "Lady Into Artist: The Literary Achievement of Anne Goodwin Winslow" (*MissQ* 22:289–302). Both her novels and short stories reveal the "traditional, decorous, humanistic, classicizing" taste of a remarkable prose stylist.

*Indiana University*

# 14. Poetry: 1900 to the 1930's

## Richard Crowder

The most impressive amount of scholarship in 1969 was on Pound. In addition to over twenty articles there were seven books, including the revision of a 1960 biography. Frost and Robinson were noticeably in second place. Crane was the subject of two books; Ransom of one (as well as of a 1967 book which has now come to our attention); and Cummings of one. A minimum of essays treated these three poets. Other books included a Millay biography and a collection of letters by Sandburg.

As for dissertations, graduate students were more interested in Frost than any other poet. Subjects included his relation to Thoreau, his epistemological dualism, his poetry of paradox, and his grammar. Pound's anti-Semitism and Fascism and Robinson's Puritanism were considered. Two studies of Vachel Lindsay included an edition of some of his letters and an examination of his role as poet and columnist. The black poet and novelist Claude McKay was the subject of another dissertation. A Hart Crane bibliography, a study of Imagism, and an edition of the letters of George Sterling completed the list.

### i. General

Only two essays attempted to examine the period as a whole. E. M. and S. B. Puknat ("Goethe and Modern American Poets," GQ 42:21–36) discuss methodically (and somewhat ploddingly) the influence of the German writer on a dozen poets, citing their verses, their prose comments, and the disclosures of their biographers and critics. The poets considered from our period include Robinson, Masters, Amy Lowell, Pound, and Crane. The authors, not unexpectedly, find that the "responses to Goethe range in tone from awe through ambivalence to rebellion."

In "Africa in Negro American Poetry to 1929" (ALT 2:32–41) Michael Furay asserts that in the period before 1930 "The New

Negroes' estrangement from American society made their symbolic journey to Africa inevitable." The principal poets involved were Claude McKay, Countee Cullen, and Langston Hughes. With the coming of the Depression, the Negro Renaissance ceased, not to be revived for over a decade.

*Fifteen Modern American Authors: A Survey of Research and Criticism*, edited by Jackson R. Bryer (Durham, N.C., Duke Univ. Press), presents a summary review of work done on four of the poets within our concern: Crane (Brom Weber), Frost (Reginald L. Cook), Pound (John Espey), and Robinson (Ellsworth Barnard). Each essay is divided into five sections: bibliography, editions, manuscripts and letters, biography, and criticism. In general each section is developed chronologically, beginning roughly in the 1920's and extending, in a few cases, into 1968. The essayists seek to evaluate the accomplishments of scholars and critics and give perspective to what has been done. They provide a background for the more detailed recent information disseminated by the annual issues of *ALS*. The essays will be referred to again in the following paragraphs.

### ii. Ezra Pound

In Bryer's *Fifteen Modern American Authors*, John Espey (pp. 322–44) points to the need for an index of the *Cantos* published since 1957 and indicates that much of the early poetry of Pound is hard to get at. He shows that a valuable contribution to Pound studies would be a vigorous effort at getting the voluminous correspondence into print. Moreover, in spite of commendable work by Charles Norman, Patricia Hutchins, and others, there is a profound lack of revealing biography. Espey is of the opinion that from 1932 to about 1952 most essays were modeled on the work of Leavis and Blackmur, but that in 1951 Hugh Kenner started the second phase of Pound criticism— examination of the entire body of poetry. To 1967, however, most subsequent book-length examinations were less ambitious. Espey concludes with a look at the chief analyses of the poetry in chronological order, beginning with the days before Imagism and concluding with comment on Eva Hesse's collection of essays in German by various scholars: *Ezra Pound: 22 Versuche über einen Dichter* (see *ALS 1967*, p. 215).

Professor Hesse's new collection, *New Approaches to Ezra Pound:*

*A Co-ordinated Investigation of Pound's Poetry and Ideas* (Berkeley, Univ. of Calif. Press), attempts to suggest to scholars heretofore unexplored areas in the work of Pound. There are several reprinted or adapted essays. Seven articles, including the introduction, are written especially for the book. The opening essay (pp. 13–53) is weighty in the Teutonic manner—thickly allusive not only to Pound and his critics but to a wide-ranging variety of other works, British, Continental, and Asiatic. The writer tries to show, partly by drawing on the essays that follow, partly through her own insights, that the *Cantos* have an "almost incredible coherence" despite Pound's own feeling of failure. A logic develops through the piling up of the *Cantos* until they offer "an inexhaustible record of the *condition humaine.*" Though Pound admittedly possesses "purblind and even vicious notions," basically he is sound in instinct and sympathy. Forrest Read ("Pound, Joyce, and Flaubert: The Odysseans," pp. 125–44) gives a more or less chronological account of the uses to which Pound put the work of Joyce and Flaubert in the *Cantos*, finding correspondences in "the Odyssean frame." In "Persephone's Ezra" (pp. 145–73) Guy Davenport actually finds "Persephone and her trees" everywhere in Pound except in passages that show abuse of nature and in "Sestina: Altaforte" (about war). Whereas Eliot and Joyce came as far as a *Purgatorio*, Pound has tried to create a *Paradiso* (cf. Persephone's trees). The *Cantos* rest on a profound, still "sense of humanity." J. P. Sullivan, in "Ezra Pound and the Classics" (pp. 215–41), reminds readers that Pound was critical of unthinking idolators of the classics, that he stressed *making it new* in his translations. In addition to actually putting the classics directly into his poetry, he found many things useful in other ways: "Melodic invention and narrative vividness . . . in Homer; economy in Sappho . . ., sophistication in Propertius; compression in Tacitus." The philosophy of all times and civilizations was never out of date for Pound. His "dialogue with Aristotle and neo-Aristotelianism is far more pervasive . . . than has yet been recognized." A different kind of exploration has been undertaken by Walter Baumann in "Secretary of Nature, J. Heydon" (303–18). Pound says that Heydon, whose name comes up four times in Canto XCI, has been "polluted." Baumann has discovered that Heydon was considered a quack astrologer in the seventeenth century. He called himself "Secretary of Nature," i.e., keeper of Nature's secrets. Following Pound's advocacy of serious study of Heydon's *Holy Guide*, Baumann proposes a fresh edition in order to "unpollute" its author. John Espey ("The Inheritance of *tò kalón*," pp. 319–30) shows the relation between Pound's devotion to Beauty and his reading of the nineteenth-century writers beginning with Coleridge and continuing through Rossetti, Lionel Johnson, Arthur Symons, and Thomas Bird Mosher, editor and publisher of *The Bibelot*, 1895–1915. The author points out that Pound at last came to the word *order* as a gloss for Beauty (i.e., that which makes Beauty possible). In a study of the complexities of metrical counterpoint in Pound ("Rhythm and Person in *The Cantos*," pp. 349–64) Albert Cook demonstrates how "rhythmical virtuosity" provides "a musical ground for the shifts and convergencies in . . . the masks and faces." He includes appropriate exegesis of Cantos XXIX and XXX. The essays in this book are illuminating and, above all, suggestive for future studies of Pound.

As if reacting to Espey's comment in the Bryer volume, Hugh Witemeyer (*The Poetry of Ezra Pound: Forms and Renewal, 1908–1920*, Berkeley, Univ. of Calif. Press) looks critically at the unreprinted poetry and prose of Pound's earliest period. The first chapter shows how the poet early began consciously to deal with literary tradition—as resource and as object of "criticism in new composition." The second chapter explores Pound's engagement with Imagism, Vorticism, and ideograms in an effort to arrive at the purpose of poetry—to seek equations for "delightful psychic experience." His poetry is "a continuous dialectic between tradition and the individual talent, between criticism and lyricism." The rest of the book (chapters 3 to 8) examines from this point of view the poetry from *A Lume Spento* through *Hugh Selwyn Mauberley*.

Concerning one group of poems in this earlier period, Wai-Lim Yip (*Ezra Pound's "Cathay*," Princeton, Princeton Univ. Press) examines the *Cathay* poems in exhaustive detail. The book is mechanically structured, starting with a discussion of the syntactical problems encountered in translating Chinese poetry, then moving to Pound's Imagist and Vorticist obsession with the seeming dichotomy of "precision and suggestion." Yip gives thorough treatment to Pound's determination to get at the "thing" in the Chinese poems. Meticulous, detailed, offering full proof with many quotations, he "anatomizes" the *Cathay* poems to see how faithful Pound is to the "internal thought-form" of the originals. Yip finds some failures in Pound's efforts to find "equivalents," but the nineteen poems in *Cathay* "provided a workshop where he could mature his poetic talent until it was ready for the explosive appearance of the *Cantos*." Following a pattern of exhaustiveness, Yip provides two appendices: excerpts from "cribs" in Fenollosa's notebooks (which Pound depended upon), and Yip's own literal retranslations of the *Cathay* poems placed opposite Pound's versions. There are a selected bibliography and four indices: names; titles by Pound; titles by others; and important concepts, topics, and terms. It would appear that nothing more needs to be done with these poems for many years to come.

Daniel D. Pearlman (*The Barb of Time: On the Unity of Ezra Pound's "Cantos*," New York, Oxford Univ. Press) defines the major form of the sprawling *Cantos* in terms of time, since there is no narrative. The author classes himself with the minority, the "integrative" critics. He achieves his analysis by considering closely only the first eighty-four cantos, arguing that, by the conclusion of the *Pisan Cantos*, the evolution of the major form had been completed.

The three "phases" of the work are not clear-cut divisions, but are played contrapuntally, each phase in turn receiving more emphasis than the other two in the development of the total structure. The pattern emerges as roughly parallel to the three parts of the *Divina Commedia*. After the prefiguring of the entire poem in Canto I, Pound proceeds through the next twenty-nine cantos to develop the theme of despair (*Inferno*)—man-made mechanical time having produced disorder in civilization. The next cantos (XXXI–LXXIII) gradually develop the concept of the richness and health to be gained from nature's time (as seen, for example, in the cyclical return of the seasons). Renewal is the only way out of chaos, based as it is on hope (*Purgatorio*). Finally, the *Pisan Cantos* present the triumphal vision of the ideal order (*Paradiso*), for out of suffering has come love. The emphasis now is on the timelessness of myth.

Pearlman gives close reading only to the passages which he has determined as "nodal points" in the evolution of the form. He does not deny the "boredom" of sections of the work, but feels justified in explicating only the parts most clearly supporting what he feels is the unifying thesis of the *Cantos*. This is a knowledgeable and significant study, complemented by the following book.

In *Ezra Pound: The Image and the Real* (Baton Rouge, La. State Univ. Press) Herbert N. Schneidau presents a thorough discussion of Pound's poetics. He investigates to some extent Pound's theory of knowledge encompassing both rationalism and mysticism, the energy thus generated creating form, the poetry growing from "Luminous Detail." Schneidau demonstrates Ford Madox Ford's influence on Pound in insisting on contemporary language, a principle Pound was soon partially repudiating in favor of "the speech of to-day, dignified, more intense, more dynamic, than to-day's speech is spoken." In establishing the Imagist movement, however, Pound took from Ford the idea of severe discipline, paring away decoration and "comment." The author dispels the myth of T. E. Hulme's part in the beginnings of Imagism, for Pound went far beyond "Hulme's demand for constant visualization," to be gained by efforts at expression of feeling by subjective processes. In Ernest Fenollosa, on the other hand, Pound found a fellow traveler toward what Schneidau calls "the real presence in the symbolic medium." Pound was totally committed to the idea that the link between scholarship and art was indispensable, providing a profound relationship with man's entire past. Vorticism was based on his feeling of the tremendous energy generated by the past and held in focus by the power of tradition. Both he and Eliot exercised a sense of history in fighting the war against mediocrity, triviality, insularity, and even nihilism. For Pound a persona did not have to be a character. This may explain the reader's frequent perplexity over Mauberley, an invention of Pound's meant to indicate what he might have become if he had not escaped to Europe and found friends and a milieu of intellectual stimulation. Schneidau suggests interesting, original ways for reading the entire group of Mauberley poems in this light. He suggests further that Pound's fervor and evangelism are related to the puritan pattern of Pound's America. Also seen as puritan is the necessity of hard work to get at the pleasure of the poems themselves. Schneidau sees the poet, not as the snob he is sometimes accused of being, but as a genuinely outraged fighter against indifference and dullness. He insists that Ford's visualization is only one side of Pound's art, that sound and hearing effect an equally important dynamism. This is a solid book, well researched. Together with Pearlman's study it will henceforth be indispensable for further Pound investigations.

Charles Norman's revision of *Ezra Pound* (New York, Funk & Wagnalls) involves a minimum of change from the 1960 edition. The author has added a few scattered lines on Pound's relationship with "Mary Moore of Trenton" and has illustrated Marianne Moore's in-

terest in the poet at St. Elizabeths. A few corrections of dates and
other inaccuracies have been made. Otherwise, the revision is exactly
like the original (including the same number of pages).

By devoting seventy-seven pages to Pound, *Texas Quarterly* (10,
iv[1967]) supplies what amounts to another small book. The first
and largest section is devoted to "Make It New: Papers Delivered at
a Symposium on Translation and Metrical Innovation: Aspects of
Ezra Pound's Work." By way of somewhat irrelevant introduction,
Pound's daughter, Mary de Rachewiltz ("Tempus Loquendi," pp.
36–39), criticizes a society that now permits "rowdy behavior" as a
form of protest but that still refuses "to blot out one national disgrace
by recognizing Pound's loyalty." Stressing the tension—and union—
between the individual talent and the tradition, Noel Stock in "Innovation Through Translation" (pp. 40–46), points to the two Pounds,
the first "essentially youthful" with an admirable freshness and the
second the disciplined man, obedient "to the rules of his heart." In
discussing "The Provençal Translations" (pp. 47–51), John Hummel,
while admitting that Provençal poetry was not a major influence, finds
that it was important in the patterning of Pound's metrical devices.
Oriental translations are given consideration by William McNaughton
and Roy E. Teele. McNaughton ("Pound's Translations and Chinese
*Melopoeia*," pp. 52–56) analyzes the poet's discoveries and employment of the so-called "musical 'charge'" characteristic of Chinese
poems. From the *Confucian Odes* the author demonstrates three traditional ornaments: repeated syllables, rhyme, and alliteration. In
"The Japanese Translations" (pp. 63–66) Teele reminds his readers
that these were done without first-hand acquaintance with the language. The results are not totally satisfactory. As for "Ezra Pound's
Classical Translations" (pp. 57–62), J. P. Sullivan maintains that the
poet's "value as a pioneer translator of ancient poetry lies . . . chiefly
in his language." He shocked the traditional scholars because his
language carried a critical, inside view (was not "literal" or "faithful"). Likewise, Hugh Kenner's thesis, in "Blood for the Ghosts" (pp.
67–79; reprinted in Hesse, *New Approaches*, pp. 331–48), is that
Pound disciplined himself to master the breathing practices (ca-
dences) of the dead writers, the way their lips and throats actually
moved. Finally, again not entirely relevant to the central topic of
translations, the curator of the Collection of American Literature, the
Beinecke Rare Book and Manuscript Room at Yale, Donald Gallup,

in " 'Boobliography' and Ezra Pound" (pp. 80–92), discloses the numerous problems—major and minor—involved in the compilation of a Pound bibliography. Pound's derogatory term was intended to indicate his impatience with excessive concern over trivia and juvenilia. The other two items in this issue of *Texas Quarterly* are biographical. David Farmer's "An Unpublished Letter by Ezra Pound" (pp. 95–104) presents a communication from Pound at Rapallo dated 3 February 1927, addressed to Samuel Putnam in Chicago, in which the poet recounts in detail his part in the "Chicago renaissance." Herbert R. Lottman ("The Silences of Ezra Pound," pp. 105–10) tells of Pound's visit to Paris in his eighty-first year, when he was disinclined to speak except in brief phrases on very rare occasions, the result of his internment at Pisa and St. Elizabeths.

Conceding that he may have gone somewhat overboard in his argument, George A. Knox ("Pound's 'Hugh Selwyn Mauberley': A Vortex Name," *Spirit* 36,ii:23–28) nevertheless invites readers to consider "Hugh Selwyn Mauberley" as "a compound, an amalgam, a mask name" deriving from T. E. Hulme, Wyndham Lewis, as well as Aubrey Beardsley and possibly even Brigadier Hugh Stephenson Moberley, with a hint of "Mobberly clock." In short, it is a Vortex name, rich in clues to the poem.

In a reading of part of Canto XCI (cf. his essay on J. Heydon in Hesse, *New Approaches*, pp. 303–18) Walter Baumann ("Pound and Layamon's *Brut*," *JEGP* 68:265–76) finds in the lines beginning "He asked not/nor wavered . . ." that Pound uses *Brut* not as history but as myth, disposing "of the apocalyptic despair of our time, scornfully intolerant, however, toward our present democracies." Marion Montgomery, in "Ezra Pound's Problems with Penelope" (*SHR* 3:114–23), explores the difficulties of finding *le mot juste*. Pound pursued precision and tolerated only what was essential in an effort "to concentrate essence." Though he rejected the idea of an afterlife, he "seems to assume a supernatural power" in his sought-after ideal language. In despair over the inability of language to bring about "the miracle of reformation," he became more and more shrill as World War II approached.

Robert A. Corrigan has worked out a detailed and fully documented account of the battle royal over Pound's Bollingen award in "Ezra Pound and the Bollingen Prize Controversy" (*MASJ* 8,i [1967]: 43–57; reprinted in *The Forties* pp. 287–95). Appended is a bibli-

ography of 149 items published in 1949 about the contested award,
arranged by date of publication.

Tom Scott ("The Poet as Scapegoat," *Agenda* 7,ii:49–58) argues
that Pound, by nature an innocent, in his insane-asylum years showed
saintly qualities: for him, those who opposed right action did so not
from sinful motives but from ignorance. His release was secured
through the efforts of many, but chiefly MacLeish, Eliot, and Hemingway, and at the last moment, in a minor role, Frost. Pound had
defended the Constitution as he understood it. Scott speculates on
the reasons for the poet's persecution. He agrees with Mary de Rachewiltz that the United States, for its own good name, should clear
Pound of all dishonor.

Two British reviews of Pound's translation of a play of Sophocles
find it successful, on the whole. Peter Levi ("Ezra Pound's Translation of Sophokles' *Women of Trachis*," *Agenda* 7,i:17–22) sees evidence that Pound understood the entire play before setting to work
on the translation of the parts. Because of his sharp vision and profound hearing, he is often more accurate than Sir Richard Jebb himself. He does not "dilute the black events" of the play, for he is here
"the Pound of the Pisan Cantos." H. A. Mason ("Creative Translation:
Ezra Pound's *Women of Trachis*," *CQ* 4:244–72) points to some ir-
ritations in Pound's work, but prefers this translation to Gilbert Murray's, which Mason now sees as banal and spuriously poetic. To
Pound's credit is his ability to see the unity of the play and to "make"
his translation around that unity.

In an earlier article Marion Montgomery ("Ezra Pound's Search
for Family," *GaR* 22[1968]:429–36) expresses the opinion that Pound
believes that a man may paradoxically select his own ancestors. Unfortunately, he does not present the opportunity for us to survive as
"members one of another," since he has set aside the natural family
in favor of the larger family of the state.

"Where Pound's later work flies apart, . . . Joyce, after the great
central effort of *Ulysses*, began to revolve in ever-narrowing circles."
This is the opinion of John Wain in "The Prophet Ezra v. 'The Ego-
tistical Sublime'" (*Encounter* 33, Aug 1969:63–70). The later works
of the two writers are "the product of an amiable and interesting
hobby rather than of any vital concern with literature."

Two essays on Pound as critic may be mentioned here. K. L.
Goodwin's "Ezra Pound's Influence on Literary Criticism" (*MLQ* 29

[1968]:423–38) focuses on English critics. Pound's influence on Eliot and others was achieved through his "practical criticism and the popularization of a few slogans" and, of course, his correspondence and conversation. Forrest Read ("'Storicamente Joyce,' 1930: Ezra Pound's First Italian Essay," *TriQ* 15:100–14) explains that Joyce was a natural subject for Pound to write about, since Joyce's fiction was of great influence on Pound at this time.

### iii. E. A. Robinson

In Bryer's *Fifteen Modern American Authors* Ellsworth Barnard discusses the chief work of Robinson (pp. 345–67). He says that the long narratives, interesting only to a few specialists and making the *Collected Poems* too bulky and expensive, have almost inevitably aided in Robinson's decline. Now that some editions of representative poems are appearing, the poet's reputation may be resurrected. The need for publication of all the known correspondence may be met by the forthcoming Harvard edition by William L. Anderson. There has yet to be written a "completely satisfactory biography." Barnard singles out Yvor Winters as a critic whose taste is highly acceptable but who "sometimes substitutes epithets for analysis; . . . his favorable judgments are often unsupported." More study is needed of Robinson's delineation of his heroes and heroines.

In spite of the centenary of the poet's birth, 1969 was not a bumper year for Robinson scholarship. One book-length study, two collections of essays, and the four issues of the *Colby Library Quarterly* constituted the bulk of the attention paid to a poet who does not deserve to die. To Richard Cary belongs commendation for the Robinson activity at Colby College. He brought together the articles in *Appreciation of Edwin Arlington Robinson: 28 Interpretive Essays* (Waterville, Me., Colby College Press), thirteen of which were culled from *CLQ* and ten of those from the Centennial Issues. The essays are arranged in chronological order, 1930–69. The chief value of the volume is the convenience of having all these commentaries in one place. (The other book of essays, original articles edited by Ellsworth Barnard for the University of Georgia Press, was not yet listed in the bibliographies for 1969. Comment will have to be postponed.)

The other book of the year is Louis O. Coxe, *Edwin Arlington Robinson: The Life of Poetry* (New York, Pegasus), a critical biography. The known facts are focused on Robinson's heroic choice to be a poet and nothing else. Coxe sees Robinson as chiefly an urban poet, even in some of the Tilbury Town pieces. No poem is "far from a dwelling, a town and a number of people." The typical Robinson "voice" is "disenchanted, cagey, reticent," though "flexible." Robinson must be read differently from his contemporaries: he is a poet generally "with a prose in view"; i.e., the irony, symbolism, and imagery are present, not, however, as an end (as in "pure" lyric), but as supporters of "an action." Robinson is a "fabulist" in his best poems, in which "the characters . . . have exemplary functions." Robinson extended the range of subject matter for poems as well as the possibilities of manner of discourse. In spite of certain eccentricities of diction, this is a useful book. The insights are based on new and responsible readings. Coxe sensibly does not undertake *explication de texte* of the long narratives and so avoids tedium and probable substitution of critcism for the poems themselves. He does remind his readers, however, that even in the short poems Robinson is never far from plot.

Richard Cary has rendered further service in editing the four Centennial Issues of *CLQ* 8(March–Dec):215–488, devoted entirely to the poet. The twenty-three contributions range from commemorative statements from fellow poets through critical and analytical studies to bibliography. In the next seven paragraphs, I shall examine these.

On the matter of influences, Lewis E. Weeks, Jr., in "Maine in the Poetry of Edwin Arlington Robinson" (pp. 317–34), says that the scenery, the weather, and the citizens (controlled by the Protestant ethic) play an indispensable role in the poetry. Though Robinson's characteristic "decay and dissolution" theme is of Maine origin, the poet transcends his region. Another early influence was the strict French forms in which he was disciplined by Dr. A. T. Schumann. Peter Dechert ("He Shouts to See Them Scamper So: E. A. Robinson and the French Forms," pp. 386–98) says that they developed in him a facility in stanzaic structure, but were inadequate for his maturing reflectiveness. Nicholas Ayo considers "Robinson's Use of the Bible" (pp. 250–65), pointing out the pervasiveness of the rebirth theme. Robinson's method was to expand rather than alter the Bible narratives he used. "How the searching mind [of the 'prophet'] evaluates the sufficiency of evidence to claim that *this* and not *that* is the truth,

and how it resolves the hazardous ambiguities of taking one's conscience as the ultimate criterion of the validity of religious experience,
must be considered a lifelong preoccupation with Robinson."

Related to this idea is David H. Burton's suggestion in "E. A.
Robinson's Idea of God" (pp. 280–94) that the chief tension throughout the poems is between the traditional concept of deity and his own
inability to go beyond "a Divine Force for Good" expressing itself in
"human fulfillment." Three forces kept him searching: idealism, science, and tradition. In "The World Is . . . a Kind of Spiritual Kin-
dergarten" (pp. 435–48) Paul H. Morrill extends the meaning of
Robinson's "Light" to include "the subconscious power of self—an
aid for one to go beyond the possible." Robinson sees both public and
private experience in a bio-social context. Morrill has worked out a
rather elaborate chart for getting at Robinson's methods of analysis.

Ronald Moran's "The Octaves of E. A. Robinson" (pp. 363–70)
shows the poet's attitude at twenty-seven and twenty-eight toward
poetry, faith, the crassness of the era, man's inability to cope with it,
and the positive quality of idealism. W. R. Robinson, in an amazingly
complex close reading of "New England" ("E. A. Robinson's Yankee
Conscience," pp. 371–85), shows the sonnet to be about the friction
between imagination and Puritan environment. The author also points
out the progression from early poems about solitary figures to poems
of "complex interpersonal relations."

Considering the case for the long narratives in "Robinson's Impulse for Narrative" (pp. 238–49), J. Vail Foy feels that the poet at
last found himself in his "verse novels." Two scholars examine the
Arthurian poems. Lyle Domina ("Fate, Tragedy and Pessimism in
Robinson's *Merlin*," pp. 471–78) sees Merlin at Broceliande as es-
caping from intellect into sensuality and returning "to this world
with a newly found wisdom," for "abstract, intellectual knowledge
has ceased to be at odds with the felt thing." In "Tennyson and Robinson: Legalistic Moralism vs. Situation Ethics" (pp. 416–33) Laurence Perrine shows that in the Arthurian poems Robinson supports
the idea that legal marriage does not automatically create sanctified
love, but can be a sinful relation.

Two studies of revisions reveal Robinson as craftsman. Robert D.
Stevick looks at two versions of the octave of "Many Are Called"
("Formulation of E. A. Robinson's Principles of Poetry," pp. 295–308)
and discovers that the use of fixed forms pointedly synthesizes the

poems, the explicit search for the right word was the result of need
for metrical control, the explicit use of relative pronouns, conjunc-
tions, and prepositions creates a sense of linguistic security, the tension between strict structure and "semantic and referential play"
results in "a characteristically ruminative poetry, modest, intellectual," nonconfessional, "and at its best . . . inevitable." Louise Dauner
("Two Robinson Revisions: 'Mr. Flood's Party' and 'The Dark Hills,'"
pp. 309–16) shows how, in the conclusions of these two poems, Robinson was able through careful changes not only to increase the unity
of metaphor and logic but also to put emphasis on "phonematic symbolism, and syntactical and rhythmic appropriateness."

Two articles call attention to Robinson as dramatist. In "The Plays
of Edwin Arlington Robinson" (pp. 347–63) Irving D. Suss says that
*Van Zorn* fails in its attempt to show "the sense of strange power that
burgeons when human beings touch the deepest currents within each
other." *The Porcupine*, too, tries unsuccessfully to probe "the pathos
of love denied," but the groups of characters are not really connected.
Contrasting *Van Zorn* and Eliot's *The Cocktail Party*, Michael C.
Hinden ("Edwin Arlington Robinson and the Theatre of Destiny,"
pp. 463–71) finds "both plays . . . metaphysical comedies," though
"Eliot . . . was able to infuse" the form "with subtlety and depth" as
Robinson could not. Hinden sees some resemblance between *The
Porcupine* and *Family Reunion*. In his play Robinson lets Destiny
be evil rather than kindly.

The other articles in *CLQ* are bibliographical. Richard Crowder,
in "Robinson's Reputation: Six Observations" (pp. 220–38), charts
the extent of the poet's critical notice through his life, lists and classi-
fies typical dissertations, develops Harriet Monroe's comment that
"the climax of [*The Man Who Died Twice*] was perhaps also the
climax of the poet's career," surveys critical comment from abroad,
looks at the book-length studies of the poet's life and work, and describes the critical comment of the past thirty years. William White
continues his good work in following up Charles Beecher Hogan's
original bibliography with "A Bibliography of Edwin Arlington Robinson, 1964–1969" (pp. 448–62). In the course of the four Centennial
Issues Richard Cary presents a compilation of the Colby library hold-
ings of Robinson materials: "Robinson Books and Periodicals: I, II,
III" (pp. 266–77, 334–43, 399–413) and "Robinson Manuscripts and

Letters" (479–87). More than a thousand letters are listed. All items, says Cary, "will continue to be available to scholars."

In the remaining Robinson articles, Hilton Anderson ("Robinson's 'Flammonde,'" *SoQ* 7:179–83) gives scholars nothing new in spelling out the similarity between Flammonde and Christ. Richard Crowder's article "E. A. Robinson and the Garden of Eden" (*CLQ* 7[1967]: 527–35) discusses the influence of the Miltonic expansion of the Eden myth, analyzes the direct influence of *Genesis,* and concludes that Robinson thought that nostalgia for the lost Eden is futile; "the Light lies ahead."

Another late-reported article is by J. C. Levenson ("Robinson's Modernity," *VQR* 44[1968]:590–610), who, after an extended explication of "Isaac and Archibald" (a poem based on the act of walking), concludes that though Robinson's tone may be informal, his poems are made with modern care; his manner may be realistic, but his symbolism is complex; though he doubted, he saw unbelief as absurd; though he had known suffering, he despised complaint and "honored honest praise."

David H. Burton (cf. his essay on "E. A. Robinson's Idea of God," above) explains that Robinson was bothered by the institutionalism and elaborate theology of the Catholic Church, but the faith of his friends increased his respect for that institution ("Robinson, Roosevelt, and Romanism: An Historical Reflection on the Catholic Church and the American Ideal," *RACHSP* 80:3–16).

In examining "An Unpublished Version of 'Mr. Flood's Party'" (*ELN* 7:55–57), Nancy Joyner finds that the final version is simpler in word choice, furthers the action rather than summarizing, surprises the reader with irony rather than washing him in nostalgia, and expresses sympathy and admiration rather than condescension and mockery.

### *iv.* Robert Frost

Reginald L. Cook's bibliographical essay on Frost in Bryer's *Fifteen Modern American Authors* (pp. 239–73) cites the need for "an extensive working bibliography." He lists what bibliographical sources are available and considers *The Poetry of Robert Frost* (New York, Holt, Rineheart and Winston), edited by Edward C. Lathem, as de-

finitive. There is no collection of the complete prose. Manuscripts
and letters are widely distributed. Lawrance Thompson's 1964 *Selected Letters* is the best available collection. Cook lists and comments on the many biographies and articles about the poet's life.
He divides the section on criticism into four parts: (i) General Estimates, (ii) Special Studies (six major areas), (iii) Explications, and
(iv) Influences and Reputation at Home and Abroad.

Donald J. Greiner's *Merrill Checklist of Robert Frost* (Columbus,
Ohio, Merrill) is selective and comes down to the Frost issue of the
*Southern Review* (Oct. 1966). Another checklist is Arnold E. Grade's
"A Chronicle of Robert Frost's Early Reading, 1874–1899" (*BNYPL*
72[1968]:611–28). This list would be useful for scholars of Frost's
development to his withdrawal from Harvard. There are three sections: (i) childhood, 13 items, 9 of which Frost's mother read to him;
(ii) adolescence, 53 items; and (iii) college years, 39 items. All entries
are annotated. Direct borrowings, however, are rare in Frost's poems.

The only book of the year was *New Hampshire's Child: The Derry
Journals of Lesley Frost* (Albany, State Univ. of N.Y. Press). Lawrance Thompson and Arnold Grade have provided notes and an index
for browsers: it includes many quotations from the journals, including, for example, under "Celebrations" Lesley's comments (as a child)
on "Birthdays," "May Day," "Hallowe'en," and so on. These journals
(in facsimile) constitute a very young daughter's account of life with
farmer Frost (February 1905 to August 1909). They are filled with
references to rural elements familiar to Frost's readers. The man
himself emerges as a good father and husband, though an indifferent
farmer.

Two articles in *TQ* 11,iii[1968] examine aspects of Frost as a man.
Wilbert Snow ("The Robert Frost I Knew," pp. 9–48) emphasizes
Frost's inability to believe in man's capacity for lasting improvement
and shows a "tragic aspect to his Muse." These reminiscences and
letters focus on meetings of the two poets at Wesleyan University
and elsewhere. Irving A. Yevish ("Robert Frost: Campus Rebel," pp.
49–55) reviews the poet's unorthodox teaching methods and analyzes
his ambivalent attitudes toward college and formal education. In
Yevish's opinion Frost differed from recent campus rebels in "being
both articulate and accommodating." Thomas P. Carpenter's "Robert
Frost and Katherine Blunt: A Confrontation" (*AN&Q* 8:35–37) is an

anecdote of interest to biographers of the way the formidable president of Connecticut College for Women twice interrupted the poet's rambling remarks one day to demand that he explain poetry to her young ladies, an exercise he was temperamentally unable to perform.

Donald J. Greiner's *Merrill Guide to Robert Frost* (Columbus, Ohio, Merrill) is a companion pamphlet to his *Checklist*, designed to introduce the casual reader to serious study. Greiner sees voice tone as Frost's distinctive contribution to our poetry. The poet uses nature as a setting for man, who must not forget that nature is, after all, impersonal.

*Robert Frost's Chicken Feathers and Other Lectures from the 1968 Augustana College NDEA English Institute* (Sioux Falls, S.D., Augustana College Press), a sixty-page pamphlet, was edited by Arthur S. Huseboe. The title lecture (pp. 9–17), by C. W. Geyer, states that between 1903 and 1905 Frost wrote and published eleven short stories and sketches in various New England poultry journals. Geyer finds them related to the spoken tradition that influenced Twain, Longstreet, and Faulkner. He says that Frost's poetry (for example, "Mending Wall") owes a debt to oral lore, proverbs as well as tales.

The remaining articles are based on explication. Bob Dowell ("Revealing Incident as Technique in the Poetry of Robert Frost," *CEA* 31,iii[1968]:12–13), by closely reading "Stopping by Woods . . . ," "Directive," and other poems, shows how Frost, in at least suggesting narrative, holds common and sophisticated reader alike, the latter because of "subtle refinement of the experience" through such devices "as irony or imagery or symbolism." J. Dennis Huston, in "'The Wonder of Unexpected Supply': Robert Frost and a Poetry Beyond Confusion" (*CentR* 13:317–29) shows some similarities between Frost and Alfred Hitchcock. But there are differences. Whereas Hitchcock treats the terrifying as an end in itself, for Frost the demonic is an imaginative way of describing energy. Huston examines "Directive" in detail to demonstrate the imagination at work in this way. Like Huston, John R. Doyle, Jr. ("A Reading of Robert Frost's 'Directive,'" *GaR* 22[1968]:501–08) sees this poem as a modern religious work. The theme is personal salvation. Though the world is in struggle and disintegration, Frost's man tries to keep a balanced serenity.

The second title of "Two Tramps in Mud Time" in *A Further Range*—"or, A Full-Time Interest"—is the basis of George Monteiro's argument in "Robert Frost and the Politics of Self" (*BNYPL* 73:309–14). As Monteiro sees it, the poem is neither an attack on collectivism nor a defense of evolution, as previous critics have claimed. Rather, Frost is here testifying to his sympathy with Thoreau's idea that man must learn "to respire and aspire both at once," which Frost translated into his own life as "I have never had a hobby in my life, but I have ranged through a lot of things."

Laurence J. Sasso, Jr. ("Robert Frost: Love's Question," *NEQ* 42:92–107) finds that Frost spent much energy trying to solve the question of whether or not it is possible to love a woman overtly without giving up some virile pride. Among the poems he considers are "West-Running Brook," "Home Burial," and "Two Look at Two." In an ingenious reading, Ward Allen in "Robert Frost's 'Iota Subscript'" (*ELN* 6:285–87) suggests that Frost's assigning the iota subscript to the letter *upsilon*—an impossibility in Greek—is in the poetic tradition of "imagining impossible situations . . . to describe the wonderful mysteries of love." In "'After Apple-Picking': Echoic Parody" (*UR* 35:301–05) William B. Stein asks, "What better phrase has been coined to describe the Fall . . .?" Almost humorous in its innocence, this poem tests the vitality of our heritage of Christian symbolism. Marie Boroff, in a sensitive reading of "Robert Frost's 'The Most of It'" (*Ventures* 9:76–82), sees the poem in the context of the totality of the poet's work. It shows the old poet reconciling longing with reality: Frost as the aged "maker" "making the most of it by making 'The Most of It.'"

### v. Ransom, Crane, Cummings, and Jeffers

Two books on Ransom serve as complements of a sort to each other. Thornton H. Parsons's *John Crowe Ransom* (TUSAS 150) and Robert Buffington's *The Equilibrists: A Study of John Crowe Ransom's Poems, 1916–1963* (Nashville, Vanderbilt Univ. Press, 1967) both concentrate on the poetry and say little about the critical prose. Parsons turns Ransom's own theory of *explication de texte* on the poems and discovers how justified the poet was in leaving all verse from his first book out of the *Selected Poems* of 1945 and later. The author se-

lects eleven of the poems as of permanent quality, poems characterized by "intensification of feeling that comes from ascetic techniques."
The "Selected Bibliography" candidly reappraises eleven critical essays on Ransom's poetry, pointing out where, in Parsons's opinion,
they have gone astray.

Buffington's book is more impressionistic than Parsons's. The author says "Eclogue" is "of high quality throughout," though he does
not support the judgment conclusively. Parsons dismisses it as "a
limp rehearsal of spiritual malaise and despair conducted by two
stagy, stodgy people, . . . unrelieved by ingenuities of characterization, metaphor, irony, or language" (pp. 140–41). Of the epitaph for
"The Equilibrists" Buffington says it "is of unqualified eloquence and
beauty." One must turn to Parsons for the means by which the poet
achieves his effects.

Nevertheless, Buffington is useful in ways that Parsons is not. He
undertakes a detailed study of "Address to the Scholars of New England," a poem which Parsons does not even mention. Whereas Buffington, on "Bells for John Whiteside's Daughter," relates the contribution
of meter and rhythm to the control of mood, Parsons is concerned in
large part with the language. Buffington lists the many revisions Ransom has made; Parsons devotes an analytical and critical chapter to
them. Buffington quotes comments of Ransom himself as well as of
other critics to support and expand his opinions; Parsons mentions
other commentators only in passing: he keeps his eyes, with only
momentary exceptions, directly on the poems. Though Parsons's may
be the better book, both can be helpful to future examiners of the
work of a man Parsons calls "the most distinguished poet of his kind"
in America.

Three articles are devoted to Ransom. George Core ("New Critic,
Antique Poet," *SR* 77:508–16) says that in spite of an apparent smil-
ing diffidence Ransom is classically severe, "ceremonious and court-
ly," though profoundly emotional and honest both in poetry and in
criticism. Colin Partridge, in "'Aesthetic Distance' in the Poetry of
John Crowe Ransom" (*SoRA* 3[1968]:159–67) finds that, because
Ransom himself remains outside a situation, he can use rhetorical
statement without artificiality, since "it is attributed to a narrator."
In "Color as Symbol and the Two-Way Metaphor in the Poetry of
John Crowe Ransom" (*MissQ* 22:29–37) Miller Williams discusses

color in terms of constant meaning for the poet. Red is "evil, passion, anger," and so on. Moreover, Ransom uses metaphor to abase people who are "already elevated, or at least sympathetic." He thus represents "the mighty fallen, and the low raised up, passion too much thought about and so unconsummated, sensibility split in two." These ideas make up Ransom's view of humanity, often symbolized by the colors of his poems.

In "Hart Crane" (Bryer's *Fifteen Modern American Authors*, pp. 63–100) Brom Weber outlines a number of problems in Crane scholarship. There is no adequate bibliography. Crane's library (at Columbia University) needs cataloguing and annotating. It is time for a thorough survey of foreign books, articles, and translations. The correspondence at Yale has not all been published. Energy should be put into a search abroad for possible "lost" manuscripts. Much biographical material is not only shallow and unbelievable, but even "embarrassing to read." "There has been a minimal amount of significant or new biographical commentary since 1948." Weber devotes twenty-five pages to outlining the criticism on Crane from 1925 to 1968. A Michigan dissertation (Stanley G. Radhuber, "Hart Crane: An Annotated Bibliography," *DA* 30:336A) "adds about 25 items to H. D. Rowe's 1955 bibliography."

A very large book (900 pages including the front material and the index), John Unterecker's *Voyager: A Life of Hart Crane* (New York, Farrar, Straus & Giroux) was ten years in the making. It is overwhelming in detail, except that the material is presented month by month without confusion. Chief among the new documents are letters exchanged between the poet and his parents and between the parents themselves. Unterecker studies thoroughly the effect of family on Crane. The father comes out as less a monster than he has often been pictured.

The poet's angers, drunken sprees, homosexual escapades, and general wildness are kept in proportion. Crane is rightfully depicted as a craftsman with a strong sense of moral responsibility, an artist whose poems were the chief instrument for rising above the pressures of everyday life. Beyond showing that Crane was his own victim—that he so wanted to "belong" that rejection (even if only imagined) turned him to his aberrations and excesses—Unterecker does not ride a hobby. Rather, he generally gives only the facts and does not insist that his opinions are gospel. Through the mass of detail appears the spirit of the poet, not just a cardboard silhouette, the result of pre-conceived notions.

This is an important book. Though one cannot rely totally on biography for interpretation of Crane's work, neither can one ignore now the part that the poet's life and contacts played as background for the creation of the poems. Though our general conclusions about Crane may remain unchanged, they are now fully reinforced by this candid but sympathetic and exhaustive book. This poet remains one of America's towering Romantics.

One awkward situation confronts Crane scholars and other devotees of documentation: there are no footnotes. One must write directly to the author (Columbia Department of English) for a copy of the sources, even for support of views in which Unterecker differs markedly from his predecessors.

Susan Jenkins Brown's *Robber Rocks: Letters and Memories of Hart Crane, 1923–1932* (Middletown, Conn., Wesleyan Univ. Press) takes its title from the name of the Connecticut country house belonging to the Browns during most of the time of the author's friendship with Crane. By means of thirty-nine Crane letters (sixteen heretofore unpublished) and extended comment and explanation, Mrs. Brown adds further details and insights to the exploration of the complex character of this difficult poet. Malcolm Cowley and Peggy Baird, Allen Tate and Caroline Gordon, and other literary people of Crane's generation figure in the unfolding story. Though the author does not gloss over Crane's faults, she does give emphasis to his pleasure in "normal" friends and his capacity for enough self-discipline to accomplish a great deal of serious work. In the middle of the book is a long "note" by Cowley explaining Crane's role in the editing of *Blue Juniata*. As a kind of appendix, Mrs. Brown has included Peggy Baird's essay "The Last Days of Hart Crane," first published in *Venture* in 1961.

J. A. Bryant, Jr., in "Hart Crane and the Illusory Abyss" (*SR* 77: 149–54), maintains that Crane's achievement is akin to Emerson's in finding "the authority for his vision" in himself, a faith now practiced by many poets in spite of Yvor Winters's warning that this path can lead only to the destruction of the self. Richard Hutson ("Exile Guise: Irony and Hart Crane," *Mosaic* 2,iv:71–86) finds Crane not so totally affirmative as many critics would have him. He mingled "the No and the Yes" simultaneously and inextricably. The complexity of his irony is found in any of the major lyrics. Hutson explicates "Praise for an Urn," "Chaplinesque," and "Lachrymae Christi." The poet's irony, he finds, consists of a "love of things irreconcilable."

In "A Voyage Through Two *Voyages*: A Study of Hart Crane's *Voyages IV* and V" (*Lang&S* 1[1968]:115–28) Susan Eve Hirshfeld and Ruth Portner analyze these two poems from a linguistic point of view. They think that "precision and definition" make "Voyages V" the superior poem. It "embraces and subsumes more, is more complex, and is more economical." The linguistic vocabulary of this essay is a barrier to complete sympathy with the method, and the findings have long been agreed upon by the best critics.

*Selected Letters of E. E. Cummings*, edited by F. W. Dupee and George Stade (New York, Harcourt, Brace & World), begins with ten letters to Cummings's grandmother and his parents written before he was nine years old and ends with a letter to Matti Meged dated less than four months before his death. The letters are marked by the same eccentricities one finds in the poems and the same open spontaneity, gaiety, and frankness. The volume includes letters to Pound, Dos Passos, Edmund Wilson, Williams, and other literary people. There are photographs of Cummings at various ages and of other people he knew. The book is an indispensable supplement to the poems.

Mick Gidley ("Picture and Poem: E. E. Cummings in Perspective," *PoetryR* 59[1968]:178–98) discloses that Cummings had not been published in England until Faber and Faber brought out *Selected Poems* in 1960. Gidley is now reviewing the English edition of *Collected Poems*. Most of his comments are already familiar to American readers. In "Cummings' 'anyone' and 'noone'" (*ArQ* 25:36–43) David R. Clark reviews the various readings of "anyone lived in a pretty how town" and concludes that it is about the uniqueness of the individual, "his difference from the group," the seeming paradox that a man's "loneliness" is his "most precious" possession.

For Jeffers "the most profound problem" was "the relationship of the individual to his time, and the uses and limitations of human freedom." This is the judgment of Robert Boyers, expressed in "A Sovereign Voice: The Poetry of Robinson Jeffers" (*SR* 77:487–507). The poet tried to explore this problem in long narratives, for which he did not have the necessary talent. On the other hand, in the shorter poems he "could blend passion and restraint, image and statement, contempt and admiration . . . often with a music . . . ripe and easy." He steadfastly refused "to counsel violence among men" and achieved for himself "a perspective wherein the violence men would and did commit could be made tolerable, in a way even absorbed into the universe as an element of necessity." His vision, then, was tragic. Boyers lists nineteen poems as representing Jeffers's best work.

Two issues of the *Robinson Jeffers Newsletter*—no. 23 (April) and no. 24 (September)—offer helps for scholars, chiefly from Robert J. Brophy. In the April issue besides two reviews Brophy supplies a bibliography, "The Tor House Library: Jeffers' Books" (pp. 4–11). In the September issue there is a section on "Robinson Jeffers in Foreign Translation" (pp. 3–4) and another bibliographical item by Brophy, "Jeffers Research: Dissertations, A Summary and Reflection" (pp. 4–9).

### vi. Sandburg, Masters, Sterling, and Cullen

In his pamphlet, *Carl Sandburg: With a Bibliography of Sandburg Materials in the Collections of the Library of Congress* (Washington, Library of Congress), Mark Van Doren praises Sandburg's poetry as "powerful, . . . distinct, . . . unmistakably poetry," even though the rhythms are those of prose. The best poems are the short ones; the long poems are accumulations of brief sections. A "threat of softness" hovers around his later work. He was always able, however, to find something of interest, something moving, in even the most obscure human being. Anna Martynova, in "Carl Sandburg and the Soviet Reader (On the Occasion of the 90th Anniversary of Sandburg's Birth)" (*SovL* 1[1968]:192–93), testifies to the love of the common Russian people for Sandburg as representative of "the best humanitarian traditions in American literature." She writes of various translations into Russian (many of them "excellent"). Herbert Mitgang has edited *The Letters of Carl Sandburg* (New York, Harcourt, Brace & World, 1968). The items are arranged chronologically, beginning with 1 May 1898, and extending to 1 July 1962, shortly after which date Mrs. Sandburg began answering the poet's mail for him. These letters supply a rich, warm, and sometimes racy addition to the well-known facts of his biography. Preceding the letters is a "detailed chronology." The book is well indexed. Where necessary, a letter is followed by explanatory notes identifying persons and situations. Chiefly of minor interest to biographers is David C. Mearns's " 'Ever and Ever, Carl'" (*MSS* 21:169–73). The essay is made up of reminiscences about the poet and biographer beginning in the days when he was collecting materials for *The War Years*.

A large issue of *Texas Quarterly* (12:4–143) is devoted to Masters. Frank Kee Robinson has compiled "Edgar Lee Masters Centenary Exhibition: Catalogue and Checklist" (pp. 2–68), which gives a descriptive listing of 155 items on display at the University of Texas during autumn 1968, ranging from Masters's own copy of his first book to a holograph letter from Robinson Jeffers and a medal of the Poetry Society of America. The checklist names all the "separately published books." There is an index. This catalogue is followed by "Posthumous Poems of Edgar Lee Masters" (pp. 71–115) with an introduction by Robinson. The twenty-nine poems were selected by the editor from a sizable number of manuscripts in the library at Texas. They show Masters still brooding "compulsively on the slavery of the human condition," in spite of which he was "an impassioned democrat and humanist." Robinson also analyzes "*The New Spoon River*: Fifteen Facsimile Pages" (pp. 116–43) to show (within obvious limits) the range of mood and characterization as well as the relatively few revisions. Charles E. Burgess ("An Unpublished Poem by Edgar Lee Masters," *PLL* 5:183–89) tells the circumstances which have kept "The Pasture Rose" from publication. Another "philosophic poetic sketch" based on characteristics of members of his family, it is quoted in full at the end of the article.

In "George Sterling: 'Prophet of the Suns'" (*Markham Rev.* [1], ii[1968]:[4–10]) Joseph W. Slade outlines the extent of the influence on Sterling of Joaquin Miller, Ambrose Bierce, Jack London, and Upton Sinclair. Sterling, however, "remained convinced that . . . beauty alone was the province of poetry."

David F. Dorsey, Jr. ("Countee Cullen's Use of Greek Mythology," *CLAJ* 13:68–77) traces Cullen's reliance on classical myth from his teen-age days. In maturity his technique was to reverse the symbolic content of the myths to support and express "the ironical content of his poetic genius."

### vii. H. D., Millay, and Others

In a large issue, *Contemporary Literature* (10,iv:431–677), under the title, "H. D.: A Reconsideration," considers her as poet, novelist, and nonfiction writer. In L. S. Dembo's "Norman Holmes Pearson on H. D.: An Interview" (pp. 435–46), Pearson, who is H. D.'s literary executor, evaluates *Helen in Egypt* as quest poetry comparable to Pound's *Cantos* and the poetry of Eliot and not related to the "confessional" poets. Pearson believes H. D.'s encounter with Freud had deep influence on her poetry in developing "her own frame of reference." Whereas Pearson calls her shy, Joseph N. Riddel ("H. D. and the Poetics of 'Spiritual Realism,'" pp. 447–73) calls her a lonely figure who through the words of her poems seeks a way out. Both Pearson and Riddel point out that Freud helped her discover how feminine she was: she needed to write to complete her subjective self. She uses gods and goddesses as "projections of her subject-object, feminine-masculine conflict." After her interviews with the psychoanalyst her poems became acts of discovery. In Riddel's words the poet is "voyaging . . . while remaining in place." H. D.'s *Tribute to Freud* is invaluable, according to Norman N. Holland ("H. D. and the 'Blameless Physician,'" pp. 474–506). Her account of her association with Freud lets readers study the insights she received and see how her inmost requirements, combined with outward acts and situations, formed her particular self as poet.

Bernard F. Engel, in "H. D.: Poems That Matter and Dilutations" (pp. 507–22), finds precision and restraint in her best poems, which are concerned with "static scene." One fault is that she expects her readers to revere the classics as she does: what she needs to do is to excite a "fresh response" through particulars. Her good poems (invariably short) are in the mainstream; the poorly executed ones are Georgian. On the other hand, Linda Welshimer Wagner ("*Helen in Egypt*: A Culmination," pp. 523–36) says all of H. D.'s work is "well worth reading" for her skill and tranquillity. Mrs. Wagner discerns what she thinks may be H. D.'s "primary artistic principle—the *montage* of memories." Cyrena N. Pondrom has edited "Selected Letters from H. D. to F. S. Flint: A Commentary on the Imagist Period" (pp. 557–86). The twenty-five letters and notes out of a collection of forty-five at the University of Texas disclose the growing rift between Pound and Imagism and H. D.'s own efforts to keep up the literary sections of the *Egoist*. Jackson R. Bryer, in "H. D.: A Note on Her Critical Reputation" (pp. 627–31), says that reviewers were at first enthusiastic because of her faithfulness to Pound's principles of Imagism. When the novelty wore off, she received less attention. When during World War II she shifted her interests to "concern with the present world," critics could not make up their minds to accept the new mode. Since her death in 1961 appreciation has been slowly mounting again. Bryer and Pamela Roblyer have compiled "H. D.: A Preliminary Checklist" (pp. 632–75), a revealing bibliography including books of verse, novels, nonfiction, translations, contributions to periodicals and to books, reprinted items, and works about the poet—in books and periodicals, including reviews.

Jean Gould's *The Poet and Her Book: A Biography of Edna St. Vincent Millay* (New York, Dodd, Mead) sometimes reads like a woman's-magazine feature, and the author almost always passes favorable judgment on the poems. She corrects the tendency in other biographers not to see that the poems finally collected in *A Few Figs from Thistles* should have been scattered throughout her work "like light color notes in a symphony." She stresses the influence of Millay's love for her mother and for Arthur Ficke (all her life). She declares emphatically that the poet was not an alcoholic, that her physical attrition was due more to "overwork" than to "dissipation." She admits —as did Millay— that the poems of World War II were propaganda and should not be included in the definitive canon. After the war she began to write again with the old joy. The author observes that the liberals and the young of the 1960's were turning again to Millay.

In the interest of scrupulosity, Norman A. Brittin ("Millay Bibliography: Additions and Corrections," *AN&Q* 8:52) adds titles of four poems appearing in periodicals (two of them reprints), four brief book notices, and two corrections of items in Karl Yost's 1937 *Bibliography*.

Harriet Monroe's associate is the subject of a forty-four-page pamphlet by T. M. Pearce, *Alice Corbin Henderson* (SWS 21). It states the basic facts of her life, including her experience in connection with *Poetry: A Magazine of Verse*, and describes the contents (little analysis, mostly "appreciation") of her four books of poems, written after she had moved to Santa Fe. Louis D. Rubin, Jr., has written an introduction to *The Yemassee Lands: Poems of Beatrice Ravenel* (Chapel Hill, Univ. of N.C. Press), a collection of this Charleston writer's best verse. After several pages of biography, Rubin turns to the poems themselves and finds the best of them distinguished by living language, bold metaphor, and comparative absence of local-color clichés and of sentimentality. Rubin then asks what it was that kept Mrs. Ravenel from breaking with her Charleston heritage enough to develop her obvious talent beyond the limits of a single book of verse and a very few more poems—an interesting problem for "students both of Southern literature and of . . . literary creativity" in general. W. Gordon Milne ("Lizette Reese Revisited," *SUS* 8:207–12) reminds us that Miss Reese from first to last worked "with an unassuming skill" marked by "austere taste and musical precision." Her romanticism is "tempered with a Cavalier flavor." Though melancholy, she is aware of the beauty and pleasure of life. Milne describes her imagery as "direct, lucid and economical," her diction as strong. The essay is chiefly an invitation to read her poems again.

*Purdue University*

# 15. Poetry: The 1930's to the Present

## A. Kingsley Weatherhead

### i. General

There were few books and essays in 1969 that surveyed this period of poetry in general, or discussed more than one poet. Among them of note is Ralph Mills's *Creation's Very Self: On the Personal Element in Recent American Poetry* (Fort Worth, Texas Christian Univ. Press), a short book, originally a lecture, which discusses the use of personality as a writing instrument among certain contemporaries. Whereas Eliot had stressed impersonality, these poets look to their own experiences and render them as unique and individual. There is a discussion of Roethke, followed by brief comments on Frank O'Hara, W. S. Merwin, James Dickey, Louis Simpson, and James Wright, with illustrations from their poems. Mills turns next to discuss Lowell and some of the confessional poets, John Berryman, Anne Sexton, Sylvia Plath. Finally, there are some remarks on the Projectivists, illustrated by passages from Denise Levertov and Gary Snyder. This book is rewarding reading: in spite of its brevity, it ranges fairly widely among contemporary poets and usefully maps out the area, and at the same time it makes observations on each poet that are new, interesting, and valuable. Paul Carroll, in *The Poem in Its Skin* (Chicago, Follett, 1968), is mainly concerned with ten separate poems, dealing with each individually: he says, "Every good poem is like a person: it has its own skin." The poems discussed are by John Ashbery, Robert Creeley, James Dickey, Isabella Gardner, Allen Ginsberg, John Logan, W. S. Merwin, Frank O'Hara, W. D. Snodgrass, James Wright. Each poem is subjected to a sensitive and knowledgeable close reading. Sometimes Carroll is prepared to "leave the poem in the mystery in which it clearly asks to remain," but more often he resolves problems of obscurity. It is a breezy and refreshing work, studded with anecdotes and digressions: in connection with his explications he repeats the story of Louis Agassiz and the fish and the history of Alcibiades; he explicates "Mending Wall." There is a long general essay at the end of the book, in which the poets whose poems have been analyzed are discussed more generally. Then the essay broadens out into consideration of techniques, themes, subjects, situations, and predicaments common to the poets of this period or shared by some of them. Speaking of Donald Allen's *The New American Poetry* (1960) and Donald Hall's *The New Poets of England and America* (1962), Robert Pack, and Louis Simpson, and declaring that "not one poet appeared in both anthologies," Carroll has forgotten Denise Levertov. He writes vivaciously and informally: it all reads like talk—good, spirited talk directed to an audience of intelligent students who have not yet grown cynical.

Some recent essays on black poetry are related to the question as to whether such work is its own genre. In "Urban Crisis and the Black Poetic Avant-Garde" (*NALF* 3:40–44) Richard K. Barksdale says that because of the strong commitment to social change, in the black poetry of the ghettos esthetic distance is unforgivable and the poet is precluded from any freedom in choosing themes. Abraham Chapman, in "Black Poetry Today" (*ASoc* 5[1968]:401–08), considers whether poetry is fundamentally personal and individual or whether the realities of racial differentiation are part of the shaping process of the black poet's vision of life.

"The New American Poetry" by Raymond Benoit (*Thought* 44: 201–18) notes the signs in our culture that truth is being redefined as no longer merely a matter of the mind but one of the whole human person. Benoit contributes appreciably to a subject that is becoming an increasingly interesting factor in contemporary literary history. He crosses the line usually drawn between the academics on the one hand and the sons of William Carlos Williams on the other to group together Gary Snyder, William Stafford, Richard Wilbur, and Howard Nemerov. He shows how contemporary poetry lets things reveal themselves.

### ii. Wallace Stevens, Theodore Roethke, Robert Lowell, and William Carlos Williams

In the number of items listed in the MLA Bibliography for poets of this period, Wallace Stevens once again leads all the rest. And the citation of three dissertation abstracts speaks of riches yet to come. The most substantial work on Stevens is Helen Hennessy Vendler's *On Extended Wings: Wallace Stevens' Longer Poems* (Cambridge, Mass., Harvard Univ. Press), a study of fourteen long poems, with particular regard to their style and what this reveals of the development of the poet. "Style" covers all the usual details of exposition such as diction, syntax, moods and voices, as well as the use of negatives, use of characters, the use of the words *this, that* and *there,* the cadence, the reduction of words to their sounds alone, and other features which have not received close attention. This book's penetrating observations at the local level and the general deductions to which these lead are an appreciable addition to our knowledge of the long poems and hence about the canon as a whole. An index would not have been superfluous.

Joseph N. Riddel has once again contributed materially to Stevens studies, this time in a thorough consideration of the criticism up to 1968, but going to press too early to cover all the work that appeared that year and thus unable to do more than name James Baird's *The Dome and The Rock,* one of the most distinguished books on this poet. Riddel's summary constitutes a chapter of Bryer's *Fifteen Modern American Authors,* pp. 389–423. In a piece of much smaller compass, "A Review of Stevens Criticism to Date" (*TCL* 15:3–18), Doris L. Eder covers some of the same materials, revealing different preferences. An example of her own criticism appears as "The Meaning of Wallace Stevens' Two Themes" (*Crit Q* 11:181–90), in which she discusses first "Reality and the Imagination" and second "The Supreme Fiction and the Problem of Belief." She has surveyed and sorted out earlier work; her article is admirable for its economy and clarity. In "Stevens' Verse Plays: Fragments of a Total Agon" (*Genre* 1[1968]:124–40) George Knox is concerned with the plays for what they anticipate of the dramatism which is to be found in the opposition and tensions of the poems. "Stevens' dramatism, beginning in the plays," he says, "becomes an amalgam of the dialogue, the dialectic, and the theatrical imagery which play out the agon between 'two sources: the imagination and reality.'" In "Wallace Stevens and Erik Satie: A Source for 'The Comedian as the Letter C'" (*TSLL* 11:811–18) Sidney Feshback deduces Stevens's interest in Satie from details that seem to have come into the poem from articles on him by Paul Rosenfeld and, to a less extent, Carl Van Vechten, and from Satie's own works. A note by J. M. Linebarger, "Wallace Stevens' 'The Good Man Has No Shape'" (*LauR* 9,i:47–49), points out that the title of this poem is ironic, since it implies that goodness cannot be incarnate, and Stevens believed otherwise.

Among the items on Theodore Roethke in 1969 are two articles of particular significance, both concerned with religious progress. "The Poetry of Theodore Roethke" (*SoR* 5:4–25) by James McMichael is a substantial and illuminating essay on Roethke's efforts to move beyond the limits of the self and the methods he used. The movement "from I to Otherwise" is traced in various earlier poems and studied with close attention to detail in "North American Sequence." One point of particular interest in this series is the retrogressive movement that McMichael discovers in the third poem; in identifying this, although retrogression is a fairly regular part of the religious process, he says he gets no support from other critics. In "The Divine Abyss: Theodore Roethke's Mysticism" (*TSLL* 11:1051–68) William Heyen reveals the debt of this poet to Evelyn Underhill, some phrases in his poem "The Abyss" being practically identical to phrases from her *Mysticism: A Study of Man's Spiritual Consciousness.* Roethke was sympathetic to mysticism throughout his career, but in later work (not only in "The Abyss") he supports his mystic intimations "with a formal understanding of its tradition." Heyen lists an imposing number of poems in which Underhill's voice is "inescapable."

Reflections of his personal biography in the works of Robert Lowell have engaged a number of critics recently. In a full and painstaking account of "The Mills of the Kavanaughs" in "Robert Lowell and the Kavanaugh Collapse" (*UWR* 5,i:1–24) Jerome Mazzaro studies the mythic meanings at the core of this difficult poem, its literary allusions, and biographical details. The last arise from incidents in the career of Commander Lowell in the Navy or from incidents in the poet's first marriage, some of which have given rise also to details in the fiction of Jean Stafford, Lowell's first wife. Mazzaro suggests that this is a *poème à clef.* And it is "a crucial, if not a necessary event in the progress of Lowell's art." Roger Bowen, in "Confession and Equilibrium: Robert Lowell's Poetic Development" (*Criticism* 11:78–93), similarly considers the confession in Lowell as a necessary part of his progress. It leads towards two freedoms: "One from the pressure of personal neuroses and an obsessive involvement with personal history, and the second from the diverting pressure of form." This essay also

discusses the autobiographical elements in "The Mills of the Kavanaughs" and mentions the devices the poet uses in his attempt "to
hide from the specific impact of details from his own life." In *Life
Studies* he achieves equilibrium. His "confessions" have made his
present dramatic productions possible. M. Byron Raizis, in "Robert
Lowell's *Prometheus Bound*" (*Studies in American Literature*, pp.
154–68), notes the differences between the Lowell and the Aeschy-
lus versions of *Prometheus Bound* and suggests reasons for them.
He finds figures from Lowell's personal life in the former version;
and he does not quite resist the temptation of naming the contemporary political figures who were the models for its villains.
Gerald Weales, in "Robert Lowell as Dramatist" (*Shenandoah* 20:3–
28), provides full descriptions of *Prometheus, Phaedra,* and *The Old
Glory,* comparing them with their respective sources and noting topical allusions. Weales finds that in spite of a lack of "theatrical validity" in his characters, "Lowell is one of the most impressive dramatists
to turn up in the 1960's." In his urbane and discursive review article,
"A Point in Time, A Place in Space: Six Poets and the Changeling
Present" (*SR* 77:300–18), F. H. Griffin Taylor spends most of his time
on Lowell's *Near the Ocean* and then concentrates on the version
therein of the Tenth Satire of Juvenal. No Roman poet, he notes, is
more relevant to the twentieth century than Juvenal, and none is so
neglected. He observes that his "towering satires are most apt in periods that see the growth of a great imperium" and cites Boileau and
Dr. Johnson as translators in their respective ages, suggesting Lowell
saw a parallel between these times and ours. There are some illuminating details about Juvenal and his anger in this article. Taylor finds
that Lowell's version fails to catch the tone sometimes and is slack
"compared with the sweep and energy of the original." Other miscellaneous articles on this poet include Rudolph L. Nelson, "A Note on
the Evolution of Robert Lowell's 'The Public Garden'" (*AL* 41:106–
10), which describes the changes made in Lowell's recasting of "David
and Bathsheba in the Public Garden" and their implications; and Paul
J. Dolan, "Lowell's *Quaker Graveyard*: Poem and Tradition" (*Renascence* 21:171–80,194), which draws attention to the relationship of
this poem to Hopkins's "Wreck of the Deutschland."

   The most distinguished item about Williams in 1969 was a general
essay on *Paterson,* "A Local Pride: The Poetry of *Paterson*" (*PMLA*
84:547–58), by Joel O. Conarroe. He describes the debts to Whitman's

*Song of Myself* and Pound's *Cantos*, noting also the similarities to *The Bridge* and the long poems of Eliot, but distinguishes the poem from all these, insisting on its uniqueness. He says it is a vast montage of images, symbols, and themes, and the individual fragments are never fully comprehensible until seen in relation to the whole; then, he claims, the larger patterns emerge. In the apparent unevenness of the poem, he grants much to Williams's strategy. The essay occasionally makes use of hitherto unpublished statements of Williams's. Conarroe takes a "close look" at passages of various poetic intensity, the parody "America the golden!" for example, and "The descent beckons." His study of the latter is particularly sensitive. In "The 'Preface' to *Paterson*" (*ConL* 10:39–53), the same critic studies the preface, directing on it what light is available from early drafts and rejected passages. Linda W. Wagner has once again contributed to Williams studies, with "William Carlos Williams: The Unity of His Art" (*Poetic Theory /Poetic Practice*, pp. 136–44). This article illustrates the principles underlying Williams's poetry, emphasizing the significance of prose, shedding new light on this subject. "Williams' 'Nude': *Kora in Hell*" (*SDR* 7,iii:3–18), by the same critic, notes the conditions under which this work was written, the 'Nude' of the title suggesting that *Kora*, though written somewhat later, was Williams's innovation equivalent to those in the Armory Show of 1913. The essay considers especially matters of pace and juxtaposition. George Monteiro, in "Dr. Williams' First Book" (*BBr* 23:85–88), recounts the private publication of *Poems* in 1909, many of which were sonnets in the manner of Keats. Monteiro quotes some of the decorative lines, comparing them with Williams's later, more familiar manner; and no one need wonder at the poet's subsequent repudiation of the sonnet form. Helge N. Nilsen is also concerned with a change in style, this one near the end of the poet's career. In "Notes on the Theme of Love in the Later Poetry of William Carlos Williams" (*ES* 50:273–83) she describes how Williams changed his style in old age from that of the early poetry, which dwelt on the commonplace and nonpoetic world and avoided direct expression of sentiment, to that which produced such a work as "Asphodel, That Greeny Flower." She discusses this poem at some length, observing that the "ultimate effect is the presentation of a few symbols which embody the total meaning" and that with the variations, the thematic recapitulations, and the coda, it is fair to speak of its structure in terms of music. The influence of Ger-

many on Williams and his creative reaction to it is detailed by Hans
Galinsky, in "An American Doctor-Poet's Image of Germany: An
Approach to the Works of William Carlos Williams" (SG 21[1968]:
74–93). He pursues the German connection into the remotest corners,
even suggesting "perhaps it is not by chance" that Linda W. Wagner,
one of Williams's first critics, should be of German extraction! It is
*an* approach, but not a fruitful one. In "William Carlos Williams:
Bibliography Review with Addenda" (*ABC* 19,vii:9–12), William
White notices Emily Mitchell Wallace's bibliography and provides
himself a checklist of materials on Williams that have appeared since
Linda Wagner's 1965 list in *TCL* (10:166–69). There is occasionally
a sense of *déjà vu* derived from reading Williams criticism, and one
wonders whether the following admonitory question of Bernard Duffey's, in a review article "Stevens and Williams" (*ConL* 9[1968]:431–
36), might not generate work from a new angle. Mentioning the need
many a poet has found "for explaining to himself the essence of his
own endeavor," Duffey asks: "If such thought has value to the critic,
is it not likely to be as aspects of the poet's whole creative effort, his
dramatization of his own creativity, rather than as expository detail?" Criticism which devolves upon the phrase "no ideas but in
things" has now reached the point of diminishing returns, and some
new departure would be welcome.

### *iii.* Marianne Moore, Allen Ginsberg, James Dickey, Robert Bly, Denise Levertov, and Richard Wilbur

Except for Stevens, Roethke, Lowell, and Williams, none of the poets
of this period was the subject of more than a handful of items. There
are, however, three books to be noticed, two on Marianne Moore and
one on Allen Ginsberg. George W. Nitchie, in *Marianne Moore: An
Introduction to the Poetry* (New York, Columbia Univ. Press), approaches the poetry by consideration of the early texts, the revisions
made upon certain poems, and the abandonment of others between
*Poems* of 1921 and the "inaccurately titled" *Complete Poems* of 1967.
He discovers relationships in poems grouped chronologically, but
finds also anomalies and contradictions. The varieties in techniques
and attitudes and the development of these as they are demonstrated
here provide a characterization of Miss Moore's work that is more
complex than the versions of earlier critics. We are shown this poet

winning the virtues by which she has come to be known: there is "the fight to be affectionate," for one eminent example. As it proceeds, the book offers many piercing glances into the poems and often clarifies what had previously been obscure; but Nitchie is sufficiently Marianne Moorish to be content to leave an insoluble poem unsolved. The style is graceful, revealing some opulence in the extent to which it can draw on literary sources: of one of Miss Moore's moments of insight, Nitchie can say, "like John Stuart Mill's discovery that he could weep, it makes life possible." In the other book on this poet, Sister Mary Thérèse, S.D.S., *Marianne Moore* (CWCP), which is the length of a long article, there are few new observations. It is upon the spiritual qualities of Miss Moore and her work that this critic focuses; and her study brings out an important quality of the poetry. Some of the conclusions about Miss Moore's spirituality are curious—"the love which comes from faith flowers spiritually as freedom," for instance; and the kinships claimed for her, at one point or another in the book, with Gabriel Marcel, St. Augustine, and Teilhard de Chardin seem a bit too easily established.

Jane Kramer's *Allen Ginsberg in America* (New York, Random House) is a series of scenes featuring this compelling protagonist in his various private and public activities. The anecdotes reveal what a consistently good-natured person Ginsberg is and what overwhelming charm he wields. The scenes are not arranged chronologically, there is no documentation, and all is seen from an omniscient viewpoint. The style is often tight-lipped, betraying no surprise at the extraordinary facts it is recounting. Ginsberg's friend Maretta had heard about India "from a meditative fellow passenger on a Greyhound bus," and she had hitchhiked there. "In the course of a job she found there teaching English to nine-year-old incarnate lamas at a Himalayan summer school, she had formally converted to Tibetan Buddhism" (p. 28). There is a fourteen-page letter from Ginsberg to John Hollander, in which he relates the motives and technical methods in *Howl*, some of which he had described earlier. There is also the old impatience with the academies. One sentiment expressed in the letter is confirmed by an increasing number of young poets: "The beauty of the writing is as Williams says, the invention, the discovery of new appropriate forms, the discovery of something you DON'T know, rather than the synthesis repetition of the things you do already know" (p. 173). The matter of discovery is brought up again in an article entitled "Allen Ginsberg: 'O Brothers of the Laurel, Is the World Real? Is the Laurel a Joke or a Crown of Thorns?'" (*MinnR* 9:50–56) by Richard Howard. Howard also discusses Ginsberg's poetry as prophecy and some other miscellaneous things about the man and his poetry. Answers to the questions raised in the title are not clearly set forth. A brief article by Thomas Parkinson, "Reflections on Allen Ginsberg as a Poet" (*CP* 2,i:21–24), describes *Planet News* as making poetry out of the debris of the planet. For Ginsberg's concern with the technological destruction of it, Parkinson compares the poet with the C. S. Lewis of *Out of the Silent Planet*, though where Lewis responds to destruction with despair and indignation, Ginsberg writes from "sad, lost affection." Like D. H. Lawrence and others, he opposes the misuse of cerebration and accordingly he extols the body; but his concern with sex diminishes as one goes through the volume. Parkinson says Ginsberg is "one of the most important men alive on the planet. We should all be grateful for his presence."

Articles on individual poets of this period have been appearing in *The Sixties* over the pseudonym Crunk, and these have been broad in their coverage, colored by strong individuality, and sensitive to nuance and scruple. One older piece by Crunk is "The Work of James Dickey" (*Sixties* 7[1964]:41–57), written for the most part ironically, the observations that masquerade as praise proving to be deadly thrusts. The article finds fairly severe fault with the irrationality in Dickey's poetry, with the narcissism, and with the "ghastly rhetoric," which goes on and on "like a compliment delivered to a Southern belle before the Civil War." A later issue of *The Sixties* (9[1967]:70–79) contains a review article, *"Buckdancer's Choice,"* by Robert Bly, the editor, in which the censure is no less hurtful for being direct instead of oblique. The review concentrates on three poems: of these, it considers "Slave Quarters" to be "one of the most repulsive poems ever written in American literature," and "Firebombing" it finds deeply middle-class in its "easy acceptance of brutality." A work of art, Bly says, can be an atonement, being able to move into regions of the memory which people cannot visit without wincing and therefore do not visit; it can pierce the mass of guilt. We know from one of his own poems, where it is exquisitely expressed, if not from other places, of the need Bly feels for atonement; and we know of his disgust at the Pentagon's operations in Asia. We may thus well suspect that these strong feelings have distorted his evaluation of Dickey's poetry. He is not by any means alone in finding shortcomings in it: Harry Morris, for instance, in a review article, "A Formal View of the Poetry of Dickey, Garrigue, and Simpson" (*SR* 77:318–25), deplores its inaccuracy, its looseness, and its prolixity. But with all its faults it is not to be judged simply upon its inability to function as atonement. "When Mr. Dickey visits college campuses for readings," says Bly, "he makes clear his wholehearted support of the Vietnam war." This does not, however, make him a bad poet. We may come, if we are not careful, to fruitless personal questions.

Speaking of Dickey in the general essay cited above, Paul Carroll is a little disdainful of "certain fellow poets and critics who seem to approve only poems which embody the pieties of the Northern White Liberal." And in a note, "On Robert Bly's Protest Poetry" (*TPJ* 2,ii: 21–22), Richard Calhoun deplores Bly's remarks about Dickey, recalling the thirties, when judgments about a piece of literature were based upon the political attitudes it manifested.

Calhoun finds the lines of Bly's protest poetry too often "merely rhetorical." Frank Steele, on the other hand, in "Three Questions Answered," in the same issue (*TPJ* 2,ii:23–28), observes some of Bly's techniques with admiration: the alternation of distance and scale for emotion, the surrealism, and especially the effects of sound. He says Bly has the ear of a master poet and can get any effect he wants. Equally strong admiration is felt by William Heyen, in "Inward to the World: The Poetry of Robert Bly" (*FPt* 3:42–50), who conveys a sense of the quality of this poetry partly through the very difficulty of articulating a description of it. Bly is a romantic, says Heyen, and his personal poetry becomes a poetry of social comment. It "assumes, from the beginning, our hurt, and our disbelief that men can do what they have done and are doing."

Another article by Crunk (pseud.) from *The Sixties* is entitled "The Work of Denise Levertov" (*Sixties* 9[1967]:48–65). He finds her main weakness to be a lack of ideas and a lack of vision. She never speaks of communism or the evil effects of usury or the horror of the bourgeoisie; only of herself. As before in this journal, there is a suspicion that social or political criteria are influencing poetic judgment, although of course this cannot be made without consideration of content. In any case, to say so is not to deny that there is value and interest in some of the curious by-ways of Crunk's discussion. The Black Mountain poets, he says, with all their talk of line length, syllable,

head, and heart, lack unity and lack the content that would supply it:
"Pound at least has content. Poets like Zukofsky or Creeley never
attack power, neither its intellectual source, nor its effect in contemporary life. In that sense, they are not true disciples of Pound."
If Denise Levertov lacks vision in one sense, the social or political,
she certainly does not lack it in another. According to Rudolph L.
Nelson, her poetry is "resident in that borderland between the tem-
poral and the eternal, the common and the mysterious." This is observed in "Edge of the Transcendent: The Poetry of Levertov and
Duncan" (*SWR* 54:188–202). Duncan's poetry resides in the same
territory. Nelson notes the kinship between the two poets, comparing
their practices in organic form and the implications of these; and he
makes useful comments on the different ways by which they move
toward the transcendent in their work: Levertov, without crossing
the threshold, finds the transcendent by probing the stuff of immediate experience; Duncan, crossing it, finds difficulty in communicating
the ineffable. Jean M. Hunt, in "Denise Levertov's New Grief-
Language II: *The Sorrow Dance*" (*UR* 35:171–77) notes that in the
latest volume there is more self-disclosure than earlier and more engagement with the detail of human character, human concerns having begun to take precedence over aesthetic ones. It is questionable
whether these conflict, however. Jean Hunt says "it is Miss Levertov's
attention to the aesthetic demands of her art that prevents the Eich-
man poems from speaking with real urgency. . . . A deeply emotional
response would seem to demand a more erratic form." One doubts
this; one doubts Dr. Johnson's similar pronouncement about *Lycidas*:
"Where there is leisure for fiction there is little grief."

There are two good essays on Richard Wilbur to be noticed. Henry
Taylor, in "Two Worlds Taken as They Come: Richard Wilbur's
'Walking to Sleep'" (*HC* 6 spec.no.:1–6,8–12), illustrates Wilbur's
sense of rhythmical rightness within the use of traditional form, his
movement from image to statement, his accounting of the discrep-
ancy between this world and that of the ideal imagination, and his
occasional venture into satire. Wilbur's latest volume, *Walking to
Sleep*, shows a departure from his earlier ways in the introduction of
a first-person speaker: Taylor says that the subject of "Running," one
of the best poems in the volume, is the self. "The Senses of Richard
Wilbur," by Gerard Reedy, S.J. (*Renascence* 21:145–50) covers some

of the same ground. Alluding to Wilbur's poem, "Love Calls Us to the Things of This World," Reedy says, "He chooses as his own the difficult stance of the nuns, a perfect image of the poet, who must maintain his balance in two worlds, one of surrender to unorganized living, sense-experience, and disorder, the other of an ideal search for form, contemplation, and discipline."

### *iv*. May Swenson. Sylvia Plath, Randall Jarrell, David Ignatow, and James Wright

Ann Stanford's "May Swenson: The Art of Perceiving" (*SoR* 5:58–75) emphasizes this poet's dependence upon her acute perceptions, which are made sometimes from unusual angles and which detect therefrom qualities in things that are normally unseen. The article is useful as it demonstrates and illustrates various techniques, the individual use of metaphor, the merging of distinct things, the return from fanciful play to the actual, the visual effects of the shape of the poem on the page, and other features peculiar to May Swenson to which criticism has not previously directed attention.

An essay about Sylvia Plath by Alicia Ostriker is equally original: "'Fact' as Style: The Americanization of Sylvia" (*Lang&S* 1[1968]: 201–12) is a breezy forthright study that takes for its point of departure not the overemphasized suicide of Miss Plath but her poetic voice. In *Ariel* the personal voice is fused with the national, which is an antibelletristic, naive strain of writing that is hostile to conventional formality. *Ariel* does not depend on tradition, as had *The Colossus*, her previous work; it asserts a totally unstable self furiously attacking an outside world which seems stupidly and brutally stable. The poetry is "continually threatening to slide into absurdity." Prosodic matters are cavalierly determined: "If something happens to fall into meter or rhyme, fine. If it doesn't, the devil with it." The imagery is valuable because it produces "verbal equivalents of physical sensation" and wraps together the *look* of something and its significance. If her work lasts it will be because her personal voice became a national one, "dealing in one of the possible valid ways with the wages of reality."

Sister M. Bernetta Quinn, "Randall Jarrell: Landscapes of Life and *Life*" (*Shenandoah* 20 ii:49–78) discusses some poems of Jarrell's which have landscapes in them, bringing early drafts and details of biography to bear in interpreting them and demonstrating their various levels of meaning.

In his survey of Ignatow's published poetry, "The Work of David Ignatow" (*Sixties* 10[1968]:10–23), Crunk (pseud.) notes the prosaic flatness at one stage of this poet's development which expressed the "poverty" of his experience and hence became poetic. Ignatow is a poet of the city, and he has tried, unsuccessfully Crunk feels, to render the suffocation of city life. He is a master, however, of the arts of the parable and of the short poem. Crunk concludes that Ignatow "speaks . . . from a comfortless underground. . . . His poems are like letters from a prison, where he has always lived, and which he himself has partly built. They are profoundly simple."

One need not agree with either the overall evaluation made about a poet or the local judgments of his successes and failures to recognize the value of this criticism. Sometimes, even when they are not political, the grounds for the approval or disapproval seem uncertain. But quite clearly Crunk reads poetry with skill. These remarks are valid also for his essay, "The Work of James Wright" (*Sixties* 8 [1966]:52–78), another full account which covers many aspects of its subject. The style is consistently clear; and if it reveals a love of language and vivid metaphor unusual in a critic, it is none the worse for that.

### v. W. S. Merwin, John Berryman, Robert Creeley, Daniel Berrigan, Louis Simpson, Richard Eberhart, Yvor Winters, and J. V. Cunningham

In his review of W. S. Merwin's latest volume, "The End of the Owls: W. S. Merwin, *The Lice*" (*FPt* 2:40–44), Vern Rutsala observes that underlying this poetry is the drama of the "abdication of available skills in favor of a skillful but bare statement." Such dispossession is now becoming a regular strategy among poets, but Rutsala declares that the change in Merwin is far more genuine, for its "openness and lack of fanfare," than it is in others where it seems to have been dictated by fashion. *The Lice* reflects reduced life: "everything is being forced to live within a shrinking margin"; and it also registers the evil that men's wills have imposed on living things.

"Congested Funeral: Berryman's New Dream Songs" (*TLS* 26

June:680) is an anonymous review article on the three hundred and eight poems. Here we are told that one may not dismiss the matter of structure in Berryman, nor, on the other hand, may the work be said to be unintelligible without a "perception of its grand design." The poem develops by accretion, and Pound and Williams are the two "obvious" models. It has a structure, but it is "inside rather than overall." The *Songs* have "almost the complexity of memory itself," and they "depend on the perception that the mind is not a unity but a plurality, and by keeping the talk going between these mental components . . . they convey their special sense of form." There is no long poem of today, it might be remarked, in which form will not be discovered by somebody.

In "Address and Posture in the Poetry of Robert Creeley" (*CQ* 4:237–43) Kenneth Cox makes some small gains in the difficult matter of illuminating the work of this poet. Cox recognizes that Creeley's writing does not easily lend itself to "conventional comparisons of style or ethic" and he has approached it with what he calls a "fundamental analysis." In this brief, dense article he finds that most of the best poems are in the form of addresses to another, thus being distinguished from lyric and drama. He explores the possibilities and conditions of such addresses. Many poems may be seen as "paradigms which attempt to provide the verbal elements of the thing required to be said"; or "they may be considered studies in the reformulation of expression whose experimental formulae have possible but unpredictable applications."

"Daniel Berrigan: The Activist as Poet" (*LauR* 9,i:11–17) by Harry J. Cargas presents some of the characteristics of Father Berrigan's poetry and the beliefs lying back of them, emphasizing particularly his idea of creation and his commitment to action in life and art. In "Louis Simpson: The Absence of Criticism and the Presence of Poetry" (*FPt* 1 [1968]:60–66) Ronald Moran quotes a number of Simpson's dicta about poetry. In " 'Walt Whitman at Bear Mountain' and the American Illusion" (*CP* 2,i:5–9) the same critic discusses Simpson's questioning of the American dream in this poem. In "The Cultivation of Paradox: The War Poetry of Richard Eberhart" (*BSUF* 10,ii:56–64) Richard J. Fein scrutinizes three war poems by Eberhart. He says that his better poems render a reaction to experience, "a beautiful unsureness," rather than arriving at logical conclusions.

Finally, there is Donald E. Stanford's essay, "Classicism and the

Modern Poet" (*SoR* 5:475–500), in which he considers the claims of
Hulme, Pound, and Eliot to be designated classic. Then, with samples of their poetry, he suggests that the true classicists are Robert
Bridges, E. A. Robinson, Yvor Winters, and J. V. Cunningham. These
combine rationalism in their poetry with nonauthoritarian political
ideals, and their work offers sounder models for the future than that
of Eliot and Pound.

*University of Oregon*

# 16. Drama

*Walter J. Meserve*

## i. Bibliographies, Histories, Anthologies, Dissertations

Although each year the number of books dealing with some aspect of American drama and theater increases, few scholars approach their material from a view larger than a single figure, and probably this is as it should be. There is much to be learned before the transcendental critic starts to work. One book which helps one see what has been accomplished thus far is Fredric M. Litto's *American Dissertations on the Drama and the Theatre, A Bibliography* (Kent, Ohio, Kent State Univ. Press). Including an author index, a keyword-in-context index, and a subject index, this work would seem to be extremely valuable for the American scholar. Unfortunately, it is not complete. One is forced back to *Dissertation Abstracts*, after all, and the book's value is sharply reduced.

The broad view of any genre, of course, makes considerable demands upon a writer. In *The Small Town in American Drama* (Dallas, Texas, Southern Methodist Univ. Press) Ima Honaker Herron attempts to catalogue plays which treat Smalltown, U.S.A.—from the "Puritan Village" through the "Yankee Village," the West, the South, the "Old Home Town," and many Main Streets to "Our Vanishing Town." It is a large thesis, and the organization becomes artificial while the information shifts from the peripheral to solid background for a discussion of the plays. Although the analyses of the plays show the limited approach that the thesis demands and the long chapter on O'Neill throws the book out of balance, there is considerable value in the references to some little-known plays as well as in the social, political, and historical commentary. Stanley Green's *The World of Musical Comedy* (Cranbury, N.J., A. S. Barnes, 1968) is a revised and enlarged edition of his 1960 book. A good review for musical comedy from 1900 to the present, this volume adds new names and brings the material on all others up to date. A third book with a genre view, Geoffrey Brereton's *Principles of Tragedy: A Rational Examination of the Tragic Concept of Life and Literature* (Coral Gables, Fla., Univ. of Miami Press) by omitting any reference to American drama simply tells us that "the legacy of Aristotle" has not yet been passed on to America.

Generally, anthologies included only plays of the modern period. The exception is the attempt by Indiana University Press to expand those well-known twenty volumes of America's Lost Plays. Volume 21, *Satiric Comedies*, edited by Walter J. Meserve and William R. Reardon, provides an introductory essay on satiric comedy in early American drama and includes *Androborus; The Trial of Atticus, Before Justice Beau, for a Rape; The Battle of Brooklyn; Darby's Return;* and *Po-ca-hon-tas*. The four-volume collection, *50 Best Plays of the American Theatre* (New York, Crown Publishers) selected by Clive Barnes and introduced by John Gassner, includes only *The Contrast, Uncle Tom's Cabin,* and *Salvation Nell* prior to the modern period. Gassner's introductions are standard and brief, while Barnes's introduction to the collection is merely a series of extremely brief paragraphs of superficial commentary. Although one might question Michael Benedict's ideas about Realism and Naturalism, his *Theatre Experiment: An Anthology of American Plays* (Garden City, N.Y., Doubleday, 1967) includes such interesting plays as Wallace Stevens's *Three Travellers Watch a Sunrise* and E. E. Cummings's *Santa Claus*. Robin Corbin and Miriam Balf's *Twelve American Plays, 1920–1960* (New York, Scribner's) is geared to secondary-school level. Unfortunately, the introduction is without value and the collection undistinguished. With only one play before 1938, the anthology is somewhat misleading in its title.

The year's dissertations are interesting both for the subjects treated and the division of labor suggested. Thirteen of the thirty-five dissertations listed in the MLA Bibliography, for example, are concerned with physical theaters or with technical people connected with the production of plays. Of the remainder, there are three dissertations on O'Neill, one each on Miller, Williams, Hellman, Maxwell Anderson, and Albee. Two dissertations treat aspects of the drama before 1915. What seems particularly encouraging, however, is the four dissertations which deal with some aspects of dramatic criticism in America—New York *Evening Post*, 1807–1830; New York *Dramatic Mirror*, 1880–1909; John Rankin Touse; Claudia Cassidy.

There is no history of dramatic criticism in America; in fact, there has been little work done on the subject. With more such dissertations, however, that history might be approached.

## *ii.* The Beginning to 1915

With reference to the drama, universities seem to spawn only scholars of modern life. There are reasons, of course. The limitations of the drama are a good one, but a generation taught to scorn literary history is another. When a study of theatrical or literary history is made, too frequently it is by an historian who senses the value of his research but lacks an understanding of the genre he is probing. *The American Playhouse in the Eighteenth Century* (Cambridge, Mass., Harvard Univ. Press) by Brooks McNamara illustrates the problem. Professor McNamara is not conversant with eighteenth-century drama and theater in America. Moreover, although he corrects some past errors of thought and adds interesting details to theater history, he sometimes misleads his reader with his pictures and quotations while occasionally depending upon rather extravagant deductions.

Vernon Lestrud provides a good comment on one problem felt by theater people in his "Early Theatrical 'Blue Laws' on the Pacific Coast" (*Rendezvous* 4:15–24), concluding that "politically, the theatre has long been vulnerable to legal restrictions." Roger E. Stoddard has created "A Guide to Spencer's Boston Theatre, 1855–1862" (*PAAS* 79:45–98). Cecelia Tichi ("Thespis and the 'Carnal Hipocrite': A Puritan Motive for Aversion to Drama," *EAL* 4,ii:86–103) shows that Puritan attitudes toward the imagination not only subdued playwriting but brought out heated arguments against actors. In another article concerned with the drama of this period C. M. Lombard ("French Romanticism on the American Stage," *RLC* 43: 161–172) explains the popularity of the French drama in terms of the current taste for sensation, emotionalism, escapism, and adventure. John R. Wolcott's essay, "A Case Study of American Production: English Source and American Practice" (*OSUTCB* 15[1968]:9–19), explores an 1817 production of *Aladdin* at the Chestnut Street Theater in Philadelphia through the letters of an Englishman who was describing a production he had witnessed.

Only two dramatists of the late nineteenth century are considered in articles. Marvin Felheim ("Bronson Howard: 'Literary Attaché,'"

*ALR* 2:174–79) concludes that the "Dean of American Drama" was
a devoted playwright who revised very carefully the few plays that
he wrote. In a well-constructed paper, A. Cleveland Harrison, "Boucicault's Formula: Illusion Equals Pleasure" (*ETJ* 21:299–309), uses
thirteen essays by Boucicault to show that playwright's belief in the
people as the arbiter of a play's effectiveness and to explain his technique of reaching that point of success through theatrical illusion.
Edward Wagenknecht's excellent critical biography of William Dean
Howells, *William Dean Howells, The Friendly Eye* (New York, Oxford Univ. Press), discusses his plays as they reveal the Howells that
Wagenknecht has envisioned. One final item to mention is Dean H.
Keller's edition of *A Fool's Errand* (Metuchen, N.J., Scarecrow Press)
by Steele MacKaye and Albion W. Tourgée. Although the play adds
little to American drama, Keller's introduction and appendices provide something of a model for this kind of edition.

### iii. Between Two World Wars

Interestingly enough, two of the book-length studies of American
drama approach the subject in terms of myth. Thomas E. Porter
(*Myth and Modern American Drama*, Detroit, Wayne State Univ.
Press) posits an examination of drama in the light of the cultural
milieu, which he describes as the "spine of drama." Building upon his
Catholic faith and an interest in the critical persuasion of Northrup
Frye, Porter analyzes eight American plays. His tendency, however,
is to reduce them to a formula. Other than these plays he sees a decline in the drama, a lack of what he calls "regeneration," and a consequent frustration on the part of the audience. Unfortunately, he
seems to be denying his original thesis by showing a reluctance to
accept the theory that dramatists reflect their culture. Hugh Dickinson (*Myth on the Modern Stage*, Urbana, Univ. of Ill. Press) shows
how ten dramatists (three of whom are American) look at traditional material. Most distinctive is his essay "Robinson Jeffers: The
Twilight of Man," in which he emphasizes Jeffers's tendency to preach
while admitting the fact that as a philosopher Jeffers undercut his
dramatic effect. The essay on "Eugene O'Neill: The Family as Furies"
explores O'Neill's use of the demonic, while in "Tennessee Williams:
Orpheus as Savior" Dickinson discusses Williams's use of the Eury-
dice legend. A single essay which should be noted is James M. Salem's

self-explanatory "American Drama Between the Wars: The Effects of Sociology" (*BSUF* 10,ii:47–54).

Two rather interesting books on the theater between the wars have appeared. Norman Nadel's *A Pictorial History of the Theatre Guild* (New York, Crown Publishers) provides a very readable history and some commentary by Lawrence Langner and Armina Marshall in addition to the pictures. *The Group Theatre, 1933–1941* (Flushing, N.Y., Queens College, Paul Klapper Library/Art Center) was compiled by Neal Richmond. It is a very slight book, but it contains pictures by Alfredo Valente, a bibliography, and notes by Robert Dierlam and Harold Clurman.

*a.* **Eugene O'Neill.** The computer makes all things possible, and there is now *An O'Neill Concordance* (3 vols., Detroit, Gale Research Co.), compiled by J. Russell Reaver. Based on the latest editions of O'Neill's plays, it is selective of plays written before 1924, but includes all plays written after that date. John Henry Raleigh's bibliographical essay appeared in Bryer's *Fifteen Modern American Authors*, pp. 301–22. He includes sections on bibliography, editions, manuscripts and letters, biography, and criticism. In the final section, however, he lists no book written after 1965 and includes essays written mainly before 1967.

Among O'Neill's plays *The Iceman Cometh* attracted most scholarly attention this year. In "The Existential Dilemma in *The Iceman Cometh*," from *Variations*, pp. 44–48, Ranjit Kaur Chopra argues that the question of "being" is the problem of the play and that the decisions of Hickey and Parrott "not to be," combined with Larry's change in belief, define the existential dilemma which controls the play. Robert C. Lee ("Evangelism and Anarchy in *The Iceman Cometh*," *MD* 12:173–86) discusses the play very forcefully in terms of two unifying symbols of destructive encroachment—evangelism and the anarchist movement—which he finds central in the character of Larry Slade. Rudolf Haas ("'Tristitia' and 'Nobiskrug': Zwei mögliche Motive in *The Iceman Cometh*," *Literatur und Sprache*, pp. 144–52) finds two motifs in the play; while Sy Kahn ("O'Neill's Legion of Losers in *The Iceman Cometh*," *The Forties*, pp. 205–13) sees the play as a comic allegory of America and a warning to a victorious country in 1946.

In "Biblical Perversions in *Desire Under the Elms*" (*MD* 11:423–

428) Peter L. Hays seems to condemn both the harsh Puritanical religion and the creation of Ephraim Cabot as a perversion of that religion "that cripples love and destroys men." A brief but perceptive essay on one of O'Neill's less-discussed plays is Gus Gey's "Unité et dualité du mythe de Dionysos dans *Lazarus Laughed* de Eugene O'Neill" (*Caliban* 6:69–72). Ulrick Hoffman covered old territory without adding much in two essays: "Ironie und Symbolik der Dramentitel O'Neills" (*NS* 18:322–35), and "Zur Symbolik der Personennamen in den Dramen Eugene O'Neills" (*Archiv* 206:38–45). Ernest G. Griffin ("Pity, Alienation, and Reconciliation in Eugene O'Neill," *Mosaic* 2,i:[1968]:66–76) attempts to place O'Neill in the modern world accompanied by some traditional concepts. In "Nietzsche and O'Neill: A Study in Affinity" (*OL* 23[1968]:97–126) Egil Törnqvist discusses Nietzsche's attitudes towards politics, religion, and man in general and suggests the influence of these ideas on some twenty of O'Neill's plays. He concludes that over the years there was no change in O'Neill's attitude toward Nietzsche. A good article with which to conclude a study of O'Neill is James M. Highsmith's "O'Neill's Idea of Theatre" (*SAB* 23,iv:[1968] 18–21), in which he argues that O'Neill fought classification, denied formulas, and never allowed himself "to formulate theories of drama."

*b.* **Clifford Odets.** Two books show different approaches to Odets's artistry. Edward Murray (*Clifford Odets: The Thirties and After*, New York, Frederick Ungar, 1968) reacts strongly to previous critics, emphasizes the structure of the plays, and provides much peripheral comment which is sometimes weakly related to his thesis. Dividing his study into two parts, he discusses three plays of the thirties—omitting *Waiting for Lefty*—and five later plays. He places a lot of emphasis on Odets's going to Hollywood, but concludes that both *The Country Girl* and *The Flowering Peach* are among the best plays in American drama. Michael J. Mendelsohn, as the title of his book suggests (*Clifford Odets, Humane Dramatist*, Deland, Fla., Everett/ Edwards) adopts a different approach to his subject. The first chapter of this book provides an impressive introduction to Odets and his period, but because of the brevity of the book the analyses of the plays are not as full as one might wish. The personal interviews which Mendelsohn had with Odets, however, are an effective part of this study.

**c. Lillian Hellman.** Miss Hellman's autobiography (*An Unfinished Woman—A Memoir*, Boston, Little, Brown) is interesting reading, particularly the first part, but disappointing for the person hoping to find comments on her plays or the theater. On these topics there is extremely little. The major part of her book is concerned with her two trips to Russia, which she explains mainly by quoting from her diary. Here the continuity may be difficult to follow, but it all reveals a fascinating life. Jacob H. Adler's pamphlet, *Lillian Hellman* (SWS 4), accomplishes rather little. Obviously, Adler's task—Lillian Hellman in 10,000 words—was difficult, but the result suggests a less than satisfactory understanding of Hellman's work, interspersed with a few interesting and unsupported observations.

**d. Connelly, Anderson, Wilder, and Hart.** Paul T. Nolan (*Marc Connelly*, TUSAS 149) attempts to show that "many of Mr. Connelly's works are worth serious attention." Although Nolan's success here is questionable because he provides very little critical argument, he does bring out new information on the Kenneth Mercer skits and shows that Connelly has written a great deal more than most people realize, including three plays since World War II. The book is a good addition to Connelly's *Voices Offstage* (1968). Laurence G. Avery has compiled a detailed *Catalogue of the Maxwell Anderson Collection at the University of Texas* (Austin, Univ. of Texas, 1968) which, in addition to doing what the title indicates, records manuscripts at the University of North Dakota, Yale University, Library of Congress, and New York Public Library. Avery provides bibliographical data and useful commentary as well. The only piece on Wilder published this year in English was Gerald Rabkin's "*The Skin of Our Teeth* and the Theatre of Thornton Wilder" (*The Forties*, pp. 113–20), which adds little to Wilder scholarship. After tracing the controversy concerning the play's sources, Rabkin concludes that Wilder was not very radical. In "The Comic Theatre of Moss Hart: Persistence of a Formula" (*TA* 23[1967]:60–87) Richard Mason argues that Hart never allowed ideas to get in the way of his comic pace, dialogue, and action.

### iv. After World War II

The most significant book, on this period is Gerald Weales's *The Jumping-Off Place: American Drama in the 1960's* (New York, Macmillan). Building upon his earlier study, *American Drama Since World War II*, and upon his reviews for *The Reporter*, Weales has produced an excellent discussion of the recent drama. After a chapter bringing Miller and Williams up to date and a very sensible and well-argued discussion of Albee, Weales comments upon the "Front Runners, Some Fading" (those who have been most active in the sixties) before developing essays on Negro drama; plays by poets, especially Robert Lowell; plays by novelists, emphasizing Saul Bellow; and the off-off-Broadway drama. His quarrel with "Happenings"—that their attempt to bring life into art tends toward dehumanization—seems tremendously perceptive. Among critics today who write for both academic and commercial audiences, Weales enjoys an absorption and understanding of American drama which allow him that intelligent and sensitive overview that distinguishes criticism. He is thoughtful, honest, never seems to duck an issue. Beyond that his lively prose style makes his writing a welcome relief to read.

The essays on drama in the volume, *The Forties*, are of uneven value. Jordan Miller's "Drama: The War Play Comes of Age" (pp. 63–82) sketches reactions to the war play by a number of dramatists but makes very little comment. The comment of "coming of age" is lost somewhere in the rapid survey. In "A Nightly Miracle: The Early Musical Drama of Rodgers and Hammerstein" (pp. 123–37) Jackson R. Bryer dips immediately into the work of these two writers, which makes the musicals of the forties distinctive, and then allots more commentary to *The King and I* (1951) than to any of the forties musicals.

One essay which deserves some particular attention is Samuel L. Macey's "Nonheroic Tragedy: A Pedigree for American Tragic Drama" (*CLS* 6:1–19). Through an examination of European plays which influenced American tragic drama, Macey concludes that American playrights O'Neill, Miller, and Williams belong to a subgenre of tragedy which he terms "nonheroic tragedy." His concept of tragedy demands more substantiation than he supplies, but his approach should provoke thought as well as disagreement.

*a.* **Arthur Miller.** The two books published this year on Miller suggest the interest this dramatist has for the broad public. Tetsumaro Hayashi's *Arthur Miller Criticism, 1930–1967* (Metuchen, N.J., Scarecrow Press) claims a completeness that does not exist. The compiler notes that all reprintings of Miller's work are listed, but he fails here; the necessity of a complete list would be questionable anyway. More important liabilities are his incomplete list of books of criticism, the limited number of foreign critical essays, the confused and sometimes awkwardly repeated entries, and the omission of reference works such as *ALS*. Most valuable is the listing of unpublished works, including manuscripts and letters. In the second book, *Psychology and Arthur Miller* (New York, Dutton) Richard I. Evans, a psychologist, interviews Miller with the seeming purpose of supporting some of his ideas about creativity—"creativity as a psychological process." Miller, however, remained unimpressed with the attempt to formalize his creative process. As Evans presents his concern for the clinical impact of drama, Miller stoutly maintains that he is an artist, not a psychologist, and not interested in curing people. The reader has the impression that here are two people speaking different languages and that they only occasionally communicate with each other.

Among the year's articles on Miller, the best was Paul Blumberg's "Sociology and Social Literature: Work Alienation in the Plays of Arthur Miller" (*AQ* 21:291–310). In a well-organized essay Blumberg shows the sociologists' interest in Miller's plays and carefully substantiates Miller's concern for the alienation of labor as a part of his theme of alienation of modern man. Lois Gordon (*"Death of a Salesman*: An Appreciation," *The Forties*, pp. 273–83) is concerned with *death* and contends that the play is both a sociopolitical criticism of American culture and a dramatization of Willy Loman as a tragic figure. Robert A. Martin's interview with Miller is misleading in its title, "The Creative Expression of Arthur Miller: An Interview" (*ETJ* 21:310–17), since they discuss mainly Miller's "Jewishness." At best it is not a very revealing interview. Raymond H. Reno's "Arthur Miller and the Death of God" (*TSLL* 11:1069–87) is concerned primarily with *All My Sons* and *After the Fall*. It is, however, a turgidly written essay and loses effect for this reason as well as for its limited approach to the Miller canon.

*b.* **Tennessee Williams.** Nancy M. Tischler, in *Tennessee Williams* (SWS 5), is limited by the pamphlet format, and although she has significant observations, there is little justification for saying that

Williams's "greatest talent lies in presenting a portion of the South." In "Tennessee Williams: Streetcar to Glory" (*The Forties*, pp. 251–58) C. W. E. Bigsby places Williams in the decade before discussing Stella as the "real hero" of *Streetcar*. It is better than most essays in this volume. In another view of the same play, "Blanche Dubois: A Re-evaluation" (*TA* 24:58–69), Constance Drake sees Blanche as "the last representative of a sensitive, gentle love whose defeat is to be lamented."

*c.* **Edward Albee.** From another part of the world, R. Parthasarathy has asked, "Who's Afraid of Edward Albee? American Drama of the Sixties" (*Quest* 55[1967]:52–55). For Parthasarathy, this most promising of the new American playwrights, whose plays are marked by force of dialogue and preoccupation with hate, is important for an articulated vision which he sees as answering some of the private needs and yearnings of an Albee audience. Obviously, Albee also answers some of the private needs of his American critics who pay more attention to his plays than to the work of any American playwright other than O'Neill. In his Twayne volume, *Edward Albee* (TUSAS 141) Richard E. Amacher provides commentary on ten of the plays. His contention that Albee writes one-act and full-length tragedies will bother some readers, as will some of the poorly supported conclusions for his explications of play texts. He seems to be most effective with *Tiny Alice*, where his formula interpretations work. In general, Amacher's assessment is fair if one accepts his critical orientation, although his argument would profit from a more balanced approach to Albee's plays. On the other hand, Ruby Cohn's *Edward Albee* (UMPAW 77), although a pamphlet, is a compellingly written and sensible interpretation as she cleverly and clearly wends her way through Albee's work. She does not consider his adaptations or his plays since *A Delicate Balance*, but with insight and without extravagant claims she presents a fine discussion. One other item which might be noted at this point is Philip C. Kolin's "A Classified Edward Albee Checklist" (*Serif* 6,iii:16–32), which corrects and updates Margaret Rule's bibliography (see *ALS 1968*, p. 269).

    *Virginia Woolf* and *Tiny Alice* attracted a considerable number of critics. Forrest E. Hazard found "The Major Theme in *Who's Afraid of Virginia Woolf?*" (*CEA* 31,iii[1968]:10–11) to be "the delicate relationship that must bind the symbolically masculine and feminine principles of creation together if life is to progress." Gretl K. Fischer ("Edward Albee and Virginia Woolf," *DR* 49:196–207) thinks of the artist rather than the play and argues that the symbolism of both writers suggests the larger issues of human progress and that the works of each indicate that healthy conditions exist only where imagination is combined with reason and action. Such a comparative essay might have been expected, but its argument is not easy to accept. Richard J. Dozier ("Adultery and Disappointment in *Who's Afraid of Virginia Woolf?*" *MD* 11:432–36) tries to stand on both sides of the street. He finds it an unsatisfactory play, halfheartedly developed and without a meaningful ending, yet concludes that it is a "good play."

*Tiny Alice* is explained in a rather elaborate fashion by Ryder H. Curry and Michael Porte as an "amazing" and "brilliant construction" of "The Surprising Unconscious of Edward Albee" (*DramS* 7:59–68). William E. Willeford, on the other hand, explores the religious mystery of the play through the figure of Alice, the God in the play who appropriates Julian at his death, who is also "The Mouse in the Model" (*MD* 12:135–45). "Symbol and Substance in *Tiny Alice*" (*MD* 12:92–98) is the approach of Alice Mandanis, who sees the play as a kind of conjurer's trick but also a compelling and serious play about religion. She compares it with Archibald MacLeish's *Nobodaddy*. William F. Lucey, in a somewhat disjointed and ineffective essay, "Albee's *Tiny Alice*: Truth and Appearance" (*Renascence* 21:76–80,110), makes some obvious comments about Albee's probing of reality.

From the foreign scene Karl Schwartz finds modern relevance in "Edward Albee's *Zoo Story*" (*NS* 18:261–67) while Paul Hübner suggests Albee's place in the modern Western tradition, "Prekäre Gleichgewichte—Albee, Hofmannsthal und Camus" (*WW* 19:28–34). Nigerian critic Dapo Adelugba, however ("Theatre Critique: Faux Pas at Ibadan University Arts Theatre," *Ibadan* 26:81–82), criticizes a production of *The American Dream* as part of an "unattractive evening," a "dreary play."

*d.* **The contemporary drama.** Having watched twenty years of what he terms a Cold War in American drama, Mordecai Gorelik

("Root-Freeze of American Drama," *Meanjin* 28:90–95) now sees hope in Barbara Garson's *MacBird!*, Howard Sackler's *The Great White Hope*, and George Sklar's *And People All Around*. Professor Gorelik, however, wants only a particular kind of "relevant" drama. The same is true of Kenneth John Atchity, another writer of passion and conviction, who produces an interesting essay in "5 Plays of Protest at the Crossroads" (*To Find Something New*, pp. 4–27). Defining "Crossroads" as the happy conjunction of drama and poetic vision, he discusses *MacBird!*, Van Itallie's *America Hurrah*, Megan Terry's *Viet Rock*, Arnold Weinstein's *Dynamite Tonight*, and Tom Sankey's *The Golden Screw*. Only in the last two, however, does he see the "crossroads" confronted and some prophecy of theater vitality. Serious treatment of another new playwright, with particular reference to language, may be found in Ren Frutkin's "Sam Shepard: Paired Existence Meets the Monster" (*Yale Theatre* 2,ii:22–30).

*e.* **The contemporary theater.** For those who wonder just what the Living Theatre does—call it drama, if you must—Richard Gilman ("Theater of Ignorance," *AtM* 224,i:35–42) makes some very sensible observations. The Living Theatre, of course, is the property of Julian Beck and Judith Malina, who began their experiment in theater during the fifties and have guided its erratic course ever since. Another director who can claim some success with the New York Shakespeare Festival, the Phoenix Theatre in New York, and the Seattle Repertory Theatre is Stuart Vaughn. In its more serious parts, his autobiography, *A Possible Theatre, The Experiences of a Pioneer Director in America's Resident Theatre* (New York, McGraw-Hill) helps one see how a play filters through a director's mind onto a stage. *The Free Southern Theater by the Free Southern Theater* (Indianapolis, Bobbs-Merrill) is a documentary of this radical black theater by Thomas C. Dent, Richard Schechner, and Gilbert Moses, complete with letters, journal and diary entries, one of the plays produced, and a running narrative. Meanwhile there is still New York and Broadway. Some of the problems here are described by Tino Balio and Robert G. McLaughlin ("The Economic Dilemma of the Broadway Theatre: A Cost Study," *ETJ* 21:81–100), who base their study of the 1938–60 period on the records of producers and producing agencies at the Wisconsin Center for Theatre Research. Clearly, all of this theater activity has a substantial effect upon American drama.

### *v.* Contemporary Black Drama

One distinctive aspect of the year's scholarship is the amount of attention being paid to black dramatists. With *The Black American Writer*, vol. 2, *Poetry and Drama* (Deland, Fla., Everett/Edwards) editor C. W. E. Bigsby is responsible for several essays on the subject, but there have also been numerous articles from other sources. As a group, these essays present a broad view of the aims and problems of black drama as well as discussions of a number of playwrights.

*a.* **Black aesthetics and the black playwright.** Seeing a new art in a changing culture, both black and white, scholars have considered basic questions. Mainly the tone of the essays has been reasonable, but not always. Black drama can be a weapon of revolution in a culture, and a number of writers show the bias as well as the bitterness that is part of revolution. In great numbers the critics of black drama preach a forceful message. Larry Neal, in "The Black Arts Movement" (*Black American Writer*, pp. 187–202), declares that the black artist must speak to the spiritual and cultural needs of the black people. The plays of LeRoi Jones, he feels, are the most advanced aspect of that movement. Melvin Dixon in "Black Theatre: The Aesthetics" (*NegroD* 18,ix:41–44) stresses a similar idea. "A functional, viable black aesthetic grows from an alliance of the artist with the community." For a more practical approach, read "Report on Black Theater" edited by Peter Bailey et al. (*NegroD* 18,vi:20–26,69–72). Like other theaters, the black theater is in "dire need of support, financial and otherwise."

Writing more specifically about black dramatists, in "The Black Playwright in the Professional Theatre of the United States of America, 1858–1959" (*Black American Writer*, pp. 113–28) Darwin Turner traces the progress of black playwrights and bases their obviously limited numbers upon an equally obvious lack of opportunity. He concludes that the black playwright is not yet a significant force in professional theater. Loften Mitchell ("On the Emerging Playwright," *Black American Writer*, pp. 129–36) presents his own bitter view with his usual force. One major creation of the emerging black playwright is discussed by Charles D. Peavey—"Satire and Contemporary Black Drama" (SNL 7,i:40–49)—who sees all satire as a Black Power weapon "to instill a Black awareness in the audience."

*b.* **Torrence, Hughes, Hansberry, Baldwin.** Perhaps one might suggest that these dramatists indicate the route that black drama has come. John M. Clum's "Ridgley Torrence's Negro Plays: A Noble Beginning" (*SAQ* 68:96–108) makes a good case for Torrence as creating a beginning for the Negro in the theater. Woodie King, Jr.'s "Remembering Langston: A Poet of the Black Theater" (*NegroD* 18,vi:27–32,95–96) is simply a reminiscence and a very readable one. One of the best essays in *The Black American Writer* volume is Jordan Y. Miller's "Lorraine Hansberry" (pp. 157–70). Judging her plays exceptional pieces of dramatic literature, Miller presents a well-supported argument for good "old fashioned plays" with people who are worth knowing. The work of James Baldwin is discussed in two essays. Walter J. Meserve ("James Baldwin's Agony Way," *Black American Writer*, pp. 171–86) approaches Baldwin through his humanitarianism—love through suffering. Mainly a thesis playwright, Baldwin is viewed as concerned with the Negro as man. Frank Silvera ("Towards a Theatre of Understanding," *NegroD* 18,vi:33–35) confines observations to Baldwin's *Amen Corner*, emphasizing his compassion.

*c.* **LeRoi Jones and others.** "Themes and Symbols in Two Plays by LeRoi Jones" (*NegroD* 18,vi:42–47) by Maria K. Mootry comments on *The Baptism* and *The Toilet*. A far more impressive essay is Louis Phillips's "LeRoi Jones and Contemporary Drama" (*Black American Writer*, pp. 203–17). Describing Jones as a militant black who wants a revolution in America, Phillips discusses the various themes that concern the playwright—the failure of Christianity, the problem of homosexuality, the inevitability of violence between black and white. C. W. E. Bigsby comments on "Three Black Playwrights: Loften Mitchell, Ossie Davis, Douglas Turner Ward" (*Black American Writer*, pp. 137–55), but with the exception of Mitchell, he provides only a few facts and observations without real evaluation. The ideas of three more black dramatists are recorded through interviews, but interviews being what they are, the ideas are generally quite scattered: "Lonne Elder III: An Interview" (*Black American Writer*, pp. 219–26); "Harold Cruse: An Interview" (*Black American Writer*, pp. 227–39); Marvin X, "Black Theatre: An Interview with Ed Bullins" (*NegroD* 18,vi:9–16).

## *vi.* A Final Comment

There are good reasons why the history of American drama has not been written. Too few scholars have an interest in the history of American drama. Confusing the drama with the theater, they are mainly aware of the present, the immediate. Each year, however, there is some good work being done outside the usual examination and reexamination of the works of O'Neill and Albee. Each year there are more book-length studies being published on American drama and theatre. And each year it would appear that the traditional animosity between "drama" and "theater" scholars is being fused to a point of understanding where each is at least aware of the value of the other. Someday that traditional wound may be healed and disappear. It is, at least, a healthy dream. In one sense the contemporary interest in "living" drama and theater and the attitude toward black drama are moves in the right direction. In these instances the scholarly concern is clearly bilateral. As for the history of American drama to this present day, an awareness of the necessary fusion and the concern for historical perspective are beginnings. One can only hope that this kind of concern for the present may stimulate a similar concern for what came before.

*Indiana University*

# 17. Folklore

## John T. Flanagan

The continually accelerating interest in folklore manifested itself in 1969 by swollen bibliographies and additional compilations. Several brief and specialized lists need to be cited first. Mary Washington Clarke's "Bibliography of Kentucky Folklore for 1968" (*KFR* 15:46–54) includes books, articles, and even newspaper items. Warren I. Titus and James H. Penrod collaborated on the folklore section in "Articles in American Studies" (*AQ* 21:425–30), which includes some fifty-five items arranged alphabetically by authors. Scattered American folklore items appear in the *Annual Bibliography of English Language and Literature* (Cambridge, Eng., Modern Humanities Research Assn., 42[1967]:83–90). Don Yoder compiled an interesting list of materials on Amish life and culture in "What to Read on the Amish" (*PF* 18,iv:14–19). A number of items appear in the general folklore section of *PMLA* and also in the American literature subsection (84:809–11, 879–80). The four numbers of volume 7 of *Abstracts of Folklore Studies*, edited by Herbert Halpert, sandwich American material among many foreign citations but are arranged by the journals sampled and cover several years. A cumulative index of both authors and titles makes the arrangement more useful. A highly specialized but unusual bibliography is a substantial part of Gerald E. Parsons's article "Cockfighting: A Potential Field of Research" (*NYFQ* 25:265–88). The author provides an annotated list of extant material on cockfighting in articles, manuals, and books. In "A Checklist of Scholarship on Southern Literature for 1968" (*MissQ* 22:155–80) Paschal Reeves inaugurates a new feature in the journal in which research is divided into five chronological areas from the Colonial to the contemporary. Folklore material is scattered throughout.

One of the most valuable regional bibliographies to appear in a long time is *A Bibliographical Guide*. The folklore chapter by Daniel W. Patterson (pp. 102–18) comprises eight sections and is extremely thorough: collections of Southern folklore, periodicals, folktales, secular songs, religious songs, cultural studies and beliefs, discography, and song style. Each section includes a short initial comment on the available material and is followed by citations of essays, monographs, and books arranged alphabetically by authors. It should be noted that material culture is omitted, Southern speech and humor are excluded because they are treated elsewhere, and riddles and proverbs are virtually absent because they have received little attention from collectors.

The annual folklore bibliography of Merle E. Simmons, assisted in 1968 by Jean McLaughlin (*SFQ* 33:135–282) shows the customary impressive coverage, all of North America plus Spanish- and Portuguese-speaking regions elsewhere. Annotations are longer and more analytical. The editor has extended his survey in the direction of folk life and popular culture, including specifically the *Journal of Popular Culture* (*JPC*); another innovation is the decision to notice reprints in order to acknowledge recent publishing tendencies, but only if the books reissued originally appeared at least twenty-five years ago. The user of this indispensable bibliography will notice that among the subject fields surveyed are anthropology, history, onomastics, ethnomusicology, and sociology.

### *i.* History and Theory

Articles comprising a wide spectrum of folklore research in history and theory appeared in 1969. Their subjects varied from the role of organized societies to collecting procedures and theories of interpretation.

Wayland D. Hand in "Folklore Societies and the Research Effort" (*KFQ* 14:97–104) examines the work of local and regional folklore societies and contends that although they fail as teaching media and can seldom accumulate archives, they can stimulate desirable folklore activity. Frank C. Brown, as Hand points out, preserved his invaluable archives in his own house. In a more comprehensive article, "North American Folklore Societies" (*JAF* 82:3–33), Hand included the reports of various individuals on some fifteen state or regional societies, most of them currently active. The reports provide capsule histories of each organization, naming officers and identifying activities. Titles of publications are also given.

310                                                                  Folklore

Methods of collecting folklore vary with the collector and the lo-
cality. In "Collecting Folklore on the Job" (*NoCF* 17:21–26) Joe Dan
Boyd reveals how a traveling editor for a farm journal can pick up
innumerable items about local customs and beliefs. He advocates the
reading of county histories and local newspapers for clues. C. Karen
Baldwin in "Humor in a Friendly World" (*PF* 18,iii:28–33) discusses
the use of a questionnaire which she devised for circulation among the
clerks of Quaker monthly meetings in order to gather material about
humor among the Friends. Ambrose Manning in "Collecting Folklore: One Procedure" (*TFSB* 35:117–23) reports on his success in
gathering songs and ballads in East Tennessee in order to establish
an archive for class use. Advertisements in the local press brought
many responses, one family alone providing almost a hundred songs.
Jan H. Brunvand in "Folklore of the Great Basin" (*NF* 3[1968]:17–
32) surveys folklore possibilities in the vast area between Utah and
the Sierras and calls attention to the potential subjects: legends of the
pioneers, Basque sheepherders, tourism, mining, and farming. Brunvand holds that comic personal anecdotes, folksongs, and miraculous
legends from the Mormon tradition remain to be collected.

In 1959 Richard M. Dorson proposed a theory of American folklore which he hoped would incite discussion and even controversy.
In "A Theory for American Folklore Reviewed" (*JAF* 82:226–44)
Dorson recapitulates his original thesis and repeats the seven fields
which he found particularly productive for American folklorists: col-
onization, the westward movement, the Negro and slavery, regional-
ism, immigration, democracy, and mass culture. In the intervening
years only three critics seriously assailed him, and their strictures he
finds easy to refute. The rest of his article is devoted to comments on
books appearing since 1959 which seem to confirm his thesis.

Américo Paredes in "Concepts About Folklore in Latin America
and the United States" (*JFI* 6:20–38) surveys the differences between
North American and Latin American folklorists and emphasizes their
mutual distrust. Folklorists in the United States seem to be empiricists
in general who are relatively short on theory and who emphasize the
primitive. Specialists south of the border, on the other hand, are accused of being authoritarian and behind the times, unconcerned about
urban folklore and enmeshed in theories which have become out-
moded. Paredes suggests that basic cultural differences explain this
disparity. Latin America has few big cities, remains largely rural, and

preserves more social stratification. Even the definitions of folk and lore, although the combined word *folklore* exists in both Spanish and Portuguese, seem to have diverse connotations.

In an article entitled "History and Folklore" (*NYFQ* 25:243–60), Richard M. Hurst attempts to distinguish between folklore deriving from history and history obtained from folklore. Some interesting examples are cited, but the contention that the student must know the culture within which he works and must examine the background and the milieu of his informants is hardly original.

The commendable effort to make the study of folklore into a recognizable discipline and to build up a body of important folklore theory has resulted in several articles which often become overingenious or are disfigured by jargon. Robert A. Georges's "The Relevance of Models for Analyses of Traditional Play Activities" (*SFQ* 33:1–23) summarizes previous scholarship in games and game theory, contends that play activities can become complex systems of behavior, and then sets up models to aid analysis of games. To at least one reader the descriptions and diagrams which follow are needlessly confusing. An even more pretentious article is Charles T. Scott's "On Defining the Riddle: The Problem of a Structural Unit" (*Genre* 2: 129–42), in which the author contrasts structural and functional analyses of a riddle without offering any useful definition of the term. Roger D. Abrahams in "The Complex Relations of Simple Forms" (*Genre* 2:104–28) defines folklore as "a collective term for those traditional items of knowledge which arise in recurring performances." He then stresses the necessary connection between performer and audience and distinguishes three levels in folklore forms: the structure of the material, dramatic structure, and the structure of content. A triple division into conversational, play, and fictive genres permits him to establish a spectrum which is neat and not especially helpful.

The ambitious attempt of J. Barre Toelken and John Wilson Foster in a two-part essay, "A Descriptive Nomenclature for the Study of Folklore" (*WF* 28:91–111), offers another definition of the materials of folklore: "traditionally exchanged expressive units existing in dynamic variation through time and space in an informal mode of transmission." Both authors feel that folklorists can benefit by borrowing terms from the natural sciences, such as ecology and taxonomy. Their examples are more interesting than their terminology, which often obscures more than it clarifies.

## *ii.* Ballads

Balladry of all kinds continues to attract students, attention centering on both Child ballads and native American products. Ben Gray Lumpkin in "Two Child Ballads from Stanly County" (*NoCF* 17:56–60) prints variants with text and music of "The Wife of Usher's Well" and "Sir Hugh." Carlos C. Drake deals with " 'Mary Hamilton' in Tradition" (*SFQ* 33:39–47), tracing the history of the ballad and commenting on changes wrought in twentieth-century versions. Bertrand H. Bronson in his valuable *The Ballad as Song* (Berkeley, Univ. of Calif. Press) collects eighteen essays, all but two previously published, dealing with balladry, texts, and music. Some reflect Bronson's memorable work on the music of the Child ballads; others deal with the relationship of tunes and texts, favorite British ballads, and ballad collectors. The essay entitled "Mrs. Brown and the Ballad" is only one of many important excursions into ballad history and appreciation.

Research in a different area is represented by Joanne B. Purcell's two-part discussion, "Traditional Ballads Among the Portuguese in California" (*WF* 28:1–19;77–90). The author collected seventy variants of twenty-seven different ballad themes and presents texts of seven ballads in the original Portuguese without translation. Comments on performance and useful analogies are provided.

A more general approach to balladry is represented by Francis Lee Utley's article, "Oral Genres as Bridge to Written Literature" (*Genre* 2:91–103). Utley selects "The Wife of Usher's Well" as a prime example of a ballad which can be used to instruct students in such qualities as irony and stylistic subtlety which they will subsequently meet in more sophisticated literature.

American ballads which attracted attention derive from various parts of the country. Norman Cohen in "The *Persian's* Crew—the Ballad, Its Author, and the Incident" (*NYFQ* 25:289–96) discusses a widely known ballad of the Great Lakes shipwrecks which was actually based on a poem by a locomotive engineer named Patrick Fennell. The vessel sank in Lake Erie in 1868. Austin E. Fife in "Border Affair" (*AW* 6:26–27) describes the singing of "Spanish Is the Lovin' Tongue" by a range rider and cowboy named Billy Simon near Prescott, Arizona. John I. White in "The Strange Career of 'The Strawberry Roan'" (*ArW* 11:359–66) surveys the song and printed history of Curley W. Fletcher's poem. "The Strawberry Roan" was not only reprinted and broadcast without authority but was actually sung in the play, "Green Grow the Lilacs," the forerunner of "Oklahoma." In another article, "Owen Wister and the Dogies," White points out that the novelist in his journal for 1893 recorded a version of the famous cowboy song "Whoopee Ti Yi Yo, Git Along Little Dogies" (*JAF* 82:66–69).

Dudley C. Gordon in "Charles F. Lummis: Pioneer American Folklorist" (*WF* 28:175–82) surveys the achievements of Lummis in the Southwest and calls attention to his printing of New Mexico folksongs in such books as *The Land of Poco Tiempo*. The collector got many of his ballads from native sheepherders in the vicinity of San Mateo and contended that the Spanish and Indian singers were natural, unlettered troubadours.

Both Child ballads and native American ballads appear in *Folksongs II*, a collection of texts and tunes edited by Thomas G. Burton and Ambrose N. Manning (Johnson City, East Tenn. State University). Four singers, only one born before 1900, provided the editors with some eighty-five ballads, including variants. All of them derive from the relatively isolated Beech Mountain area of North Carolina. In addition to "Barbue Ellen" and "The House Carpenter" there are versions of "Tom Dooley," "Casey Jones," and "Little Mohee." Strong elements of social protest occur in such songs as "Tobaccer Union." The editors provide succinct annotation.

An interesting collection of lumberjack ballads appeared during the year, Edith Fowke's *Lumbering Songs from the Northern Woods* (Austin, Univ. of Texas Press). Many of the sixty-five ballads included here are Canadian in origin and virtually all the singers were domiciled in Ontario and Quebec. But the editor prints a number of ballads previously collected in the American logging camps and familiar to large audiences: "Michigan-I-O," "Jimmy Whelan," and "Jack Haggerty" in particular. Tunes accompany the texts and the annotation is thorough and accurate.

### *iii.* Popular Song

Research in popular song seems to be one of the most rapidly growing areas of folk study. The material examined ranges from Negro field chants and children's games to protest songs and verse inscribed in autograph albums.

Sterling Stuckey deals with Negro folklore in "Through the Prism of Folklore: the Black Ethos in Slavery" (*MR* [1968],9:417–437) and contends that slaves in the old South expressed emotive, intuitive, and aesthetic values through their folklore. Adept in both storytelling and singing, Southern blacks expressed their emotions in memorable ways and found song especially suitable for an expression of their grief and suffering. Spirituals like "Samson" and chants like "Jubilo" confirm the slaves' sense of injustice and their tendency to produce songs with obvious double meanings.

In several articles W. K. McNeil drew upon autograph albums for evidence about nineteenth-century taste in popular song. Sheet music and published collections, he argues, are insufficient indexes; autograph albums often reveal telling aspects of popular culture. In "Popular Songs from New York Autograph Albums, 1820–1900" (*JPC* 3:46–56) and in "From Advice to Laments: New York Autograph Album Verse, 1820–1850" (*NYFQ* 25:175–94) he quotes liberally from manuscript sources. Fragments from familiar songs like "Old Smokey," lines from hymns, tags from music-hall ballads ("no Irish need apply") appear frequently. The verse is banal and sentimental, prolix and sober, often sententious or proverbial. Indeed in "Proverbs Used in New York Autograph Albums, 1820–1900" (*SFQ* 33:352–356) McNeil concentrates on the axiomatic nature of album verse and cites many examples. In still another article, "A Schoharie County Songster" (*NYFQ* 25:3–58) McNeil prints the songs found in a book kept by Ida Finkell, most of them dating from the period just after the Civil War. If one finds the familiar "Grandfather's Clock" and "The Battle Cry of Freedom" here, one also reads with interest minstrel show hits, temperance ditties, murder tales, parodies, and sentimental ballads. All reveal a good deal about popular taste a century ago.

Juvenile jingles interested Barbara Castagna. In "Some Rhymes, Games, and Songs from Children in the New Rochelle Area" (*NYFQ* 25:221–37) she collects jump-rope rhymes, counting-out rhymes, parodies, and jeers. A characteristic one follows:

> Baby, baby
> Stick your head in gravy,
> Wash it out with kerosene
> And send it to the Navy.

Nineteenth-century folksongs stimulated various writers to collect and discuss popular song. Ben Gray Lumpkin in "Folksongs of the Early 1830's" (*SFQ* 33:116–28) comments on half a dozen texts without music preserved in a folio manuscript in the possession of the Withers family of Virginia. Although two or three are unfamiliar, everyone will recognize a variant of "Will the Weaver." John W. Foster in "Some Irish Songs in the Gordon Collection" (*NF* 3[1968]:16–29) prints six examples of Irish songs found in an old notebook, representative of the comic or satiric ditties in the collection. "The Calibar" deals with a canal boat while others are often nostalgic laments on leaving the old sod of Erin. Quite different is the article by Jerome L. Rodnitzky, "The Evolution of the American Protest Song" (*JPC* 3:35–45), which summarizes the development and decline of songs which were primarily social criticism. Such songs, Rodnitzky argues, are of necessity topical and ephemeral. Most of the angry I.W.W. songs of the *Little Red Songbook* have disappeared, while modern protest songs try to cover too wide a spectrum and thus scatter their effect. Woody Guthrie, who combined a personal style with genuine protest, was the most successful bard; today commercial singers tend to replace the genuine folk singers who were spoiled by their own success. A similar essay is R. Serge Denisoff's "Folk-Rock: Folk Music, Protest, or Commercialism?" (*JPC* 3:214–30) which concentrates on the period between the rise of the Kingston Trio or the Brothers Four and the fame of Bob Dylan and Joan Baez. Folk music, the author contends, has begun to merge with popular music; at least what is esoteric one day may well become exoteric the next, since the mass media have discovered the profitability of vicarious deviance.

Another perennial subject for the student of popular song is the blues. John Q. Wolf in "Aunt Caroline Dye: the Gypsy in the 'St. Louis Blues'" (*SFQ* 33:339–46) identifies the Aunt Caroline who figures in W. C. Handy's famous song as an old Negress who lived in Newport, Arkansas. Traditionally a centenarian, she was probably about seventy-eight when she died in 1918, but she had a wide reputation as a clairvoyant, counsellor, and sybil. She read palms and used decks of cards to help her prognostications. In "The Blues as a Genre" (*Genre* 2:259–274) Harry Oster defines various kinds of blues (talking blues, classic blues, free-form three-unit blues) and discusses versification, structure, personal and social context, irony, and even the blues as catharsis.

The best collection of popular songs to appear during the year is *Cowboy and Western Songs, A Comprehensive Anthology* (New York, Clarkson N. Potter), edited by Austin E. and Alta S. Fife. Some 128 individual songs are included, from "Shenandoah" to "A Cowboy's Prayer." The material is arranged under fourteen headings, such as The West Before the Cowboy, Frontier Realism, Red Men and White, Cowboy Lovers, Outlaws, and The Last Roundup. All the familiar western songs are here but often in variant and still authentic texts. The Fife sources include phonograph records, newspapers, obscure journals, the Lomax and Dorson archives, and the Library of Congress. Some editorial revision has been done to eliminate merely eccentric spelling, but in general authenticity has been the criterion. One notes with interest that the editors prefer the compositions of Harry McClintock, Slim Critchlow, and Woody Guthrie.

Among the spate of articles about folk and popular singers that were published during the year, three might be cited as representative. "An Interview with Judy Collins" (*Life* 66,xvii[2May]:40A–46) is a personal story about the young girl who had classical training on the piano, suffered a bout with polio, and then successfully switched to folk singing. Tom Dearmore's "First Angry Man of Country Singers" (*NYTM* 21Sept:32–57) is a detailed account of the background and accelerating reputation of Johnny Cash, the modern exemplar of country music. Susan Braudy's "As Arlo Guthrie Sees It . . . Kids Are Groovy. Adults Aren't" (*NYTM* 27 Apr:57–80) chronicles the rise of Woody Guthrie's well-known son and the story of "Alice's Restaurant."

### iv. Folk Tales and Legends

Folk tale scholarship like ballad scholarship is diversified and extensive. Lloyd Hustvedt in "The Folktale and Norwegian Migration" (*JPC* 2:552–62) points out that the 750,000 Norwegians who emigrated to America between 1825 and 1915 brought few viable folk tales with them, but that certain Norwegian stories such as "Little Freddy and His Fiddle," "The Parson and the Sexton," and "The Boy and the Ale Keg" taught lessons in social democracy which the newcomers found important. Moreover, the familiar ashlad theme became important in Rölvaag's fine novel, *Giants in the Earth*. On the other hand, German or Pennsylvania Dutch settlers preserved in the late 1880's the story of Belsnickel and his sooty crew. Eleanor R. Wilcox remarks in "It Was Belsnickel, the Demon Helper of Santa Claus" (*Baltimore Sun Mag* 21 Dec) that the ritual was more closely associated with Christmas than with St. Nicholas's Day.

The study of North American Indian tales continues to develop. C. E. Schorer prints another of C. C. Trowbridge's Indian tales in "The Ornamented Head" (*SFQ* 33:317–32). The main theme here is the success of the hero in gaining a wife, a hoard of game, and the leadership of the tribe. Schorer in elaborate notes cites analogies presented by Schoolcraft, Boas, and Thompson. In "*Grizzly-Bear* Woman in Nez Perce Indian Mythology" (*NF* 3[1968]:1–9) Dell Skeels analyzes the character of his protagonist in fifteen stories and stresses her ferocity, jealousy, penchant for kidnaping victims, and ready emission of blood. He finds Grizzly-Bear Woman to be "the projection of libidinal and aggressive forces from the id." Navaho lore provided J. Barre Toelken with his material for "The 'Pretty Language' of Yellowman" (*Genre* 2:211–35). Familiar with the Navahos of southern Utah, Toelken concentrates on a typical Coyote story in which the mischievous predator with the aid of Skunk kills and eats some prairie dogs. Coyote is presented through the narrator Yellowman as more than a trickster; he is also an actor whose deeds enable him to bring certain ideas into the field of possibility. Coyote stories of this type are not primarily comic or meant for juveniles; they have important cultural values. An interesting collection of Indian tales is Anna Moore Shaw's *Pima Indian Legends* (Tucson, Univ. of Ariz. Press, 1968). The stories are etiological and moralistic, deal primarily with animal characters in a mythical age, and are full of magical transformations, pursuits, and reductions of size. The tales, presented by a full-blooded Pima Indian who has lived on reservations and in Phoenix, are given without analysis.

Legends of a very different sort were collected by folklore students in Indiana and are presented by Linda Dégh in "The Haunted Bridges Near Avon and Danville and Their Role in Legend Formation" (*IF* 2:54–90). In "I Swear to God It's the Truth If I Ever Told It" (*KFQ* 15:1–54) Chuck Perdue records the tales of John and Cora Jackson from Virginia. They vary from jokes to anecdotes and deal with hoop snakes, ghosts, fabliaux, and an enormous mountain boar with a voracious appetite which weighs 1800 pounds. Similar windies appear in Charles S. Guthrie's "Some Folktales and Legends from the

Cumberland Valley" (*KFR* 15:61–65), in which a madstone, a witch, and an excessively lazy man appear. The entire annual 1968 issue of *Northeast Folklore* (10:1–74) is given over to C. Richard K. Lunt's "Jones Tracy: Tall-Tale Hero from Mount Desert Island." In it we see a farmer and hunter gifted as a narrator who told local variants of the wonderful-hunt theme, the bent gun that could shoot around corners, the split bullet that could kill game on both sides, and the man who indicates directions by pointing with a plow. Lunt finds analogies to Tracy in John Darling, Gib Morgan, and Oregon Smith, all equally adept in spinning extravagant yarns.

A somewhat more serious type of tale is illustrated in William A. Wilson's article "Mormon Legends of the Three Nephites Collected at Indiana University" (*IF* 2:3–35), in which variants of stories deriving from the area around Bloomington are given. Nephite tales are still narrated, but probably more for entertainment now than out of conviction. Durward T. Stokes, on the other hand, reprints, in "A Newly Discovered Letter from the Fool Killer" (*NoCF* 17:3–8), a tale written by the Carolina editor Charles Evans in 1876. Evans invented a character named Jesse Holmes the Fool Killer and chronicled his adventures in several issues which had wide circulation.

In *Old Greasybeard: Tales from the Cumberland Gap* (Detroit, Folklore Associates) Leonard Roberts brings together some fifty tales from eastern Kentucky, the majority reported by students in his folklore courses. Divided into animal tales, hero and giant tales (including witchcraft), and humorous or tall tales, they are in many cases American variants, in somewhat degenerate form, of well-known European stories. The reader will recognize at once, even without the elaborate notes provided by the editor, versions of such Grimm tales as "The Bremen Town Musicians," "Cinderella," "The Brave Little Tailor," and "Frau Holle," plus the Münchhausen story of the deer with a peach tree growing out of his back. It is interesting to meet giants, specters, kings, and devils in the Kentucky mountains, not to mention speaking animals, magical objects, and transformations. Roberts's survey of folk-tale scholarship for each narrative item is excessively detailed, but one welcomes his careful identification of sources and types.

The dozen stories retold by Julius Lester in *Black Folktales* (New York, Richard W. Baron) are streamlined and modernized versions of familiar African and American narratives. The four divisions include origin tales and tales of love, heroes, and people. Lester explains the genesis of butterflies and retells the adventures of High John the Conqueror and Stagolee (the last being derivative from the familiar ballad of a Negro bad man). It is surprising to find allusions to submarines, the draft, computers, and Vietnam worked into these traditional stories.

The exploits of fabulous animals continue to attract attention. The Argentine writer Jorge Luis Borges's *Book of Imaginary Beings* (New York, Dutton), based on a smaller Spanish original of 1967, contains an astonishing amount of lore about monsters, demons, and mythical creatures. Borges combed mythology, legend, and natural history for his data. The American examples include the Haokah or Thunder God of the Sioux; the Squonk, said to inhabit the Pennsylvania hemlock forests; and certain companions of Paul Bunyan in the Great Lakes lumber camps such as the Goofus Bird, the Pinnacle Grouse, and a kind of North Woods dachshund known as the Axehandle Hound.

More regionally appropriate is Walker D. Wyman's *Mythical Creatures of the North Country* (River Falls, Wis., River Falls State Univ. Press), in part the editor's own contribution and in part a reprinting of William T. Coxe's *Fearsome Creatures of the Lumberwoods*. Here the reader will again encounter the Squonk and the Axehandle Hound in the company of the Hodag, the Agropelter, the Hugag, and the fur-bearing small-mouth bass. Illustrations by Helen B. Wyman do much to make these creatures more convincing.

### v. Folk Speech

Specialists in folk speech, rural humor, or occupational idiom cover a wide area. J. Rea in "Seeing the Elephant" (*WF* 28:21–26) traces the history of an old phrase which was once very familiar and defines it either as seeing all there is to see or as gaining experience the hard way. George Boswell reports the result of his collecting amusing sayings, proverbs, or verse in "Humor from the Kentucky Hills" (*NoCF* 17:71–76). A good example is the following quatrain:

> Little Patty had a watch,
> She swallowed it one day;
> Now she is taking castor oil
> To pass the time away.

In "Humor from the Hills" (*ArkHQ* 28:231–33) Nancy McDonough quotes five expressions or sayings deriving from actual events in Yell County. Mac E. Barrick in "Pulpit Humor in Central Pennsylvania" (*PF* 19,i:28–36) records amusing anecdotes and jests from a variety of sources in the vicinity of Carlisle. Thus, an itinerant minister had just sat down to a chicken dinner at a layman's house when he heard a rooster crow loudly. When he asked why the cock made such a din at that hour, he was answered, "You'd crow, too, if your son had just entered the ministry."

Gordon Wilson contributed three collections of regional sayings, proverbs, and maxims to the *Kentucky Folklore Record* (15:12–21,37–44,69–74). His "Some Mammoth Cave Sayings" includes traditional remarks about the weather and domestic animals, derisive or bantering humor, and generally familiar maxims. Certainly "Everybody has to bear his own cross" and "No pains, no gains" are not limited to Kentucky. In "The Briar Joke in the Middle Miami Valley" Clifford M. Stamper defined the "briar-hopper" as a scornful term for a Kentucky hillman, usually the butt of a moron joke (*KFR* 15:35–36). One briar, for example, spent three days in Sears looking for a miscarriage.

Sometimes comedy combines speech and action. Robert S. Thurman in "'Twas Only a Joke" (*TFSB* 34:86–94) describes mimicry, ridicule, and practical jokes played on greenhorns in the mining area around Joplin, Missouri. The idiom of the loggers is collected by L. G. Sorden in *Lumberjack Lingo* (Spring Green, Wis., Wisconsin House), a 149-page compilation of occupational slang and technology. "The lumberjack had a language all his own," Sorden contends, sometimes place names converted into verbs (to *St. Croix* or *Saginaw* a log), sometimes useful technical terms (*wanigan* or *peavey*), sometimes inverted euphemisms (*pine hog* for timber baron, *dunghister* for farmer). Occupational speech is also reflected in John Michael Bennett's "Folk Speech and Legends of the Trade of House-Painting" (*SFQ* 33:313–16), an article which stresses the fact that each craft develops its own jargon.

George Monteiro, on the other hand, collected examples of what might be called language depreciation. In "Religious Parodies" (*NYFQ* 25:59–76) he discusses parodies in general circulation as represented by radio, television, and journalism. Thus, "Bread cast on the waters must return wet," or "Mine eyes have seen the glory of the coming of the Lord; now I'm pregnant."

One of the more unusual books to appear in 1969 is Roger D. Abrahams's *Jump-Rope Rhymes, a Dictionary* (Austin, Univ. of Texas Press). Abrahams collected from many sources, both native and foreign, the rhymes that children sing when they jump rope. Most of them are twentieth-century, as the many allusions to cartoon or television characters and political celebrities confirm. The verses serve the jumpers, generally girls, as counting-out rhymes, taunts, or insults, but many are simply nonsense syllables or pointless repetitions. In any event they are true folk speech. Abrahams has arranged the examples alphabetically, has printed many variants, and has provided such extensive sources and analogues that they sometimes dwarf the examples. But the book is uniquely useful.

Students of onomastics frequently unearth extraordinary appellations. The September 1968 issue of *Names*, edited by Jan Brunvand, includes much relevant material. Brunvand in his introduction (16: 197–206) observes that several lines of research are open to students of namelore: the applications or explanations of names according to custom and usage; the names that appear in traditional texts such as proverbs and tales; the names for traditional artifacts and activities, ranging from quilts and fences to games and gestures. In the same issue Robert M. Rennick writes on "Obscene Names and Naming in Folk Tradition" (16:207–29), providing a fascinating list of proper names with vulgar or erotic connotations. He observes that personal names which Americans today find obscene were not so regarded historically: Cock, Crappe, Urine (Cornish Euren); while such old names as Outhouse, Backhouse, and Leake were once deemed thoroughly inoffensive. Rennick also enumerates four categories of names which would today evoke displeasure: general obscenita, names alluding to intimate parts of the body, names suggesting bodily functions, and names connoting erotic activities. Thus persons bearing the names of Damm, Wetmore, Hore, Stink, and Swindler might well go to court for legal permission to change their cognomens. In another article Rennick covers some of the same substitutes, although he concentrates on the evolution of personal names. "Successive Name-Changing: a Popular Theme in Onomastic Folklore and Literature" (*NYFQ* 25:119–28) gives the familiar example of the Jew who was Mortimer Brooks in New York City but had been Morris Fountain in London, Maurice La Fountain in Paris, Moritz Wasserspritzer in the Rhineland, and Moisher Pisher in his original Warsaw.

### vi. Folk Heroes

The traditional American folk hero, according to at least two specialists, needs to be reexamined. Gerald Parsons in "Second Thoughts on
a 'Folk Hero'; or, Sam Patch Falls Again" (*NYFQ* 25:83–92) discounts
the notion that the celebrated waterfalls jumper was a genuine folk
hero; he was actually a crackpot and a braggart. Parsons argues convincingly that Patch was never remembered by the folk and was not
immortalized in ballad or legend, two important criteria for folk heroes. Fred H. Schroeder in "A Bellyful of Coffee" (*JPC* 2:679–86)
contends that the old American folk heroes became obsolete with the
passing of the frontier. Among their replacements the truck driver
looms large, a man who is primarily mobile, but who is celebrated in
contemporary popular song for his independence, social responsibility, and flamboyant potency. General recognition of the truck driver
as folk hero has lagged, Schroeder thinks, because he is too familiar,
too close to his audience.

Mody C. Boatright examined hundreds of popular magazine stories for his article, "The Formula in Cowboy Fiction and Drama"
(*WF* 28:136–45), and reduced the possible plots to seven standard
types. He finds the typical protagonist to be a roving cowhand, often
with a buddy serving as foil, who might be suspected of a crime of
which he is innocent, who avenges a crime involving someone close
to him, or who migrates to a new country and there builds an empire.
The reader of these stories is apparently not deterred by their appall-
ing sameness.

### vii. Superstitions and Beliefs

An enormous amount of material involving superstitions and beliefs
remains available to the assiduous collector, whether he concerns
himself with rural or urban areas. These range from practices and
cures to magic and witchcraft.

Thad Stem writing on "Aphrodisiacs" (*NoCF* 17:61–66) produces
a kind of literary essay but alludes to many plants in North Carolina
which have legendary qualities. Men seeking potency apparently use
artichokes, ginseng, and mushrooms, not to speak of ground flesh from
the loins of alligators. Lila G. Scrimsher in "The Medicinal Herbs of
Our Forefathers" (*NebrHist* 50:309–22) surveys a multitude of home

remedies for all conceivable ailments, the best having some merit as sedative, purgative, or tonic. But some pioneers treasured frog spit as a salve and skunk cabbage as a panacea for coughs. Similar cures are discussed by Wayland D. Hand in "Folk Medical Magic and Symbolism in the West" (*Forms Upon the Frontier*, pp. 103–18). Hand used archival material from California and Utah to illustrate beliefs in the transference of diseases to animals or plants, in the elimination of warts, and in the curing of cancer by having toads suck the poison from the system. Some Pennsylvania folk beliefs about medicines are dealt with by Betty Snellenburg in "Four Interviews with Powwowers" (*PF* 18,iv:40–45). Powwows or faith healers presumably owned the power of healing warts, bleeding, erysipelas, and especially rheumatism or lumbago, but they would not touch cancer or broken bones. Biblical verses were an important part of their ritual. In parts of California, according to Keith A. Neighbors in "Mexican-American Folk Diseases" (*WF* 28:249–59), certain afflictions such as *empacho*, a form of indigestion, and *mal ojo*, the evil eye, resist any treatment by physicians and are restricted to Mexican Americans. Older women operating traditionally can effect cures, but sometimes professional healers or *curanderos* are resorted to.

Writing on "Folk Beliefs Popular in the Lower Snake River Valley" (*NF* 3[1968]:12–15), Janice S. Jones reports some sixty different beliefs about cures, weather, and crops. Many are familiar, such as "If you bite your tongue, then you have recently told a lie." Lucile F. Newman in a more specialized article entitled "Folklore of Pregnancy" (*WF* 28:112–35) lists pregnancy beliefs held by white, Negro, and Mexican-American women in Contra Costa County, California. White prospective mothers are most concerned about the sex of the coming child, Negroes about the possibility of its death. The commonest belief is the interdiction against reaching up, since if this is done the cord will strangle the baby. In "American Folk Customs of Courtship and Marriage" (*Forms Upon the Frontier*, pp. 138–58) Frances Tally deals with love divination, the use of mirrors, the placing of salt or wedding cake under the pillow. The tradition of a honeymoon is apparently reinforced by the fear of spending the wedding night in the first permanent home.

Gordon Wilson with various collaborators published three articles on "Folklore in Certain Professions" (*TFSB* 35:1–5,75–80,113–16), one on physicians, one on ornithologists, and one on pharmacists.

Wilson points out the passing of old remedies and the elimination of the practice by druggists of concocting their own pills. Likewise folk misconceptions about birds are slowly dying out. But people still use euphemisms when they are afraid to name diseases (for example, "female trouble").

A variety of early medical beliefs and superstitions appears in Joseph D. Clark's article, "Folk Medicine in Colonial North Carolina as Found in Dr. John Brickell's *Natural History*" (*NoCF* 17:100–24). Clark compiled from an early book on North Carolina a list of some forty-three types of cures for diseases ranging from asthma and scrofula to baldness and cachexy. Among the examples given are the belief of rustics that lice can cure jaundice or consumption, roasted bat will cure children from eating dirt, and the dung of a cuckoo given in canary wine helps the bite of a mad dog. As Clark comments, "In short, some of the stuff is genuine, some is experimental, and some is hilarious."

Not all beliefs in folk medicine are associated with rural life, however, as David J. Winslow proves in "Bishop E. E. Everett and Some Aspects of Occultism and Folk Religion in Negro Philadelphia" (*KFQ* 14:59–80). Everett, both a Negro pastor and proprietor of the Calvary Religious and Occult Store on the side, dispenses snake oil, graveyard or goofer dust, High John the Conqueror roots (St. John's wort), lodestones, and many kinds of oils and candles which his parishioners buy in quantity and at substantial prices.

Several articles deal with the prevalence of nautical beliefs. In "Varieties of Sea Lore" (*WF* 28:260–66) Jerry Foster divides the living folklore of the sea into practical skills, sea language, and rites or ceremonies still performed. As examples he cites such tasks as handling ropes and sails, proverbial expressions ("any port in a storm"), and the rituals of launching a new vessel or crossing the equator. Superstitions held by both Negroes and whites among the fishermen of the Texas Gulf Coast provide the material for two essays by Patrick B. Mullen. In "The Function of Folk Belief Among Negro Fishermen of the Texas Coast" (*SFQ* 33:80–91) Mullen distinguishes between magical and pragmatic beliefs held by this in-group. Black fishermen observe taboos against beginning a trip on a Friday, having a black suitcase or black cat on board, and saying aloud the word "alligator." But a horseshoe and a porpoise are good-luck tokens. "The Function of Magic Folk Belief Among Texas Coastal Fishermen" (*JAF* 82:214–

22) uses much of the same material but links folklore with religion (thus the taboo against working on Sundays). Mullen concludes, "Folk beliefs have persisted in modern American society despite the encroachment of education, urbanization, science, and technology."

Witchcraft is no longer as prevalent as magic, but an interest in its operations remains viable. In "Witchcraft and Spirit Possession in Grimm's Fairy Tales" (*JPC* 2:627–48) Henry Carsch examines various stories familiar to American readers and discusses the witches active in them. The witches are usually old, hunchbacked, ugly, with wrinkled skin and red eyes; they are shortsighted but have a keen sense of smell, and they lure people into their grasp by lies and false promises. Tracey Peterson in "The Witch of Franklin" (*SFQ* 33:297–312) deals with Mrs. Augustine Charpentier of a small Louisiana community who was widely recognized and admired for her hoodoo practices. Among her methods of divination were fortunetelling by cards, writing in blood, and working with a glass of water and a raw egg. Mrs. Charpentier was rarely maleficent, but did work spells on birds and animals which ravaged gardens. Apparently some of her powers were passed on to her daughter and granddaughter.

In a full-length historical study, *Witchcraft at Salem* (New York, Braziller), Chadwick Hansen traces the history of witchcraft in Europe and then concentrates on its manifestations in New England. He stresses the fact that witchcraft did exist and that people believed in it throughout the seventeenth century. The folklore interest of the book is limited to the descriptions of witches and the tests to which they were subjected. An interesting miscellany of witchcraft was compiled by F. Roy Johnson in *Witches and Demons in History and Folklore* (Murfreesboro, N.C., Johnson Publishing Co.). Johnson argues that witchcraft was not limited to New England and that many charges of diabolical practice were brought against women in Virginia and North Carolina, although no one was executed. Using examples from travelers and journalists or provided by informants, Johnson enumerates the usual practices of a witch and suggests some of the cures or preventives preserved in the legends. A section about the devil and his pranks concludes the volume. Although carelessly written and badly proofread, the book is a rich collection of occult lore.

Dowsing, unlike witchcraft, seems to retain both the interest and the support of many people. Nor is it limited to rural practitioners.

John Quincy Wolf in "Two Folk Scientists in Action" (*TFSB* 35:6–9) describes dowsing in rural Arkansas. But Linda K. Barrett and Evon Z. Vogt in "The Urban American Dowser" (*JAF* 82:195–213) prove that the dowser is not unknown in cities. Water is not always his goal; he is called on to locate oil, minerals, lost metallic objects, forgotten pipes or cables, and he even seems to have some validity in the detection of disease. The authors describe the equipment and training of the successful dowser and suggest a relationship between dowsing and extrasensory perception, both to be sure nonscientific.

### *viii.* Literary Use of Folklore

The extensive use of folklore by American authors becomes clearer as critics examine fiction from this point of view. Donald W. Hatley in "Folklore in the Fiction of Barry Benefield" (*MissQ* 21[1968]:63–70) discusses Benefield's novels of East Texas and points out his use of occupational and Negro folklore in such books as *The Chicken-Wagon Family*. A peddler, a hoodoo woman, and a herb doctor illustrate folk beliefs and practices. Geoffrey A. Grimes in " 'Brandy and Water': American Folk Types in the Work of Artemus Ward" (*NYFQ* 25:163–74) argues that Lincoln's favorite humorist introduced folk types into his regional sketches and perhaps anticipated the paradigms of Constance Rourke in *American Humor*. But the discussion is thin and needs further substantiation. In "Folk Medicine in the Writings of Rowland Robinson" (*VH* 37:184–93) Ronald L. Baker provides a careful examination of the work of the famous Vermont regionalist and shows how Robinson introduced plants and herbs into his stories. As Baker concludes, "One value of Robinson's stories is that they preserve a number of folk cures from an age in which no systematic folklore collections were made." In a rather superficial survey of diabolical folklore, "The Devil Outwitted in Folklore and Literature" (*NoCF* 17:15–20), J. T. McCullen and Jeri Tanner discuss the role of the devil in stories ranging from Rabelais and Ben Jonson to Richard Chase and Stephen Vincent Benét. Special attention is given William Faulkner's *The Hamlet* and Flem Snopes's visit to Hell.

Brief references to folklore items occur in two articles. George R. Mowrer in "The Kentucky Tragedy: a Source for *Pierre*" (*KRF* 15:1–2) contends that Melville may have used the gory Kentucky story in his New York novel. David J. Burt in "A Folk Reference in Warren's

*Flood"* (*MissQ* 22:74–76) comments on the use of the old ballad "Cotton-Eye Joe" in Warren's novel. On the other hand, John R. Milton devotes a full issue of the *South Dakota Review* to the work of Isaac Lamoreaux Udell (7:9–105). "In the Dust of the Valley" analyzes the work of this painter and writer and points out many of the Southwestern folklore elements in it.

An extensive article by John T. Flanagan, "Folklore in Faulkner's Fiction" (*PLL* 5:119–44) discusses the sources and amplitude of Faulkner's use of folklore, the result primarily of his Mississippi background and environment, and illustrates the novelist's familiarity with superstitions, cures, omens, proverbs, fabulous animals, and such practices as dowsing. In another article Flanagan calls attention to what is probably the first reference in the American press to the famous foolish-wise man of Turkish legend. "Long Live the Hodja" (*SFQ* 33:48–53) cites an article in the New York *Spirit of the Times* in 1846 which includes many of the most familiar anecdotes involving Nasreddin Hodja.

One of the most attractive books to appear during 1969 is N. Scott Momaday's *The Way to Rainy Mountain* (Albuquerque, Univ. of N.M. Press), a melange of Kiowa tradition, anthropology, and personal experience. Momaday, himself of Kiowa extraction, describes the legendary emergence of the Kiowa tribe from a hollow log, the migration from the slopes of the Rockies to the Southwest, the transformation from foot hunters to expert horsemen, and the famous figure of the image Tai-me in the Sun Dance. Interspersed with this saga are excerpts from the accounts of observers like Mooney and Catlin and the author's own recollections of life with his people in Oklahoma. The book is poetically written and its appeal is augmented by the illustrations of the author's father, Al Momaday. In *The Way to Rainy Mountain* folklore becomes literature.

### ix. Material and Miscellaneous Folklore

Research into folk art and folk craft continues to engage many scholars, tempted probably by the vast field inviting exploration. This interest is especially reflected in the volume *Forms Upon the Frontier*, a collection of papers presented at a conference at Logan in the summer of 1968. The subjects include architecture, medicine and recipes, folk customs and ethnic groups, and arts and crafts. An unusual example of the last is the survey by Jan Brunvand and John C. Abramson entitled "Aspen Tree Doodlings in the Wasatch Mountains" (pp. 89–102), which describes and illustrates carvings found on aspen trees at high altitudes. Carvings of animal heads are most frequently found. Quite different is Don Yoder's article, "Sectarian Costume Research in the United States" (pp. 41–75), which is primarily concerned with Pennsylvania German, Mormon, and Quaker female costumes. Most of the papers in the collection are represented by abstracts, however, and the résumés are unfortunately brief.

Similar themes were explored by a variety of other writers. Gene Christman contributed a pictorial article on fences to the *American West* (6:33–39) with excellent photographs of fences made of wood, stone, wire, adobe, cactus, or granite posts. In "The Long Shingle" Robert C. Bucher discusses the red oak shingle once familiar to Pennsylvanians which often measured two and a half feet in length and half a foot wide (*PF* 18,iv:51–56). Carlos C. Drake considers "Traditional Elements in the Cooperage Industry" (*KFQ* 14:81–95), basing his discussion on a family shop at Martinsville, Indiana, which began operations just after the Civil War. Specific details are given about the materials and patterns used for kegs of various sizes, only a few of which were destined for distilleries. In an essay entitled "The Kreutz Brothers: Craftsmen in Glass" (*NYFQ* 25:100–18) Robert Atkinson surveys the work of four brothers from Czechoslovakia who settled on Long Island and produced fine glass for many years. A decanter is a typical product. Most of the summer issue of *Foxfire* (3:9–68) is given over to a staff-written account of the building of a log cabin, special attention being accorded the materials and implements used, the hewing and notching of the logs, and the final chinking.

The most ambitious recent study of folk architecture is the work of Henry Glassie, *Pattern in the Material Folk Culture of the Eastern United States* (Philadelphia, Univ. of Pa. Press, 1968), based on extensive field work and historical research. Glassie is concerned chiefly with the Mid-Atlantic section, although he derives illustrations from both New England and the Carolinas. He contends that a material object must have form, construction, and use—criteria which he then applies to various examples. He finds that certain tools, quilt patterns, fence types, and cabin patterns are common to all the regions he considers. The book has a long and somewhat miscellaneous bibliography, but no index and oddly enough no table of contents. In an unrelated short article Glassie describes "A Central Chimney Continental Log House" (*PF* 18,ii:32–39), proving that a log house in almost total disrepair can still provide useful data about design and pattern.

A good deal of planting lore appears in Jim Wayne Miller's "The Vocabulary and Methods of Raising Burley Tobacco in Western North Carolina" (*NoCF* 17:27–38); the author not only surveys the year-round operation of growing tobacco but also cites many local terms familiar to the tobacco farmer.

Harry E. Smith's "The End of the Horse and Buggy Days" (*PF* 18,iii:2–25) is both nostalgic and miscellaneous. It contains material ranging from childhood games and rural activities to superstitions about weather changes, bad luck, and seasonal duration. Smith also deals with the Lancaster almanacs of John Baer, long the Pennsylvania farmer's scripture, and the hex marks of the region.

An odd folk custom interested Allison Yeager. Her "Historic Egg Fight" (*TFSB* 35:41–43) describes an Easter custom of East Tennessee in which the residents of a particular "holler" match brightly colored Easter eggs to see which will be last to crack. One woman, determined to win, fed her chickens crushed oyster shells and emerged triumphant. Another folk custom, butter making at home, is described by Judy Brown in "Churn Your Own Butter" (*Foxfire* 3:17–19) and is followed by Chuck Perdue's "Come Butter Come" (*Foxfire* 3:20–24, 65–72), mostly a collection of churning chants used by girls and women during the laborious process of transforming clabbered cream into butter. As one might expect they are coaxingly repetitious.

Wooden folk sculpture is discussed in "This Heavy Folk Thing: An Interview [by Joseph Slate] with David Hostetler" (*KR* 31:97–121). Hostetler, an Ohio craftsman, fashions tall thin figures, usually female, out of elm logs from his own farm and generally eschews the use of power tools. Traditional gouges of various sizes are his customary implements.

A more theoretical essay is Robert A. Barakat's "Gesture Systems" (*KFQ* 14:105–21), devoted to traditional gestures which he has observed in the Middle East and in Trappist monasteries, but which have wider currency. He defines four classes of gestures based on their origins: autistic or personal; culture-induced; semiotic or folk; and invented. Individual gestures have their own names: the Shanghai gesture, sign of the fig, sign of the horn. Gestures, it should be noted, have a special significance for American auctioneers, truck drivers, crane operators, and monks vowed to silence.

Erik Wahlgren's article in *Northwest Folklore*, "Scandinavian Folklore and Folk Culture in the Trans-Mississippi West" (3[1968]: 1–16), is a real Swedish smörgasbord. Wahlgren surveys Scandinavian folklore from all over the West and considers historical and geographical lore, folk dancing, cookery, festivals, handicrafts and customs, balladry, and what the Swedish specialist Von Sydow called the *memorat*. His examples are legion. Such dishes as *lutefisk* and *ostkaka* are popular wherever Scandinavians gather. Kansas Swedes drink King Oscar brand coffee and honor St. Lucy's Day (December 13). Limpa bread, lingonberry jam, and *glögg* find their way into many households, and in regions settled by people of Finnish descent the sauna has been domiciled. Wahlgren concludes his article with allusions to Finnish charms, proverbs, and lullabies, some of them strangely akin to the runes of the *Kalevala*.

The most interesting anthology of folklore to appear during 1969 is John Greenway's *Folklore of the Great West* (Palo Alto, Calif., American West Publ. Co.). Basically it consists of reprinted selections from the *Journal of American Folklore*, some fifty-seven narratives and songs representing the eighty-three years of the periodical's existence. The material includes "The Good Old Days" (the longest section), treatments of the Indian, cowboy and other ballads, tales of the gold rush, stories of outlaws and mythical heroes, witchcraft, and party activities. Greenway pays scant attention to folk speech, medical superstitions, and popular beliefs, and he ignores material folklore —this last omission being its own comment on the editorial policy of the *JAF* since 1888. But the collection is important and representative of folklore collecting and interpretation in the United States. Greenway's own comments are especially lively and unconventional. The introductory sections are a delight to read.

*University of Illinois*

# 18. Themes, Topics, and Criticism

## G. R. Thompson

The coverage for this chapter requires a word of explanation. First, limited space requires that discussion of a number of studies of individual figures not covered elsewhere in *ALS* (mainly social critics and philosophers or historians) be postponed. Second, because of general inaccessibility, I shall discuss several foreign studies as a group in next year's volume. Finally, I have chosen to put heavy emphasis upon literary history and criticism. There is good reason for this. The rapid development of American Studies, Black Literature, and related phenomena has tended to reduce our awareness of developments in more traditional areas of concern. Yet throughout the last decade important change has been quietly occurring in the practice and theory of criticism and literary history—change so fundamental that it may be said to imply that we are in the midst of a major revaluation of literary study. As the sixties end, then, it seems most pertinent to emphasize in the "Themes, Topics, and Criticism" section of *ALS* these newer developments in literary criticism and literary history. Black literature and other ethnic, and regional, studies will be given full coverage in the next volume.

### i. Toward a Critical Literary History: Some European and American Parallels

American scholars intent upon their own national literature have largely ignored an energetic modern European criticism which is determined to find a firm theoretical base for both criticism and literary history. Although several of our critics have in the past few years seen somewhat beyond the orthodoxies of American New Criticism, studies in the broader themes and forms of American literature are characteristically provincial. Willis Wager's promisingly titled *American Literature: A World View* (New York, N.Y. Univ. Press, 1968), for example, is mainly a conventional, genteel survey in the manner of

W. F. Taylor's *Story of American Letters* (rev. ed., 1956). Indeed, it has been only in this decade that the achievements and limitations of our New Criticism have been at all systematically analyzed, in Richard Foster's *The New Romantics: A Reappraisal of the New Criticism* (1962), Robert Weimann's *"New Criticism"* (1962), Walter Sutton's *Modern American Criticism* (1963), and Lee T. Lemon's *The Partial Critics* (1965); and if a decline in the influence of New Criticism is not yet fully clear, at least reaction against the too vigorous exclusion of historicism by the New Critics has been growing for some time.[1]

The increasing frequency of indictments of New Criticism notwithstanding, it is still with something of a shock that most of us will come upon Peter Brooks's essay, "Nouvelle critique et critique nouvelle aux Etats-Unis" (*NRF* 17:416–26); for here he explains to French readers what American New Criticism *was*. Although the essay is largely an introductory survey of the major New Critics in America, Brooks offers two arresting observations. One is that although American New Critics have provided us with instruments to deal with the rhetoric and structure of the poem-as-specific-poem, their rhetorical methods have developed little in recent years, so that they ignore many questions about the nature of literature and the act of criticism, in contrast to the energetic inquiries of the French "Newer Critics." The second observation is directly related: American New Criticism, in its exclusive and almost spiritual focus on the poem as immediate aesthetic object, no longer satisfies a growing number of those who insist on asking what literature has to offer beyond a pattern of images and ironies. And while Peter Brooks explains to the French a moribund American criticism, Americans find themselves increasingly confronted with this very active *Critique nouvelle française*, presently engaged in its own battle with academicians. A fair amount of the writing of these "structuralists," as some of them call themselves, is concerned with American writers (notably Poe), and traces of their techniques are noticeable in the year's work in American literature by American scholars. Thus it is with symmetrical appropriateness that we find David Paul Funt explaining the *Nouvelle*

1. For a random sampling of recent (1968–69) articles calling for a "newer" criticism of one sort of another, see Claudio Guillén (*CL* 22:193–222); Lubomir Dolezel (*Style* 2:143–58); P. K. Saha (*Style* 2:7–31); William Baker (*Style* 2: 1–5); Mark Lester (*CE* 30:366–75); Thomas J. Roberts (*CE* 31:1–24); Walter E. Meyers (*CE* 30:518–26); Michael H. Means (*UDR* 2:37–47); Richard L. Lanigan (*P&R* 2:61–71).

*critique* to Americans in a series of related articles: "The Structuralist Debate" (*HudR* 22:623–46), "Roland Barthes and the *Nouvelle critique*" (*JAAC* 26[1968]:329–40), and "Newer Criticism and Revolution" (*HudR* 22:87–96).

The structuralists take a stance between empiricists who see the world as discontinuous and existentialists who see the world as continuous but man as alienated from it. They contend that principles of order are not to be found in theology, ideology, or psychology, but in that repetition and "structuration" which is most evident in *language*, for in language a series of discontinuous elements give rise to a continuity of sense. Like linguists, structuralists are more interested in how any system *comes* to mean than in *what it means*. They contend that a thing has meaning only by virtue of its oppositions to other items in the same culture system; hence the same item may have any number of different meanings depending on the system in which it is engaged. Funt surveys the thinking of five central structuralist figures in France today, of whom Roland Barthes has special importance for literary criticism. Barthes's main focus is on what makes literary language literary as distinct from other uses of language, and on how the writer attaches himself to or detaches himself from his society. Since language is a system of interrelated structures (linguistics, semantics) contained in larger structures (the various organizational patterns and oppositions of the work) within larger structures (for example, genres) within larger structures (culture and its various institutions), and since this structure of structures is perceived by readers who bring their own psychological and intellectual patterns to bear on it, the critic's first job is to "decompose" the work. That is, he sorts out repeated units in order to find the patterns of recurrence and opposition (in elements empty in themselves) that embody the style, the form, the action, and so on. Then he "reconstructs" these elements in a "model" that will reveal the "rules of association" by which the literary assemblage comes to have different kinds and levels of significance. One kind of "model-building strategy" is to look at a work not in terms of its conventional "thematic" organization (which, however, is *one* of its structures) but in terms of recurring elements that are not necessarily coextensive with any particular theme (but which are presumably coextensive with the author's consciousness in some way). The sensitivity to certain special kinds of relationships revealed in a writer's habitual choices of comparison, for example, can reveal not only his thematic concerns but also *how* he relates things, how his individual consciousness interacts with the "givens" of his world. At least one of the major thrusts of structuralism, then, is the reintroduction of a "new" historicism back into literary criticism, all the while keeping the literary work, and its author, at the center of attention, in contrast to the "old" historicism which buried the work in historical and social details.

This "newer" critical awareness is endorsed in America by the "Johns Hopkins school," a taxonomy no doubt influenced by the presence of Leo Spitzer and the development of "stylistics" at Hopkins.[2] Testimony to the structuralist interest at Hopkins is the new symposium, *The Languages of Criticism and the Sciences of Man: The Structuralist Controversy* (Baltimore, Johns Hopkins Press), the title of which suggests a simultaneous concern to relate literary criticism to all human activity and to achieve some sort of "scientific" methodology. From another direction, American scholars informed by the insights of structural linguistics are also beginning to develop an approach to the literary work as a "structure of structures" that should eventually merge with the structuralist strategy of inquiry, especially in the concern to build "models of consciousness." Thus we have had recently *Essays on the Language of Literature*, edited by Seymour Chatman and Samuel R. Levin (Boston, Houghton Mifflin, 1967), which contains an illuminating essay, "Linguistics and Poetics," by Roman Jakobson, one of the original Russian formalists.[3] This essay was first published in 1960 in *Style in Language*, edited by Thomas A.

2. Those who may wonder at the territorial imperative implied here may want to consult the 1966 double issue of *Yale French Studies* nos. 36–37, the whole of which is devoted to structuralism. Moreover, the Hopkins school is not merely an emulation of structuralism, for critics like J. Hillis Miller fall into another context, that of the so-called Geneva school of existentialist criticism. This group has been studied by Sarah Lawall in *Critics of Consciousness: The Existential Structures of Literature* (Cambridge, Mass., Harvard Univ. Press, 1968), but their approach has had, so far, less impact on American criticism. The point is that Johns Hopkins has distinguished itself for being on the forefront of innovative literary criticism.

3. The writings of the Russian formalists in the twenties composed a matrix of systematic critical theory very similar to but farther ranging than the more applied criticism of the American New Critics in the thirties and forties. The ideas of the formalists were, in part, brought to this country by René Wellek, but it has only been recently that the activities of the formalists have been surveyed and codified, by Victor Erlick in *Russian Formalism: History—Doctrine* (rev. ed., The Hague, Mouton, 1965), with a preface by Wellek, and in an exemplary article by Judith Garson, "Literary History: Russian Formalist Views" (*JHI* 31:399–412).

Sebeok (Cambridge, Mass., MIT Press) as part of the continuing joint investigation of Indiana, Harvard, and MIT linguists into the question, What makes a verbal message a work of art? And now we also have a brief statement by Noam Chomsky, addressed to humanists in general, on the topic of the contributions of linguistics to the study of the way the human mind works. In his three Berkeley lectures on language and the "structures of consciousness," collected as *Language and Mind* (New York, Harcourt Brace & World, 1968) Chomsky attempts to outline what has been discovered about the "deep structures" of the mind.

The latest volume in the Princeton series Humanistic Scholarship in America, Karl D. Uitti's *Linguistics and Literary Theory* (Englewood Cliffs, N.J., Prentice-Hall), is one of the major studies of the year if only for its lucidity in surveying the forefront of a "newer" criticism. The book is divided into three parts. In Part I, Language, Thought, Culture, Uitti gives a long, difficult, and interesting account of culturally determined theories of language and language systems from Plato to Coleridge. Part II deals with the techniques of literary and linguistic study in the present century, describing the attempt of the Prague Linguistic Circle (which included René Wellek) to achieve a firm theoretical basis and a scientific rigor for literary criticism, and as well describing with great concision the rise of Russian formalism, the New Stylistics, and American New Criticism. He attributes the development of French structuralism to the "disciplinary paradigm" of the Prague Circle, and in a subchapter called "Literary Criticism and the Science of Literature in America" succinctly reviews modern American critical schools in relation to linguistics. In Part III, Uitti deals with conclusions that presently seem valid and remarks that what is most striking is the recurrent idea that literary language must be viewed "above all in cultural terms," that is, as a "formal function" of "historical traditions" in their "expressive relationships."

Also indicative of the rapprochement of linguistics, semantics, formalist criticism, and literary history is the recent establishment in this country of new journals devoted to style and the structures of signs, notably *Style* (with an annual bibliography of stylistics), *Language and Style*, and *Semiotics*. In addition, *Genre* and *New Literary History* seek to provide vehicles for formalist criticism within broader frameworks. Ralph Cohen, editor of *NLH*, invites articles on the concept of form "and its alternatives," on "periodization," on theories of literary history old and new, and on "the intersection of the arts."

A systematic investigation into the study of the relations between style, literature as institution, and society—and therefore of criticism and history—is the recent book of Vytautas Kavolis, whose essay "Art Content and Social Involvement" appeared in *American Studies: Essays on Theory and Method* (Columbus, Ohio, Merrill, 1968). Kavolis's *Artistic Expression—A Sociological Analysis* (Ithaca, N.Y., Cornell Univ. Press, 1968) is a study of the large forms and institutions of change in artistic style. The book presents difficulties because it does not engage specific literary works and because it is written in prohibitive sociologese. Although this work does not focus on American literature, it contains relevant chapters on artistic styles as "determinants" of economy, politics, and the "community" structure; and on style in relation to religious, philosophical, and other systematic rhetorics of values. There is also a chapter "Abstract Expression and Puritanism," and the book concludes with "Social Evolution and Modern Styles" and "Notes Toward a Sociology of the Imagination."

### ii. Aesthetic Historicism: New Versions of American Literature

Walter Sutton discusses the relations between literary theory and the social and political assumptions of a democratically organized society in a brief but provocative paper in the *Actes du cinquième congrès international d'esthétique* (The Hague, Mouton, 1968). In "The Idea of a Democratic Literary Theory" (pp. 482–85) Sutton speculates that the old idea of "natural" rights has unfortunately reinforced the current New Critical emphasis on the "organic" form of the individual poem and suggests that we must come to see that a society which constantly revises its institutions consequently encourages an unlimited variety of acceptable literary forms. He suggests that the "general 'form-sense' of modern man" beginning to be manifest in literary theory has also been conditioned by science and concludes that literary theory can best be sustained and developed by adopting the methods of the structural sciences and continuing to explore the relations of literary form to environment. John O. McCormick, however, in "Notes on a Comparative American Literary History" (*CLS*

5[1968]:167–79) takes issue with much of the current concern for a "scientific" approach to literary history as an "institutional" problem. He argues that literary history is a blend of "provable" data with "subjective" critical judgment on specific literary works. Because Americans are "positivistic" and treat literature as a "social" problem, the American "canon" includes "all manner of marginalia, journals, political polemic, letters, and laundry-lists"—things "pertinent to the history of culture but hardly to a history of literature rigorously conceived." McCormick has a point, but he is clearly unaware of the "scientific" yet antipositivistic attitude of European criticism and does not see that literature can be institutionally described if these institutions are cast as aesthetic modes. As he himself says, the true tasks of the literary historian are to indicate the nature of the artist's *solutions* to his *technical* problem and to see the artist's aesthetic problems and solutions in broader contexts. This is much like the formalist, linguistic, and structuralist insistence that the history of literature, like the language which embodies it, is primarily the continuing life of expressive forms.

Roy Harvey Pearce's *Historicism Once More: Problems and Occasions for the American Scholar* (Princeton, N.J., Princeton Univ. Press) is not the culminating work his followers have looked forward to. For one thing, he has not revised and refined his twelve essays (eight of which are focused on individual writers) in such a way as to justify their publication as a book. The long first essay, "Historicism Once More," for example, is laborious in the extreme, not so much from clogged sentences as from repetition of a single idea in different sets of abstract terms. Pearce attempts to develop (in the general context of New Criticism) a theory of the reader's dual response to a work of another age, and his basic idea is quite simple. The reader participates in the sensibility of that age as shaped (in and through literary forms and language) by the author's mind working with the "givens" of his culture. Simultaneously, he is aware of his own perspective from a different time and culture (and with a somewhat altered value-laden language). But it takes a while to see what Pearce is getting at.

Another problem is Pearce's romanticism, connected first of all with a belief in the old verities about the "human spirit" or *humanitas*, which turns out to be in Pearce's theory a universal "constant" in the flux of ever-changing systems or modes of literature and culture.

In all the concrete particularity (linguistic and cultural) that gives a literary work its vivid value, this overriding spirit remains at the center. It is this *humanitas* that we all share that allows us to read the works of other eras, of other cultures; it is the "self" at the center, which, when it interacts with the external "givens" in the culture, is a means of its own definition, a dialectic of external particulars with the internal universal. Man is thus defined, especially in literature, by outer forms and inner essence.

This inner "essence," however, might more profitably be investigated in terms of Chomsky's findings regarding the "deep structures" of the mind instead of asserting a mystical continuity to human life. For what allows translation from one language to another would seem to be some sort of deep logical-linguistic structure in the human brain rather than the "divine" in us all; and by extension it would be this structure that allows us to read the records of other minds, in other cultures, in other times. This is an especially pertinent matter because Pearce otherwise frames his discussion of literature in the way the linguists and the practitioners of the *Critique nouvelle française* do. That is, literature is an "institution," a conscious, communal, "mythic," conceptual model or system of expressive forms that change slowly but constantly. New Historicism is in part the study of these changing forms, in which we both see the world and define ourselves.

Another aspect of Pearce's romanticism likely to cause initial difficulty is his implicit belief in Progress, in some sort of evolution toward a Great Society, which along with a belief in that universal essence called *humanitas* and a dialectical method, all point to the (perhaps unconscious) presence of Hegel in the background of Pearce's thought. Once this Hegelian mystique of progress through higher and higher levels of cultural articulation toward the fruition of that Divine Plan Hegel called *Humanität* is seen informing Pearce's thought, much of the vagueness of Pearce's position is reduced. Pearce's reiterated "humanistic" concerns come to the point that a critical literary historicism will allow us actually to "meet our students" instead of giving them those unrelated aesthetic artifacts which are the product of nonhistorical New Criticism.[4]

4. Here mention may be made of a most timely dissertation relevant to an understanding of Pearce's position. W. A. Morris in "The Rediscovery of Historicism in Contemporary American Literary Theory" (*DA* 29: 4013A–14A) notes

Three other recent book-length works of applied historical criticism in American literature partake of the methodology and rhetoric of the newer criticism and the new historicism, however unconsciously or incompletely. John F. Lynen in *The Design of the Present: Essays on Time and Form in American Literature* (New Haven, Conn., Yale Univ. Press) addresses himself to the problems of an evaluative formalist historicism by means of a theme-and-form study. His approach is based on what at first looks like a stunningly simple observation of a significant polarity. Lynen suggests that American writers habitually conceive of any particular, isolated "present" moment against a background of "eternal" time, a habit apparently derived from the Puritans, though Lynen disavows attributing causal relationships. The characteristic "habit of mind" ( read "model of consciousness") of the Puritans was to see immanence and transcendence simultaneously, to hold the concrete present in some sort of tension with a sense of eternal time and its implications of divine order. Thus Lynen accounts for the American "didactic impulse" as a structure of consciousness resulting from our characteristic sense of time as the "Eternal Incarnate." It is hard to see, however, that a Catholic or a Jewish tradition, in any country, would produce a different paradigm.

In six loosely chronological essays that he considers only partially historicist, Lynen pursues his thesis with reference first to the Puritans and then to Edwards and Franklin, Irving and Cooper, Poe, Whitman, and Eliot. The essays are somewhat overlong and characterized by redundance and unclear theorizing. Lynen seems to make critical mountains of commonsense molehills. Nevertheless, one may find a number of sensitive observations in the book. Lynen's discussion of Poe, for example, which is attuned to current views of Poe, surveys the fiction in relation to *Eureka* and comes to the conclusion that embodied in the tales is an unresolved polarity of cosmo-

that the "older" aesthetics of historicism, characterized by a belief in the "relatedness" of all "human knowledge and activity," is essentially a romantic nineteenth-century philosophy which "asserts the dynamic nature of history in opposition to the static neo-classical world view." In the twentieth century Morris sees two similar yet fundamentally distinct "new" historicisms. One is that embodied in the writings of Marius Bewley, R. W. B. Lewis, F. O. Matthiessen, Paul Goodman, Frederick Hoffman, Harry Levin, and Roy Harvey Pearce; the other is that of Charles Feidelson, Jr., Leo Spitzer, Eliseo Vivas, and Murray Krieger. The first kind of historicism, he suggests, attempts to include formalism selectively, and the second attempts to accommodate formalist techniques and theory.

logical unity and individual separation; although this division seems intellectively resolved in *Eureka*, the work is actually informed by the same wavering nihilistic consciousness that permeates the tales. This is well observed; and when Lynen comes to Whitman and Eliot (one need think only of "Song of Myself," "Crossing Brooklyn Ferry," and "Four Quartets"), he has made-to-order materials for a tradition of time consciousness that puts these writers into an interesting paradigm. It is significant that Lynen is concerned to build a criticism which will reveal methods by which we may "experience the value-system" embodied in the work and avoid a "sterile aestheticism." Great works of literature "engage our humanity," giving us a perception of value more important to our lives than the work's own artistry. But they do it *through* their form, which embodies the author's own time and world view.

David L. Minter's *The Interpreted Design as a Structural Principle in American Prose* (New Haven, Conn., Yale Univ. Press) is less historicist theoretically and less pretentious philosophically. He too suggests that there is a "genre" in American prose which involves a sense of vast cosmology, and he builds a structural model which brings together a number of unlikely works. This "genre" involves two major figures in a narrative. One is a doer, a man of action with a large vision or "design" that he wants to bring into existence; the other is an observer or "interpreter" who relates the story of the other man's fortunes as he pursues his vision. Like Lynen, Minter begins with the Puritans, who came to the American wilderness to construct a new society "whole." But as loyalty to the Puritan vision waned, succeeding generations reinterpreted the design of their fathers in the form of the "Jeremiad," or fast-day "lamentation" intended to review failings and to promote reform. As time wore on, the Jeremiad became a mode for minimizing failures instead of examining them, and eventually did no more than memorialize a "design that had failed" (the major though not quite the exclusive motif of the genre Minter takes it to be). Moving on from this introductory analysis of one mode of American thinking, Minter proceeds to discover two major forms of his genre. One is an autobiographical form, including Edwards's *Personal Narrative*, Franklin's *Autobiography*, Thoreau's *Walden*, and Henry Adams's *Education*. The other is a fictional form, including Hawthorne's *Blithedale*, the major novels of Henry James, Fitzgerald's *Gatsby*, and Faulkner's *Absalom, Absalom!*

Several of these fit the pattern well, like *Gatsby*, others less well. And yet, once the model (this new genre) has been constructed, there is a provocative coherence to it, as illustrated by Franklin's *Autobiography* and Adams's *Education*. After all, Adams chooses to speak of his younger questing self in the third person, with all sorts of interpretive commentary on "him." And although Minter is unconvincing on Franklin's "failed design" of living a life of (thirteen) virtues, Franklin's basic metaphor, as he looks back on his programmatically successful life from the interpretive perspective of old age, is that of "errata" in a book he now wishes he might correct here and there. Commendably, Minter's book is a trim 200 pages that move us rapidly through the model. Although it is true that Minter runs the risk of too large and reductive a pattern, he does provide a model which allows us to break away from some of the traditional conceptions of genre.

Even more interesting, both in the specific works brought together and in the way they are brought together, is A. D. Van Nostrand's *Everyman His Own Poet: Romantic Gospels in American Literature* (New York, McGraw-Hill, 1968). Curiously enough, this work too is a study of the American "cosmological" sensibility, for what Van Nostrand means by a "Romantic Gospel" is a "single theory of all events to explain everything that plagues you"—a cosmology with the "self" at the center, and therefore "romantic." Such cosmologies emphasize the "dramatic persona" of the author and embody the "processes" of his consciousness as he attempts to build a universal system out of words. The general model set up here is somewhat like Minter's, though Van Nostrand uses his more flexibly. In fact, he sets up a number of paradigms within the general model described. As he says: "The strategy of the paradigm intrigues me . . . the use of a model to convey the whole subject in its complexity. The basic configurations of the subject are inherent in the paradigm, but they are not all at once apparent . . . this is the problem." His strategy therefore is to present "successive paradigms to discover and reveal whatever there is in the subject. . . . Possibly, I can discover the literary and historical significance of these cosmologies by discovering a kind of critical syntax as I go" (p. 7). The newer critical technique of model building could not be clearer, though Van Nostrand does not mention any of the newer critics.

Van Nostrand sets up five paradigms of cosmologies in all. Paradigm One brings together Wolfe's *Of Time and the River* with William Carlos Williams's *The Great American Novel*; Paradigm Two, Emerson's *Nature*, "The Poet," and "Merlin" with Whitman's *Leaves of Grass* and Hart Crane's *The Bridge*; Paradigm Three, *Walden* with *Moby-Dick*; Paradigm Four, Henry James's novels with Faulkner's; and Paradigm Five, Adams's *Education* with Poe's *Eureka* and Williams's *Paterson*. All this is most promising: each paradigm, besides deriving from the large model, is supposed to have its own organizational principles, which have been discovered in the works brought together; that is, certain recurrent unities have been sorted out from the works and reconstituted as the paradigms. For example, like Minter, Van Nostrand sees *Walden* and *Moby-Dick* as structured around an observing self interpreting the more active self. But that Van Nostrand achieves something different and potentially richer than Lynen and Minter can be illustrated by the model he builds in the chapter called "The Theories of Adams and Poe." He examines the recurrent metaphors of an unlikely pair of works, the *Education* and *Eureka*, in terms of their developing narrative argument. In each, he sees an unconcluded search for an epistemology; in each, the author struggles to come to terms with the physical universe in relation to the mental processes; in each, the author conceives of existence, history, and mind in a series of scientific analogies. For Adams, temperature, pressure, volume, energy, describe the history of the world and the evolution of his own thinking. For Poe, electricity, gravity, irradiation, concentralization, attraction, repulsion, similarly shape his view of the universe and define his conception of the process of thought. Both works are *different* from the particular similarities *Walden* and *Moby-Dick* display in the other paradigm; but they are similar to *Walden* and *Moby-Dick* in the larger model of "Romantic Gospel." The problem is that Van Nostrand does not lay it out clearly in this fashion; the reader has to construct his own model of how Van Nostrand intends the total configuration to be seen, at least as methodology. He writes like a "gentleman of letters" who has not endeavored to be rigorously systematic, a very strange thing for so innovative a reader as Van Nostrand shows himself to be.

Van Nostrand also leaves largely unexplored the question of why this cosmological "genre" should exist. By failing to deal with the writer's motive for constructing a work of this genre, he misses an opportunity to construct an aesthetic historicism that explores the interaction between individual consciousness and cultural givens, between materials and devices. In any event, though Van Nostrand does not consider these matters, his work reflects the view of the newer critics that the historicist sense interpenetrates the critical, and in the final analysis is integral to the critical. Suffice it to say, then, that a "newer" criticism does exist, and that there is a growing desire on the part of university teachers to go beyond the "intrinsic" patterns of the individual work itself without, however, abandoning the focus on the poem-as-poem. Moreover, it is clear that American New Criticism and New Historicism are but versions of a larger worldwide intellectual movement toward a firmer critical theory and toward a critical literary history as yet but incompletely noticed in America.

### *iii.* From Romantic to Modern: Pastoralism, Adamism, Existentialism

To turn from attempts at a "newer" criticism, no matter how incompletely successful, to more conventional studies is apt to produce a sense of lower intensity. Some of the works discussed here complement one another, notably those on the themes of romantic pastoralism and romantic existentialism. But others seem merely repetitive rather than adding to our cumulative knowledge, as though faddism were not merely the province of our students. Paradoxically, collections of essays, usually lacking sharp overall focus, are often more valuable than, say, the continuing flood of studies on the American Adam in his various disguises.

For example, we have had recently *Essays on American Literature in Honor of Jay B. Hubbell* (1966), *Essays in American and English Literature: Presented to Bruce Robert McElderry* (1967), *Patterns of Commitment in American Literature* (1967), and *Studies in American Literature in Honor of Robert Dunn Faner* (*PLL* 5 suppl.:1–172). A very full example of such volumes is the somewhat misleadingly titled *Themes and Directions in American Literature: Essays in Honor of Leon Howard*, edited by Ray B. Browne and Donald Pizer (Lafayette, Ind., Purdue Univ. Studies). The title is misleading in the sense that the volume does not quite have the focus indicated, though a few of the essays pick up recurrent themes in the year's work. It contains in addition to memorabilia of Howard, fifteen essays, eleven on individual figures from Holmes to Randall Jarrell, and only four on broad topics. Norman S. Grabo examines the psychological dimension of Puritan devotional literature, linking it with literature of the Romantic period and after. John Stafford surveys the importation of the idea-cluster "Sympathy" to America in various guises at the end of the eighteenth century. Richard D. Lehan rather conventionally explores the admiration of French existentialists for American fiction. And James E. Phillips picks up several themes that recur in the year's work in American literature when he suggests that, contrary to conventional literary history, classical pastoralism did not die a hundred years ago but instead took the form of the American cowboy convention, in which cattle replace sheep, the cow-hero replaces the shepherd, and the ranch replaces Arcadia. Against this "pastoral" western setting the corruptions of society are measured.

Focused on psychology from the Romantic period to the present, Edward Stone's *A Certain Morbidness: A View of American Literature* is another volume in the Crosscurrents series that Southern Illinois has been issuing too hurriedly throughout the sixties (Carbondale, Southern Ill. Univ. Press). Stone attempts, with only limited success, to study the movement from the "nonrational" to the "morbid" as phases in American literary history. He encloses his chapters on sample individual works with an opening chapter called "Notes on the American Muse as Psyche" (the title of which neatly describes the focus of the book) and with a closing chapter on "association theory" from Poe to the present.

As these works suggest, Romanticism and the romantic impulse continue to evoke much study. Two works relevant to important French influence on that transitional period from Enlightenment to Romanticism are Richard Switzer's new translation of *Chateaubriand's "Travels in America"* (Lexington, Univ. of Ky. Press) with an introduction, and Paul M. Spurlin's *Rousseau in America, 1760–1809* (University, Univ. of Ala. Press). Spurlin corrects facile generalizations regarding the reception and influence of Rousseau in America. It turns out that since Rousseau was a man of many books, Americans regarded him in different ways, depending on the context. As a writer, his best received works were *The New Eloisa, Emile,* and *The Savoyard Vicar.* Surprisingly, *The Social Contract* "played no significant role in influential contemporary thinking on contractual or any other theory." As a man, Rousseau was found to be distasteful, and the *Confessions* did great damage to his image in America.

*American Romanticism: A Shape for Fiction,* edited by Stanley Banks (New York, Putnam's) is a useful collection of excerpts and essays on the craft of writing by the major Romantic fiction writers: Brown, Irving, Cooper, Poe, Hawthorne, Melville, Simms, along with selected reviews of their works by their contemporaries. In his introduction, "American Romanticism, Literary History, and the Romance" (pp. 7–16) Banks emphasizes the efforts of the American Romanticist to keep in balance the shape his individual art had to take, the demands of his audience, and the pressures of literary tradition. In particular, Banks notices the similarities between the American romance and the classical romance and the recurrence of adapted "pastoral themes."

James E. Mulqueen in "Conservatism and Criticism: The Literary Standards of American Whigs, 1845–1852" (*AL* 41:355–72) gives a detailed survey of the relationship between the political and literary principles of American Whigs as set forth in the *Whig Review* for the eight years. "The Whigs stressed unity and harmony in politics and art, espousing the organic theory for both society and literature." Literature was considered an organic part of society, with religion at the center, and the critic's role was to guide the public in right thinking. At one point, Mulqueen observes that "stability is always a prime objective of conservative thought, which fears nothing so much as to have the existing social order 'tampered and trifled with by quacks and demagogues . . . who, unable to see anything but evil in the existing state of things, cry "down with it! destroy! destroy!" ' " Mulqueen's quotations are from the 1845 *Review.*

About the same time Ruskin's influence becomes noticeable in American criticism of the arts, as documented, rather repetitively, by Roger Stein in *John Ruskin and Aesthetic Thought in America, 1840–1900* (Cambridge, Mass., Harvard Univ. Press, 1967). In particular, critics embraced Ruskin's "moral" approach to literature, though in the second half of the century his inattention to technical matters began to work against his authority in America.

Tony Tanner in "Notes for a Comparison Between American and European Romanticism" (*JAmS* 2[1968]:83–103) explores differences between American and English Romanticists in terms of the hackneyed theme of "open space," but with a few new twists. Tanner suggests that a sense of alienation with nature causes the American writer to try to "fill in the spaces between self and environment"; he throws out filament, filament, filament of a verbal web with which "to sustain himself in the vastness," whereas the British Romanticist more typically speaks of "harmonious reciprocities between landscape and mind." American Romanticists place unusual stress on a "visual" relationship with nature, which is to say that they are "watchers" rather than participators, indicating again a state of alienation, in contrast to the "auditory" emphasis of British Romanticists. Thus, basically "alone," whether "alone in his house or sporting in fields of air alone," the American writer creates a dreamlike world of his own making. Finally, just as there is "wilder image" of the land as opposed to the "trace of men" in the European landscape, so also the American Romanticist seems to want a solitary escape from time itself, while the European exploits both memory and past history.

Tanner remarks that when he says "the American Romantic writer" he is also largely talking about "the American writer." Several articles make a point of the same observation. Mohan Lal Sharma, for example, discusses, once-over-lightly, philosophical parallels between nineteenth-century writers and moderns in terms of "The 'Oriental Estate,' Especially, the *Bhagavad-Gita* in American Literature" (*ForumH* 7,i:5–11). Herbert London in a pungently ambivalent essay, "American Romantics; Old and New" (*ColQ* 18:15–20) observes that the "hippie is not so hip as he has led a receptive audience to believe . . . but is only the most recent manifestation of an old, romantic tradition." London draws a number of parallels, among them the espousal of Oriental philosophies, an antipathy for the machine age, and a fear of compromise, all "translated into a back-to-nature exodus."

Leo Marx, exploring further some of the ideas of his *Machine in the Garden* (1964), also treats this back-to-nature theme as a continuity between centuries in a fine essay, "Pastoral Ideals and City Troubles" (*JGE* 20:251–71). Many of our literary heroes follow the mythic pattern of retreating from a community with a "mechanistic system of value" into the forests, where they explore for a while a more harmonious way of life which produces a sense of relatedness to the cosmos. Often, however, this idyll is interrupted. Peace is sometimes shattered by the violent intrusion of a machine (as symbol). Other times, the hero discovers the dark side of nature: that there are "two hostile forces which impinge, from opposite sides of the symbolic landscape." The third phase of the mythic pattern is the return of the hero to society, though it is usually clouded with ambiguity.

All this, Marx says, is "a peculiarly American version of romantic pastoralism." Invoking the myth of Arcadia, Marx explores the continuing hold of pastoralism upon the literary imagination of the twentieth century, especially in Frost and Hemingway. In Frost's poems there are three sectors of symbolic landscape: the farm and village community, the middle pasture, and the dark woods beyond, through which the persona journeys in varying degrees of psychological retreat and return. Similarly, Hemingway casts his landscapes in symbolic thirds. In "Big Two-Hearted River," Nick goes from the fire-blackened town to the middle psychological area of his camp in the woods to the tentative encounter with the swamp beyond. Marx concludes with general comments on the "machine" as emblematic of a system with no goals but its own ceaseless expansion, on the "pastoral" as emblematic of the impulse to withdraw in order to "recapture a human situation beyond or anterior to technological order," and finally suggests that we need rural renewal as well as urban.

The basic frame of the latest psychoanalytic archetype study by Leslie Fiedler is similar. In *The Return of the Vanishing American* (New York, Stein and Day, 1968), he surveys the genre of the American "Western." In the Old Western, a Paleface refugee from Europe, having just escaped from a domineering female society, faces a Redman in the American Wilderness. We experience for a while the good times of the Paleface and his Redskin buddy in the free Wilderness. In the new Western, the escape westward has become an escape into psychological freedom, through social revolution and drugs and the like. In another archetype study cast in a very similar frame, David Noble deals with eighteen novelists from Cooper to Saul Bellow; but despite his focus on the novel, Noble does not engage fiction as literature. The literary analysis of *The Eternal Adam and the New World Garden: The Central Myth in the American Novel Since 1830* (New York, Braziller, 1968) consists mainly of plot summary. The book is actually more in the tradition of the history of ideas, but his thesis is the not very original one that the central American myth is the transcendence of time, imaged as a tension between two conceptions of man, presented by two versions of the archetypal figure of Adam. The "Eternal Adam" is the sinful, time-bound, and community-bound man; the new version of him in the New Eden is the American Adam who is free of the past, free of guilt, and as yet free of community restraints. Walter Allen picks up several of these themes in *The Ur-*

*gent West: The American Dream and Modern Man* (New York, Dutton). He studies the American obsession with national identity in terms of a "dream" of establishing a perfect society which takes the form of an "Arcadian" western myth. But his chronological discussion of the major American writers from the Puritans to Ginsberg is an error-plagued, plot-summarizing outline with only general pertinence to his thesis.

Here may be the place to mention Peter Schmitt's basically non-literary but much better book, *Back to Nature: The Arcadian Myth in Urban America* (New York, Oxford Univ. Press). Schmitt attempts to chronicle the impact of the nature sense or nature myth on America's city dwellers from the last decade of the nineteenth century to the early thirties of the twentieth. City people, when they turned "back to nature" rather than "back to the land" responded to a "philosophy only faintly related to the pattern of thought which Richard Hofstader and others have called 'agrarianism'." This "urban response valued nature's spiritual impact above its economic importance; it might better be called 'Arcadian.'" The bulk of Schmitt's work is a cultural study, with statistics from the 1889 Bureau of Biological Survey and the like, though he does have one chapter on "The Wilderness Novel," in which he surveys the works of popular writers—Gene Stratton Porter, Owen Wister, Jack London, Stewart Edward White, James Oliver Curwood, and others. Here too is probably the place to mention the latest casebook in the series Perspectives in American Literature being issued by Odyssey Press. *Agrarianism in American Literature*, edited by M. Thomas Inge, tends to be somewhat less literary and more idea-oriented than the preceding volumes on *The Social Rebel, The Young Man,* and *The Frontier* edited by various hands, but all of them are quite useful.

Anthony C. Hilfer in *The Revolt from the Village, 1915–1930* (Chapel Hill, Univ. of N.C. Press) explores the other side of the rural vs. urban feeling of the same period. Hilfer notes a double tradition regarding rural life: on the one hand, it was regarded as a refuge from the corruption of city life; on the other hand, it was regarded as the "buried life" of provincial intolerance and hypocrisy. Hilfer notes two phases: first, the criticism of the realists (Eggleston, Howe, Garland, Frederic, Stephen Crane, Mark Twain) in the last years of the nineteenth century; second, the criticism of writers like Cather, Van Wyck Brooks, Mencken, Anderson, Lewis, Wolfe, and others in the second and third decades of the twentieth century. Hilfer notes that the literature that developed out of this dissatisfaction with village life more often than not tended to adopt a tone or stance that became more important than plot or character; and in his last chapter Hilfer remarks on the irony that saw the very critics of the "thinness of American culture" trapped by those "banal categories of American thought" which they attacked; for they submitted themselves to shallow American culture in the very process of attacking it, to the detriment of their art.

Samuel Hux links modern American writing with another aspect of the "romantic tradition," and adds something at least a little new to the American Adam complex, in a graceful essay "On American Literary Existentialism" (*ForumH* 7,i:37–42). Exploring the possibility of an "indigenous" American existentialism, Hux surveys the American myth of a "new man" in a "new world." Both "Adamism and Existentialism presuppose a man relieved of the burden of *a priori* definition of who he is." Remarking that both the American Adam and the existentialist man are "outsiders," Hux suggests that when the Romantic myth of the "new man" collapsed, American writers turned from a "celebration of a fortunate alienation" to an "exploration of an unfortunate alienation" no longer informed with value by "a national faith." This produced the characteristic tone of contemporary American literature, which, however, is not the "no-exit rhetoric" of Sartre, but a kind of "comic and frenetic" affirmation of faith in human possibility. In the course of his remarks, Hux happens to see William James in just the way John Wild does in a recent booklength study of James. Noting James's large debt to Emerson, Hux sees in pragmatism a striking parallel to existentialist thinking: the tendency to distrust metaphysics and to believe instead in "instrumentality," and, in the romantic tradition, to conceive of man as a "transcendent being, a process, creating himself as he goes along through the agency of his own will and choices."

Little of this "new man" sensibility, however, is very evident in two volumes devoted to the 1940's. *The Forties: Fiction, Poetry, Drama*, edited by Warren French (Deland, Fla., Everett/Edwards), contains in addition to an introduction and three general essays on the fiction, the poetry, and the drama, about twenty essays by various hands on such works as *The Heart Is a Lonely Hunter* and *Reflections in a Golden Eye, A Curtain of Green, The Skin of Our Teeth*, and musicals of Rogers and Hammerstein, *The Bulwark*, "Notes Toward a Supreme Fiction," *The Hucksters*, *All the King's Men*, *The Iceman Cometh*, *Under the Volcano*, *Lord Weary's Castle*, *The Middle of the Journey*, *A Streetcar Named Desire*, *Other Voices Other Rooms*, *Death of a Salesman*, *The Pisan Cantos*, *Never Come Morning* and *The Man with the Golden Arm*, along with an essay on the apocalyptic "post-Bomb imagination." Preceded by French's *The Thirties* (1967), this volume is to be followed soon by *The Fifties*. Complementing French's volume is *The Survival Years: A Collection of American Writings of the 1940's*, edited by Jack Salzman (New York, Pegasus), with some fifty selections of poems, stories, and essays. Part I deals with how writers of the forties saw the war. Part II deals with three major controversies of the period: fascism at home, Pound and the Bollingen Prize, and the relevance and morality of the New Criticism (a contemporary critic noted its "alienating and paradoxical . . . social rejection"). This is followed by selections from the new poetry and fiction.

### iv. Authorship, Publishing, and Magazines

*The Profession of Authorship in America, 1800–1870: The Papers of William Charvat*, edited by Matthew J. Bruccoli (Columbus, Ohio State Univ. Press, 1968) is a major work despite the fact that it was unfinished at Charvat's death. Moreover, despite its focus on the economics of authorship, it is clearly the beginning of what probably would have been in the mode of a structuralist literary history, at least insofar as literature is approached through the "institutions" of culture. As Howard Mumford Jones points out in a foreword, Charvat conceived of the literary work as the product of "the three-fold tensions of public production: the judgment of the author in creating the work and submitting it for publication; the judgment of the publisher both of the aesthetic or philosophic importance of the manuscript and its potential sales; and the judgment of the reading public, expressed in opinion and purchase, on the validity of the work as amusement, edification, or illumination." Literary history, in short, was the interplay between producer, distributor, and consumer. Moreover, unusual critical insights come from this historical economic approach. Charvat shows that because Longfellow was a shrewd bargainer and had a certain market position, it was expected that he would produce a certain kind of work. He had become "typed." Later he attempted to become "untyped." In between he engaged in a double-edged struggle to be responsive to his public and yet give utterance to his genuine concerns. Of the fifteen essays, six are previously unpublished. Along with seven essays on Cooper, Longfellow, Melville, and Poe (one of the least successful of the essays), there are eight on such broader themes as "American Romanticism and the Depression of 1837," "James T. Fields and the Beginnings of Book Promotion," and so on.

Three books on the relations of author, editor, publisher, and the reading public in this century have appeared: *The Writer's World,* edited by Elizabeth Janeway (New York, McGraw-Hill); *Editor, Author, and Publisher: Papers Given at the Editorial Conference, University of Toronto, November, 1968,* edited by William J. Howard (Toronto, Univ. of Toronto Press); and *What Happens in Book Publishing,* edited by Chandler B. Grannis (2d ed., New York, Columbia Univ. Press, 1967). An historical study of a special aspect of publishing is Paul S. Boyer's *Purity in Print: The Vice-Society Movement and Book Censorship in America* (New York, Scribner's, 1968), which covers the period from the Civil War to the early part of this century.

In 1966, W. J. Stuckey studied *The Pulitzer Prize Novels.* Complementing this study, we now have *American Winners of the Nobel Literary Prize,* edited by Warren G. French and Walter E. Kidd (Norman, Univ. of Okla. Press, 1968), a collection of seven essays by various hands on each of the prize winners. The general career of each is reviewed, along with critical estimates of his works and an account of the ostensible reasons for the awarding of the prize. Walter Kidd in an introductory essay notes the varying quality and reputation of the seven and remarks on the paradox that despite the stipulation that the prize be given to a writer whose work shows "an idealistic tendency," the American winners (with the exception of Pearl Buck) have been deeply pessimistic.

Literary magazines meanwhile continue to attract a good deal of notice. Besides an almost alarming number of dissertations on American magazines from the eighteenth century to the present, no fewer than seven booklength studies, a major research tool, and a goodly number of articles have been published recently, along with several studies of little newspapers. William Free examines the influence of one magazine in the Romantic period in *The "Columbian Magazine" and American Literary Nationalism* (The Hague, Mouton, 1968).

Volume 5 of Frank Luther Mott's *History of American Magazines* has been published as *Sketches of 21 Magazines, 1905–1930* (Cambridge, Mass., Harvard Univ. Press, 1968). This volume, the last of the projected six that will appear, discusses most notably the *American Mercury* and has a cumulative index for all five volumes. Nicholas Joost in *Years of Transition: "The Dial," 1912–1920* (Barre, Mass., Barre Publishers, 1967) chronicles the change of the Chicago *Dial* from a conventional reviewing organ to an avant-garde magazine in the twenties, with such contributors as Van Wyck Brooks, John Gould Fletcher, Amy Lowell, Harold Laski, Randolph Bourne, and Marianne Moore. *A Return to "Pagany": The History, Correspondence, and Selections from a Little Magazine, 1929–1932*, edited by Stephen Halpert with Richard Johns (Boston, Beacon Press) is basically an anthology of contributions and letters to the editor by well-known writers—Cummings, Pound, Gertrude Stein, and others. In the introduction to *New Masses: An Anthology of the Rebel Thirties*, edited by Joseph North (New York, International Publishers), Maxwell Geismar rather curiously characterizes the thirties as "the last true outburst of our social and literary creativity before the somnolence of the 1940s and the silence of the 1950s." *New Masses*, he writes, "was *the* magazine of the period." If so, the selections of the poetry, fiction, reportage, and essays do not overwhelmingly bear him out.

G. A. M. Janssens's *The American Literary Review: A Critical History, 1920–1950* (The Hague, Mouton, 1968) is less a critical history than a "genealogy" (as Janssens calls it at one point) of the years of the *Dial* (1920–29), *Hound and Horn* (1927–34), *The Symposium* (1930–33), *The Southern Review* (1935–42), and, in the forties, the *Kenyon Review*, *Sewanee Review*, and *Partisan Review*. In an introductory essay, "The Tradition of the Literary Review," Janssens links the American magazines with a long line of European magazines. Janssens also examines the connection between two American magazines in an article on *"The Dial* and *The Seven Arts"* (*PLL* 4[1968]: 442–58), coming to the conclusion that *The Dial* was less influenced by the earlier magazine than has been supposed.

Walter Goodman in "On the (N.Y.) Literary Left" (*AR* 29:67–75) reviews several current New York leftist journals, primarily the *New York Review of Books*, *Dissent*, and *Commentary*. He notes that although these journals are "unrepresentative of the divisions within the nation or even within Manhattan," they have had considerable influence beyond the numbers of their circulation. He observes that these magazines have been the product mainly of "second-generation East European Jewish" intellectuals, and that they are at war with each other in intricate ways: for example, he remarks of the *New York Review of Books* that it serves in large measure as "a vehicle of vengeance upon the anti-Communist left."

In "What a Rich Uncle Can Do" (*SR* 77:338–49), a review essay on the 1968 volume of *The American Literary Anthology* (New York, Farrar, Straus & Giroux), Frederick K. Sanders observes that although the anthology does not encourage experimental or avant-garde writing, it does present a good selection of the "best" stories, poems, and essays from established small-circulation literary magazines. He expresses the hope that the anthology, sponsored as it is by the National Endowment for the Arts, will avoid becoming what the *New York Review of Books* has become: "an organ for political essays of an exclusively one-sided political orientation."

It would be hard to think of a magazine that has had as much literary impact as the *New Yorker*. Robert O. Johnson has now produced the first volume of *An Index to Literature in the "New Yorker": Volumes I–XV, 1925–1940* (Metuchen, N.J., Scarecrow Press). Johnson has carefully searched not only through the issues of the *New Yorker* but also through the files of the magazine's library in an effort to identify the authors of unsigned and pseudonymous pieces.

### *v.* American Studies

Some of the failings of American Studies as an academic discipline along with possible "new" directions are discussed, rather summarily, by G. N. D. Evans and Leonard Quart in "American Studies: An Approach for the Urban Sixties" (*JGE* 21:177–82). Their basic complaint is that American Studies has not yet developed into a true interdisciplinary study of American civilization but instead remains a "double major" of English and history. Moreover, they claim that most undergraduate students interested in American civilization do not have predominantly historical or literary interests. The authors suggest studying American culture through the "myths" of various institutions: politics, sports, the barroom, television and movies, folk-rock, and so on; and they emphasize the need for more field work. If Evans and Quart are right, the situation is perhaps even more disappointing than they indicate, for American Studies students characteristically do not so much display a "double major" of English and history as they do a "double minor." Unfortunately, something similar seems to hold for scholars as well. In its avowed attempt to integrate various aspects of culture, American Studies ought to provide a framework for a critical literary historicism as a system of structures. But for all its aspirations toward "relatedness," the American Studies approach to literature remains critically naive—this despite the fact that many people writing in the area are literary scholars. It is as though the scholar had a different head that he puts on for the occasion. Literary discussion, American Studies style, tends to be both obligatory and *ad hoc*. This can be illustrated by reference to what should have been a good collection of essays, *Landmarks of American Writing*, edited by Hennig Cohen (New York, Basic Books). The volume contains thirty-two brief essays of about ten pages each on books that marked "turning points" of some kind in our culture (never precisely specified) from *Of Plymouth Plantation* to *Profiles in Courage*. Most of the essays have a similar pattern: they place the work in the cultural environment of the author's career, make a comment or two about style, and conclude with the "relevance" of the work to the social, economic, political background of both its time and ours. Thus, surprisingly, we find Richard Harter Fogle assuring us that *The House of the Seven Gables* is "thoroughly relevant to the social, the psychological, and the religious history of colonial America and the young republic." And Edwin H. Cady remarks that Stephen Crane's *Maggie* is a "great book" because it is an "ecological" study of the slum child. *Landmarks* concludes with an essay by Cohen on the American pattern that so many have noted recently, only with chic, up-to-date, relevant terms: the American begins as "involved," then "drops out," eventually to return to society.

*Frontiers of American Culture*, edited by Ray B. Browne, Richard H. Crowder, Virgil L. Lokke, and William T. Stafford (Lafayette, Ind., Purdue Univ. Studies, 1968) addresses itself in a forthright way to its real concern, "popular culture." The twelve essays tend to be broad in scope, though four of them focus upon individuals: W. W. Story, Styron, Melville, Charlie Chaplin. Of the other essays, E. McClung Fleming studies six major personified images (the Indian Princess, the Neo-Classic Plumed Goddess, American Liberty, Columbia, Brother Jonathan, Uncle Sam) as an "iconography" for America from 1775 to 1885; C. Hugh Holman discusses the ambivalencies of "cheap" book publication at two different historical periods; Leslie Fiedler offers a small version of his *Return of the Vanishing American*; Virgil L. Lokke studies American utopian fiction in the last quarter of the nineteenth century; Leslie B. Rout discusses Jim Crow and jazz; Walter Robert discusses electronic music; Richard M. Dorson advocates more folklore studies in the discipline of American Studies; and William H. Gass attacks the study of popular culture as pretty much a waste of time, comparing it to a mirror with nothing falling into it yet reflecting itself in an endless "mockery of light." It is admirable of Browne to conclude his collection with such an attack. His *Journal of Popular Culture*, now in its third year, is even better. Although it carries a high percentage of essays on American culture, it also carries a number of articles on other cultures. Thus in the Winter 1969 issue we find, on the one hand, essays on Ginsberg, Mailer, Vidal, *Playboy*, Marlboro cigarettes, adventure comics during the depression, the popular novel in America, fictional renderings of the fighting man in the Vietnam War, and the like. On the other hand, we also find essays on the German backgrounds of the new occultism of the under-thirty subculture, the flute in French-Spanish Basque culture, the transition from nationalism to nativism in Britain from 1829–1848, the popularity of *Steppenwolf*, the Jew in the "Holy Protestant" empire. All in all, the variety within the approach is illuminating.

Among other works of value for those interested in American culture is John W. Ward's *Red, White, and Blue: Men, Books, and Ideas in American Culture* (New York: Oxford Univ. Press). Ward collects seventeen essays under four headings, History and Culture, American Culture and the American Imagination, The Culture of Freedom, and The Values of American Culture: The Intellectual and the University. Among the subjects of his essays are "The Meaning of Lindbergh's Flight," Franklin and "American Character," Dos Passos, Cooper, Stowe, Howe, Cozzens, Kennedy, radicalism, Marxism, individualism, and so on. In the first few essays, Ward articulates a concept of the history of culture as the study of the "consciousness of men in the past" made "manifest in symbolic action" of various kinds, giving rise to conceptual models, myths, or institutions whereby men live. His approach to literature is also in these terms, only like most

American Studies scholars he entirely neglects aesthetic "institutions." Nevertheless, as a record of a lively mind, it is a rewarding collection.

When the study of American civilization takes the form of history of ideas, it comes off considerably better than when it tries to engage literature as literature. The positive side of American Studies is well illustrated by two works on single themes. Richard Weiss lucidly explores *The American Myth of Success: From Horatio Alger to Norman Vincent Peale* (New York, Basic Books). In seven chapters, Weiss discusses the "emergence" of the myth in the Renaissance and its special forms in the American Gilded Age—in particular the novels of Horatio Alger, the "Christian" novel of success from the Civil War to World War I, and the "how to succeed" writing of the same era. In addition, he discusses the "revival of the Transcendentalist Dogma" at the turn of the century, concluding with the American "mystique of the mind." In his introduction, Weiss traces the success myth from Puritanism to the nineteenth century in terms of a Protestant ethic which became altered to "mind-power." The rise of a "self-help" cult of pseudo-psychology whereby man could will his way to success is still with us, and, as Weiss points out, a sound mind was and is conceived of in much the same way as a regenerate spirit.

Ernest Lee Tuveson's *Redeemer Nation: The Idea of America's Millennial Role* (Chicago, Univ. of Chicago Press, 1968) studies the concepts of "chosen race, chosen nation; millennial-utopian destiny for mankind; a continuing war between good (progress) and evil (reaction) in which the United States is to play a starring role." It is this religious self-concept of a "redemptive mission" that Tuveson attempts to explore. He sees it as an outgrowth of a seventeenth-century "reversal of the Augustinian concept of history." According to Augustine, the mystic body of the faithful (the City of God) must live separate from the world of action; but this concept gave way to the idea that the kingdoms of earth could in literal fact become the kingdom of God. From such an historical context derives the statement of President Wilson that the mission of the United States was "the redemption of the world," an idea still plaguing us. In six chapters (and an appendix, "*A Connecticut Yankee* in the Mystical Babylon"), Tuveson traces a vast complex of millennial ideas from a wide variety of sources. In his last chapter (on the concept of "The Ennobling War"), he observes that two extremes have alternated in our history. One is isolationist withdrawal, wherein America is conceived of as an innocent nation in a wicked world—as a new Eden to be preserved inviolate. The other is that of active messianism, a generally less powerful idea, but one which, like a recessive gene, from time to time becomes dominant. Although Howard Mumford Jones has written an unfavorable review in which he points out Tuveson's several inconsistencies and omissions, *Redeemer Nation* is nonetheless a mine of historical information that throws into high relief the messianic tendency so manifest in the current radical movements. Tuveson remarks at one point, for example, that "Americans are inclined to expect each crisis to be final, to think each must be solved by a permanently decisive conflict. Nothing could be more characteristic of an apocalyptic attitude."

Two less successful books are John G. Sproat's *"The Best Men": Liberal Reformers in the Gilded Age* (New York, Oxford Univ. Press, 1968), which shows for one thing that the liberals of the last years of the nineteenth century were not very liberal; and Elizabeth Stevenson's *Babbitts and Bohemians: The American 1920's* (New York, Macmillan, 1967) a somewhat inconsistent history of the decade focused on personalities. A book likely to be infuriating to both the fifties-style liberal and the sixties-style new leftist is Ronald Berman's *America in the Sixties: An Intellectual History* (New York, Free Press, 1968), for Berman takes a jaundiced view of intellectuals as they ineffectually wrestle with religion, politics, racism, and the like. One of the virtues of the book, though at the same time it becomes a bit tedious, is that it is crammed with quotations long and short. As Berman says, quotation is often superior to paraphrase if one's object is "to transmit the tone of the decade, and to make the book a repository of information." The eleven chapters move from general commentary on the decade and on the American intellectual in relation to religion (politics is the new religion) and history, to the role of the Negro in the sixties (more a symbol than a human being), to three chapters on the vagaries of the New Left (which he finds basically divisive in and of itself and of the nation), to a chapter on conservative and liberal attitudes (one of the effects of radicalism has been to reveal the moderate liberal's conservatism to himself). The last three chapters are generally literary, on writers, writing, and "culture heroes." Berman finds that the culture hero of the sixties is basically existentialist. He takes two forms, one of power, the other of suffering. Among the new intellectuals' power heroes are Castro, Mao, Lumumba, and even Nasser, all admired as opposites of the old "liberal hero." Existential suffering heroes turn out to be an assortment of "criminals," notably Caryl Chessman and Eldridge Cleaver. Berman's bias is often heavy, but it is still refreshing to have a moderate's sensibility play in a lively way over the repetitive material of the "age of the demonstration." Curiously, however, he speaks of the tumult of the sixties as if it were all over.

*Washington State University*

# Index

This index gives references to literary and historical figures who are referred to throughout the book, as well as to authors of the literary scholarship therein surveyed. Works are cited only for those authors given chapter coverage. Literary movements and genres are not indexed as such, since the organization of the book makes pertinent pages clear for most such studies.